RESEARCH METHODS IN CONFLICT SETTINGS

Increasing numbers of researchers are now working in regions experiencing high levels of conflict or crisis, or among populations that have fled violent conflict to become refugees or internally displaced persons. Understanding of these conflicts and their aftermath should be shaped not only by the victors and their elite companions but also by the local people whose daily lives become intertwined with the conflict – and it is this "view from below" that this volume's authors seek to share. Yet conducting rigorous research in these kinds of field contexts presents a range of ethical, methodological, logistical, and security challenges not usually confronted in nonconflict field contexts. This volume compiles a rich variety of lessons learned by experienced field researchers, many of whom have faced demanding situations characterized by violence, profound and well-grounded distrust, and social fragmentation. The authors offer options, ideas, and techniques for studying the situations of people affected by conflict and, by focusing on ethical and security issues, seek ways to safeguard the interests and integrity of the research "subjects" and of the researchers and their teams.

Dyan Mazurana is Associate Research Professor at The Fletcher School of Law and Diplomacy, Tufts University, and Research Director of Gender, Youth, and Community at the Feinstein International Center, Tufts University. Mazurana's areas of specialty include women's and children's rights during and after armed conflict, armed opposition groups, serious crimes and violations committed during armed conflict, and remedy and reparation. Her most recent books include *After the Taliban: Life and Security in Rural Afghanistan* (2008 with Nojumi and Stites) and *Gender, Conflict, and Peacekeeping* (2005 with Raven-Roberts and Parpart). She has published more than seventy scholarly and policy books, articles, and international reports in numerous languages.

Karen Jacobsen is Associate Research Professor at The Fletcher School of Law and Diplomacy, Tufts University, and Research Director of the Refugees and Forced Migration Program at the Feinstein International Center, Tufts University. Jacobsen's current research focuses on urban refugees and internally displaced persons in countries of first asylum, and on livelihood interventions in conflict-affected areas. She works closely with UNHCR and other refugee aid agencies. Her book, *The Economic Life of Refugees*, was published in 2005, and she is finishing a book on refugee camps. She has published a range of scholarly and policy articles and reports on displacement, livelihoods, and research methods.

Lacey Andrews Gale is Visiting Fellow at the Feinstein International Center, Tufts University, and Research Associate in the Africana Studies Program at Bowdoin College. Her current research and consulting work focus on community leadership, mental health and resilience, intergenerational relationships, and storytelling among refugee diasporas in the United States. Gale has worked with refugee populations in West Africa and the United States since 1998. She has published scholarly and policy articles on issues of gender and family, child fostering, youth leadership, durable solutions, host-refugee relationships, and transnational connections and remittance sending among refugee diasporas.

Research Methods in Conflict Settings

A VIEW FROM BELOW

Edited by

DYAN MAZURANA

Tufts University, The Fletcher School of Law and Diplomacy and
the Feinstein International Center

KAREN JACOBSEN

Tufts University, The Fletcher School of Law and Diplomacy and
the Feinstein International Center

LACEY ANDREWS GALE

Feinstein International Center, Tufts University

CAMBRIDGE
UNIVERSITY PRESS

CAMBRIDGE
UNIVERSITY PRESS

32 Avenue of the Americas, New York NY 10013-2473, USA

Cambridge University Press is part of the University of Cambridge.

It furthers the University's mission by disseminating knowledge in the pursuit of
education, learning and research at the highest international levels of excellence.

www.cambridge.org
Information on this title: www.cambridge.org/9781107502819

© Cambridge University Press 2013

First published 2013
First paperback edition 2015

A catalogue record for this publication is available from the British Library

Library of Congress Cataloguing in Publication data
Research methods in conflict settings : a view from below / [edited by] Dyan Mazurana
Tufts University, the Fletcher School of Law and Diplomacy, Karen Jacobsen, Tufts
University, the Fletcher School of Law and Diplomacy, Lacey Gale, Feinstein International
Center, Tufts University
   pages   cm
Includes bibliographical references and index.
ISBN 978-1-107-03810-3 (hardback)
1. Social conflict – Research.   2. War and society – Research.   3. Violence –
Research.   I. Mazurana, Dyan E.   II. Jacobsen, Karen.   III. Gale, Lacey Andrews.
HM1121.R465   2013
303.6072–dc23   2013002763

ISBN 978-1-107-03810-3 Hardback
ISBN 978-1-107-50281-9 Paperback

Contents

Contributors   *page* vii
Foreword by Valerie Amos   xv
Acknowledgments   xix

INTRODUCTION

A View from Below: Conducting Research in Conflict Zones   3
Dyan Mazurana, Lacey Andrews Gale, and Karen Jacobsen

PART I REPRESENTATION

1   **The Other Side of the Country: Filming the Human
Experience of War**   27
Catherine Hébert, Translated from French by Valerie Vanstone

2   **Negotiating Identity, Space, and Place among Iraqi Women
Refugees in Jordan**   56
Isis Nusair

PART II DO NO HARM

3   **Reflections on Ethical and Practical Challenges of
Conducting Research with Children in War Zones: Toward
a Grounded Approach**   81
Michael Wessells

4   **Researching Social Life in Protracted Exile: Experiences
with Sudanese Refugees in Uganda 1996–2008**   106
Tania Kaiser

PART III SAFE SPACES

5   "I Love My Soldier": Developing Responsible and Ethically
    Sound Research Strategies in a Militarized Society   129
    Cathrine Brun

6   Power Dynamics and the Politics of Fieldwork under
    Sudan's Prolonged Conflicts   149
    Jok Madut Jok

PART IV TRUST

7   Reporting the Story: Thoughts for Reporting on Violent
    Groups in a Turbulent Environment   169
    Molly Bingham and Steve Connors

PART V RESPONSIBILITY

8   Establishing a Policy Research Organization in a Conflict
    Zone: The Case of the Afghanistan Research and
    Evaluation Unit   223
    Paul Fishstein and Andrew Wilder

9   Conducting Research in Conflict Zones: Lessons from the
    African Great Lakes Region   254
    Timothy Longman

PART VI PRACTICALITIES

10 Preparing for Research in Active Conflict Zones: Practical
    Considerations for Personal Safety   277
    Dyan Mazurana and Lacey Andrews Gale

AFTERWORD

    Reflections on the Challenges, Dilemmas, and Rewards of
    Research in Conflict Zones   293
    Elisabeth Jean Wood

    Index   309

Contributors

Valerie Amos is the current Under-Secretary-General and Emergency Relief Coordinator (USG/ERC) for the United Nations. In this role Ms. Amos is responsible for the oversight of all emergencies requiring United Nations humanitarian assistance. She also acts as the central focal point for governmental, intergovernmental, and nongovernmental relief activities. Ms. Amos has a long-standing commitment to development, particularly on the African continent. As a Minister in the British Government, she worked with colleagues globally to tackle poverty in Africa by increasing aid flows through debt relief initiatives and promoting private-sector investment on the continent. She has been active for more than thirty years in the promotion of human rights, social justice, and equality on the African continent. Ms Amos was the first black woman appointed to a British Cabinet and the first black Leader of the House of Lords. In the United Kingdom, she has played a central role in the Government's broader diversity and community-cohesion agenda. She is currently Chair of the Royal African Society, a member of the Fulbright Commission, and a Fellow at the Centre for Corporate Reputation, University of Oxford.

Mònica Bernabé is a Spanish freelance journalist working in Afghanistan for the newspaper *El Mundo*. She first traveled to Afghanistan in 2000, during Taliban rule, and established the Association for Human Rights in Afghanistan (ASDHA), which assists Afghan women and victims of the war. As President of ASDHA, Bernabé works with women's rights activists in Afghanistan. She has lived in Afghanistan since 2006 and is the only reporter from Spain permanently established in that country. In 2010 she was awarded the Julio Anguita Parrado Prize for international journalism. Bernabé's most recent publication is a book entitled *Afganistán, crónica de una ficción* (*Afghanistan, chronicle of a fiction*) (Debate, 2012).

Molly Bingham has worked since 1994 as a freelance photojournalist covering international stories, and she recently launched a new project addressing journalism's future called Transforming the Media (http://www.transformingthemedia.com). She has worked widely in Africa and the Middle East, including Rwanda, Burundi, DR Congo, Gaza, Iran, and Afghanistan and Iraq. During the U.S. invasion of Iraq in 2003 Bingham was arrested by Saddam Hussein's security services along with three other journalists and held in solitary confinement in Abu Ghraib. She and her colleagues were released unharmed to Amman, Jordan, after eight days. In addition to her journalistic projects Bingham worked in a documentary capacity as the Official White House Photographer to the Vice President from 1998 to 2001. She has also reported several special projects for Human Rights Watch. Since 2003 Bingham has expanded her journalistic work to include written stories and film. With her colleague Steve Connors she coreported, directed, and produced a documentary film called *Meeting Resistance* (http://www.meetingresistance.com) about the Iraqi resistance, which was released in theaters in 2007. Bingham's written work has been published in *Vanity Fair, Nieman Reports*, and others as well as op-eds in the *New York Times* and the *Boston Globe*. She is a graduate of Harvard College and was a Nieman Fellow.

Cathrine Brun, Ph.D., is Associate Professor in Development Geography at the Norwegian University of Science and Technology. Her teaching and research are in the areas of gender, humanitarianism, and displacement due to conflict and disaster. Her main geographical area of study is Sri Lanka, where she collaborates with universities, aid agencies, and citizen groups. She has published widely; some recent publications include "Birds of freedom: Young people, LTTE and representations of gender, nationalism and governance in northern Sri Lanka" (*Critical Asian Studies*, 2008); *Spatialising politics: Culture and geography in postcolonial Sri Lanka* (with T. Jazeel, Sage, 2009), and "A geographer's imperative: Research and action in the aftermath of a disaster" (*Geographical Journal*, 2009).

Steve Connors has worked since 1984 as a freelance photojournalist. He began taking photographs while serving as a British soldier in Northern Ireland in the early 1980s. After leaving the military in 1984 he worked for London newspapers and housing charities and then spent the early 1990s covering the wars following the breakup of Yugoslavia and later spending time in Russia. Connors has worked for most of the world newspapers and magazines including *Time, Newsweek*, and the *New York Times* in the United States; the *Guardian*, the *Observer*, and the *Telegraph* in London; and in Europe he has worked for *Der Spiegel, Stern,* and *Paris Match* among others. Connors worked in Afghanistan for fifteen months starting in November 2001 and then went to Iraq during the 2003 invasion. Of the fourteen months Connors worked in Iraq (April 2003–June 2004), ten months were devoted to filming the documentary *Meeting Resistance,* which he coreported, directed, and produced with fellow photojournalist Molly Bingham. The film, an intimate exploration of the motivations and methodology of Iraqi antioccupation fighters, was Connors's directorial debut. *Meeting Resistance* was released in theaters across the United States in 2007. Since finishing touring with the documentary, Connors is focusing his attention on the field of conflict prevention and resolution.

Paul Fishstein, M.S., is currently a Research Fellow at the John F. Kennedy School of Government at Harvard University. He is conducting research on the relationship between aid and security in Afghanistan for the Feinstein International Center at Tufts University, and on the role of economic policy in building state legitimacy. In 2004, Fishstein joined the Afghanistan Research and Evaluation Unit (AREU), a Kabul-based policy research institution, as Deputy Director, then served as Director from 2005 to 2008. From 2002 to 2004, he worked in Kabul and at provincial levels on USAID-funded initiatives to strengthen the management of health care delivery. He first worked in Afghanistan during 1977–1979 as a teacher trainer in Kabul and northern Afghanistan and from 1989 to 1993 managed refugee assistance and "cross-border" reconstruction activities in Quetta and Islamabad, Pakistan. Fishstein has also worked as a Researcher at the World Bank, focusing on agricultural policies and food security in India and Africa, and he has provided assistance on financial analysis, organizational development, and sustainability planning to health organizations in developing countries.

Lacey Andrews Gale, Ph.D. (coeditor), is Visiting Fellow at the Feinstein International Center, Tufts University, and Research Associate in the Africana Studies Program at Bowdoin College. Her current research and consulting work focuses on community leadership, mental health and resilience, intergenerational relationships, and storytelling among refugee diasporas in the United States. Gale has worked with refugee populations in West Africa and the United States since 1998. She has conducted research and published scholarly and policy articles on issues of gender and family, child fostering, youth leadership, durable solutions, host/refugee relationships, and transnational connections and remittance sending among refugee diasporas. Lacey is an editorial consultant for academic centers and development agencies and leads contemplative, nature-based retreats through her organization littleseed (www.littleseedmaine.org). She holds a Ph.D. in Cultural Anthropology from Brown University.

Mélanie Gauthier began her career as a consultant for digital editing in image and sound with the National Film Board of Canada. Since 1999, Gauthier has been part of numerous teams as a sound recordist and sound designer. She travels around the world creating sound tracks and sound atmosphere for documentary films. Gauthier has compiled a sound library of thousands of hours that she uses to create sound tracks for a variety of projects. Gauthier won Best Sound in Documentaries at the 2008 Gemeaux Awards, which honors French-language achievement in Canadian television, for her work on the film *The Other Side of the Country* (Catherine Hébert, 2007).

Sébastien Gros was originally trained in the fine arts and photography. For the last fifteen years, he has been working in film. The majority of the films he has worked on are fiction, including both feature-length films and television series. Over the last several years, Gros has become increasingly interested in camera work for documentaries. Unlike films of fiction or television, where the focus of camera work is lighting and technical aspects, in documentary filming, the focus is on how the camera person interacts with and approaches people. Gros has a natural ability to put his characters at ease, and the results are an intimate look into people's daily lives and emotions through his camera.

Catherine Hébert is Director and Producer of Mango Films Independent Film Production (www.mangofilms.ca). She holds a degree in international journalism from Université Laval and the École supérieure de journalisme in Lille, France. Her deep interest in human rights, history, and politics is the cornerstone of her work. In 2002, she began directing news reports for *Points Chauds*, an international news program broadcast on Télé-Québec. Her first documentary, *Tea at the Embassy*, describes the struggle of an eighty-year-old activist and former prisoner of war from the Japanese concentration camps. In 2004, she filmed *Mangos for Charlotte*, a news report on the conflict in northern Uganda. Her news report, *The Face I Once Had*, called attention to acid attacks on women in Bangladesh and won Best News Report at the 2006 Gémeaux Award, honoring French-language achievement in Canadian television. In 2006, she filmed the award-winning feature documentary *The Other Side of the Country*, released in theaters in 2007. The film is an immersion into a Uganda ravaged by twenty years of war. Hébert's recent film, *Notes on a Road Less Taken*, is her most personal film to date, told in the form of a quest for stories during her walk from the Strait of Gibraltar to Bamako, Mali. *Notes on a Road Less Taken* ran in theaters for many weeks and won the Grand Prize for Best Canadian Feature at Rencontres internationales du documentaire de Montréal in 2011.

Karen Jacobsen, Ph.D. (coeditor), is Associate Professor at the School of Nutrition and Science Policy, Tufts University, and teaches in The Fletcher School of Law and Diplomacy (Tufts University). She is based at the Feinstein International Center, where she leads the Refugees and Forced Migration Program. Jacobsen's current research focuses on urban refugees and IDPs in Africa, and on livelihood interventions in conflict-affected areas. She directed the Alchemy Project, which provided grants and conducted research and impact evaluations on microenterprise initiatives in displaced communities in Africa, from 2001 to 2005. She has worked with IRC on a survey of Burmese migrants in Thailand, and with IDMC on surveys of urban IDPs. Her most recent book, *The Economic Life of Refugees*, was published in 2005. She teaches courses on field research methods and on forced migration. Her earlier research investigated security and protection issues in refugee camps, a study for UNHCR on self-settled refugees and local integration, and research on security problems in refugee camps, on the environmental impact of refugees in asylum countries, and on the policy responses of host governments in Africa and Southeast Asia to refugees. She holds a B.A. from the University of the Witwatersrand (Johannesburg) and a Ph.D. in Political Science from the Massachusetts Institute of Technology.

Jok Madut Jok, Ph.D., was born and raised in Sudan and studied in Egypt and the United States. He is trained in the anthropology of health and holds a Ph.D. from the University of California, Los Angeles (UCLA). Jok is a Fellow of Rift Valley Institute and a Professor in the Department of History at Loyola Marymount University in California. He is currently the undersecretary in the Ministry of Culture and Heritage in South Sudan. He has also worked in aid and development, first as a humanitarian aid worker and subsequently as a consultant for a number of aid agencies. He is the author of three books and numerous articles covering gender, sexuality, reproductive health, humanitarian aid, ethnography of political violence, gender-based violence, war and slavery, and the politics of identity in Sudan. His latest book, *Sudan: Race, Religion and Violence*, was published in 2007.

Tania Kaiser, Ph.D., is a Senior Lecturer in Refugee Studies, School of Oriental and African Studies, University of London. She specializes in East Africa, particularly Uganda and Sudan, West Africa, and Sri Lanka. She has conducted research and written on issues of conflict, gender, and development; humanitarian protection and assistance; and social research methods. She has degrees in Literature and Anthropology from the Universities of Bristol and Oxford.

Kate Lapides is a freelance photographer and writer based in Colorado. She has photographed and produced stories on humanitarian issues for non-profits working in Africa, Asia, Central and Latin America, and the rural United States. Clients include Save the Children, the International Rescue Committee, Resurge International, United Somali Women of Maine, The Family Intercultural Resource Center, and Ronald McDonald House Charities. Lapides is the recipient of two Individual Artist grants from the Colorado Council on the Arts for her work creating community photography projects for immigrant and Native American communities and underserved youth in Colorado. She was a National Press Photographers Association Women in Photojournalism National Juried Show finalist and has been a visiting instructor for Anderson Ranch Arts Center's summer workshop programs for children since 2010. Her editorial documentary work has been exhibited at Telluride Mountainfilm, the New Orleans Photography Alliance, the Rhode Island Humanitarian Film Festival, and, most recently, the Red Brick Center for the Arts in Aspen, Colorado. Her writing has been published in *Mountain Gazette, Women's Adventure, Trailrunner,* and the former *Silverton Mountain Journal.* She is a regular contributing writer and photographer for *Breckenridge* magazine and works as the Marketing Editor at Colorado Mountain College.

Timothy Longman, Ph.D., is Director of the African Studies Center and is Visiting Associate Professor of Political Science at Boston University. Prior to arriving at Boston University, he taught for twelve years at Vassar College. He has also taught in the International Human Rights Exchange at the University of the Witwatersrand in Johannesburg, South Africa, and at the National University of Rwanda. In 1995–96, Longman served as director of the field office of Human Rights Watch in Rwanda. He has subsequently served as a consultant for HRW, the International Center for Transitional Justice, USAID, and the State Department in Rwanda, Burundi, and Congo. Longman is the author of numerous journal articles and book chapters and of the book *Christianity and Genocide in Rwanda,* forthcoming from Cambridge University Press. His work focuses primarily on religion and politics, human rights, ethnic identity and politics, and gender and politics. His research is primarily focused on Rwanda, Burundi, and Congo.

Dyan Mazurana, Ph.D. (coeditor), is Associate Professor and Research Director of Gender, Youth, and Community at the Feinstein International Center, Tufts University. She teaches graduate courses on armed conflict at The Fletcher School of Law and Diplomacy, Tufts University. Mazurana's areas of specialty

include women's human rights, war-affected children and youth, armed conflict, and peacekeeping. Her books include *After the Taliban: Life and Security
in Rural Afghanistan* (Rowman & Littlefield, 2008) with Neamatollah Nojumi
and Elizabeth Stites; *Gender, Conflict, and Peacekeeping* (Rowman & Littlefield
2005) with Angela Raven-Roberts and Jane Parpart; *Where Are the Girls? Girls
in Fighting Forces in Northern Uganda, Sierra Leone, and Mozambique* (Rights
& Democracy, 2004) with Susan McKay; and *Women, Peace and Security:
Study of the United Nations Secretary-General as Pursuant Security Council
Resolution 1325* (United Nations, 2002) with Sandra Whitworth. She has published more than seventy scholarly and policy books, articles, and international
reports in numerous languages. Mazurana works with a variety of governments,
UN agencies, and human rights and child protection organizations regarding improving efforts to assist youth and women affected by armed conflict,
including those associated with fighting forces. Her current research focuses
on efforts of communities to heal (physically, mentally, spiritually), rebuild
individual and societal relations, and restore moral boundaries in the midst or
aftermath of extreme violence. She has worked in Afghanistan, the Balkans,
and Nepal, as well as southern, West, and East Africa. Her current research
focuses on accountability, remedy, and reparation in Uganda.

Isis Nusair, Ph.D., is Associate Professor of Women's Studies and International
Studies at Denison University. She teaches courses on transnational feminism;
feminism in the Middle East and North Africa; and gender, war, and conflict.
Her current research focuses on the impact of war and displacement on Iraqi
women refugees in Jordan. Nusair previously served as a researcher on wom-
en's human rights in the Middle East and North Africa at Human Rights
Watch and at the Euro-Mediterranean Human Rights Network. She is the
coeditor with Rhoda Kanaaneh of *Displaced at Home: Ethnicity and Gender
among Palestinians in Israel* (SUNY Press, 2011).

Michael Wessells, Ph.D., is Professor at Columbia University in the Program
on Forced Migration and Health. A longtime psychosocial and child protection practitioner, he is former Co-Chair of the United Nations Inter-Agency
Standing Committee Task Force on Mental Health and Psychosocial Support
in Emergency Settings. Recently, he was co–focal point on mental health
and psychosocial support for the revision of the Sphere humanitarian standards. He has conducted extensive research on the holistic impacts of war
and political violence on children, and he is author of *Child Soldiers: From
Violence to Protection* (Harvard University Press, 2006). Currently, he is lead

researcher on interagency, multicountry action research on strengthening community-based child protection mechanisms by enabling effective linkages with national child protection systems. He regularly advises UN agencies, governments, and donors on issues of child protection and psychosocial support, including in communities and schools. Throughout Africa and Asia he helps to develop community-based, culturally grounded programs that assist people affected by armed conflict and natural disasters.

Andrew Wilder, Ph.D., is the Director of Afghanistan and Pakistan Programs for the United States Institute for Peace. Prior to joining the Institute, Wilder served as Research Director for Politics and Policy at the Feinstein International Center at Tufts University. From 2002 to 2005, he served as founder and Director of Afghanistan's first independent policy research institution, the Kabul-based Afghanistan Research and Evaluation Unit (AREU). This was preceded by more than ten years managing humanitarian and development programs in Pakistan and Afghanistan, including serving as the Director of the Pakistan/Afghanistan program of Save the Children, as well as holding positions with the International Rescue Committee and Mercy Corps International. Wilder is the author of *The Pakistani Voter: Electoral Politics and Voting Behaviour in the Punjab* (Oxford University Press, 1999) and has written numerous book chapters, journal articles, and other publications. His recent research explores issues relating to state building, reconstruction, and stabilization efforts in Afghanistan, specifically examining the effectiveness of aid in promoting stabilization objectives. Wilder has also conducted extensive research on subnational governance, elections, and police reform efforts in Afghanistan, and on electoral politics and the politics of civil service reform in Pakistan.

Elisabeth Jean Wood, Ph.D., is Professor of Political Science at Yale University. Her current research focuses on sexual violence during war. She is the author of *Insurgent Collective Action and Civil War in El Salvador* (Cambridge University Press, 2003) and *Forging Democracy from Below: Insurgent Transitions in South Africa and El Salvador* (Cambridge University Press, 2000), as well as various scholarly articles. She previously taught at New York University (1995–2004) and has been a visiting scholar at the University of Cape Town and the Universidad Centroamericana José Simeón Cañas (San Salvador) and a scholar at the Harvard Academy for International and Area Studies (1995–97). She is also a Professor at the Santa Fe Institute and serves on the editorial boards of *Politics and Society*, the Contentious Politics series of Cambridge University Press, and the *American Political Review*.

Foreword

The incidence of conflict in the world and the proportion of the world's people suffering from its consequences has steadily decreased over the past hundred years. Many of us have far less of a chance of dying a violent death than our grandfathers or grandmothers did. Most conflicts today are characterized by regions or nations turning in on themselves with devastating consequences for ordinary people. The distinction between combatant and noncombatant, so central to the Geneva Conventions and the protection of civilians, is all too often disregarded. In many conflicts the destruction of a people, and the direct targeting of women, children, the elderly and their way of life, are seen as a goal, or a justifiable means to an end. We label such inhumanity war crimes, crimes against humanity, or acts of genocide. Such acts are brutal in their execution and leave behind deep psychological and physical injuries that linger long after the fighting has ended. The effects of today's armed conflicts extend over time and space far beyond the defined battlefield and often shape the lives of generations to come.

The humanitarian agencies of the United Nations, Red Cross, and Red Crescent Societies and humanitarian NGOs (international and local) seek to help people affected by conflict, by keeping alive the notion of a shared humanity and the importance of the innate dignity of each person. It is not about charity. It is fundamentally about values, and a belief about "people helping people." To do our job well, we need a profound understanding of the politics and power dynamics of those waging war. When active armed violence ends and rebuilding begins, sustainable recovery depends on development structures that are responsive to available resources as well as the capacity and aspirations of the particular conflict-affected community. Context is everything. Without an understanding of context, humanitarian aid can be ineffective and postconflict reconstruction fails to materialize, leaving people vulnerable.

Exploring, describing, verifying, and understanding the situation in which people find themselves require knowledgeable, courageous, and highly skilled researchers, journalists, and filmmakers. These researchers, journalists, and filmmakers show the harsh reality of conflict to the outside world. They help amplify the voices of those in harm's way. People working in conflict-related settings confront a range of ethical, methodological, logistical, and security challenges not usually confronted in nonconflict field situations. If such researchers, journalists, and filmmakers are to be credible, and are to build a coherent body of knowledge that shapes our understanding of what really is going on in conflict and its aftermath, they have to learn, develop, refine, and practice critical skills that allow objective and rigorous work to be carried out in conflict zones and among deeply distrustful and distressed communities.

Research Methods in Conflict Settings: A View from Below is a compilation of rich insights and lessons learned by experienced field researchers, journalists, and filmmakers, all of whom have worked in demanding situations. The authors offer options, ideas, and techniques for studying the situations of people affected by conflict and, by focusing on ethical and security issues, raise key questions and seek ways to safeguard the interests and integrity of those being researched and of themselves and their teams.

The authors of this book all write from many years of experience working in conflict settings. They draw lessons from their work in conflict-affected countries around the world including Afghanistan, Burundi, Colombia, Democratic Republic of Congo, Iraq, Lebanon, Pakistan, Rwanda, Sierra Leone, South Sudan, Sri Lanka, and Uganda, among others. They demonstrate that it is both possible and necessary to conduct sound and rigorous research and documentation in the challenging contexts of conflict zones. All of them have worked under harsh and challenging conditions and continue their efforts to expand our collective knowledge and improve our collective ability to understand better the realities on the ground and give relief and the hope of a better future to conflict-affected communities.

Their insights will benefit students, professional researchers, advocacy or action researchers, and journalists seeking to work with people affected by conflict, as well as governments and humanitarian and development policy makers. Governments and humanitarian organizations that commission research to inform their policies and programs can better understand how to conduct and evaluate research projects.

The United Nations Charter speaks of us as "One people." One humanity. Peace, prosperity, freedom from fear, and human dignity are inalienable rights of us all. The contributors to this volume through their attitudes, approaches, and insights help us to understand how we can make progress in turning those values and principles into reality.

Valerie Amos
Under-Secretary-General for Humanitarian Affairs
and Emergency Relief Coordinator
New York, March 2013

Acknowledgments

We wish to thank Peter Walker for his intellectual contributions to the development of this volume. The Feinstein International Center and the Norwegian Aid Council offered critical financial support for the writing of the book. Rosa Pendenza and Beth O'Leary provided administrative support. We also wish to thank our colleagues who assisted us in identifying our superb contributors and offered critical feedback at crucial points along the way, including Anita Garey, Laura Hammond, Jennifer Leaning, Dan Maxwell, Rosalind Shaw, Peter Uvin, Kim Wilson, and Helen Young. Thanks to the professional photographers who generously allowed us to use their striking images, in particular Mònica Bernabé, Molly Bingham, Mélanie Gauthier, Sébastien Gros, Catherine Hébert, and Kate Lapides. Anonymous reviewers gave critical feedback as we completed final edits. Our editor, John Berger, and his staff at Cambridge University Press enthusiastically and patiently supported publication of the volume. We wish to recognize and thank our colleagues, collaborators, and research assistants who live in the countries described in this book and make it possible for us to do our work well. Finally, we wish to thank the people who have given of themselves so that we might learn from their stories.

INTRODUCTION

A View from Below: Conducting Research in Conflict Zones

Dyan Mazurana, Lacey Andrews Gale, and Karen Jacobsen

WITNESSES TO WAR

Think for a moment of the men, women, and children who live in the world's
armed conflict zones.[1] At the time of this writing, these people would include
those living in parts of Afghanistan, Darfur, eastern Democratic Republic
of Congo, Colombia, Gaza, Iraq, southern Somalia, central Sudan, and the
towns of Libya, Syria, and northern Mexico (now engulfed in a drug war) – to
name just a few. Unlike those fortunate enough to live in areas not experiencing armed conflict, people in conflict zones must confront daily life in a highly
compromised and challenging environment. In addition, they have to share
their domestic setting with three groups that usually do not have a salient presence in more peaceful regions – armed forces and groups, the humanitarian
aid industry, and so-called observers or witnesses of the conflict.

A conflict zone is one in which armed forces and/or groups are present
and are actively engaged in acts of violence and warfare. Armed forces refer
to state forces, including state-backed militias, as well as state forces operating as part of NATO, African Union, or United Nations or other multilateral military missions. Belligerent forces are those that the state or a body of
authority (such as the United Nations) has recognized as belligerents to a war;
usually this designation is given to sovereign states. Nonstate armed groups
can also be considered belligerents, but only if they are recognized as such
by the state or a body of authority. However, such state-generated recognition
is rare as it triggers certain rights for the belligerent forces under the Geneva
Conventions and their Additional Protocols. Nonstate armed groups also
include insurgents, a term designating a group that has taken up arms against

---

[1] The term "armed conflict" is used here to describe conflict of varying degrees of inten-
sity. A precise definition of the term is not provided in any treaty body; see United Nations
(2004, 8).

a recognized, constituted authority (usually a sovereign state) and that is not recognized as a belligerent to the conflict.[2] For example, in both Afghanistan and Iraq multiple insurgent groups are engaged in armed conflict against state forces, multilateral forces, and, in some cases, each other. Insurgencies also arise where there is a complete breakdown of the state and different factions vie for control, as in Somalia in 1998–2006 (Bruton 2010). Nonstate armed groups also include organized armed criminal groups, such as the drug cartels of Colombia and Mexico, or roving groups of bandits with shifting alliances such as are found, for example, in Darfur, Somalia, and many areas where insurgent groups are present.

A second group with whom people living in conflict zones share their environment is humanitarian aid workers, there to provide relief and humanitarian assistance. Humanitarianism is based on the principles of impartiality, neutrality, and independence (Walker and Maxwell 2009, Sphere Project 2011), although the extent to which these principles are followed by humanitarian agencies or are perceived by the recipients of humanitarian assistance is subject to debate (Barnett and Weiss 2011, Barnett and Weiss 2008, Keen 2008). Humanitarian aid workers are associated with an ever-expanding number of secular and nonsecular local, national, and international organizations and have a wide range of agendas (Webster and Walker 2009, Stoddard, Harmer, and Taylor 2010, Donini 2008).

In conflict zones there is also a third group that the local population must accommodate, at times in their actual homes. These are the observers or witnesses of the conflict – the journalists, researchers, filmmakers, and others who come to document and understand what is happening and then communicate their findings back to a variety of audiences. This third group is potentially as important to the people living in conflict zones as the first two groups. By conveying their impressions of what is happening to people living outside the conflict zones, these observers can influence advocacy and underpin change. They can also play a role in enabling or obstructing peace. How these observers go about their work – conducting research, gathering stories and interviews for the media, and making films – is the topic of this book. Our purpose is to capture some key lessons from their experience for the benefit of other researchers, journalists, and filmmakers, experienced and novice alike.

---

[2] Within international law, the term "belligerency" indicates the legal status of two or more entities, usually sovereign states, engaging in war. Belligerents may also include rebel forces if such forces are recognized as such by the sovereign state or an authority such as the United Nations. However, if the rebel forces are not recognized as belligerents, then their actions to rebel constitute an insurgency.

The book's conceptual point of departure is that it is both possible and necessary to conduct sound and rigorous research and documentation in the challenging contexts of conflict zones. It is important to carry out such research because new networks and new forms of power, wealth, marginalization, and social reordering emerge in conflict zones (Mazurana 2004, Duffield 2001, Duffield 2002, Nordstrom 2004). These dynamics should be not only documented but puzzled over and understood as they will have tremendous implications for people's lives and the futures of their countries. This history should not only be written by and about the victors and their elite companions, but also about local people whose daily lives become intertwined with the conflict. As Elisabeth Wood points out, information flowing from conflict zones is characterized by "the absence of unbiased data from sources such as newspapers, [and] the partisan nature of much data compiled by organizations operating in the conflict zone" (2006, 373). This bias is all the more concerning when media sources or organizations are largely controlled by a state that is party to the conflict, as is the case with conflicts in Afghanistan, Iraq, Myanmar, Sudan, Russia, and Uganda. The need to challenge and correct biased reporting makes independent research, reporting, and filmmaking all the more important.

Rigorous research, reporting, and filmmaking can also present alternative perspectives and narratives of any armed conflict. It is often to the benefit of the architects of war to ensure that the realities of war are not presented or presentable. Carolyn Nordstrom's writings are among the most elegant and illuminating on this subject. Nordstrom likens the behavior of the architects of war to that of a story she is reading of a magician performing magic.

> The illusion is performed out of doors, often in a dusty field. The magician works inside a circle surrounded by spectators, assisted by a young girl, his obedient daughter. Near the end of the show, the magician suddenly and unexpectedly takes a hold of the girl, pulls a dagger from beneath his cloak and slits her throat. Blood spurts, spattering their smocks and sometimes the clothing of the spectators nearby. The magician stuffs the body of the girl into a bulb basket he has used throughout the show. Once she is inside, he covers the basket with a cloth, and mutters incantations. Removing the cloth he shows the audience that the basket is empty, the body of the girl gone. Just then the spectators hear a shout from beyond the circle. They turn to see the girl gaily running through the crowd into the magician's waiting arms. (2004, 182)

Nordstorm writes that in reading this description, she realizes that for those most marginalized and violated during war, "the illusion refers to the very real, and very dangerous, politics of power. The purveyors of war suddenly pull out daggers and slit throats, and then for the grande finale – peace – they attempt to show that no one really died, that no harm was really done, that no war-orphan street children exist" (2004, 182). Researchers, journalists, film-makers, and others working in conflict zones can directly challenge this process of sanitizing, mystifying, and obscuring the realities of war, and as such their findings have very real implications for peace.

Many of us living outside conflict zones believe in the importance of giving a voice to, and relating to, the daily experiences of those living in conflict zones – especially those who have been displaced, brutalized, marginalized, or impoverished by the conflict. This book, *Research Methods in Conflict Settings: A View from below*, joins a long intellectual tradition of according epistemic privilege to socially marginalized communities. This tradition is founded on the idea that those on the margins of power actually have a better understanding of the center than the center does – either of itself or of the margins (Marx and Engels 1998, hooks 1990, Spivak 1988, Bar On 1993).[3] As contributor Tim Longman writes in this volume:

> Everyday people are important sources of information not simply because public opinion affects the success or failure of policies but also because ordinary people – the kind who may not have finished school, who work with their hands, who are often struggling for daily survival – offer a perspective that comes from the grassroots. Living in communities where they are overlooked or discounted by the more powerful members of society, common people often have access to information that the elite do not. Sadly, they frequently bear the brunt of war-related violence and other human rights abuses, so they have important eye witness accounts to report.

Our authors also explore the ways in which the experience of oppression, marginalization, and violence is not only an experience of powerlessness and despair, but also a site of critique, alternative realties, and agency through resistance to victimization and violation (hooks 1990, Bar On 1993).

The populations written about in this book have experienced state and insurgent violence and conflict, punctuated by periods of peace or "times of not-war not-peace,"[4] often for generations. In seeking to gain insight into and reporting on the experiences of marginalized, conflict-affected populations,

---

[3] See, for example, Marx and Engels's epistemic privileging of the proletariat and bell hooks's and postcolonial theorist Gayatri Chakravorty Spivak's writings on marginality as a space for the production of counterhegemonic discourse.

[4] This term is used by Nordstrom to characterize times during which states or international actors may proclaim the conflict to be over, but civilian populations are still bearing the brunt of continued violence at the hands of armed actors (Nordstrom 2004).

our authors faced a range of challenges – gaining access to these populations, gathering data in insecure and challenging locations, and presenting findings to multiple audiences. Conflict environments are often rapidly evolving, requiring that researchers be flexible and able to adapt their methodologies. Furthermore, as Wood points out, "the ethical imperative of research ('do no harm') is intensified in conflict zones by political polarization, the presence of armed actors, the precarious security of most residents, the general unpredictability of events, and the traumatization through violence of combatants and civilians alike" (2006, 373). All researchers face ethical dilemmas and problems, but in conflict zones these issues can sometimes mean people's lives are at stake.

While nothing can substitute for time spent in the field, researchers can prepare themselves to meet the challenges presented in conflict settings. Apprenticing with an experienced researcher can help a lot but is not always possible. One of the most productive approaches is for externally based researchers to partner with an organization based in the conflict zone and staffed with local people. Finding the right partner and developing the partnership are worth dedicating time and resources, including where possible a separate field trip before the research commences.

All of the authors have spent considerable portions of their professional lives exploring the experience of people living in conflict zones. Their chapters recount their struggles and dilemmas – practical, ethical, intellectual – and the ways they have addressed them. From these experiences we can identify three common themes and conceptual dilemmas that are important to consider in carrying out research in situations of armed conflict: the responsibility attached to representing oneself and others in violent environments, the careful choosing of research methods in conflict settings, and the skill of accessing, creating, and ultimately understanding the fluidity of safe spaces to carry out research.

RESPONSIBILITY AND REPRESENTING ONESELF AND OTHERS IN VIOLENT ENVIRONMENTS

One of the primary concerns of researchers working in situations of armed conflict is the responsibility of communicating their findings. Iris Marion Young, in arguing for developing principles for ethically sound and socially responsible research, suggests that research has the potential, and indeed obligation, to expose and transform unjust structures (Young 2006). Our contributors are motivated by different goals – to advocate, to gain information to assist, to represent unheard voices, or to reveal marginalized or suppressed experiences or perspectives – and all pay attention to the analysis of power. They seek to understand how the struggle for power within conflict zones plays out in people's daily lives, at the levels of gender, age, ethnicity, wealth group, and religion. Some, as in the chapters by Tim Longman and Paul Fishstein and Andrew Wilder, are able to convey their research findings to international human rights bodies or national governments to influence and push for change. Other contributors pursue deeper understanding of the conditions creating marginalization and violence and seek to make a difference. For example, Jok Madut Jok's work on sexuality and violence led him to receive training as a midwife and eventually to open a girls' school in South Sudan.

Independent researchers, journalists, and filmmakers routinely have to negotiate the way they represent themselves, their allegiances and objectivity, and the influence they seek to gain through their research findings. The lines between aid workers, journalists, military, private contractors, and researchers have blurred. Journalists are embedded with fighters from different armed forces and groups. Anthropologists and social scientists collect information for state military intelligence. Military bases house both military and civilian personnel. Private contractors provide personnel security but also conduct field research for development or humanitarian agencies. Some private military and security contracting firms have sought to link with research universities to win large competitive bids for work in conflict zones worth millions of dollars. In such a mix, it is important for researchers, journalists, and filmmakers to be clear about their independence.

Our contributors consider carefully how they will represent themselves in and out of "the field," and how they will represent their research communities and the violence permeating their lives. This includes, for example, how researchers introduce themselves and their projects and their dress, manner, and behavior in the field, as Dyan Mazurana and Lacey Andrews Gale and Molly Bingham and Steve Conners stress in their chapters. In her chapter, Catherine Brun writes, "We are part of the field both when we conduct fieldwork and when we are away from the locations we define as our field. This has implications for how we understand our position as researchers." Brun and others rightly remind us that the field is not simply a set geographic space that a researcher moves in and out of. The field is also a social terrain, constructed through processes operating on multiple levels, always involving complex power relations (Gupta and Ferguson 1997, Brun 2009).

Another key consideration for independent researchers is how to represent violence and violent environments, both to understand and to communicate the realities of people living within situations of armed conflict. Hugo Slim advocates against overly abstract analyses that talk "easily and intellectually about violence without recognizing it for what it really is" (2008, 8). Slim contends that research and writing (or filmmaking) on violence should incorporate actual civilian experience to affect the reader or viewer emotionally at the same time he or she is conceptualizing and intellectualizing the violence. The key, Slim writes, is to select the telling of those experiences carefully to ensure they are necessary and illuminating for the discussion and respectful of the victims. As filmmaker Catherine Hébert writes in this book:

> You do not film Misery, War or Hunger. At best, you film the *experience of* misery, war and hunger ... we can understand many things just by seeing how people live. When Caroline walks 10 miles from her village to the city, morning and night, to avoid being captured by the rebels, that's the war we're seeing. When little Dennis, the street child, sleeps under a shop awning with ten other kids and gets up at dawn to "look for some light" and to scrounge for food, that's the war we're seeing. When elderly Anguleta takes us to the ruins of what was once her village and sighs as she looks at the skeletal remains of her hut, that too is the war. It's the war in the everyday.

Margaret Urban Walker's insights into the linkages and amplifiers of violence in situations of armed conflict also provide important contributions to understanding how to study and represent violence. She finds that violence and harms[5] are often linked and "create destructive synergies of loss and suffering" that can expose victims to additional violence and harms, even when the victims are not the primary target (Walker 2009, 20). These destructive synergies of loss and suffering come about because "some forms of violent harm or loss precipitate further losses that enlarge the impact of, and may in the end be worse or less manageable than, the original violation or loss itself" (Walker 2009, 52). Isis Nusair's chapter on Iraqi refugees in Jordan is, in part, so poignant because she brings forth these synergies. As one of the women she interviews says, "We live in exile, and there is no stability or security.... There is no stability from the inside. We always feel that there is something missing.... You speak two languages, Iraqi inside the house and Jordanian outside. The psychology of it all is hard and the way people treat you is hard as well." A number of our contributors engage in revealing, exploring, and representing the linkages and multipliers of violence experienced by the people they encounter, from torture and rape victims, to peoples who have been forcibly displaced, to those crossing armed check points, to persons involved in insurgent forces.

---

[5] Harm refers to physical or mental damage, an act resulting in injury, or a material and tangible detriment or loss to a person.

Walker's theories of the discontinuity and rupture of violence in people's everyday lives are also instructive. Walker challenges theories that posit violence in war as a continuum of violence, in which conflict-related violence is understood as an extreme projection of everyday violence and the structural discrimination and inequalities faced by marginalized or disempowered populations during periods of peace. Rather, she contends that one must pay attention to the lived experiences of people and understand

> the shattering experience of discontinuity, the sense of enormity and outrage, or the terror, despair, and social ruin of victims in many actual instances of violence in conflict. What theory reconstructs conceptually as a continuum may not correspond to victims' shocking and traumatizing experiences of violence in conflict and repression situations. (Walker 2009, 29)

To illustrate, a woman who because of social, cultural, religious, and family pressure accepts without complaint her husband's beating and demands for sexual relations, is in no way prepared for being beaten by strangers, raped in public (at times by males her children's age), or kidnapped and abused (Walker 2009). Studying and representing violence necessitate an ability to discern the discontinuity and ruptures when they occur, recognizing them not as an amplification of an earlier manifestation but as a break, something that should be scrutinized for the new meanings and realities that are being produced. In noting and analyzing these discontinuities and rupture, one is better able to think through both the short- and long-term implications of how people are being (and will be) affected by violent acts and processes going on within conflict zones. Michael Wessells in this book engages directly with the ruptures and the long-lasting ripple effects caused by children forced to become fighters, the rape and sexual abuse of elderly women and girls, and the violation of cultural taboos and practices. Bingham and Connors deal intellectually and practically with these ruptures when news and images of the abuse and torture of prisoners in Abu Ghraib break during their work.

The writings of Duffield (2001) and Nordstrom (2004) encourage us to pay attention to the realities and complexities of daily life in conflict zones, revealing that much of what is occurring is not in and of itself violent but is instead the actions of highly adaptive and resourceful people trying to improve their lives in extremely challenging circumstances largely beyond their control. Nusair's contribution in this book on her work with Iraqi refugees clearly illustrates these points. Additionally, Nordstrom's and Nusair's empirically grounded research throws into question not only conceptualizations of, but representations of violence, peace, war, conflict, postconflict, perpetrators, victims, refugees, winners, losers, development, and destruction. How these dynamics, and the actors involved in them, are represented determines how conflicts are understood.

The subjects or others that the book's authors seek to understand are diverse and complex figures. Depending on one's vantage point, these subjects can occupy a number of categories. In conflict zones, many of these subjects inhabit particular legal categories that impart certain legal rights, entitlements, and responsibilities, such as the categories of civilians, children, refugees, protected persons (i.e., medical and aid workers), victims of serious crimes and violations, belligerents, and hors de combat.[6] Other categories of people fall outside legal definitions that provide additional protection, and as such these people can at times find themselves with fewer legal or structural options to meet their needs, rights, and demands. These persons include internally displaced persons[7] and insurgents or rebels,[8] among others. Yet the clarity suggested in these legal categories is often challenged as people's status changes over time as the conflict shifts, people take on different roles, or people move from one role or location to another.[9] Nusair's chapter on the layers of lived roles and realities experienced by the Iraqi women she interviews and Wessell's writings on research with war affected children poignantly illustrate this point.

RESEARCH METHODS IN CONFLICT SETTINGS

"In research on or during conflict, ethical issues do not dramatically change but they get sharpened and become more difficult to resolve" (Cramer, Hammond, and Pottier 2011, 8). In much the same way, the research methods used in

---

[6] These categories are defined within a number of international and regional conventions and covenants, most notably the Geneva Conventions of 1949 and their two Additional Protocols of 1977, the Convention relating to the Status of Refugees (1951), the International Covenant on Civil and Political Rights (1966), the Convention on the Elimination of All Forms of Racial Discrimination (1969), the International Covenant on Economic, Social and Cultural Rights (1976), the Convention on the Elimination of All Forms of Discrimination against Women (1979), the Convention against Torture and Other Cruel, Inhuman or Degrading Treatment or Punishment (1984), the ILO Indigenous and Tribal Peoples Convention (No. 169) (1989), the Convention on the Rights of the Child (1990), the Rome Statute of the International Criminal Court (1998), and the Optional Protocol on the Rights of the Child on the Involvement of Children in Armed Conflict (2000), among others.

[7] The Guiding Principles on Internal Displacement are soft law adopted by the UN Commission on Human Rights and the UN General Assembly in 1998.

[8] See footnote 2.

[9] A good example of the fluidity of these categories is Hoffman (2011), which exposes the mutability of such groupings – licit/illicit, state/nonstate, rebel/soldier, ex-combatant/combatant, peacekeeper/profiteer – as he traces fighters from multiple armed forces and groups involved in the wars within the Mano River region of West Africa.

conflict zones are not qualitatively different, yet require heightened sensitivity to an ever-changing, high-stakes context. In conflict zones, as in all field settings, researchers often rely on a mix of qualitative and quantitative research approaches, including participant observation, formal and informal interviews, focus groups, and surveys. Once they arrive in the field, many researchers realize that the questions they so carefully honed require substantial reformulation or that their intended study subject or methods will not work. While this situation is not unique to conflict zones, the contributors to this volume offer detailed accounts of the methods they use and how they adapted them in high-stakes situations. For example, in her work with Sudanese refugees in Uganda, Tania Kaiser found it essential to adopt different research approaches and styles depending on the topic and context of the research:

> Any researcher in the domain of conflict and forced migration studies is aware that the flow of information – who controls it, who possesses it, and who seeks to share and disseminate it is highly charged, contextually specific and always political. Information sharing is never neutral, especially where it can increase or decrease your security, affect your capacity to generate income, and/or raise or lower your prestige in the eyes of your community.

Many of our contributors draw upon ethnographic methods to gather information. Anthropologist Rosalind Shaw, who has spent much of her professional life writing and researching in Sierra Leone, summarizes the usefulness of ethnographic methods:

> In ethnographic research, which typically consists of a combination of participant observation and informal ethnographic interviews, anthropologists and others seek to understand particular processes, events, ideas and practices in an informant's own terms rather than ours. This entails building up relationships rather than making a single visit, and spending time in ordinary conversation and interaction, preferably before introducing the more directed form of an interview....What we learn through ethnography thus has more potential to challenge our assumptions, often forcing us to unlearn as much as we learn. It is this that makes ethnography such a powerful tool for challenging received wisdom and for understanding events and processes on the ground. (2007, 188)

Participant observation, or what one can think of as "seeing and being seen," involves "getting close to people and making them feel comfortable enough with your presence so that you can observe and record information about their lives" (Russell 1995, 136). Seeing and being seen involve spending time where informants live, work, market, eat, and socialize; our contributors Hébert, Jok, and Bingham and Connors all met their subjects and carried out their work in this way. They attended weddings, baptisms, funerals, rallies, and other key social events, and at times they went to places of work with their subjects. In nonconflict settings, there is less at stake when planning one's presence at social events. While some events may be off limits because of one's gender, nationality, age, or social status, for the most part, there is low risk involved with attending such events. However, in conflict settings a meeting place or social event that is safe one day may not be the next. Spending time in a particular location or with certain people can mark researchers as partisan or supportive of particular groups and make them easier targets for violence, as experienced by several of our contributors.

For a researcher, being seen allows people to observe you and assess your legitimacy. By spending time in a place, the researcher becomes part of the known landscape, and this in turn increases access to a broader swath of the local population. If a researcher does not spend some time in particular locations, certain groups and individuals may not know that you're there, or how to contact you without being noticed, or may be suspicious of your activities. Bingham and Connors drank countless cups of tea through the course of their documentary project in order to be accessible. Kaiser followed standard protocol by meeting with the refugee committee and other official "gatekeepers" about the subject of her research, but she says that nothing was as convincing to those she worked with as the fact that she became their neighbor in the refugee camp. Kaiser was told by one of her neighbors, "Of the fourteen thousand people here, you are the only one who chose to come." For Nusair, her identity as a Palestinian woman and her teaching English at a community center for Iraqi refugees helped her gain access and legitimacy among her study population.

Cultivating local contacts and resources – by "hanging out" – enables researchers to develop sensitivity to changes in volatile environments and to understand subtle gradations of power and influence. Witnessing how members of the community treat informants can be instructive about power structures. Research in conflict settings requires careful triangulation of information so as to sort out rumor from knowledge. However, rumors are revealing in and of themselves as to what they disclose about the communities' view of those in power and of the power dynamics affecting their daily lives. What people do and say in the presence of others may in fact be more revealing about their views and priorities, sense of security, strategies for survival, and relationships than what is said during an interview.

Hanging out and observing give insight about community power dynamics, allowing researchers to go beyond relying on those who claim to represent a community or who are the first ones to present themselves to researchers. As the filmmaker Hébert writes in her chapter:

> "Listening time" is where we truly learn to set aside the things that differentiate one person from another, and to notice, in an organic way, the ways in which we are alike. Transposed to the screen, this identifying with the Other operates between the character and the viewer. Understanding how this identification process works keeps us from indulging in sentimentality: for a brief moment, I *am* that Other.

Particularly in a rapidly changing context in which uncertainty, rumor, insecurity, and violence may be pervasive, actions often speak louder than words. Walking the ten kilometers with a child trying to stay alive through the war to the quarry where she sat and broke rocks all day taught Hébert and her film crew more about the life of the displaced child in northern Uganda than a formal interview with the child.

Several contributors attest to the importance of listening to people on their own terms by observing and participating in daily events. Such methods are often appropriate in conflict zones, where people may be suspicious of more formal techniques of data gathering. They may be unsure of how the information might be used, the neutrality of the researcher, and the confidentiality or anonymity of their responses. For those who have been badly treated by government authorities, people with notebooks recording details about their lives can appear threatening, especially if they are using translators and recording in a language the informant does not understand. Informants in stressful situations are likely to feel that nothing useful will come out of the research and do not want to waste their time and energy answering questions. It takes time to build relationships in communities and to understand the power dynamics, especially when those with knowledge about particular topics may not be interested in making themselves available to outsiders.

Yet we recognize that spending long periods in the field becoming acquainted and building trust is not always possible in conflict settings because of safety concerns and logistical problems. Also, while single case in-depth studies are an important part of understanding conflict, this kind of research does not facilitate comparative studies – a significant gap in contemporary research on conflict (Dancygier 2010).

ACCESSING AND CREATING SAFE SPACES

Creating a safe space in conflict zones is a fraught exercise. "In contemporary conflicts, researchers can no longer predict the full array of likely consequences for those who participate in the fieldwork encounter" (Cramer et al. 2011, 8). Several of our contributors talk about finding or creating spaces that felt safe for informants to talk with them. In Western terms, privacy is usually equated with confidentiality, and a safe space often translates as a private space. If researchers are able to establish a trusting relationship with informants, they may be invited to their homes or other private settings, where in-depth and longer conversations can take place. Once inside a family space, researchers are faced with the challenge of understanding and managing informed consent in situations where information is gathered through "hanging out" and informal interactions in private spaces such as people's homes and family gatherings (see also Norman 2009)

In some societies, however, private conversations and one-on-one interviews are regarded with suspicion and sometimes considered rude, as Fishstein and Wilder found in Afghanistan. Gender norms in particular influence the terms and conditions in which men and women can talk together or even be seen together. In such circumstances, public spaces (even if secluded) are safest for frank discussions. As with other aspects of research, while the issue of privacy is an important consideration in all field contexts, in conflict settings, it becomes more charged and salient. It is important that the researcher understand the implications of meeting space, and that in a conflict-affected community there could be multiple views of why people are meeting. Public spaces might be preferred also because the informant (or the researcher) can leave quickly if need be, and neither party is responsible for guaranteeing the other's safety. Such spaces include restaurants, public parks, and hotels.

In her chapter on Sri Lanka, Cathrine Brun argues the importance of long-term relationships in allowing access to safe spaces, especially intimate, gendered safe spaces. Brun writes:

> I have spent much time in the kitchen part of families' compounds, chatting with women of all ages during the preparation of lunch and dinner. During these sessions, the chatting might result in casual references to such past experiences as a daughter's or son's last meal before joining the LTTE; a description of an old kitchen prior to displacement; how a soldier entered the kitchen to take their food; the way they hid kitchen utensils and other valuables when they had to leave their homes; or the experience of seeing their old kitchen in ruins when returning to their homes after displacement. I gained a deeper understanding of their past and present lives from these passing references to past experiences than what I had learned from interviewing them earlier. Perhaps they had kept silent in the previous interview because they considered such details irrelevant or perhaps the subject was too painful or awkward to talk about.

Creating a safe space can also mean taking a step back from your study populations if the timing or conditions are not right, as demonstrated by Wessells in Afghanistan, Bingham and Connors in Iraq, and Brun in Sri Lanka. Kaiser describes her assessment of the situation as she tried to document the forcible relocation of refugees from her research site.

> Several encouraged me to use the small back roads to bypass the main gate and government offices and enter the settlement to see the damage, and talk to witnesses and victims of the violence. Doing so would have been easy, but I realised that my refugee friends left behind when I returned to the UK would likely be blamed and punished directly or indirectly for facilitating my visit. My own future research access would also have been seriously compromised. Instead, refugees continued to come to me in Bweyale where I could transcribe their accounts and pass their reports to refugee rights organizations in Kampala. Meanwhile, a trusted and courageous refugee friend volunteered to photograph the physical evidence in the form of destroyed houses, so that I could also pass this material on.

Both Hébert in her filmmaking and Brun in her research write that silence itself at times constituted a safe space. Jok discusses how his women informants would sometimes act naive or become silent when male family members were present and would only continue their discussion once the men had determined little of value was being said and left them to talk alone with Jok. Nusair writes of how Iraqi women chose at times not to speak so that their accent could not mark them as refugees and open them up to further discrimination.

Silence itself is a key consideration when collecting information from informants and deciding what to reveal about what one learns and experiences, and in how one is treated. In Shaw's work (2005) in Sierra Leone, she writes about the considerable difference experienced by victims of grave violence between being forced into silence and choosing silence. Laura Hammond (2011) explores the layers of silence that formed after a particular event, in this case, an unexpected military attack by the Ethiopian government against insurgent forces that led to her imprisonment. She describes the multiple silences that coexisted around that experience: silence as a survival strategy constructed by the victims of the attack, the hegemonic silence of the Ethiopian government concerning the attacks and their treatment of Hammond and her colleague, the complicit silence of the United States government in not claiming Hammond as a citizen, and finally Hammond's own sixteen-year silence as a protective mechanism for herself and her Afar hosts. Her example reveals the power structures that enforce and require silence, as well as the multiple meanings that underlie the practice of silence as a safe space.

OVERVIEW OF THE BOOK

Given the increased recognition of the importance and challenge of carrying out research in situations of armed conflict, *Research Methods in Conflict Settings: A View from Below* joins a handful of notable publications focused on the dilemmas and experiences of conducting research in conflict zones.[10] This book seeks to provide depth and reflection on some of the conceptual and practical challenges facing independent researchers, journalists, and film-makers working in conflict zones and with conflict-affected populations. We organized the book under section headings that reflect these key multifaceted conceptual and practical considerations: Representation, Do No Harm, Safe Spaces, Trust, Responsibility, and Practicalities. We invited contributors with a range of experience, including conducting academic research, document-ing human rights violations, writing or filming for commercial media, and research institution building. We asked our authors to reflect on their research experience, beginning with the conceptual stage, through the field visits, to their use of their findings to influence policy and practice. All the contributors write about the issues they were trying to understand, why they chose particu-lar methods, and how they adapted their methods in response to challenges. They discuss the logistical, security, and ethical challenges they encountered and how they dealt with them, and whether and how these challenges cre-ated threats to the validity of their research. We asked them to reflect on their efforts to make a difference with their research, reporting, and films. Most of our authors have cultivated connections with national and international policy makers, governments, humanitarian and human rights organizations, and local organizations, in part so that their findings can help shape decision making by those bodies.

Part I: Representation

What does war look like? Television and sensationalistic documentary films feature images of blood, bombs, and mothers crying over their sons' bodies. However, violence in situations of long-term conflict such as northern Uganda is insidious; it is in the denial of the conflict by the government, the inabil-ity of the population to feed itself, and the ever-present, almost palpable fear that permeates each generation. For each abducted child there are desperate

---

[10] One of the first volumes to address this subject was Nordstrom and Robben (1995). Recent substantial contributions include Richards ed. (2005); Sriram, King, Mertus, Martin-Ortega, and Herman eds. (2009); Institute of Development Studies (2009); and Cramer, Hammond, and Pottier eds. (2011).

parents trying to find and recover their missing child. Grandparents are stuck in camps, trying to get back to their land. Thousands of children leave their villages every night to seek safety in towns. How do journalists and filmmakers expose this type of violence? Catherine Hébert's chapter addresses these questions by critically revisiting the process of making her film, *The Other Side of the Country*. In particular, Hébert discusses her decision to show the causes and consequences of the war through the stories of five characters, providing witness to a day-to-day life lived amid war.

Isis Nusair provides a portrait of the lives of Iraqi women who live as refugees in Jordan who are poets, journalists, artists, disabled persons, mothers, wives, and widows. Nusair's translation of their voices – both linguistic and figurative – offers the reader powerful insight into the effects of violence and displacement on women's lives. Her work underscores the importance of speaking the language (and/or working with excellent interpreters). She explores how feminist scholarship has the potential to affect policy and whether such research should have humanitarian and community-level objectives. She focuses on the ethics of questioning subjects who have experienced trauma, arguing that the repeated telling of one's story has the potential both to open wounds and to produce silence. Nusair examines the usefulness of the research findings to the women involved, as well as the consequences for her – a Palestinian woman – being identified as a researcher in this community.

Part II: Do No Harm

Psychologist Mike Wessells provides examples of ethical, practical, and logistical dilemmas he encountered over the last twenty years straddling the worlds of research and humanitarian aid. Wessells is squarely positioned in the front lines of providing aid and negotiating the complex web of power relations and cultural divides that arise when doing humanitarian research. His chapter focuses on working with children and youth and their communities in different cultural settings. Wessells explores the tensions between creating generalizable lessons about working with children in conflict and creating unique research programs and interventions suited to specific cultural contexts. He questions the primacy of Western concepts and theories regarding psychological well-being and trauma, as well as blind adherence to international standards without attempting to understand how they play out in the complexities of the particular context. His chapter also provides important insights into the problem of translating research into action on the ground.

Tania Kaiser describes her research in Uganda over the last twenty years, some of which was carried out while living in refugee camps. Hers is a cautionary tale, underlining the need for flexibility in security situations and the complicated issues that arise when working with mobile populations stuck in in-between places. Multiple contacts and relationships made it possible for her to respond to these changing dynamics. Through relationships with aid agencies, refugee neighbors in camps, and various layers of state bureaucracy, she was able to conduct research over the long term, while continually changing her focus and questions in response to on the ground practicalities. Her sense of responsibility to do no harm meant that she does not always tell the most dramatic stories. Often she held back information that might be damaging to her informants and did not take advantage of illicit access options when she was refused permits by the government, even though she had the local contacts to make it happen and wanted to document killings in an IDP camp firsthand.

Part III: Safe Spaces

Catherine Brun is a geographer whose work focuses on the conflict in Sri Lanka. Her chapter discusses the field and fieldwork as concepts to be unpacked. She offers the concept of "complex citizenship," which maps out the range of actors in conflict settings and the dual identity civilians must adopt in order to survive. Brun grapples with her reservations about whether researchers should be in the field at all during conflict, and explores when it is and is not appropriate to conduct research. She also explores the nature of our obligations to the people with whom we work and socialize in the field – our research assistants, collaborators, informants, and friends.

Jok Madut Jok is a cultural anthropologist who has returned to his country of birth, Sudan – now South Sudan – to conduct research over the last twenty years. His chapter provides a provocative perspective on anthropology and its limits. His work explores the ways in which sexual and gender relations have changed after decades of war. Jok grapples with the tension of simultaneously occupying several (often contradictory) roles in a high-stakes situation. He is at the same time humanitarian worker, researcher, prodigal son, insider, and outsider. Jok continually struggles with the question of what the right thing to do is, given his knowledge and power.

Part IV: Trust

Photojournalists Steve Connors and Molly Bingham spent ten months in Iraq in 2003 and 2004, interviewing members of the Iraqi resistance to the U.S.-led occupation. Their chapter shares their reporting experiences in Iraq and draws on their cumulative thirty years of living and reporting in conflict zones. They lay out the questions they were trying to answer, why these questions were chosen, and how they addressed challenges related to surviving and completing the project. They explore the challenges and benefits of working as a team, the importance of transparency, and the ethical issues involved in working with a research assistant and the complexities of establishing trust with informants.

Part V: Responsibility

Paul Fishstein and Andrew Wilder's chapter traces the formation of the Afghanistan Research and Evaluation Unit (AREU) in Kabul, and reflects on the challenges, successes, and failures of establishing an independent policy research institution in a country experiencing war. They discuss issues of security such as how to balance staff security with the need to conduct research outside the "Kabul bubble" and how then to communicate politically sensitive research findings. They explore how to use the relative strengths of international and Afghan staff to gain access to Afghan institutions and communities, and the competing priorities of building local research capacity and producing high-quality policy research that is credible and relevant to both global and local audiences. They also address the intersection of research and policy, examining the tension between the need to do good-quality, in-depth research and the importance of being timely and relevant in a rapidly evolving political and security environment with high turnover of key policy makers.

Political scientist Tim Longman writes on the need for and responsibility to produce independent research in situations of pervasive serious crimes and violations. He draws upon examples from his research for Human Rights Watch and as an academic in Rwanda, Burundi, and the Democratic Republic of the Congo. Longman writes:

> Yet even in places where violence is endemic and governments regularly persecute people who criticize them, good, systematic research is still possible. People are often much more willing to speak openly than one would expect. And it is not simply civil society activists and other elites who will be willing to provide information. Average people – farmers, day laborers, market women – are not only much better informed than most elites. Even when people are afraid of the consequences of speaking out and evade questions or tell untruths, a well developed knowledge of the local culture can help a researcher break through this barrier and get people to open up.

He challenges those who research and report on conflict to get the appropriate training to do their work well and pushes independent researchers, journalists, and filmmakers to see that their findings are used to improve the lives of those in conflict settings.

Part VI: Practicalities

Dyan Mazurana and Lacey Andrews Gale's chapter, "Preparing for Research in Active Conflict Zones: Practical Considerations for Personal Safety," provides a practical look at key issues for those who are interested in working in sites of active armed conflict. They discuss a variety of issues including personal safety and health protocol, conflict analysis, developing security plans, check-ins, medical care, trauma and vicarious trauma, and other practical measures. They argue that researchers who lack the knowledge, ability, and/or discipline to make good decisions to stay physically and emotionally healthy and safe are a risk to themselves, the other people on their team, and the people they are interviewing.

The book concludes with an Afterword by the political scientist Elizabeth Jean Wood. Wood draws on her own experience, as well as that of some of her students, to discuss the challenges as well as the promise of gathering data in such settings – including the importance of participant observation alongside more structured encounters with subjects, the complexity of the construction of trust with subjects, and the role of respect for the agency of our subjects. She assesses the process of "learning from the field," including subjects' capacity for resilience as well as suffering, the dilemmas of working with research assistants or partners, and the importance for most projects of deep local knowledge on the part of the researcher, which often implies returning time and again to the same setting. She discusses the ethical challenges and dilemmas that researchers confront in conflict settings and argues that the ethical principles held central by academic researchers and institutions of "do no harm," data security, and informed consent are particularly challenging to implement in such settings. Throughout, her discussion makes frequent reference to the volume's overarching themes of representation, do no harm, safe spaces, trust, and responsibility, as well as practicalities.

BIBLIOGRAPHY

Bar On, Bat-Ami. 1993. Marginality and privilege. In *Feminist epistemologies*, eds. Linda Alcoff and Elizabeth Potter, 83–100. New York: Routledge.
Barnett, Michael and Thomas Weiss. 2008. *Humanitarianism in question: Politics, power, ethics*. Ithaca, NY: Cornell University Press.
    2011. *Humanitarianism contested: Where angels fear to tread*. New York: Routledge.

Barnett, Michael. 2005. Humanitarianism transformed. *Perspectives on Politics* 3: 723–40.

Bronwyn, Bruton. 2010. *Somalia: A new approach*. New York: Council on Foreign Relations.

Cramer, Christopher, Laura Hammond, and Johan Pottier. 2011. *Researching violence in Africa: Insights and experiences*. Leiden and Boston: Brill Publishing House.

Dancygier, Rafaela. 2010. *Immigration and conflict in Europe*. Cambridge: Cambridge University Press.

Donini, Antonio. 2008. *The state of the humanitarian enterprise: Humanitarian agenda 2015: Final report*. Medford, MA: Feinstein International Center, Tufts University.

Duffield, Mark. 2001. *Global governance and the new wars: The merging of development and security*, London: Zed Books.

2002. War as network enterprise: The new security terrain and its implications. *Cultural Values* 6: 153–65.

Harvey, Paul, Abby Stoddard, Adele Harmer, and Glyn Taylor. 2010. *The state of the humanitarian system: Assessing performance and progress*. London: ALNAP.

Hoffman, Danny. 2011. *The war machines: Young men and violence in Sierra Leone and Liberia*. Durham, NC, and London: Duke University Press.

hooks, bell. 1990. *Yearning: Race, gender and cultural politics*. Boston: South End Press.

Institute of Development Studies. 2009. Violence, social action and research. *Institute of Development Studies Bulletin* 40.3.

Keen, David. 2008. *Complex emergencies*. Cambridge, UK: Polity Press.

Marx, Karl and Friedrich Engels. 1998. *The Communist Manifesto*, introduction by Martin Malia. New York: Penguin Group, 1998.

Mazurana, Dyan. 2004. Gender and the causes and consequences of armed conflict. In *Gender, conflict, and peacekeeping*, eds. Dyan Mazurana, Angela Raven-Roberts, and Jane Parpart, 29–42. Oxford and Boulder, CO: Rowman & Littlefield.

Nordstrom, Carolyn. 2004. *Shadow wars: Violence, power and international profiteering in the twenty-first century*. Berkeley: University of California Press.

Nordstrom, Carolyn and Antonius Robben. 1995. *Fieldwork under fire: Contemporary studies of violence and survival*. Berkeley: University of California Press.

Norman, Julie. 2009. Got trust? The challenge of gaining access in conflict zones. In *Surviving field research: Working in violent and difficult situations*, eds. Chandra Lekha Sriram, John C. King, Julie A. Mertus, Olga Martin-Ortega, and Johanna Herman. London: Taylor & Francis.

Richards, Paul ed. 2005. *No peace no war: An anthropology of contemporary armed conflicts*. Oxford: James Curry.

Shaw, Rosalind. **February** 2005. *Rethinking truth and reconciliation commissions: Lessons from Sierra Leone*. Washington DC: United States Institute for Peace. Available at http://www.usip.org/publications/rethinking-truth-and-reconciliatio n-commissions-lessons-sierra-leone (accessed January 12, 2012).

Slim, Hugo. 2008. *Killing civilians: Method, madness and morality in war*. New York: Columbia University Press.

Sphere Project. 2011. *Humanitarian charter and minimum standards in disaster response*. Geneva: The Sphere Project. Available at http://www.sphereproject.org/ content/view/720/200/lang,english (accessed January 12, 2012).

Spivak, Gayatri Chakravorty. 1988. Can the subaltern speak? In *Marxism and the interpretation of culture*, eds. C. Nelson and L. Grossberg, 271–313. Basingstoke: Macmillian Education.

Sriram, Chandra Lekha, John C. King, Julie A. Mertus, Olga Martin-Ortega, **and** Johanna Herman, eds. 2009. *Surviving field research: Working in violent and difficult situations*. London: Taylor & Francis.

United Nations. 2004. *Final Report of the Special Rapporteur, Terrorism and Human Rights. UN Sub-Commission on the Promotion and Protection of Human Rights. Final report of the Special Rapporteur, Kalliopi K. Koufa*, E.CN.4/Sub.2/2004/40, June 25, 2004.

Walker, Peter and Daniel Maxwell. 2009. *Shaping the humanitarian world*. London: Routledge.

Webster, Mackinnon and Peter Walker. 2009. *One for all and all for one: Intra-organizational dynamics in humanitarian action*. Medford, MA: Feinstein International Center, Tufts University.

Wood, Elisabeth. 2006. The ethical challenges of field research in conflict zones. *Qualitative Sociology* 29: 373–86.

Young, Iris Marion. 2006. Responsibility and global justice: A social connection model. *Social Philosophy and Policy* 23(1): 102–30.

PART I

REPRESENTATION

Figure 1. "Filming" April 2006, Gulu district, northern Uganda.
Photographer: Mélanie Gauthier

During the shooting, we were constantly looking for new ways to film the
internally displaced person (IDP) camps in order to show their unimaginable
expanse. We found that high-angle shots – such as the one we took on top of
a termite mound – were often the best way to do it. And, of course, we had
dozens of voluntary assistants.

The Other Side of the Country: Filming the Human Experience of War

Catherine Hébert, Translated from French by Valerie Vanstone

We must not miss anything from this journey, we cannot overlook or lose anything, because we are going to have to give an account of our experience, write a report, a story; in other words, we will have to examine our conscience.

Ryszard *Kapuściński, The Other,* 18

INTRODUCTION

The Victoria Nile River twists and turns across Uganda, dividing the northern and southern regions of the country. To enter the north, you cross Karuma Bridge where it spans the Nile's strong currents and waterfalls. On the far side is a different, ruined country, one where few villages are inhabited, roadside shops have been abandoned, no cattle graze, and fields have lain fallow for a long time.

I wrote that in May 2004, the first time I set foot in northern Uganda. With support from Dyan Mazurana, a university professor and researcher who had been working for several years in northern Uganda, I was doing a reportage aimed at lifting the veil on the war that had been ravaging the country for twenty years. Equipped with a small camera, I shot and produced a twenty-two-minute feature called *Mangos for Charlotte,* outlining the main elements of the conflict.

My brief stay in Uganda troubled me deeply. I could not believe that a country devastated by two decades of war had received so little attention and even less response. Barely a year earlier, the UN special adviser to the secretary general on humanitarian affairs, Jan England, had described the situation in northern Uganda as "the world's most neglected humanitarian crisis."

Moving among the people felt as though I were walking through the heart of a wound that would not stop bleeding. My reportage gave a brief summary

of the conflict but I felt it remained essentially superficial. I promised myself
I would return to Uganda, this time to make a documentary, a personal film
that would not settle for simply reporting on the conflict but would bring it
alive from the inside, through the eyes of its characters. I would like to be clear
from the start that I do not particularly care for the word "character" in relation to documentary film. My feeling is that the word dehumanizes people,
reducing them to the status of "film objects." For the purposes of this chapter,
therefore, the word should be read only in its technical sense to mean "people
who appear on-screen."

The war in Uganda must be guessed at rather than seen. To communicate the insidious nature of the violence Ugandans living in the northern
region endure, the documentary would have to be more than a political film;
it would *also* have to be atmospheric. For me, an atmospheric film is the
antithesis of a didactic film. It expects the viewers to understand more than
what they see or hear. It lets you see beyond a simple plotline, offering keys
to understandings that are implied rather than explained. The most telling
illustration of an atmospheric film is the scenes in which characters' emotions are revealed, not by their words but by their silence. Many things are
revealed by seeing how people live. The atmospheric film allows for those
moments where the action has no other goal than to enable an emotional
rather than logical understanding. Rather than follow a single narrative
thread, the atmospheric film presents a complex, layered vision that asks
the viewer to connect and interpret sequences without an explanatory note
attached to each one.

In 2006, I spent nearly three months in northern Uganda: one month of
field research and just less than two months of shooting. The process of making the film was hugely transformative for me, both personally and artistically.
It resulted in a feature-length documentary, *The Other Side of the Country*,
subtitled *What Do You Do When War Engulfs You*, and *Your Government Tells
You There Is No War?*

After completing journalism studies in Quebec and in France, I began my
professional life doing feature reporting. It did not take me long to realize
that, although it is a genre I respect enormously, I was unsuited to it. The
fast pace and "quickie" interviews made me uncomfortable. I prefer to enter
a world where I can spend time, both with and without a camera. I also like
to get off the beaten track, turning my gaze elsewhere while most are fixed
on the same points of interest. In Quebec, the window for international news
is very small. Mainstream media narrowly focus on one or two stories or
geographic locations at the expense of hundreds of other salient stories and
realities.

For these reasons, I was drawn to documentary filmmaking. It is a genre that lets me devote myself to alternative topics. Documentary provides the kind of space needed to create original cinematic work that focuses attention on critically important but neglected subjects. For me, film is an essential medium in that it lets significant and extraordinary stories be brought to light and then allows the viewer to watch them unfold. By making it possible to recount real-life experiences, documentary film moves such narratives and realities from the margin to the center.

WITHOUT BLOOD

Cinema has often tried to film pain, the wounded self, using sometimes questionable methods with even more questionable results. Today, compassionate voyeurism has become almost a genre in itself, and documentary has not escaped that trap. I thought it was crucial, therefore, to film *The Other Side of the Country* in human terms: to make the characters' suffering palpable without self-indulgence or affectation. It was clear to me I needed to show not only the daily tragedy but people's dignity as well. Why? Because war, hunger, and death are not commodities to be exploited. And there was dignity. Courage too. After all, these people had survived more than twenty years of war.

The surroundings in northern Uganda were indescribably beautiful, despite the war. The light was amazing, the vegetation luxurious, and the Acholi and Langi people speak with a softness and grace that, for a Westerner, are surreal.

And therein lay the challenge of capturing the war in northern Uganda.

The violence in Uganda is not manifest; it is insidious. What struck me was that no generation north of the Nile had been spared, from the children abducted and forcibly recruited by the LRA to the elderly people forced into the displaced person camps. Among the most common forms of violence in northern Uganda and most difficult to render on film, were government denial and complicity in the war. But first, let me briefly describe the roots of the conflict, to help us not only understand how it came about but why it continues.

ORIGINS OF THE CONFLICT

In 1986, the man who would become Uganda's president, Yoweri Museveni, toppled the elected government and took power. Regulars from the defeated Ugandan army fled north, to the traditional lands of the Acholi and Langi people. Since the country's independence in 1962, the Acholi and Langi had held positions of authority in the Ugandan army. Museveni, afraid that soldiers loyal to the deposed regime (where the now deposed president hailed from) would turn against him, ordered his army to occupy the north to quell any attempts at rebellion. One of the most enduring armed groups to rise up against him was the "Lord's Resistance Army," or LRA, led by the mystic Joseph Kony.

At first, the LRA claimed it was fighting to overthrow Museveni and "free" northern Uganda. But over the years, its political goals became less clear, and Kony focused more on its strange mix of religion, spirituality, and extreme violence against civilian populations and his own troops. Kony, who had earlier set himself up to challenge those in power in Kampala, then seemed to turn the violence inward, against his own Acholi people and the neighboring ethnic groups. He had been losing their support and responded by abducting children and adults and forcing them into serving his armed group. Beginning in 1993, weapons, support, and safe bases for the LRA to pursue the conflict were received in large part from the Sudanese government, in retaliation for Museveni's support of the rebel Sudanese People's Liberation Army (SPLA) in southern Sudan.

Among the cruelest outcomes of twenty years of war have been the so-called protected villages, the government's description of squalid camps for internally displaced persons or IDPs. At the time we were filming, the count was close to two million IDPs in northern Uganda. Ninety percent of the population in Acholiland and a third in neighboring regions of northern Uganda had been forced by the government to abandon their villages and move to the filthy, overcrowded camps. We counted more than two hundred IDP camps in the north. Museveni's government was moving the population – emptying villages – often with threat and force on the pretext that people would be safer from the rebels in the camps. But rather than security zones, the camps simply made the LRA's work easier. The camps became "one-stop centers" (as James Otto, a northern Ugandan human right activist, calls them in the film) for rebels who no longer had to cover dozens of kilometers to find children to kidnap, women to abduct for "wives," and food to steal; now they just had to visit one camp. Museveni's soldiers were too few in number to prove capable of protecting the camps' bruised, impoverished people. It was the weakest who paid the highest price.

President Museveni had on many occasions over the twenty-plus years of the war declared that the conflict was nearly over or that it had in fact ended. Yet the conflict continues to this day, claiming more lives not only in Uganda, but now in Sudan, the Democratic Republic of Congo, and the Central African Republic. Without diminishing the brutality of the LRA, most political analysts agree that Museveni and the heads of Uganda's national army have used the conflict to inflate military budgets, enrich themselves, and maintain power. Uganda receives nearly half its total annual revenues from international donor governments, and Museveni has in the past siphoned those funds away from intended social programs and into defense ministry coffers. Despite a military budget that has more than tripled since the conflict began, Museveni's army has proven both unable and unwilling to adequately protect people in IDP camps or to end the conflict. Where are the government soldiers? Why are they unable to protect the camps? These were some of the troubling questions the film sought to answer.

Since 1987, the LRA has left tens of thousands dead in its wake. More than sixty thousand young people have been abducted into the LRA – girls and boys forced to fight or be killed. Because it did not have the support of the population, the LRA took people by force, to commit atrocities or become slaves.

For each abducted child, dozens of others feared they would suffer the same fate. Every evening, tens of thousands of children fled the countryside for the cities. The humanitarian aid workers called them "night commuters" because they appeared only in the night, seeking shelter from LRA abduction raids on their camps. At twilight, we would see these night exiles hurrying along the roads, desperately trying to reach the city before darkness fell.

THE STARTING POINT: ONE GIRL'S STORY

Despite the complexity of the conflict in Uganda, I did not want to make a didactic film. For the reasons outlined earlier, I had set myself the task of making a film that would be both political and atmospheric. Every good film tells a story, and in that sense, a documentary is no different from a fiction film. Among all the horrific stories about the war, one has become tragically infamous – that of the "Aboke Girls." On the night of October 9, 1996, at Saint Mary's College Aboke, a boarding school run by Italian nuns, the LRA abducted 139 schoolgirls. Carrying burning torches, the LRA broke into their dormitory and took the girls away, as the sisters looked on helplessly. Tied together like slaves, the girls were swallowed up into the night. Parents waited for their girls to return, knowing they were being used as fighters and slaves by day and sexually abused by the captor "husbands" by night. As the years passed, some of the girls did manage to escape, some returning with children born of rape, and all weighed down by the heavy silence of those who have seen the unspeakable.

It was the Aboke girls' story that would become the starting point for *The Other Side of the Country* and eventually lead us to other characters whose lives had been shaped by the war. The characters had parallel stories that would converge at a single reality: that of an insidious, seemingly endless war, with no battles raging to be filmed and no high-tech arsenal, but omnipresent nonetheless.

GRAY ZONES

In northern Uganda, we saw the links in a chain of destruction – unspectacular but extraordinary – that had touched an entire society. And destroyed it was. For each abducted youth, there were desperate parents and grandparents. Thousands of other children were fleeing their homes nightly to avoid the same fate. Villages had been emptied – by rebels and by the government. Thousands of young women had been abducted and given as "forced wives" to LRA commanders as rewards. When they returned, so too did their children born of rape. Fear was part of everyone's daily life.

But like a light shining in the darkness, there were also northern Ugandans who refused to live in terror, who fought back in whatever way they could. I wanted to film this stubborn resistance of people who had survived two decades of conflict, caught between government hypocrisy and rebel machetes. I did not want to make a film that would romanticize their suffering, which I saw would be of no use to anyone and expand no one's thinking. I was afraid of making a film that would only reinforce prejudice that would allow viewers to respond to the Ugandan conflict with "Just more Africans killing each other – leave them to it." It pains me to write so bluntly. Yet that is the kind of automatic reflex that television portrays when, if at all, conflicts in Africa are shown. Reserving little time for in-depth coverage, television news is necessarily reductionist. I remember watching a report on national radio (Radio-Canada), by a journalist I respect, and being horrified as I realized that she was in northern Uganda, showing how the government was doing the impossible to protect its people. Her evidence? The havens of peace and security provided by IDP camps. Inside I cringed.

Scouting without a Camera

When I show *The Other Side of the Country* to audiences, one of the questions that always arises is, How did I, or more precisely we, get so close to the characters? My response is always the same: the time spent beforehand with the people you plan to film ensures the closeness that will appear on-screen. As crucial as the time spent filming is the time spent *before* the shoot – without the camera. Nowhere is that more true than in dealing with a people racked by twenty years of war. A film crew is, by definition, intrusive. Turning a camera on someone creates a one-way gaze; it is not easy exchanging glances with a lens. The sound boom with a microphone hanging off the end feels like the sword of Damocles. While the crew can demonstrate all the empathy in the world, the physical bulk of the equipment and the fact they show up in a group (director, camera operator, sound recorder, and translator) are still intimidating for the person being filmed. That is why it is vital to establish from the outset that the film will be made *with* them and not *about* them. To make sure that future characters are true partners in the film, they of course need to know why we are making it and, even more importantly, why they should take part. What is the benefit to them? What do they have to gain by exposing themselves in this way?

Scouting before the actual shoot was a privileged opportunity to explain to people what it means to take part in the film. I tried to explain how there could even be some benefit to helping others understand what is going on, even if that benefit seems abstract at the time and remains, all things considered, quite small. As a documentary filmmaker, I spend almost all my time asking other people questions. And I am delighted when someone challenges me. Right away, that makes the relationship one more of equals: me, interested in their stories, and them, curious about why I'm there. That kind of opening is impossible to create if you pull up with a full crew and all your equipment. The process of gaining trust in this first encounter is premised on the fact that people are under no pressure to be in the film. That kind of pressure, as unintentional as it may be, is inevitable when a film crew arrives and starts unloading equipment. By going out first to meet people on my own, I gave them the latitude to decide whether or not to take part. My main focus was to ensure that no one felt coerced.

I remember going to the IDP camps while I was doing field research and the crowds that would gather around. A white woman – a *toubab!*[1] Did that mean sacks of rice were on the way? Or salt? Or a visit from the children's doctor? What NGO do you work for? Where is the logistics truck? "No," I told them humbly – and pitifully – "I'm only here to listen to your stories. So that you can tell me what it's like to live with war every day." Invariably at that point, three-quarters of the throng would walk away, disappointed. Each time it happened, I told myself I would have done the same. But a few curious onlookers stayed. They watched me, half-amused, half-skeptical. A foreign woman wants to listen to us? Why? That simple question – "Why?" – became

---

[1] A white person.

the way into a conversation. And so it was with that mutual curiosity that we began our conversations.

The Camp Settings

In the camp the filth was inescapable. Here were people whose traditional homes would have been spaced well apart from each other, each surrounded by their fruit and nut trees, their agricultural garden plots, and their livestock. Now, they were pushed together "like animals," they told us, and living practically on top of one another. They explained how it was impossible to maintain their hygiene and hence their dignity as they had in the past. The people struggled to survive on meager rations from the UN World Food Program, supplemented often with just a few manioc roots dried in the sun. In that context, how do you convince people it is important they should tell their story to an audience on the other side of an ocean? How do you explain that their testimony may help make a few policy makers more aware? That their words may help awaken slumbering consciences? In the end, the filmmaker has only "maybes" to make the argument. It is not the best form of persuasion the world has ever seen.

In this kind of undertaking, it is hard to be too modest. You always feel slightly ridiculous saying that a film is only one link in a long chain, that it cannot stop the war or open the floodgates of food aid, but that it can give a voice to the voiceless, and that every word we carry back with us may have some impact. All I can offer is the act of listening, and the promise that their stories will be heard. By whom? And with what result? These are questions for which there is never any answer. The skepticism of the people I talk to is palpable. In their eyes, I read: "You, foreign person, you're going back to your comfortable country afterward? Why should we trust you? Why should we agree to do this film with you?" I give my answer to the translator in the hope his words will convey more than my French-laced, halting English. "Only because I am interested in you. I came all the way here because I think your stories are worth telling and deserve to be widely heard, and because together, bit by bit, perhaps we can make a difference. If you agree, I will come back with other foreigners and we will spend more time with you." "Ah. You are coming back?" (Meaning: So you really are interested in what happens to us?) "Of course," I answer. "And I won't be alone. There are others who are ready to join me in listening to you." In them I sense the first glimmers of trust.

The promise to return proves I am genuinely interested in them. They invite me over to the shade. They begin to talk to me. That was the moment the film began. The actual shooting would occur much later.

Shooting in Secret

In 2006 when I was shooting the film, the government of Yoweri Museveni, calling itself a "single-party democracy," forbade journalists to go more than fifty kilometers outside the capital city of Kampala without government permission and a military escort. Reporters and filmmakers were not allowed to travel to the northern part of the country and, if they did, were accompanied by security personnel and intelligence officers, often posing as translators, who showed them how well the government was protecting the people in IDP camps. There was never any mention that the government sent no food aid to the camps (it was the World Food Program who did that). Or that, at the height of the war, more than one thousand people died of preventable disease in IDP camps every week (rates well above humanitarian emergency levels). Or that, according to human rights organizations, concentrating people in the camps had not offered increased protection nor enabled the government military to defeat the LRA.

We were not interested in propagating more government stories about the conflict. There was no question, therefore, of our asking official government permission for anything. The film would have to be shot in secret. When I say "secret," I often hear "oohs" and "aahs" from people half-thrilled and half-admiring. It is a word that excites fear but also excites the imagination. But this was not a case of wearing camouflage jackets and taking pictures with a telephoto lens from behind a window. The word "secret" or "clandestine" as it is used here means only an "unannounced" shoot. We had decided to go ahead without a film permit and had invented a reasonable story in case of a problem. At that point, we had no choice but to film with the utmost discretion, avoiding all the military barracks.

In this case, filming in secret was more than an issue of feasibility; this type of shooting contributed to the quality of the film. A clandestine shoot meant I did not have the luxury of wandering too far afield or being sidelined by secondary concerns. My film proposal had been narrowly defined and the scenes to be filmed, chosen with care. Now I needed to focus on the essential – the human experience. I aligned myself more closely with my characters. Paradoxically, the country's being at war helped us in a way. To explain: northern Uganda had essentially been abandoned by the government and left to its own devices. It was not a war zone of frenzied military activity. The soldiers posted there were poorly equipped, badly dressed, badly paid, and largely uninterested in protecting the people or tracking and fighting the rebels. So they left the people pretty much to themselves. Once past the military roadblocks, the crew had a fairly easy time getting around. It was the rebels who posed the greatest threat. Our Ugandan associates were on the lookout and helped us move safely.

A piece of Uganda's social fabric had been destroyed by the war, but another part turned out to have been strengthened. The people I worked with had an uncanny ability to know where the rebels were, an ability that defied any technology. They alerted me to the rebel detachments' movements with surprising accuracy, using a word-of-mouth technique perfected, sadly, over twenty years of war. Thanks to our Ugandan friends – and I can never thank them enough – we were able to do our work in relative safety.

Technical Constraints

I want to stop for a moment to talk about technical constraints, because, while espousing a noble philosophy about cinema is all well and good, making a film remains a technical operation.

Smoothly running equipment is the secret to a good shoot. Consider what happens if there is a technical glitch during the filming: the people you are filming wonder what is going on (and often think they have made some mistake), you lose concentration, the camera operator or sound recorder begins to fiddle nervously with the equipment (which you had worked so hard to make the person forget) – and at that point you may as well accept that your scene is ruined. In Uganda, we could do little against sun, heat, rain, wind, or dust – the archenemy of the electrical circuit – but we could respond to an electrical blackout with something as small as a car battery to recharge our equipment. The advance scouting, therefore, also served to identify technical issues (power outages created the most problems) and potential solutions.

The other challenges were those that arise in any war zone: ensuring a minimum of comfort for the crew, traveling on collapsed roads, communicating with the production team in Montreal, and so on. After one scouting expedition, I immediately decided that the filming would be done in two blocks: the first, lasting one month; and the second, about two weeks. That decision, although revisited several times for budget reasons, was among the best I made. Not only did it allow the crew to recharge their own batteries, it also gave me a chance to look carefully at the footage, with the editor, and do a first assembly. With hindsight, I can state with certainty that this two-step process was a key step in creative terms. By the time we returned to Uganda for the second shoot, the film had a life of its own; it had taken shape and found its voice. We knew what kinds of scenes did not belong and were not worth pushing to get. And so I began the second round of filming guided by the insights gained from those initial screenings. It was during that second round that we shot some of our most beautiful scenes, including those in which an elderly women named Anguleta takes us to the place where her village once stood and where her children were taken from her and killed.

Once again, the film's greatest ally turned out to be time; because we had been there before, we had returned, and we had given her time to reflect, Anguleta decided on her own to take us to her former village and the site of some of her greatest sorrow.

Anguleta had never been back to her village, now a field of wild grass with a few skeletal huts still standing. She had told me she never wanted to set foot in it again; that the place where her children had died was cursed, haunted by evil spirits. I had not insisted. The village was a place I could go back to alone, with the crew. There was no need to unearth the grim memories of a mother, now grandmother, already so grievously tested by life. Time passed. We spent several days filming with Anguleta: on her long walk (over dozens of kilometers) to collect firewood that began in the pitch dark at three in the morning, on her walk to fetch water, as she prepared meals in her hut. There was nothing remarkable, but we were there with her as she went through her daily routine. I will never know how, but the idea of seeing her village again had been quietly working away inside Anguleta's head. One day, she told me: "Let's go." I was so surprised, I had to ask the translator to repeat it. Affirmative.

You should have seen Anguleta climbing into the truck! Her fleshless arms straining to hold on to the door handle told me this was the first time she had ever been in a motor vehicle. She was overcome with laughter. And so were we. It was a moment of pure childish delight that we did not film. You have to know when to protect these fleeting moments that an overly ambitious camera would have spoiled.

A few hundred meters away from what was now essentially a ghost town, we stopped to film Anguleta's slow progress along the deserted dirt road. It was a risk to film here: the grass was high; the rebels move through here. But our Ugandan colleagues had heard and detected no rebel activity, so we stepped out. A fine rain had begun to fall, as though the weather was attuned to this fragile moment. Anguleta was barefoot, as usual. After a few moments, she stopped. "Here," she said, pointing to a mound of grass standing higher than our heads. Then she glanced at us slyly, with a hoarse little laugh. For me, that complicit glance meant: "I must be completely crazy to have come back here with you. And you are probably just as crazy as I am." It was a pure – and all too rare – "documentary moment," a moment of pure authenticity, one that would have unfolded in exactly the same way if the camera had not been there.

Figure 2. "Anguleta" April 2006, IDP camp in Lira, northern Uganda.
Photographer: Mélanie Gauthier

The afternoon this image was taken, we were sitting with Anguleta and some
other women from the IDP camp. We could feel the great despair of the mothers
and grandmothers. They could not bear seeing their children leaving the camps to
become street kids in town, in search of food. The transmission of culture – most
importantly the farming of the land – was vanishing.

I keep insisting on the importance of time in documentary filmmaking.
I like to remind myself that we work with human beings, not machines,

and that creating trust takes time – especially with people ravaged by war. Whenever I remember that scene, I think, Trust takes time.

Choosing the Characters

In northern Uganda, the social fabric has been roughly torn, its resources slashed away. For twenty years, people have been dying wondering why, in a silence as embarrassing as it is inexplicable. I was struck by the fact that not one generation has been spared, a realization that would determine the choice of characters for the film: everyone, from children to grandparents, would give the war a face. Each of their stories would give us access to a different aspect of the war, and by putting them together, the vast tableau of this strange conflict would emerge. I decided ahead of time, therefore, that there would be five main characters. Some remained until the end; others fell away during the filming or editing.

I would like to be clear that my documentary method and the way I find my characters have nothing to do with a "case study" approach. I did not decide ahead of time on a profile for each character. I wanted to share the way the characters experienced the war, not by observing them but by being with them, as a partner, for a short time. Clearly, that kind of "complicity" did not always happen. Unlike a case study in which one person is chosen to represent a wider reality for many victims, my approach consisted in spending time with an individual I had selected but without pretending that his or her life was representative of others or of war. My role as a documentarian is to go out and meet people in order to share that precious thing that is the human experience. The documentarian thus becomes a person who wonders – about other humans, with other humans. Not to formulate certitudes but to reformulate life's essential questions in human terms.

ANGELINA

Angelina is the mother of Charlotte, whose story inspired my feature film *Mangos for Charlotte*.[2] She had become an activist after the abduction of her daughter, and she was a natural starting point for the film. She had also become a Ugandan figurehead in the movement to rescue children held by the LRA. She was accustomed to the media and easy to film. Tall, with a

[2] The title of the film represents Angelina's hope for her daughter's return. At the end of the feature report, in her garden full of flowers, Angelina showed me a heavily laden mango tree. She told me she had planted the tree after her daughter's kidnapping and expressed the wish that Charlotte would come back some day to eat some of the mangos.

dignified walk, charismatic and politically aware, she perfectly embodied
the cause of parents whose children had been stolen. At the point we went
back to shoot the film, two years had gone by since the writing of the script.
During this time, a happy and unforeseen event had occurred: Charlotte had
returned. She was deeply traumatized, and carried two children born of rape
in her arms, but she was alive.

Clearly, her daughter's return had transformed Angelina's life. The reunion
she had waited for so long had finally happened. Her relief knew no bounds,
and her mother's heart could finally find some rest. After eight years of fierce
struggle, the nervous fatigue was clear throughout Angelina's body. She
was exhausted. She wanted to continue being an activist, but she no longer
wanted to take centre stage, which was understandable. The film put her in
a dilemma. She did not want to abandon the cause, or the other parents still
waiting for their children to return. But going back yet again over the story of
Charlotte's kidnapping held no appeal. She did not say it in so many words,
but the unreturned phone calls spoke volumes.

I too was in a dilemma. My grand theory about not asking people to relive
their trauma left me stranded. If Angelina decided not to take part in the film,
the entire thread of my story would unravel. Watching me struggle with the
situation, Abdallah, my friend and driver, collaborator, and cultural interpreter[3]
as I enjoyed calling him, came to my aid. He advised me to invite Angelina to
supper and simply explain my dilemma to her. She was strong enough that she
would make her own decision at that point. I took his advice, though I was very
nervous. Angelina listened patiently. A few days later, she called: OK, she would
go with us to Aboke College to tell us about the night of the kidnapping.

I have to admit, it was not a particularly relaxed shoot. I spread the word to
the crew: on no account were we to ask Angelina to go over anything twice.
This was our one chance, and we had to focus to get everything on this one
take. I wanted to intervene as little as possible so that Angelina would feel at
ease, telling the story at her own pace without my interrupting to ask her to be
more precise. She told us everything, from A to Z, without leaving out a single
detail. It was her experience as an activist that shone on the screen that day.

In the end, the scene we filmed in the dormitory where Charlotte and her
classmates were kidnapped was a moment of pure grace.

Did I disobey my own documentary code by pushing Angelina? Did she
benefit from the experience at all? If I had it to do over, would I go about it the
same way? I don't know. I only know that the dormitory scene with Angelina

---

[3] Jackson, who appears in the film, works as a driver in real life but he was not our crew driver
during the filming.

is the basic arc that underlies the entire film. It begins the dramatic arc as the film opens, and it closes that arc at the end. I also know that many parents identified with Angelina, and that thanks to her, an entire aspect of the war in Uganda was better understood. Angelina was able to appeal to audiences with a rare skill. "In your country," she told me, "if a parent goes to pick up their child after school, and the child is not there within five minutes, they panic. Five minutes.... Imagine eight years."

I know that my filmmaking craft is a fluid one. The experience in Uganda taught me that I would have to redefine the limits of that craft with each new film I made; that documentary method cannot be set in stone; that sometimes you have to cross a line you yourself have drawn. My approaching Angelina is a good example of that.

JACKSON

Jackson was not our official driver (as you might believe from seeing the film), but he *was* a driver for a local human rights organization. I met him early on in the research process, when he was assigned to take me around the country. At that point, I had absolutely no intention of making him a character in the film. One day, he told me: "Tomorrow is Sunday. My day off. I want to take you to an IDP camp. I want to show you what my people have to endure. *I'm* going to show you how they live." Of course, I accepted his invitation. All the way out to the camp, at the camp, and on the way back, Jackson vented his anger. He was a bottomless pit of words. Despite all the human misery I had seen that day, I went home feeling less burdened after the time I spent with Jackson. I wondered why. And then I understood that Jackson was a release valve for me. His outpourings embodied and externalized *my* anger, *my* revulsion, *my* disgust. What a relief that was! What he said was profoundly political (I'll return to that). Ugandans have been so beaten down by war that any rebellious spirit – which could attract the ire of the army or the rebels – has been smothered for a long time. Not because they do not feel it, but because expressing it openly would probably mean their death. You have to choose your battles if you want to survive. My own rebelliousness thus found a voice, an emergency exit, in Jackson. If I could identify with him, I had no doubt that audiences would do the same. And so, after that achingly awful Sunday drive, Jackson entered the film.

ANGULETA

I have already talked at length about Anguleta, a grandmother sentenced to spend her last days in a fetid, anonymous camp, far from her little plot of

Figure 3. "Amuru Camp" April 2006. IDP Camp outside Gulu, Northern Uganda
Photographer: Mélanie Gauthier

> We wanted to show the vast geographic reach of the IDP camps and the crowded
> conditions under which people were living. But we were finding a gap between the
> not-so-dramatic images we were shooting and the gravity of the situation. After
> much trial and error, we found that a high-angle shot was the most graphic, and
> we shot many camps climbing on our truck roof. Amuru camp, population 44 000,
> was one of them.

land and the shea trees she had tended with such good care and from which
she had made her living. I want to tell you more about how we met. I already
knew I wanted to film an elderly person in an IDP camp. Northern Uganda
had once been known as the country's breadbasket. The Acholi and Langi
people are herders and farmers, and forcing them to leave their land, abandoning them in IDP camps, was to condemn them to hunger, misery, and even
death. Worst of all, when they were taken off their land, the farmers could
no longer hand down their knowledge to their children. So it was the entire
heritage of an ancestral farming culture that was being lost – another prime
example of the insidious violence of the war. You don't notice it at first; it is

invisible. The children do not go to school. But they are not learning to raise crops either. This second privation, being cut off from traditional learning, is probably the more tragic; for the Acholi and Langi people, the results are likely to be devastating.

In deciding to film an older person, I wanted to show this loss of ancestral culture and values. I visited many IDP camps, first greeting the camp leader and explaining why I was there. They would kindly spread the word, assembling dozens of older people willing to talk to me. I generally ended up with about fifteen older people waiting patiently for my questions. Here again, I did not fully grasp the formal – and necessary – structure of this kind of Q&A. It always felt as though the person before me wanted to meet expectations I did not have and was formulating answers based on those expectations. It was so very refreshing to set foot in Anguleta's camp and encounter a group of older women who were bright, curious, and unruly. I outlined my project and then asked, as I always do, whether they had any questions for me. "Do you have any children?" one of them threw out. "No." I realized my credibility had just taken a hit. "But you're married?" another woman asked. "Uh, no. Not married either." Clearly, I was only making matters worse. They burst out laughing. "Well then, you are like our daughter!" I could hear them thinking: "The poor *toubab*. She's thirty-one and she's dressed like a boy. She hasn't been able to find a husband back home. She must be unhappy and needs to be gathered up into some motherly arms." I told them I'd be glad to be their daughter and hoped to be officially adopted by a Ugandan grandmother. That's when Anguleta spoke up. I had noticed her big toothless laugh from the start. She would be glad to be my adoptive grandmother. She was a sly one. We were going to get along.

The discussion with the women began. They told me about losing their land, and the impossibility of educating their children and teaching them the values they had always known. About children running away from the misery in the camps to become street children in the city. About the men withdrawing, drowning the loss of their pride in home brew made in the camp. Anguleta told me about the disappearance of her village and her children. I asked to see the box where she kept her things. We sat down beside each other, our backs leaning against the hut. We did not talk much that day. There was no need.

DENNIS

Talking with the women had got me wondering. I had already noticed the gangs of children hanging around the streets in Lira. I learned that the phenomenon of street children had been unheard of in that city before the war. Then, the children had been at school or in the fields, not grubbing through urban garbage for something to eat or sell. I was also following a radio program that broadcast the voices of children who had returned from the bush. The person responsible for the radio show was Christine, a policewoman who also did social work, trying to convince children abducted by the LRA not to believe the rebels' propaganda that returning children would be killed, trying to convince street children to return to the camps, and working to make parents more aware. "Do whatever it takes to keep your children close to you," she told them. "In the city, they are condemned to wander the streets." When I broached the subject with her, Christine offered to take me on her nightly rounds. I would see for myself where and in what conditions the street children slept. It was on those rounds that I met little Dennis. The image that remains with me is that of a scrawny, unclean body in a mauve school-uniform shirt that was much too big. His mother had died "at the camp," he said. His father beat him. His grandmother was sick and could not take care of him. And so he had run away to live on the streets of Lira town. When I asked him how old he was, he said, "My father told me I was seven." A little boy, lost, ageless. He was the smallest in the group, and every night, Christine told me, he had to fight for a place to sleep. The older kids didn't like the new ones. Dennis was captivating.

We followed Dennis at dawn, when the children go looking for a bit of light; that's how they refer to it. Seeking to get away from the darkness, they rise in the morning and say to one another, "let's go looking for some light." We followed Dennis and the children to the police station, where Christine tried to imagine with him ways he could go back to life in his camp. That was how I filmed an important scene that did not appear in the film: Christine going back to the camp with Dennis to learn that the father had run off long before, and the grandmother was dying in the rundown hospital. The women relatives with whom Christine talked were firm: they could not take Dennis back into the camp. He was a difficult child who was always running away. They had trouble feeding their own children as it was. In other words, Dennis was unwanted. Finally, Christine turned to face me, to say she could do nothing more for Dennis. The scene was laden with despair. During our four months of shooting, we asked ourselves: Did that scene belong in the film? What did it add to the story? It revealed nothing we did not already know, which was that Dennis was at a dead end. In test screenings, opinion was unanimous: the film respected people's dignity except for that one scene, which was too close to exploiting human misery.[4] It was at odds with the tone of the rest of the film.

---

4   This screening was held during the filming process (after several weeks of editing, what we call the first cut) with a small audience to help us identify what works and what does not work in the film.

The line between empathy and exploitation is a thin one, and we could not cross this line.

CAROLINE

I have already talked about the night commuters, unique to Uganda: the children who walk into the city each night in search of a safe place to sleep. This sorry state of affairs had been going on for years, and a group of "volunteer parents," revolted by the fate of "their" children, had set up centers where the children could spend the night. Among these improvised shelters was Noah's Ark. Built on a large property at the edge of the city of Gulu, it consisted of two wooden buildings and several large white tents supplied by UNICEF. Inside the tents, we were struck by the din as hundreds of children got ready for bed, boisterously unfolding their woolen blankets – one to use for a mattress and the other as a cover. The children arrived by the hundreds and every inch of the floor was put to use, the tiny bodies lining themselves up in neat, parallel lines. Once our ears were accustomed to the noise, it was the stench of the woolen blankets that was overwhelming – a rancid mix of humidity and sweat.

Noah's Ark is where I met Caroline. The volunteer parents had asked some of the boys and girls (I will return to this later) to talk to me. I met many children, each with a story more somber than the last. All were fleeing the LRA raids at the camps; some had been taken but had managed to escape; others had seen a brother or a sister taken away. That was the case for Caroline. She had watched the rebels take her big brother as she herself managed to escape with her little brother clinging to her back. She and her little brother survived; her older brother she believes was eventually killed by the rebels. From our first meeting, Caroline watched me, her eyes inquisitive. Her smile, shy at first, quickly became teasing. It seemed she found my company hugely amusing. She was twelve, tall for her age, and I quickly realized she would be the one to give the night commuters a face.

Of the twenty or so children I met, why did I "choose" Caroline? Meeting a character for a film is not unlike the kinds of encounters we all have in our lives. There are people we spontaneously want to see again and spend more time with, and others we will never see again. When I'm doing field research, as in life, I don't walk around with a checklist. The research at that stage has more to do with emotion than analysis.

Caroline had a determined quality I found astonishing. You could see it in the way she walked – her head high and her footsteps quick and sure. The crew had a hard time keeping up! At times there was also something very childlike and playful about her, and it was probably that quality that won me over. In a country at war, where childhood is often the first casualty, Caroline's freshness was welcome indeed. My only criterion (because yes, I did have one, of primary importance) was not to film a child traumatized by the war. It was entirely out of the question that I risk "retraumatizing" a child for the purposes of a film. That leads me to the delicate topic of how to gather testimony from people who have lived through – and continue to live through – the horrors of war.

The Pitfalls of "Humanitarian Cinema"

The term "humanitarian cinema" has been used to describe *The Other Side of the Country*. I would like to challenge the term. If the word "humanitarian" is used in its strictest sense to mean humanity, the human experience, then fine. But if that same notion is applied in the sense of a cinema that sacrifices itself to make the fate of the unfortunate better known, then I cannot condone it. When I filmed *The Other Side of the Country*, I was not on a mission to help anyone directly. I intended to film a fragment of the human experience, one that was at the very least unfortunate but that was part of a much broader reality. You do not film Misery, War, or Hunger; at best, you film the *experience of* misery, war, and hunger. Human experiences, then, often qualitatively different from our own, are human just the same.

If I reject the expression "humanitarian cinema," it is because it is sometimes used as an excuse to put "victims" on camera to deliver their testimony with no regard for the psychological or security impact that it may have on them. I feel uncomfortable watching a film when I sense that the person on-screen has some reservation, where there is a sense of unease that suggests the person's consent was only partially given, or feigned. A film crew, by its presence alone, exerts a power that can convince people their testimony is somehow "owed" to them. For me, that is an obstacle to any filming.

We must never lose sight of the fact that cinema is an expensive medium, and for each day of filming lost, huge amounts of funding go up in smoke. Talking about money may seem out of place here, but it would be dishonest to pretend it is not an issue. If I do mention money, it is to explain that, obsessed as we are by the end result – making a good film – we sometimes forget a basic truth: that our raw material is human beings. No cause, no principle – as honorable as those may be – and no film can justify any disrespect toward them. The person always comes before the film – never the other way around. And when there is any doubt, I think it is the film that must be sacrificed.

In some cases, people consumed by anger want to howl against their fate. There is no great skill in putting their testimony on film. That was the case with our driver, Jackson, whom I mentioned earlier. He commanded me to take his message across the Atlantic! But my reflection involves people who have been traumatized – women who have been raped, children who have been kidnapped, old people stripped of everything they own. Impressed by the camera and crew, they may agree to speak because they think they "have" to. Again, the line between freely given consent and so-called necessary consent is very thin.

The people in Uganda have been diminished. They have been terrorized for two decades. Any change in their surroundings can mean some new deterioration in their situation. Three relatively well-dressed and visibly well-nourished French-speaking foreigners pulling up in a truck one day make an impression. Whether we mean to or not, our appearance alone gives us power. Most people I met in Uganda were vulnerable and they knew it. Many would not have dared say no to our requests out of fear it would make their situation worse. As Westerners living in a world where freedom of expression is alive and well, we assume that a person who does not want to talk to us will decline our invitation to be interviewed. That did not seem to be the case in Uganda.

When I began looking for a child to talk to us about the life of a night commuter, I explained the project to the volunteer parents at Noah's Ark. Arriving at the shelter the next day, I found twenty children waiting for me, one line of boys and another of girls. Someone had probably told them, with the best intentions in the world: "A foreign person wants to hear stories of children in the war. You have one. Go line up and she's going to ask you some questions." I remember that evening at Noah's Ark very well. I wanted the ground to swallow me up. There I was, perched uneasily on a bench with the children waiting in lines in front of me. But I could not run away. I thought about gathering them into a group and talking to them all at the same time but changed my mind. I had done that once, and it doesn't work with children. And so I resigned myself to talking to each of them in turn. The only good idea I had that night was not to talk about the war if the child did not mention it. I remember one boy who told me he was fifteen but looked about ten. He had the face of an adult but his body was that of a child. He sat down and before I had time to even open my mouth, he told me how his father had been shot before his eyes, how he had been kidnapped by the rebels, and how he himself had killed – all with such cold dispassion it froze my blood. Here was a child who clearly needed help; putting him in front of a camera was not the way to give it to him.

To all intents and purposes, that little boy had a heart-rending story. Yes, he was ready to talk. Yes, he would have been a "good" character for the film. But it would have been unethical. I believe that revisiting his past, and all the horror it contained, without a social worker or a psychologist on the team would only have made him a victim once more. This is what I mean when

I say the people we meet are more important than the film and that we must not take advantage of our position in the name of "humanitarian" or "human rights" cinema.

Protecting the Characters

The safety of the film crew (Quebecers and Ugandans) was my responsibility since I was officially the team leader. In fact, when the time came to choose a camera operator and sound recorder in Quebec, my first criterion was that these future colleagues not have any children. I don't know whether that was overly scrupulous, but I was not dealing with people with extensive field experience and the ability to evaluate risk. One of my two technical crew members had never set foot in Africa. If something happened, I would not be able to hide behind the excuse that "they knew what they were getting into." The problem was that I *did* know, and I could not slide out from under the responsibility that knowledge entailed. For the Ugandans on the crew, I did not have the same concerns. They knew better than I did the risks they would be facing. Still, the safety of the crew is crucial, and we had to include the characters as full members of that crew. I never forget that when the filming is over, we have a return ticket and the people we have been filming do not. They stay where they are, and if anyone has to live with the consequences of the shoot, it's they and not us. I knew I therefore had to reduce the risks to the characters as much as possible. And my greatest concern was that two of our five main characters were children.

I had made a rule for myself that I would film people telling me about their everyday lives, inevitably shaped by the war, but not speaking openly about anything political. As I have written, we can understand many things just by seeing how people live. When Caroline walks ten miles from her village to the city, morning and night, to avoid being captured by the rebels, that's the war we're seeing. When little Dennis, the street child, sleeps under a shop awning with ten other kids and gets up at dawn to "look for some light" and to scrounge for food, that's the war we're seeing. When elderly Anguleta takes us to the ruins of what was once her village and sighs as she looks at the skeletal remains of her hut, that too is the war. It's the war in the everyday. And it was my goal to show what was happening in their everyday lives.

There's no need to put everything in political terms. The only people in the film who openly criticize the government are two well-known Ugandan human rights activists, who knew only too well the risks they were taking by speaking out, and Jackson, our infamous driver. Despite all our warnings, he insisted on giving us his acerbic political opinions. "Our president isn't right in his head," he told me in one interview. I said: "Jackson, come on! You can't say those kinds of things while we're filming! I won't be able to use it! You're putting yourself at too great a risk!" His response: "I risk my life every single day in this war! What do I care if I die for the cause? I want to say what I think, and I think our President is crazy. How are you going to know how things hang together here if I don't tell you? Listen to me, and then tell the people in America."

The man seemed to have considered the risks, and his desire to denounce the political dealings that were prolonging the war won out. And so I listened and I filmed. All of it.

If I want to be the echo of these people, I must echo their anger as well as their misery. Everything comes down to common sense. After all, I wanted the film to be a political film as well as a work of art. Here again, of course, we edited the interview with Jackson as we did for all the characters, taking out what we thought might spark a visit from the army or other security forces. The messages coming out in the film were powerful enough, and there was no need to risk more with Jackson.

Protecting Young People during the Filmmaking

I have already talked about filming characters at the human level without asking them directly about the war. I made that decision in order to reduce the risks to the film's protagonists: a government agent would not subsequently be able to accuse them of dissidence. For the children in the film, however, that precaution seemed inadequate. They were vulnerable in ways that called for special protection.

I took additional measures, therefore, to ensure that the children would be impossible to trace. An example is the scene in the office of the Concerned Parents Association in which Angelina shows us ID cards of children who had escaped the LRA. In postproduction, we blurred the names to make them unreadable. When Dennis went to the police station with the other street children, he gave his full name to the policewoman in charge of their reintegration. In the soundtrack, we edited out his family name. We also cut the family names of the children identifying themselves to the security guards at Noah's Ark at night. Seemingly ordinary, these measures are vitally important.

While I did not mention the topic of war to the children, it did emerge naturally in ways that had no negative impacts. Caroline herself addressed it in a scene that still troubles me today. In order to survive, Caroline was working in a stone quarry. We followed her into a vast grey moonscape bathed in yellowish light. In the scene, Caroline sits down and determinedly grasps her little hammer. She strikes a medium-sized rock until it breaks. The sound of Caroline's hammer is one of dozens echoing in the quarry. With each blow, her face tightens. Occasionally, she lifts her large, candid eyes to see whether we are still there. She tells us a little about her work and then, still hammering, makes the following penetrating comment: "If peace returns, I will give up this work and go home."

What we needed to understand about war as experienced in the mind and body of a child is contained in that one scene and that one statement.

Decisions about scenes like these are always made in tandem with my editor, Annie Jean, an invaluable partner with whom every image in the film is thought through. Another decision about which we thought long and hard revolved around the filmmaker's need to *show* things and the issue of how to protect people who trust themselves to us. The scene in question occurs near the end of the film. A young woman, one of the Aboke girls we talked about earlier, tells us about the eight years she spent as a captive of the LRA. She desperately needs to tell her story to someone. We are spared nothing. The film suggests that it is Charlotte, Angelina's daughter, who is speaking. Perhaps it is; perhaps it is not. The imprecision I deliberately leave in the film makes the young woman's testimony universal. It is not only her story that is involved here, but that of all the adolescent girls who have been kidnapped, beaten, and raped. Here is an excerpt from her testimony:

> For the past eight years I have been in the bush. I was totally cut off from the world. It's like being put in a tomb; you are still breathing, but you are in there. (long pause) In the bush it was always horrible.
>
> I didn't understand at first what they were talking about (hesitantly), you know, someone very old, in his late fifties. (sigh) You cannot imagine, you know (long pause), I thought maybe he was out of his head, not joking, because I have never seen any of them joking. But after that, they just (hesitates), they just have to tie you up and somebody rapes you, just like that (sadly and very faint).
>
> I was always, always afraid they might ask me to kill somebody; I was always, always afraid to do that. (long pause) One day some girl tried to escape, and they asked us, all thirty of us girls, to come. We went there not knowing what was going to happen (pause) – they gave us all big sticks and they ordered us to beat her to death (very sad and with a gasp). We could not imagine doing this and (heavy sigh) we refused; we refused (trails off). We refused, but we were beaten so badly, to the extent that we all had to beat her to death (very faintly and sad) and so we did (trails off).
>
> There was no day when you would get up and smile to see the sun rise, because every day you would think, maybe today, maybe today will be the end of me.

The young woman whose voice we hear never appears on-screen. The things she confides to us are recited during a long, low-angle shot looking up into the canopy of a eucalyptus forest at twilight. You hear the young woman speaking, but you also feel the oppressive power of the bush, the terror of the approaching night, and the inexorable threat of captivity.

I used to think that the most extreme act a human could commit was to kill. After hearing the young woman's story, I now believe there is something more sinister: to be forced to kill.

The young woman had agreed to talk to us with her face uncovered. She talked for two hours without stopping. Nevertheless, in the editing process, after lengthy consideration, we decided not to show her on-screen. As an "Aboke girl" she had already been ostracized, and her mother was being pressured by the government to stop her activism demanding that the children be freed. Putting her testimony on-screen would make both of them more vulnerable and increase the risk of reprisals. Anonymity was called for. And because creativity often emerges when restrictions are imposed, the sequence in which we hear her testimony is, in visual terms, one of the most beautiful in the film. Moreover, by not showing the young woman, we avoided falling into the trap of sensationalism, no matter how unintentional. It is her words that take on the greatest importance, and the long nighttime shot encourages us to listen. To truly listen.

Political Understandings without Talking Politics

The political underpinnings of the war in Uganda are, nonetheless, extremely important. The war is driven by political and economic interests I did not want to ignore; that would have been to miss the target completely. Once you have shown the everyday face of the war, you do have to take the time to explain the "why" of that war. If not, the film remains superficial. I therefore had to find a way to communicate what was at stake at the political level, without being didactic.

I had an immense stroke of luck. I found Andrew Mwenda. A popular – and controversial – radio personality, he was the longtime host of a show on KFM, a private radio station (of which there are few in Uganda). A clear-sighted political analyst and skilled interviewer, Mwenda had met with Uganda's top political players in his studio – including the president himself – before his show was pulled from the airwaves and he left the country for a while. There was nothing mealymouthed about Mwenda. He once asked an army general why the president had a private security force of fifteen thousand men when some IDP camps with populations in the thousands were protected by only fifteen soldiers. In another show, Mwenda collared Museveni himself: the military budget in Uganda had reached $100 million; with that kind of money, how could the government *not* have managed to quell the LRA? The guests on his show sputtered and mumbled, tripping over their answers. Their responses were so vague that they were practically useless for the purposes of the film. It didn't matter: it was Mwenda's *questions* that gave us almost all the clues we needed to understand the political and economic issues that fed into the war. All I had to do was add explanatory slides in which each carefully chosen word filled in the logical steps of Mwenda's line of questioning. Thanks to those radio clips (which we accessed on the Internet from Montreal), I was able to assemble a political story without burdening the film with expository interviews. The clips passed the editing test: with Mwenda's questions at the top of a sequence, scenes from everyday life took on another dimension. We began to understand how the destinies of Caroline, Dennis, and Anguleta had been shaped by shadowy political forces for whom people like them were simply not a concern. The war feeds a world of power and money that is built on the backs of the Carolines, Dennises, and Anguletas of northern Uganda.

Once the basic issues in the war had been identified, each of the characters' actions could be seen in a new light. Each action became an act of resistance. Caroline commuted to survive. As for Dennis, he preferred to take refuge in the city rather than end up dead in an IDP camp. Anguleta walked for eight hours to collect wood to cook manioc. With these gestures, the characters were refusing to assume the role of victim. They emerge with greater dignity. And it was that dignity I wanted to jump out of the screen.

Government Denial

People asked me why I did not interview representatives from Museveni's government. My answer was simple: Why would I? The "duty" to provide airtime for protagonists on either side of an issue is for journalists, not documentarians. The government's role in the war is clear. There was no need for me to listen to the mouthings of politicians to find out what was happening. Give the government a platform from which to justify itself? Absolutely not. Give the government credibility while it abjured all responsibility for the people dying in the north? It was simply out of the question.

And besides, you *can* find the official government position in the film. Thanks to Ugandan friends in the media, who took courageous risks in order to help me, I got hold of archival footage in which Museveni states – yet again! – that the war is over. In his words, "Kony is finished." An interesting fact: because the quality of the footage I had available to me was so poor, I submitted an official request to the Information Ministry of the Ugandan government to purchase footage of that speech. After a long process (and a great deal of money changing hands for the so-called transfer of the images), I received a cassette tape. Museveni's speech was on it, but the excerpt in which he states that the war is over was not. It had been censored. No comment.

Going Home

One of the questions that haunt me as a documentarian is how to handle the fact that I pack up and go home once the filming is done, leaving my characters behind. In reality, I do not handle it; I endure it. I know full well that I am going back to a surfeit of comfort and security while the people I have been filming, in the case of Uganda, stay behind in hunger, violence, and fear. I have found no way to resolve that dilemma.

My feelings of unhappiness are inconsolable. I manage to address the situation – if only partially – with a strictly intellectual response. If as a documentarian my aim is to be the conduit of human stories and experiences, then leaving is part of my work. That response offers cold comfort, but it does allow me to *stay focused*. If I did not respond in that way, the film might never be made and the entire foundation of my work would crumble. I constantly have to keep in mind that it is neither my role nor my place to set up an NGO, build a school, or open a dispensary. Other filmmakers have done those things. I salute them. Some people can take on more than others.

When I left Uganda, I reminded myself that if I wanted to keep my promise and make the voices of northern Ugandans heard, I did have to go back to Montreal. Over and over, I repeated Jackson's words: "How will people in America know what is going on here, unless I tell you?"

Clearly, all the reasoning in the world cannot resolve the moral dilemma of leaving children behind in a country at war. I have no defensible position on the matter. My only response was an imperfect and patently inadequate gesture. It was out of the question that I leave Caroline or Dennis on the street. I found adults who were able to look after them, and both children are now in boarding school. I get their report cards every year. I realize I acted in response to a specific situation. I don't worry about whether I could or should send every child I will ever film to school. "All the children I will ever film" do not yet exist. I was concerned solely for Caroline and Dennis, two children in the "here and now." I was not about to deprive them of the chance to go to school on the basis of some abstract principle that says: "You cannot put every child you film in school." My solution is not a universal one to be applied on every shoot. It was a specific response to one moment in my life, during the making of one particular film.

Finally, among the difficulties of coming home is the absence of any sort of debriefing. The camera operator and sound recordist go on to make other films. In a way, they are "forced" to move on. The director, on the other hand, continues to live with the characters for several more months, screening the footage and doing image and sound assemblies. Returning from the shoot, I felt somewhat lost. I had few people with whom I could share what had happened during the filming. I had been deeply affected by my time in Uganda, and it would have been helpful, even healthy, to have had a team or professional family on whom I could lean for support. My craft has this "defect" of the solitary homecoming, and I have yet to find a way to avoid it.

Conclusion

I imagine all documentarians define their filmmaking role in their own way. And all would probably want to fine-tune that definition with each new film they made. I myself can offer no firm guidelines as to what I do as a filmmaker. My craft is a fluid one, and the way I approach each film depends on the setting, the subject, and the characters themselves.

As far as my experience in Uganda is concerned, I now understand that my role was to gather and document human experiences so that the film would become an expression, an exploration, and a wondering about the everyday nature of the war. I got as close to the people as I could, and they allowed me to do that, so that the wondering was theirs too. In filming the characters day after day, I wanted their reality to speak for itself.

Time is a fundamental component of my approach. Filming the human experience takes time – for me, and for the people I film. I need to go slowly, learning to adopt the pace of my surroundings.

It is the time spent with people – the impressions, reflections, and questioning that emerge during that time – that gives birth to the film. I do not disembark somewhere with a preconceived notion of what I'm looking for. I have the broad strokes of a project in mind, but the film itself emerges from the encounters I have. This encounter, this listening, takes time: it is a "listening" time, a "time without borders" that exists in and of itself.

"Listening time" is where we truly learn to set aside the things that differentiate one person from another, and to notice, in an organic way, the ways in which we are alike. Transposed to the screen, this identifying with the Other operates between the character and the viewer. Understanding how this identification process works prevents us from indulging in sentimentality: for a brief moment, I *am* that Other.

Time operates on the characters, with whom I form a close relationship and who become full members of the filmmaking team, as well. For me, as for the film's protagonists, the research stage is a time of reflection. They too reflect on where they belong in the film, and in the end, it is they who give the film its true color. These characters – who are, after all, essentially strangers – are the documentary. They open their homes to us and invite us into their hearts. The least we can do is respect the time they give us and the rhythms of their lives. Being accepted into their space and time is the first step toward creating any documentary art.

BIBLIOGRAPHY

Kapuściński, Ryszard. 2009. *The Other*, trans. Antonia Lloyd-Jones. Brooklyn and London: Verso.

2

Negotiating Identity, Space, and Place among Iraqi Women Refugees in Jordan

Isis Nusair

A vague picture with no homeland, and no stable place of residence. I cannot see my future. It is as if you are shackled and they say walk to freedom. But where is freedom?

~An Iraqi woman refugee in Jordan in her mid-twenties

Those who live in Al-Khadra [Green Zone] have hospitals and schools. They have everything except for the people. They live in a different Iraq.

~An Iraqi woman refugee aid worker living in Jordan

I started to document my memory [after the 2003 invasion]. I am a witness. I walk at Al-Rashid Street. I see the shops, books, music, school and the teachers who taught me.... At least I try to capture memory before it fades away. If Iraq [under the Ba'th regime] was a big prison, now it is a small prison because people are confined to their homes.

~May Muzafar, an Iraqi poet

INTRODUCTION

This chapter focuses on the complex negotiation of identity that happens during refugee displacement. This process is further complicated by the gendered aspects of living in exile. I discuss the uncertainty of the Iraqi refugee women's situation, the limitations on their space, and the effect it has on the research process itself. I examine the gendered and sexual politics of being a refugee, as well as the ethical, practical, and methodological challenges that I faced when conducting research with Iraqi women refugees in Jordan in 2007 and 2008. I address the ways in which feminist scholarship could effect change in policy and whether research conducted with urban women refugees should have humanitarian and community-level objectives. I discuss the usefulness of the research findings to the women involved and what it has meant to me to be associated as a researcher with this community. I then end this chapter with an analysis of the networks of support that the women employ to sustain their agency in this prolonged state of instability and displacement.

I have been teaching courses on the gendered impact of war and conflict since 2003. My dissertation research focused on the gendered politics of location of three generations of Palestinian women in Israel. Troubled by the images of torture at Abu-Ghraib that were released in spring of 2004, I wrote an article analyzing the gendered, racialized, and sexualized nature of the abuse and its orientalist representations of the other (Nusair 2008). I wanted to travel to Iraq to examine the impact of the United States–led invasion on women but was unable to do so for security reasons. Since I had worked previously in Jordan with Human Rights Watch (HRW) and with the Euro-Mediterranean Human Rights Network and given the large number of Iraqi refugees in Jordan, I decided to travel to Amman in 2007 to conduct research with Iraqi women refugees.

Over the course of three research trips, I conducted eighty interviews with Iraqi women refugees (including four with the women's husbands) and with independent researchers and activists.[1] I also carried out interviews with representatives of the United Nations and national and international aid organizations. I attended a 2007 meeting for Iraqi and Jordanian human rights organizations to assess the conditions of Iraqi refugees in Jordan and the internally displaced in Iraq. I used a snowball approach to reach women with different social, political, religious, and economic backgrounds in Amman and Zarqa. The majority of Iraqi refugees live in the capital, Amman, hoping to find jobs and to improve their access to aid services. Some of the refugees interviewed chose to live in Zarqa as the cost of living there is cheaper than in Amman. I did not ask about the women's religion, though some women mentioned their religion when describing the social context in which they lived in Iraq or when describing the current challenges they face as women refugees in Jordan. I chose not to ask about religion in order not to privilege it over class, ethnicity, and political and educational backgrounds.[2] I also wanted to keep my questions as open as possible in order to allow for the women to construct their narratives as they saw fit. The interviews were conducted in Arabic at a place of the women's choosing, and the names of the women have

---

[1] I conducted more than one interview with some of the women and with representatives of national and international aid organizations.

[2] Hyndman and de Alwis argue that a "more comprehensive feminist approach to such programs [of development and humanitarian aid] takes gender into consideration but also attends to other bases of marginalization and/or displacement, such as ethnicity, ability, sexuality, caste, and age" (85).

been changed to protect their identity. It was a challenge for me at times to translate the interviews into English while maintaining the eloquence of the narratives.

I also volunteered to teach English to Iraqi women refugees in a community center in East Amman. Initially, some of the women at the center were hesitant to talk to me about their experiences, but as they got to know me, they agreed to take part in the research project. The majority of the women I interviewed arrived in Jordan after the 2003 United States–led invasion of Iraq, with most arriving between 2005 and 2006. Some arrived in Jordan for mostly economic reasons during the sanctions period in the 1990s. The women's age ranged from eighteen to seventy-two, and I deliberately chose to interview women who were from different parts of Iraq and who had different economic, educational, and political backgrounds. Importantly, the place of residence of Iraqi refugees in Amman reflects their economic status. Those who live in East Amman arrived in Jordan with little savings and rely mostly on aid organizations to survive. It was emotionally wrenching at times for me to move among different parts of the city and witness the huge economic disparities among the refugees.

My research is informed by feminist participatory research methodology and educational theory. I am very aware of the need for relational/reflective approaches and historicization of the women's context. These were important factors in my structuring and analysis of the interviews. Throughout my work, I privilege an ethnographic approach in which the voices of the women frame my conceptual understanding and analysis of their situations. Rather than apply theoretical frameworks to their narratives and in this way hem in and constrain the meaning I might derive, I instead reflect on the multiple layers of meaning in what the women reveal. I then consider what theoretical insights can help deepen my understanding of their discourses and shifting, lived experiences.

A Note on Context and Terminology

It was important for the majority of women I interviewed to emphasize that the United States–led invasion of Iraq in 2003 is part of a larger continuum of war and conflict that they have lived through since the Iran-Iraq war in 1980–8, the Iraqi invasion of Kuwait in 1990, the Gulf War in 1991, and the United Nations–imposed sanctions of 1990–2003. Jordan and Iraq had close economic ties in the 1970–80s. Waves of migration from Iraq under the Ba'th regime started in the 1980s as individuals and families left the country to escape the oppressive policies of the regime and conscription in the military during the war with Iran. This migration intensified in the 1990s and included

Iraqi men who traveled abroad, including to Jordan, to seek jobs because of the United Nations–imposed sanctions (see Chatelard, forthcoming). Iraqi refugees did not leave immediately after the United States–led invasion in 2003. The majority left in 2005–6 to neighboring countries of Syria and Jordan, especially after the bombing of the mosque in Samarra in 2006.

Jordan and Syria have the largest number of Iraqi refugees. There are approximately one million Iraqi refugees in Syria and half a million in Jordan.[3] Neither Syria nor Jordan is signatory to the United Nations 1951 Refugee Convention. Jordan signed a memorandum of understanding with the United Nations High Commissioner for Refugees (UNHCR) in 1998 concerning the treatment of asylum seekers and refugees in which Jordan agrees to admit refugees and asylum seekers and respect UNHCR refugee status determination. The memorandum also adopts the refugee definition contained in the United Nations Refugee Convention and forbids the refoulment of refugees and asylum seekers.[4]

FIXED TEMPORALITY

The politics of being a refugee has as much to do with the "cultural expectation of certain qualities and behaviors that are demonstrative of 'authentic' refugeeness (e.g., silence, passivity, victimhood) as it does with legal definitions of regulations" (Nyers 2006, xv). I refrain from using the term "guests" to describe Iraqi refugees in Jordan. "Guests" is the official term used in Jordan to connote hospitality and the temporary nature of the Iraqi refugees' presence in the country.[5] Many refugees referred directly to this contradiction and explained the lack of rights associated with the term and the fact that many of them have been "guests" in Jordan for a number of years. The majority described their presence in Jordan as temporary and explained that the main reason behind their leaving Iraq was to seek safety and protect their children from violence.

---

[3] Some scholars and activists contest these numbers. See Geraldine Chatelard's "Iraqis in Jordan: Elusive numbers, uncertain future."

[4] According to the 1951 United Nations Convention Relating to the Status of Refugees (the Refugee Convention), a refugee is a person who "owing to a well-founded fear of being persecuted for reasons of race, religion, nationality, membership of a particular social group or political opinion, is outside the country of his nationality, and is unable to or, owing to such fear, is unwilling to avail himself of the protection of that country or return there because there is a fear of persecution."

[5] Nyers (2006), on the other hand, asserts that "'hospitality' allows for encounters with refugees without pretending that anxiety and conflict are absent but also without negatively characterizing refugees as bestial beings to be feared and controlled" (xvii).

Hana, a widow in her fifties, described the situation as up in the air. "We do not know our destiny. The Jordanian government might ask us to leave at any moment .... There is no rest for a guest. It is heavy, if we were to work, the situation could have been better.... I am responsible for the house and the kids. The responsibility of a daughter and a disabled child is on me." An artist couple in their forties said, "There is no guarantee for us and for our children here .... We are like prisoners, like the torn album thrown in the wind .... We are not refugees because we do not have rights as refugees .... We are dispersed and not refugees." Suad, a woman in her early sixties whose house was broken into and who was kidnapped in Iraq in 2006, added, "There is no stability. Our living in Amman is temporary as they might ask us to leave at any moment. If it were not for my kids, I would not be here." She concluded by saying that the situation in her country will take a long time to resolve and that her extended family is dispersed in the Arab Gulf States and in Europe.

This sense of no return was reiterated by the majority of the women I interviewed. Sameera, born in 1958, has been in Jordan since 2007. She traveled to Jordan with her children after the assassination of her husband in 2007. Sameera is not registered with the United Nations. She described how she does not have any ambition to go back to Iraq, and that not much is left of this life. She concluded, "We have seen a lot." Nadia, an Iraqi painter in her early seventies, described how people were afraid to say a word under the Ba'th regime, and how she does not interact much with the Jordanian society. "Nothing is left.... Our group [family] is dispersed. This is our situation, some are in Qatar, New Zealand, and Sweden.... When they [the Americans] occupied us, they did not bring a democratic life and the situation became worse. Now we miss the Saddam days .... Many families do not have money to go back and visit their homes. This is a long-term stay for us for where could we go?" Nadia, as were many women interviewed, was steadfast and emphasized that life continues despite the cruelty of the situation. "We are still better than others.... I do not have hope that Iraq will return. At times, my husband and I say, 'What have they done to us?' We have lost a lot."

ETHICAL, PRACTICAL, AND METHODOLOGICAL CHALLENGES

Sama, an Iraqi performance artist in her early fifties, started the interview by saying, "I do not like the word refuge. I prefer shelter .... There is no security and if it was not for my son, I would not have left .... I do not like to philosophize. Before we were able to dream and work to achieve our dreams. Today we only have one dream and we are even afraid to dream it." She described how in the last five years she has been unable to perform despite the proposals that she receives. "I feel that I cannot reflect what the country [Iraq] is going through." This sense of paralysis was echoed by many women refugees who were traumatized by what they went through before their arrival in Jordan (see Dahl 2005). They expressed the limits on their space and the contradictions they live through, especially that they entered Jordan seeking security and found instability instead. This instability is a product of the temporality of their presence in Jordan as they constantly have to pay fees to renew their visas and avoid deportation. In addition, refugees in Jordan cannot work legally unless they deposit large sums of money in the bank and show willingness to invest in the country. Those who register with the United Nations are in a state of waiting for resettlement in a third country.

Sana, a woman in her mid-twenties, said, "We sacrificed everything for security . . . . The main thing is to feel stable and to be respected as human beings. If there is work, no one is incapable." Nyers argues that "the refugees' relationship to the political can be described as a kind of 'inclusive exclusion.' Refugees are included in the discourse of 'normality' and 'order' only by virtue of their exclusion from the normal identities and ordered spaces of the sovereign state" (2006, xiii). He elaborates further, "Refugees are people deprived of their human rights first and foremost because they are denied access to a political space that allows for a meaningful political presence" (17). My interviews exposed the level of political invisibility of Iraqi refugees in Jordan and how being labeled as "guests" by Jordanian officials amplified this invisibility. This is in stark contradiction to the presumed economic visibility of some members of the Iraqi middle and upper classes who sought refuge in Jordan and now are invested in the Jordanian economy. It is also in stark contradiction to widespread claims and complaints among the Jordanian public that the presence of Iraqis in the country is contributing to rising prices and increased unemployment.

Rabiha, a journalist in her late fifties, described this contradiction between visibility and invisibility when talking about her job. She publishes daily and weekly articles in a major Jordanian newspaper, and her articles are translated regularly into different languages. Although she is a well-known journalist in the region, she was granted residency in Jordan through her son's work permit and not through her credentials as a journalist. She says, "The person that does not have a country does not have protection. Iraqis are not treated well because no one protects them and defends their rights. This was also the case during the sanctions regime . . . . There is no security and the poor suffer the most. If the situation remains as is, we will all be poor."

Sana, who has been living in Jordan since 1994, elaborated on the contradiction in her life of being an Iraqi refugee in Jordan by saying, "We are breaking the law, there are no permits for work and no stability.... You feel like a stranger .... It is important that the situation becomes stable, and salaries need to increase. There needs to be security, and you need to be strong; otherwise you could be exploited." Sana acknowledged throughout the interview that her family's situation in Jordan will not improve and that it is better that they return to Iraq. Yet, she emphasized that as long as the situation does not improve in Iraq, they will be afraid to go back. She concluded by saying, "We live in exile, and there is no stability or security .... There is no stability from the inside. We always feel that there is something missing .... You speak two languages, Iraqi inside the house and Jordanian outside. The psychology of it all is hard and the way people treat you is hard as well. The situation is normal now as a result of what we went through. We laugh despite the circumstances."

Refugee identity is not merely the negative, empty, temporary, and helpless counterpart to the positive, present, permanent, and authoritative citizen (Nyers 2006). The humanitarian discourse around refugees is "dominated by a problem-solving mentality that defines refugee movement as a technical problem in need of rapid solutions" (3). Humanitarian solutions to the phenomenon of the refugee "enact a spatial reversal of the binary citizen-refugee to transform the refugee's lack into a positive presence. These solutions take the form of restoring statist identities and communities to refugees" (settlement in a third country or repatriation, 22). Since both of these options are mostly unavailable for Iraqi refugees in Syria and Jordan, what is needed are perspectives that are open to the "possibility of political and ethical engagements that do not reproduce the sovereign codes that doom refugees to the status of 'speechless emissaries'" (24).

ETHICS, BENEFITS, AND IDENTITY

In a context where many refugee women are in dire need of aid, it was imperative for me to emphasize that the research I was carrying out will help expose the issues but not necessarily resolve the problems. This challenge exposed the limits of the research process itself in effecting meaningful change in the life of the refugees (see Bloch et al. 2000). The women were well aware of this limitation. Suha said, "Iraqis are tired and need solutions and not surveys and application forms. We need tangible things." Many women emphasized that despite these limitations they had a need to make their stories heard. Hajdukowski-Ahmed et al. argue that through "voice and voicing, agency and power are reclaimed by marginalized groups, particularly women" (2008, 13). Olujc (as quoted in Nordstrom and Robben 1996) further refines their point by reminding us that we may give voice to the victims of violence, but we can never restore their lives. Many of the aid workers I interviewed emphasized how difficult it was to provide psychological aid to Iraqi refugees who have other pressing material needs.

I conducted the research with a firm political engagement to analyze the gendered nature of Iraqi refugee experience in Jordan that raised questions about where research ends and intervention begins. Recognizing my location, complicity, and distance, identification and personal involvement were constant reminders of power differentials and the need to pay attention to issues of subjectivity and accountability. My activist background and academic training in feminist analysis push me to link theory with practice and think of research as a space for social change. The invisibility of the consequences of the United States–led invasion of Iraq in 2003, particularly its impact on population displacement, prompted concerns about accountability and the impact of the war on the day-to-day lives of Iraqis in general and refugees in particular. The question of Iraqi refugees remained absent from American public discourse until 2006. To illustrate, only 406 Iraqi refugees were admitted into the United States between 2003 and 2006, as admitting more Iraqis into the country would have acknowledged the Bush administration's failure to bring "democracy, freedom and stability" to Iraq. It was not until an international conference was held in Geneva, Switzerland in 2007 and a series of reports were published about the plight of Iraqi refugees that Congress introduced in 2007 the Responsibility to Iraqi Refugees Act.[6]

My initial concern of being an outsider to the community quickly disappeared as the women shared their stories with me or when I was recommended by a trusted friend (see McMichael 2002). There were times that my

---

[6] There are a number of reports that track the U.S. response to Iraqi refugees, such as the report of the 2008 joint hearing at the House of Representatives on the United States response to the Iraqi refugee crisis (http://www.internationalrelations.house.gov/110/41229. pdf [accessed October 15, 2012]). There is also a 2008 staff trip report to the Committee on Foreign Relations titled "Managing chaos – the Iraqi refugees of Jordan and Syria and internally displaced persons in Iraq" (http://www.gpo.gov/fdsys/pkg/CPRT-110SPRT41773/ pdf/CPRT-110SPRT41773.pdf [accessed October 15, 2012]) and the 2009 report by the Congressional Research Service titled "Iraqi refugees and internally displaced persons: A deepening humanitarian crisis?" (http://www.fas.org/sgp/crs/mideast/RL33936.pdf [accessed October 15, 2012]). As well, Human Rights Watch has issued a series of reports starting in 2006 with "The silent treatment: Fleeing Iraq, surviving in Jordan" (http://www.hrw.org/ sites/default/files/reports/jordan1106webwcover.pdf [accessed October 15, 2012]) and another in 2007 titled "From flood to trickle: Neighboring states stop Iraqis fleeing war and persecution" (http://www.hrw.org/legacy/backgrounder/refugees/iraq0407/iraq0407.pdf [accessed October 15, 2012]). Finally, the special issue for the Forced Migration Review in June 2007 was titled "Iraq's displacement crisis: The search for solutions" (http://www.fmreview.org/ sites/fmr/files/FMRdownloads/en/FMRpdfs/Iraq/full.pdf [accessed October 15, 2012]).

being Palestinian helped as the women referred to the commonalities between their experiences and the displacement of Palestinians, and the irony of how some of them were advocates of Palestinian refugee rights in the past and are now advocating for their own rights as refugees. My multiple locations, especially my living in the United States, allowed for many women to critique the American government's lack of attention to the refugee problem directly with the hope that the research might help expose some of these limitations.

I was constantly reminded, as I conducted the interviews, of the need to be attentive to the complexity embedded in the women's narratives and their coping mechanisms. Should the interview become a space to vent and express sadness, anger, and frustration? How could the interview address questions of trauma, especially given that the majority of the refugees fled Iraq because of direct threats and attacks on their lives? Or, as stated by an interviewee in her forties, "We witnessed wonders between 2003 and 2005." Does the interview become another site for that witnessing act? It is worth noting that the majority of the women did not elaborate or provide graphic details of what they went through before leaving Iraq. They positioned their experiences as part of a larger collective and made clear connections between the hardships they had to endure while living under the Ba'th and sanctions regimes and in the aftermath of the United States–led invasion in 2003. Zeina, a medical doctor who was kidnapped and severely harassed for five days in 2004, said that she went to Jordan to overcome the shock that she went through. "I need security to go back. We are thankful to Jordan but the prospect of return worsens by the day.... There was a loss of security, and everything collapsed."

References to trauma as well as paralyses were particularly present in the narratives of younger women who were still navigating their personal and professional paths. Nadine, a woman in her early twenties who studied computer science in Iraq, said, "My life passes me by, stops, like a machine that has not been used for a long time. I need to get out of this paralysis that I am in .... Sometimes I see my future as black, that my life will end here with no chance to advance, and that the situation will become worse ... [we are] like refugees with no past, present or future. All this could be overcome as long as I have my family with me and I feel settled and comfortable where I live. Work [in Jordan] is a waste of time, and you cannot advance."

Nadine described how she was followed in 2006 by a car with militia men while in Iraq and how she had to flee with her mother to Amman as her father and brother remained behind. She emphasized throughout the interview that if her country were to return to the way it was, she would immediately go back. For her, the Iraq she knew and grew up in is no longer there.

Nadine described how she has been unable to work or develop in her field and that the work conditions for Iraqi refugees in Jordan are exploitative.

This was echoed by Hanan and Zeina, two sisters who fled to Jordan with their father and other sister as their mother and brothers remained behind. They fled because of threats made against the older sister, Hanan, who worked as a translator with the Americans. Zeina, a schoolteacher by training, described how depressed she feels and how she gained weight as she mostly stays at home cooking and watching TV. She described her eighteen-month experience of working in a factory in Amman in 2006–7 as exploitative with no opportunity for advancement. "They would not pay for work permits or health insurance. There is no stability, no stability. I feel like an intruder; I am not for this place and nothing in it connects me to it.... We as Iraqis hope that they will give us asylum and a place to settle. There is no security, neither here nor there. Everything is hanging." Hanan, on the other hand, described her inability to organize for Iraqi refugee rights politically in Jordan and how the Mukhabarat (General Intelligence Directorate) called her for questioning about her activities.

Suha, a divorced woman in her late thirties with three children (one of whom is disabled), described how she felt alienated and denied identity. "There are lots of people without families. They do not have self-confidence and they have no confidence in others.... Iraqis are tormented.... I am alone and my burden is heavy.... I need a home where I could settle down.... The hope is to leave. That is how we could get our rights and feel secure. We are supposed to be refugees but not here. Here is temporary.... Despite the Saddam regime, Iraq was our country ... the situation today is barbaric.... We got used to exile and difficulties, yet change might help make things better." She concluded the interview by saying, "Maybe it will be better in a foreign country.... Things will not improve in Iraq even after ten years.... It is hard to see the country fall apart in front of your eyes. This is what hurts. I live in constant worry yet I am optimistic and won't despair.... My hope is to gain independence and immigrate." Suha's persistence in sustaining her presence as a woman and as an Iraqi is illustrated in her wish, "I want to be able to say in the future that this is my home; I do not want people to control me."

Nyers (2006) argues that refugee situations should be understood as complex and multidimensional sites of identity. Within this context, a crisis situation is a contested social construction involving a variety of competing political, cultural, and identity practices. He warns against emptying all notions of political agency from refugee subjectivity, especially given that the prevailing attitude in conventional analyses of refugee movements is one that "provides no place for refugees to articulate their experiences and struggles or to assert their (often collectively conceived) political agency. Refugees are silenced by the very discourses that attempt to provide solutions to their plight. This silence is not natural or inevitable but something that is produced by power relations that require explanations and critical analysis" (xiv).

The open-ended nature of the interviews, where the focus was on the causes that prompted the women to leave Iraq and the transition and challenges they currently face as Iraqi women refugees in Jordan, opened a space for the women to reflect on their experiences and construct a narrative that analyzed their situation and visions for the future. It also allowed them to address the power differentials between us and the objectifying nature of the research process itself. Although I had minimal intervention in what they said and passed no judgment on what they were sharing with me, I was the one taking notes and expected to write about their lives. The women were comfortable in general with this style despite its limitations. This was not always easy as some of the narratives raised the pain, loss, and trauma that they lived through. This was also hard on me as I was deeply affected by their stories and felt helpless to provide tangible solutions to their problems.

Hardgrove argues that as families work to balance demands with capabilities, they are constantly in the process of interpreting their circumstances by assigning meanings to themselves and their context (2009, 484). Relating to the refugee experience as a process emphasizes the connection and continuum between their life before and after their arrival in Jordan. The term and act of becoming a refugee are political and involve a process of becoming. "This process is not a seamless, sudden, or otherwise dramatic shift from one static state to another (i.e., from citizen to refugee). Rather, it is a site of struggle, a continual process of identity construction, and one that highlights how the activity and practices of refugees are recasting the terms of ethical and political discourse" (Nyers 2006, xv).

The majority of Iraqi women interviewed described the militarization of their lives and the continuities between the past and present, their current status in Jordan and their living through the Iran-Iraq war, the Gulf War, and life under the sanctions regime. Sama vividly recalled living under the Ba'th regime. She said, "Terror was implanted even among the members of the same family.... When I remember it now, I feel the bitterness more than when we lived it. We live in exile; we flee from the unknown." She spoke about the impact of the Iran-Iraq war: "It was then that things started to deteriorate. We lived as if suffocated and pretended to be living.... I used to walk by the wall [to protect herself from the Ba'th regime] and if my death would have made a difference I would have sacrificed myself." Suha recalled how under the sanctions regime, they were unable to achieve anything. "You were unable to develop, only sleep and eat." These were the same words that many women refugees used to describe their situation in Jordan. Suha added, "The war [with Iran] started when we were children. We grew up with war and bombing, and something died inside. We lived from one war to another; we were barely living."

BODY POLITICS AND THE CONTINUUM OF VIOLENCE

Cockburn (2004) and Kelly (2000) analyze the continuum of violence before, during, and in the aftermath of conflict as well as the link between sexual violence and other forms of violence. Violence in this context is not only about power but about lived experiences and how power is reproduced and maintained (Nordstrom 1996, 8–9). As bodies are vested with gendered and sexualized meanings, women's experiences of their bodies are produced through multiple social and political relationships defined by religion, class, race, sexuality, and ethnicity (see Zarkov 2007). The body of the Iraqi woman became a site of contestation of power structures and a struggle over the meanings and constructions of masculinity and femininity, especially during the Iran-Iraq war, under the sanctions regime, and in the aftermath of the 2003 United States–led invasion. The Ba'th regime's attempt to increase birth rates during the war with Iran in 1980–8 limited access to contraceptives and highlighted the masculine image of the Iraqi male war hero (Al-Ali 2007). Yasmin Al-Jawaheri (2008) and Nadje Al-Ali (2007) describe the effects of the sanctions regime on Iraqi women and their increased insecurity and vulnerability in light of economic destitution, a changing social climate, and decline in educational and employment opportunities. Under the sanctions and especially in the aftermath of the United States–led invasion, women's bodies became a contested site for marking the political, religious, and social identity of the new Iraq (see Al-Ali and Pratt 2009).

This vulnerability and insecurity were illustrated by many of the women interviewed. Jamila, a university professor in her early sixties, said, "Under the sanctions, there was hunger and some women sold their honor to leave Iraq in all ways possible. When the woman leaves with nothing, all she has is her body." Hanan emphasized throughout the interview how the instability of the situation and of being a refugee falls on the woman. "It is hard financially on the man; he feels lost and this has negative consequences on the family.... It is not only that I am not legal; I also do not like to be threatened with that and with the fact that they could deport me at any second .... I am tired and my brain is frozen.... People hide their Iraqi identity and when you speak with

an Iraqi accent, you get higher prices and they ask you political questions."
Nasra, an accountant in her early forties, said, "When asked, I say that I am
Sunni and not Shi'a, and I am able to imitate the Jordanian accent. To be a
woman and on your own is hard. They harass you sexually because you are
Iraqi. They ask whether you are married, engaged, and speak dirty to you."
She cries and adds, "Isn't it enough what we went through, and on top of that
we are being harassed."

Nasra emphasized, "We are strangers and cannot talk even if they step on
our head." She repeated a saying that I heard from many women refugees on
how as strangers they should be polite (*ya gharib kun adib*). Here the connection was clear between being polite and being invisible as a refugee. Nasra
ended the interview by stating that Iraqis are concentrated in certain areas
in Amman. "I am an Iraqi citizen and if my country goes back to how it was,
I refuse to go to the USA. I am a citizen seeking asylum and no more." This
emphasis on the need to keep silent and negotiate the different terrains of what
it means to be a woman refugee in Jordan was echoed by Suha. She added,
"I worked as a secretary for two years. The owner was good in the beginning
but then his son would say, 'Watch out from my father' [that he might ask
for sexual advances].... As a consequence, I left work and started to wear a
headscarf. I should have rights where I live." Suha described how she changed
her place of residence to be close to the Iraqi community in Amman, and
how she changes her accent when leaving that community in order to pass as
non-Iraqi.

The refugee as an "other" is never only ethnic but also always gendered and
sexualized, albeit in ambiguous and conflicting ways. Within this context, refugee women constitute an extreme form of the "other" that is both vulnerable
and an object of domination, and where the physicality of the body can hardly
be separated from the symbolic meanings vested in it (see Zarkov 2007). Many
of the women described the limitations on their space as a result in part of
preconceived notions dominant in Jordanian society about Iraqi refugees in
general and women refugees in particular. The impact of these limitations
on the day-to-day life of refugee women resulted in the gendering of their
experiences and restrictions on their access to the public sphere. Lower-class
women interviewed described how hard it was at times to walk in the street
or use public transportation let alone find a job because of the harassment
they faced. This prompted many of them to change their accents and the way
they dress to pass as Jordanians. Both lower- and upper-class Iraqi refugees
tended to be concentrated in certain neighborhoods in Amman, which gave
them more visibility in those areas yet limited their interaction with the larger
Jordan society.

The role of displaced women as leading family income earners has not led to a growing sense of empowerment within the family or communities, as other studies have shown (Buck 2000). On the contrary, gender roles in many conflict situations have remained clearly delineated. Women are still expected to perform traditional household duties of feeding and caring for their children, even after long and difficult days of work outside the house. Segregation from local communities and a lack of permanent residence have had adverse effects on the political rights of displaced women (Buck 2000). The case of Iraqi women refugees in Jordan illustrates the contradictions embedded in their presence as refugees in Jordan. On the one hand, they are able to work illegally and are less threatened than men with deportation by the Jordanian border police. Yet, they are constantly harassed in the public sphere as a result of the prevailing social assumption that marks them as sexually available. This differs across class and place of residence, and the probability of being sexually harassed while using public transportation is higher for lower-class women.

Although sexual harassment is a problem in Jordan, and I was sexually and verbally harassed on more than one occasion while conducting the research, it was clear that my association with Iraqi women refugees gave people the liberty to make assumptions about my work. Whenever a taxi driver would ask me about my research, I could hear the changing tone in his voice as I replied that I conduct research with Iraqi women refugees. Haines describes how the violation of women's bodies acts as a symbol of the violation of the country (as quoted in Zarkov 2007). Violence against women is regarded as a "natural" circumstance of war and conflict, and women frequently face social stigma if they are living alone or accusations of promiscuity (Zarkov 2007). This was the case with many single, divorced, and widowed women I interviewed.

Suha made clear throughout the interview that she does not reveal to her neighbors that she is divorced. Women are expected, even under the conditions of forced displacement, to take care of the family and to uphold gender roles. This expectation holds even when women are abandoned by their husbands, left without a home or work, and without any family or community support. Khawla, a woman in her mid-thirties, said that her husband, who was a member of the Ba'th regime, was assassinated in 2004. She was scared for her children and went to Jordan a year after. She has three children; the oldest is ten years old. "We came to Jordan seeking aid and I had to become independent. I used to work as a hairdresser before I got married. I came back to work to support my children. I am the mother, father, head of the household and everything.... The kids are confined. I am managing and my neighbors are good. They are always watching because I am on my own. They are always watching." Khawla added, "The owner of the house rang my doorbell once at four in the morning asking for water. I told him to come in and showed him my three kids who were sleeping on the floor. He left immediately." Khawla emphasized how she wants her children to learn and absorb the situation, yet she admitted that she does not have time to sit with them and help with homework. "Our kids are tired from what they went through. They want to purchase things and there are no places for entertainment. I won't go back to Iraq; Iraq is lost." She added that she worked in different places and was at times mistreated and exploited. Although there is demand for hairdressers, the money is not hers and she is paid a fixed salary of 110 JD. She sells part of the ration that she receives through the United Nations to help with the house expenses. "I had a big house in Baghdad, but Baghdad is in the past. If it wasn't for good and generous people, I would not have made it." Khawla acknowledged that she cannot afford not to work and that she is barely making it financially.

This steadfastness and resistance were present in many of the women's narratives. Sama expressed optimism and insistence on how she wants to sustain her life in the simplest of ways. Although she is enduring, she described herself as weak in asking for her rights. Her first priority is to keep her family and her husband together. She described how the majority of Iraqi families are dispersed, and how women have lost everything. She sees women's role as protecting the family and keeping the memory alive from one generation to the other. This emphasis on women's roles as keeping the family together was echoed by both women refugees and aid workers. According to Nada, who is in her late twenties, women should endure despite the circumstances. Nada's husband was kidnapped in Iraq and left on the street to die. He survived and Nada is thankful that her family is still together.

Suha echoed Nada and Sama's narrative by saying, "The Iraqi woman is strong. She endures and is very patient. That is our nature.... We are tired [emotionally and physically]. I wish someone will ask the woman what she wants and how she could get comfort. Nobody asks us what we want. My stability is that of my family." Suha's emphasis on both the need to be strong and keep the family together and her complaint that no one asks the woman what she wants illustrates both the empowerment opportunities and constraints that result from these gendered family roles. Nasra added, "My family is not here; I have no one here .... God wrote this for us. I do not trust people, with all due respect to you." Since Nasra is living on her own in Jordan, she expressed throughout the interview how strong she needs to be in order not to be taken advantage of. Nasra mentioned how she was attacked and forced out of her job by members of the Ba'th regime in Iraq. She, as well as many other interviewees, expressed the level of fear and mistrust that they lived through in Iraq. Some went as far as expressing similar mistrust in humanitarian aid organizations and even in me as a researcher.

AGENCY AND NETWORKS OF SUPPORT

The prevention and protection dimension of humanitarian interventions are particularly important for an effective response to women's different demands at the local level (Meertens 2010, 160). Humanitarian actions that focus especially on gender sensitive risk analysis and thoughtfully designed prevention and protection measures can make a significant practical contribution to the overall process of providing humanitarian assistance to the displaced (see Meertens 2010, Schmiechen 2004). Buscher (2007) adds that protection of internally displaced women, children, and youth is inextricably linked to providing what we all need for normality and well-being – safety, health care, education, and economic opportunities (16). Yet, health care, education, and economic opportunities are lacking for the majority of Iraqi women refugees in Jordan. Although well-to-do families can pay for health services and for the private education of their children, they are still not allowed to work legally in Jordan unless they deposit large amounts of money in the bank.

The Humanitarian Response Review in 2005 prompted a further effort toward improving coordination and enhancing collaboration among humanitarian actors to strengthen the technical capacity and service delivery on the ground (Austin 2008, 12). This was emphasized in my interviews with United Nations and national and international humanitarian aid workers in Jordan. In addition, there is an equally urgent need for health organizations to recognize the reproductive health needs of those affected by conflict and natural disaster and mainstream effective response for reproductive health into their institutional and field operations. Iraqi refugee women in Jordan lacked preventive care, and as they struggled to provide basic needs for their families, they usually made their needs and health a second priority, as has been shown in other situations (Doliashvili and Buckley 2008).

Respect for the dignity of women can be embedded both in research and in ways services can respond to their needs (Hajdukowski-Ahmed et al. 2008, 18). Refugee women find themselves in "continuous situations of crisis, that is, etymologically at turning points that create challenges but that also elicit critical judgment and open up new possibilities" (ibid). CARE International had implemented a community-level research model that many refugee women described with great appreciation. Nasra, who volunteered with CARE and served on their committee, said, "Our voice is being heard at CARE; we talk about violence in the family, in the street and at work. Although there is more [illegal] work for women refugees, they suffer from sexual harassment at home, at work, and everywhere." Nasra added that aid organizations cannot cover all of people's needs. "After the collapse of the Ba'th regime, we established civil society organizations. I wanted women's voices to be heard and was active in Iraq as well as in Jordan .... We get stronger from one war and tragedy to another. Even death is now normal. When you hear that people are dying, this becomes natural." Nasra recognized throughout the interview the structural limits of her agency and ability to organize as a refugee woman in Jordan.

The women's narratives reflected the complexity of identity and erosion of agency in various situations and power relationships, as well as the contradictions and counterdiscursive practices. May Muzafar, an Iraqi poet living in Amman since the early 1990s, insisted that I use her real name in my research. She said "I am hopeful even if I have only one day left in my life. I am still defending my existence and memory. I aim to preserve the quality of our presence outside." May emphasized throughout the interview how she uses her writing and creativity to resist. She also acknowledged her advantageous position as her family and friends are close by and she has financial stability. Nadine's mother, Arwa, who is in her fifties, described how she relies on herself as she lives with her daughter in Amman. She emphasized how she does not trust anyone and shared how she changes her accent and wears sunglasses in public in order to pass as non-Iraqi. Arwa is well aware of the limits of her agency, especially that she does not have health insurance and is barely surviving in Jordan with the remittance that her husband and son send from Iraq.

Austin (2008) argues that migrant women show greater resilience and adaptability than men because they maintain household and child care routines, which provide them with occupation and with self-confidence during the stressful period of uncertainty in exile (see also Franz 2003, Buijs 1993). Meertens's (2010) concept of the victimization of refugee women – and in particular the rupture from the known elements of their daily domestic life and of the social and emotional uprooting brought about by their displacement from their world of primary relations – is also important to consider when analyzing the changing gender roles among Iraqi women refugees in Jordan (140). According to Meertens, the destruction in the "before" phase has meant the destruction of social identity far more for women than for men, whose freedom of movement, access to information, and control of free time were taken as given and who were accustomed to dealing with a wider geographic, social, and political space. For women, the rupture of the social fabric at the family and neighborhood levels has produced the sensation of being adrift: like a boat with no harbor. Although the majority of Iraqi women refugees felt adrift, as did those in Meertens's study, they were at times freer than the men to move around Jordan, as they and their children were less likely to be deported by the Jordanian authorities. In addition, many of the women survived living in Iraq under severe conditions during the sanctions period. The attitude among all the women and men interviewed, as well as the aid workers, is that Iraqi women are strong and are expected to keep their families together.

Meertens argues that these possibilities have had greater force for those women whose previous organizational and leadership experiences help them to overcome the tragedies of displacement and undertake personal and collective reconstruction in their new urban lives (145). Despite the increased responsibilities for Iraqi women, they are confined to limited spaces for social and political action. Lower-class women were extremely dependent on aid services to sustain their daily living. For the middle- and upper-class women interviewed, residency problems in Jordan, as well as the instability of the political situation in Iraq, affected their ability to take initiative and reconstruct their lives. Jamila said, "I was not afraid then; now I am afraid. How I endured, I do not know ... the strange thing is that you do not know who they are [she was threatened by militia groups because she is an independent and single woman, and a presumed Ba'th supporter].... I left Iraq forced.... I am not comfortable and there is a problem with my residency. It took eight months for them [Jordanian authorities] to give me residency [to teach part time at the university in Amman]. Neither my sister nor my nephew have residency. I got mine one month ago. I did finally register with the United Nations as I was afraid that if they deport us we would have no place to go." Jamila described how in the aftermath of the United States–led invasion in 2003, she was no longer able to drive her car in Baghdad. She also described how for the first time in many years, she has been unable to write a book or conduct research. "My pain and suffering as a woman is hard.... I feel that my hand eats me. There is no respect for my health or dignity. Now I only live on my salary. I am managing but cannot afford luxury. The Jordanian society does not want to accept us." She wondered out loud whether it was solely the responsibility of Jordanian society to absorb Iraqi refugees. "I cry bitterly for myself, the homeland, and what happened to us. I do not leave the house much because going out costs me financially and psychologically. I am in pain. Sometimes I wonder whether it is better to go back to Iraq and die there." Jamila added, "I am well known in Iraq; I was patriotic ... suddenly, I am a refugee. I did not expect this in my age. I am here and my situation is not stable. After serving [at the university in Iraq] for thirty years, I need to start from zero." Jamila described how she was harassed by the Ba'th regime and arrested for forty days in the aftermath of the Gulf War in 1991 and the following uprising in the south of Iraq. She acknowledged that she was tortured. "I used to walk on the edge of the sword in order to survive. Now it is worse. I was hoping that the situation will improve."

Many interviewees and aid workers described how Iraqis were repressed under the Ba'th regime, and how they lacked the capacity for national and collective organizing. Civil society groups were severely restricted and only those associated with the Ba'th regime were allowed to operate. Many activists went underground or left the country in the 1970–80s (Ismael and Ismael 2000). Hikmat, an Iraqi art dealer in her fifties, described how Iraqis had an unspoken agreement with the Ba'th regime and how if you wanted to survive you had to limit yourself to certain boundaries. That is why many activists focused on cultural rather than political issues. "We talked more about culture.... The effect of the war with Iran and its consequences are present until today." This view was echoed by Jamila and the majority of the women interviewed from all generations.

CONCLUSION

The urgency of the Iraqi refugee situation prompts me to think of more than one venue to share my work with the women and the larger community – especially in the United States – as the subject of Iraqi refugees remains mostly invisible despite the increasing number of refugees admitted to the country. I returned to Jordan in December 2011 to follow up on my research and share my work with the women interviewed. I had already established contact with those who recently immigrated to the United States and decided to expand the scope of the research to include women refugees who arrived here in the last few years. In addition to publishing my work in academic journals, I am in the process of collaborating on making a documentary film about Iraqi women refugees that describes the challenges they face during this prolonged state of displacement.

My analysis focuses on how Iraqi women refugees constructed meanings and practices to deal with the challenges they face on a daily basis as women refugees in Jordan. I wonder about the consequences of the transient nature of displacement and the impact on the physical and mental health of Iraqi women refugees. Could women refugees (especially those from the lower classes) rely on aid for decades, and what is the impact of this prolonged state of displacement on social networks and communal support systems? Women refugees from East Amman and Zarqa relied on social networks to exchange information about aid agencies and the variety of resources available that could help in addressing the health and educational needs of their children. For the majority of women from the lower and upper classes, being around Iraqi refugees sustained a sense of community and a feeling of home, even if a limited one.

The longer refugees remain in exile, the more difficult and complicated it may be to return (Bloch et al. 2000). Since the prospects of local integration or return for Iraqi refugees are not foreseeable in the near future, most of the Iraqi women I spoke with were interested in repatriation into a third country. With the current economic global crisis and the dwindling number of countries willing to grant asylum to Iraqi refugees, this option is becoming quite impossible to achieve as well. Since viable options were almost entirely outside the realm of the control of refugee women, they were still resilient and constantly searching for ways to improve their situation. Yet, can they sustain this situation for the short and long term, and can they continue to live for years in this third space, which grants them no chance to seek asylum, return to Iraq, or settle in Jordan?

BIBLIOGRAPHY

Al-Ali, Nadje. 2007. *Iraqi women: Untold stories from 1948 to the present*. London: Zed Books.

Al-Ali, Nadje and Nicola Pratt. 2009. *What kind of liberation? Women and the occupation of Iraq*. Berkeley: University of California Press.

Al-Jawaheri, Yasmin Husein. 2008. *Women in Iraq: The gender impact of international sanctions*. Boulder, CO: Lynne Rienner.

Austin, Judy et al. 2008. Reproductive health: A right for refugees and internally displaced persons. *Reproductive Health Matters* 16(31): 10–21.

Bloch, Alice et al. 2000. Refugee women in Europe: Some aspects of the legal and policy dimensions. *International Migration* 38(2): 169–90.

Buck, Thomas et al. 2000. *Aftermath: Effects of conflict on internally displaced women in Georgia*. Working Paper No 310. Washington, DC: Center for Development Information and Evaluation, U.S. Agency for International Development.

Buijs, Gina, ed. 1993. *Migrant women: Crossing boundaries and changing identities*. Oxford: Berg.

Buscher, Dale and Carolyn Makinson. 2007. Protection of IDP women, children and youth. *FMR/Brookings-Bern Special Issue*. 15–16.

Chatelard, Géraldine. Forthcoming. *The politics of population movements in contemporary Iraq: A research agenda*. In *Writing the history of Iraq: Historiographical and political challenges*, eds. Riccardo Bocco, Jordi Tejet, and Peter Sluglett, 359–78. London: World Scientific Publishers/Imperial College Press.

Chatelard, Geraldine. Iraqis in Jordan: Elusive numbers, uncertain futures. Available at http://www.academia.edu/189411/Iraqis_in_Jordan_Elusive_numbers_uncertain_future (accessed November 30, 2011).

Cockburn, Cynthia. 2004. *The continuum of violence: A gender perspective on war and peace.* In *Sites of violence: Gender and conflict zones,* eds. Wenona Giles and Jennifer Hyndman, 24–44. Berkeley: University of California Press.

Dahl, Solveig et al. 1998. Traumatic effects and predictive factors for posttraumatic symptoms in displaced Bosnian women in a war zone. *Journal of Traumatic Stress* 11(1): 137–45.

Doliashvili, Khatuna and Cynthia J. Buckley. 2008. Women's sexual and reproductive health in post-socialist Georgia: Does international displacement matter? *International Family Planning Perspectives* 34(1): 21–9.

Forced Migration Review. 2007. Iraq's Displacement Crisis: The Search for Solutions. Available at http://www.fmreview.org/sites/fmr/files/FMRdownloads/en/FMRpdfs/Iraq/full.pdf (accessed October 15, 2012).

Franz, Barbara. 2003. Bosnian refugee women in (re)settlement: Gender relations and social mobility. *Feminist Review* 73: 86–103.

Hajdukowski-Ahmed, Maroussia et al. 2008. *Introduction. In Not born a refugee woman: Contesting identities, rethinking practices,* 1–24. Oxford: Berghahn Books.

Hardgrove, Abby. 2009. Liberian refugee families in Ghana: The implications of family demands and capabilities for return to Liberia. *Journal of Refugee Studies* 22(4): 483–501.

Human Rights Watch. 2006. The silent treatment: Fleeing Iraq, surviving in Jordan. Available at http://www.hrw.org/sites/default/files/reports/jordan1106webwcover.pdf (accessed October 15, 2012).

———. 2007. From flood to trickle: Neighboring states stop Iraqis fleeing war and persecution. Available at http://www.hrw.org/legacy/backgrounder/refugees/iraq0407/iraq0407.pdf (accessed October 15, 2012).

Hyndman, Jennifer and Malathi de Alwis. 2008. *Reconstituting the subject: Feminist politics of humanitarian assistance.* In *Not born a refugee woman: Contesting identities, rethinking practices,* eds. Hajdukowski-Ahmed, Maroussia et al., 83–96. Oxford: Berghahn Books.

Ismael, Jacqueline, and Shereen Ismael. 2000. *Gender and state in Iraq.* In *Gender and citizenship in the Middle East,* ed. Joseph Suad, 185–211. Syracuse, NY: Syracuse University Press.

Kelly, Liz. 2000. *Wars against women: Sexual violence, sexual politics and the militarised states.* In *States of conflict: Gender, violence and resistance,* eds. Susie Jacobs et al., 45–65. London: Zed Books.

McMichael, Celia. 2002. "Everywhere is Allah's place": Islam and the everyday life of Somali women in Melbourne, Australia. *Journal of Refugee Studies* 15(2): 171–88.

Meertens, Donny. 2010. Forced displacement and women's security in Colombia. *Disasters* 34(s2): 147–64.

Nordstrom, Carolyn and Antonius C.G.M. Robben, eds. 1996. *Fieldwork under fire: Contemporary studies of violence and culture.* Berkeley: University of California Press.

Nusair, Isis. 2008. *Gendered, racialized and sexualized torture at Abu-Ghraib.* In *Feminism and war: Confronting U.S. imperialism,* eds. Robin Riley, Chandra Talpade Mohanty, and Minnie Bruce Pratt, 179–93. London: Zed Books.

Nyers, Peter. 2006. *Rethinking refugees: Beyond states of emergency.* New York: Routledge.

Schmiechen, Malinda M. 2004. Parallel lives, uneven justice: An analysis of rights, protection and redress for refugee and internally displaced women in camps. *Saint Louis University Public Law Review* 22(473): 473–520.

U.S. Committee on Foreign Relations. 2008. Managing chaos: The Iraqi refugees of Jordan and Syria and Internally Displaced Persons in Iraq. Available at http://www.gpo.gov/fdsys/pkg/CPRT-110SPRT41773/pdf/CPRT-110SPRT41773.pdf (accessed October 15, 2012).

U.S. Congressional Research Service. 2009. Iraqi Refugees and Internally Displaced Persons: A Deepening Humanitarian Crisis? Available at http://www.fas.org/sgp/crs/mideast/RL33936.pdf (accessed October 15, 2012).

U.S. House of Representatives. 2008. A joint hearing on the United States response to the Iraqi refugee crisis. Available at http://www.internationalrelations.house.gov/110/41229.pdf (accessed October 15, 2012).

Žarkov, Dubravka. 2007. *The body of war: Media, ethnicity, and gender in the break-up of Yugoslavia*. Durham, NC: Duke University Press.

PART II

DO NO HARM

Figure 4. "Jump Rope" December 2003, Kono, Sierra Leone.
Photographer: Kate Lapides

We were sitting under the shade of a tree watching children jump rope when
the UN peacekeepers walked out of the garrison for a midday exercise. The
UN peacekeeping force in Sierra Leone was composed of battalions from
different countries. In Kono, the battalion was called "Pakbat," shorthand for
the Pakistani battalion. We were struck by the contrast of play and war, an
everyday experience for these children.

3

Reflections on Ethical and Practical Challenges of Conducting Research with Children in War Zones: Toward a Grounded Approach

Michael Wessells

For the past twenty years, I have worked as a practitioner-researcher on issues of children affected by armed conflict. My orientation as an intervention researcher reflects my strong belief that good practice must be guided by robust evidence, which is often lacking in humanitarian settings. From this standpoint, research is not a completely separate enterprise from practice but an integral part of a process of systematic documentation, testing, and learning that helps to identify which practices are effective, which components work and how, which approaches are cost-effective and sustainable, and what are the unintended consequences of one's practice. By using the insights from systematic program evaluations and from intervention research that embodies higher standards of evidence to guide efforts to improve programming, one can strengthen practice, ensure high levels of accountability, and advance applied science that aims to address significant social problems.

My commitment to using research to strengthen practice is matched by an awareness of the enormity of the ethical complexities associated with research in war zones. These complexities, which are the focus of this chapter, are best illustrated by an example pertaining to well-intentioned efforts to respect children's participation rights as guaranteed under the United Nations Convention on the Rights of the Child. In Sri Lanka, which experienced decades of armed conflict in which large numbers of children had been recruited into the Liberation Tigers of Tamil Eelam (LTTE), a research team gathered groups of ten or so teenagers for focus group discussions. Their intent was to learn directly from young people about their challenges and hopes and to give them voice in a situation that had rendered them invisible. But the politically tense atmosphere meant the discussion was perceived by adults having diverse political views as a political meeting to recruit youth as fighters. As a result, the discussions put the youth at increased risk of being detained or attacked by state forces, the LTTE, or both. Thus even research guided by a strong commitment to human rights can cause unintended harm. This example illustrates the broader principle that all research in war zones, no matter how carefully conceived and conducted, has unintended consequences, including negative consequences that violate the humanitarian imperative "Do No Harm."

The possibility of causing harm becomes even greater when the research concerns children (people younger than eighteen years of age), who typically constitute half or more of the population of war-affected countries. Children who grow up in war zones already face many sources of vulnerability: separation from their families, attack, displacement, multiple losses, gender-based violence, trafficking, recruitment, deprivation of basic needs, chronic poverty, disruption of education, recruitment into armed groups, and HIV and AIDS, among others. While researchers attempt to conduct their work on war-affected children in an ethically sensitive manner, this effort is impeded by factors related to the humanitarian enterprise. For example, in an emergency, NGOs must produce data quickly in order to compete for limited donor funds. Not uncommonly, this strong press for data encourages the use of shoddy methods that yield data of questionable quality. This raises ethical issues, since weak data will likely misguide the flow of humanitarian aid, denying it to the most vulnerable people.

Additional obstacles to conducting research in an ethical manner include the standards gap and the evidence gap. The "standards gap" refers to the lack of consensus on ethical standards for research that fit the fluid circumstances and the contextual diversity of war zones. For example, many wars occur in cultures and societies in which a young person is regarded as an adult once he or she has completed the culturally prescribed rite of passage (e.g., an initiation process and ceremony) or marries and does the work of an adult. In Sierra Leone (West Africa) and Angola (Southern Africa), for example, this typically occurs around the age of fourteen or fifteen years, whereas in Western societies, eighteen years demarcates the transition into adulthood. In countries such as South Africa, national law defines people as youth until they have reached thirty-five years of age. The fact that the concept of childhood is socially and politically constructed – and varies considerably according to context – makes it very challenging to develop universal standards regarding what counts as ethical treatment of children. The ethical standards and review processes by Institutional Review Boards that are commonplace in the United States offer little in the way of contextualized guidance for how to manage this and other complexities encountered routinely in war zones.

The "evidence gap" refers to the fact that the field of child protection and psychosocial support in humanitarian emergencies is still young and lacks a solid evidence base about which interventions are effective, particularly in terms of how they work and their feasibility, cost-effectiveness, and usefulness on a large scale. Furthermore, there is a paucity of evidence regarding the consequences of using particular research methods in war zones. Methods that appear promising because they help to guide useful interventions may have harmful consequences that outweigh the benefits. The inability to identify the cost-benefit ratio associated with particular methods and interventions makes it difficult to decide which approach is most appropriate in a particular context. In turn, the shortage of evidence makes it difficult to set standards.

The combined result of these considerations is substantial uncertainty on both a personal and a professional level about how to conduct research on children in war zones in an ethical manner. As humanitarians and researchers, we are thrust into a situation that is well described by the maxim that "we don't know what we don't know." However, the difficulties posed by this situation are no cause for throwing up one's hands and abandoning the search for pathways to ethical research and practice. Through critical analysis, self-reflection, and dialogue with people (including war-affected children) who have different perspectives on research ethics, humanitarian workers and researchers can increase their ethical sensitivity and move into a better position to avoid causing harm.

In this spirit, my chapter is a reflection on some of the main ethical and practical challenges to the conduct of research on children in war zones and on my evolving approach in trying to manage these challenges. I write not from the high moral ground of someone who knows the answers and professes to be fully ethical but from the humbler ground of one who continuously wrestles with the issues, is subject to the same pitfalls that affect all humanitarians and researchers, and is in a process of learning. The chapter begins with a discussion of how I became involved with research on war-affected children and how my understanding of war-affected children has evolved. The main part of the discussion identifies and reflects on important ethical challenges I encounter and my strategies for managing them. Because of space limitations, the chapter makes no attempt to consider all the ethical and practical challenges that arise in working with war-affected children but focuses on the subset of challenges that I have found to be most pervasive and difficult to manage. Because my own research is often tied to informing the structure and delivery of humanitarian assistance for affected children, throughout the analysis I reflect deeply on the intertwining of research and humanitarian response.

ORIGINS AND EVOLUTION

The story of how I became involved in work with war-affected children and of how my thinking has evolved about war-affected children is far from linear. Broadly, I have passed through numerous stages: feeling compassion and empathy from afar, becoming a psychologist who integrates psychology into a multidisciplinary perspective while focusing on peace and youth concerns, and then taking the plunge into practice while keeping one leg in academe. Through field experience, I have learned the value of bracketing the scientific knowledge I was trained to hold in very high regard. For example, in Angola, where people in rural areas have very different ideas about who is a child, I learned not to begin research discussions with local people with questions about older children who were between fifteen and seventeen years of age because such young people were regarded locally as adults. Asking the question in a manner that put forward my own assumptions about childhood simultaneously marginalized local views and put me in a position of imposing my views rather than learning about local views. Gradually, I learned to temper a technical approach with a more grounded approach of colearning, starting with open-ended questions and methods such as ethnography that are designed to enable learning about local views.

I also learned to maintain a robust criticism of the humanitarian enterprise and my place within it, struggling daily with the complexities of the ethical issues attending my research. My approach became less steeped in Western notions of childhood and psychology and more grounded in local understandings and approaches. I gained a better understanding of children, their place in their families and societies, and how they had been affected by seeing them in a different light. As my appreciation for the agency and resilience of young people in war zones grew, I moved away from the deficits approaches – such as the emphasis on trauma that has characterized Western analyses of children's psychosocial condition – in favor of approaches that emphasize coping and resilience.

A resilience orientation invites researchers to investigate people's strengths and assets in the cognitive, social, emotional, physical, and spiritual domains and to analyze how to build on those strengths. A resilience lens views people not as passive victims but as agents who actively cope with adversity, attempt to make meaning of their difficult experiences, and usually remain able to function without excessive suffering. Too often, the emphasis on trauma depicts war-affected people as damaged goods and as such unable to carry out basic tasks such as working and parenting. Yet in most war zones, the majority of people are not overwhelmed and dysfunctional but are actively struggling to cope with and adapt to their difficult life circumstances. A resilience orientation avoids pathologizing and labeling people, emphasizes the importance of self-help, and avoids implying that everyone needs counseling or psychotherapy. To say that people are resilient, however, does not imply that they do not need support. War-affected people who are able to function reasonably well still need support in the arenas of education and livelihoods as well as access to basic services and information about access to services, including legal services.

THE ORIGINS OF MY INTEREST

My interest in researching and learning about children who grow up in war zones had its origins in my involvement in the protest against the Vietnam War during my undergraduate days, particularly in the period 1968–70. The horrific photographs of napalm bombed children and families running naked down the streets triggered my shock, anger, and involvement in antiwar activism. They also sparked a strong desire to help the young people who, for the most part, had no part in starting the war but who suffered its ravages on a daily basis.

Accompanying this desire to help was my growing awareness of the moral, political, cultural, and other complexities associated with humanitarian aid. Having read *The Ugly American* in eighth grade and having had lengthy discussions of it with friends, I had an elementary awareness of the ways in which well-intentioned efforts cause harm and had an appropriate wariness of a starry-eyed charity model wherein outside helpers deliver aid to passive victims. By my second year in university, it seemed clear that one of the reasons why the United States had become enmeshed in such an ill-conceived war was that we had very little understanding of who the people of North Vietnam were and why the Vietcong fought and were so willing to suffer – by Western standards – enormous casualty rates. Analyses from outside the mainstream of political science and anthropology indicated that we knew very little about the people's culture and identity, sociohistoric context, and political orientation. I was concerned that if we did not know who the North Vietnamese were, we were not in a good position to help. In an inchoate way, I was beginning to realize the importance of linking action with research.

The problem, however, was that I needed to learn how to do research and develop the analytic skills that seemed necessary for making a positive contribution. Uncertain whether my future lay in research, practice, teaching, or some combination of these elements, I decided that doctoral training in basic science would provide the best preparation and engagement in research. My chosen field was psychology, which was inherently interesting to me and offered a useful lens for analyzing the subjective worlds of people in different societies and understanding one's own perceptions, motives, and behavior. In 1970, I entered the Ph.D. program in experimental psychology at the University of Massachusetts, Amherst. Conducting hard-nosed scientific research, which resulted in an initial publication in *Science* magazine, was exhilarating and drew me into a community of scholars, which expanded as I took my first academic post at Vassar College in 1974 and subsequently moved to Randolph-Macon College in Virginia in 1981.

Ultimately, however, a strong focus on basic science seemed too distant from the problems of the world. Also, a split had occurred in my professional and personal lives. By day, I worked as a psychology professor who had multidisciplinary interests. After hours, I continued my peace activism. The birth of my son in 1982 made me hold up the mirror and ask, "What am I doing to help build a better world for his generation?" This question had considerable salience since at the time the United States and the former Soviet Union were deadlocked in the cold war. Escalating tensions between the superpowers were intensified, with the likelihood that an escalation of one of the various proxy wars fought in Latin America and the Middle East could unleash the horrors of global nuclear war. The more I reflected on the importance of building peace for future generations, the more I wanted to integrate my work in psychology with my work for peace.

A Kellogg National Leadership Fellowship in 1983–6 enabled me to bridge activism and profession by turning my work toward issues of preventing armed conflict. Working with mentors in Russia, Sweden, and China as well as in the United States, I studied broadly in political science, history, and anthropology, and used my travels as an opportunity to learn from young people about their views on war and peace and their hopes for the future. During that period, I connected with peace-oriented psychologists, including developmental psychologists who studied the impact of the nuclear threat on children or who worked with young people as peace builders. Wanting to integrate peace issues with my work as a psychologist and educator, I devoted the following five years to revising my teaching responsibilities to include courses on peace psychology, aggression, and dynamics of conflict. These courses emphasized the importance of conducting research and of taking diverse cultural perspectives in addressing issues of peace. They also analyzed the importance of socializing children for peace as a means of transforming the global war system. This theme was reinforced by discussions I had with youth during travels to Syria, Jordan, Occupied Palestinian Territories, and Israel during that period.

YOUTH NARRATIVES – AGENCY AND RESILIENCE

The discussions I had with Palestinian youth, including refugees living in squalid, overcrowded camps in Jordan, drove home three key lessons that had significant influence on my subsequent research. First, youth who have been victimized by oppression and in many cases by direct violence show a degree of resilience that is at odds with most Western psychological analyses. The latter have emphasized negative effects such as trauma (particularly posttraumatic stress disorder or PTSD), depression, and anxiety. In the hands of journalists, these analyses have led to simplistic images of war-affected youth as traumatized or as a "Lost Generation." Problems such as trauma were present, particularly among youth who had been detained and tortured. However, most of the youth were better off than most deficits theories would have predicted.

Many youth were quite functional in that they performed the roles (e.g., student) expected of them and were not obviously debilitated or overwhelmed. To be sure, the youth needed support such as viable livelihoods in order to be able to marry and care for their families. Also, many struggled with issues such as loss of hope and needed support in managing their feelings. Some, particularly torture survivors, said they needed counseling or a specialized psychotherapy. Overall, these experiences of youth resilience led me to avoid in my research a singular emphasis on deficits and to place equal emphasis on resilience.

An equally compelling lesson was the youths' high degree of agency. Far from being passive victims, they actively engaged and coped with hardships by talking with their families and friends or by practicing their religion. Living in collectivist societies in which the good of the individual is less important than that of the group, they felt keen responsibility for their families, leading most to work after school. Among the many youth who were political activists, some engaged in the nonviolent resistance tactics of the first Intifada, whereas others said that either they or young people they knew were turning to violence as a means of fighting the daily oppression and humiliations the Palestinian people suffered. Either way, their level of agency and sense of empowerment were very strong and suggested the value of research approaches that actively engaged youth as researchers. This lesson planted the seeds for my subsequent engagement in participatory action research in which young people themselves are the researchers, the architects, and the participants in interventions of their own choosing.

An important methodological lesson was the value of learning from the narratives of young people. Many clinical psychologists approach their research as if they know how to analyze youths' problems and how to develop solutions for them. Yet there was a disconnection between these adult "expert" perspectives and those expressed by the young people themselves. In the refugee camps, for example, NGO psychosocial workers measured trauma and depression and prided themselves on their quantitative data and scientific approach. Although this practice had its value, it was not complemented by a more humane, grounded approach of listening to the youth, learning how they understood their situation, and responding to their greatest felt needs. The overreliance on quantitative approaches was also not good science, which normally employs a mixture of qualitative and quantitative methods to answer different kinds of questions. These lessons about resilience, agency, and listening were the seeds; my subsequent research in Africa and Asia helped these seeds to germinate and grow into a new approach to research in conflict settings.

TOWARD A GROUNDED APPROACH

The lessons learned from Palestinian youth took on new importance as I began in 1995 to work with Christian Children's Fund (CCF, now called ChildFund), a nondenominational NGO headquartered in Richmond, Virginia, near my home. CCF needed methodological support in evaluating a large-scale psychosocial program for war-affected children in Angola and invited my assistance. At that time, following the advice of international consultants, an all-Angolan team was implementing a program that focused primarily on traumatized children. Its main evaluation tools were scales for measuring traumatic exposure and impact, with the latter focused primarily on symptoms such as nightmares and rapid heartbeat. The team reported that these tools, which had been used in various war contexts, were helpful but did not apply to some children's greatest self-reported problems. In one case, a ten-year-old girl whose home had been attacked and who had seen her parents killed wanted to talk about her problems. Her biggest problem, she said, was that she had had to run away before she could conduct the appropriate burial rituals for her parents. When asked why that was so important to her, she said that where she lived, people believed that without the conduct of burial rituals, the spirits of the dead cannot transition to the realm of the ancestors. Trapped and angry, the spirits inflict harm on the living, causing problems such as illness and food insecurity, among others. This girl, who was visibly distressed, said that what she needed most was to be able to conduct the *obito*, the traditional burial rituals, for her parents.

A related case occurred several months later amid work to support the reintegration of formerly recruited youth. A fourteen-year-old formerly recruited boy said that he was unable to sleep at night because he was visited by the spirit of the man he had killed. The spirit asked, "Why did you do this to me?" creating terror since the boy believed that the spirit had the power to harm him and other people. Asked what might help, the boy said that it would help for a traditional healer to conduct a cleansing ritual that would rid him of the angry spirit.

Together, these cases indicated the importance of spiritual sources of distress and of so-called traditional practices as sources of psychosocial support. They put the Angolan team's dilemma in sharp focus: Should the program continue with its focus on trauma or should it reorient itself to address children's spiritual distress and to work with traditional healers? Programmatically, it was a significant question because the donor (USAID) had supported a trauma program and there was uncertainty about how they might respond to a call for reorientation. In addition, it was unclear how to incorporate local cultural dimensions into the program, and a reorientation would cause delays since extensive capacity building of staff would be needed.

The situation posed equally significant questions regarding evaluation: Should the data collection be driven by the trauma model that was based in Western science and fit the initial program objectives? Or should the data collection also emphasize indicators that reflected local beliefs and cultural practices? To include the latter could be seen as valorizing traditional healing, which sat outside the house of Western science and on which there was little empirical evidence regarding effectiveness. After extended dialogue with many stakeholders, the Angolan program team and the international evaluation team decided to reorient the program, blending trauma and cultural elements. From the standpoint of evaluation and learning, this meant conducting research on traditional practices, shifting to an evaluation design that considered local understandings and practices, and broadening evaluation measures beyond purely quantitative assessments of trauma.

The fact that this reorientation was needed itself raises a significant ethical issue – the imposition of outsider approaches that did not fit the local context. The initial trauma focus had originated with international psychologists and consultants who carried the imprimatur of Western science and who had been viewed as "experts" by the Angolan team. They had developed a program and evaluation framework that neither reflected nor responded to local understandings and practices. In essence, psychology in this situation had become a form of neocolonialism, with trainings used as a means of moving local people away from their own beliefs and practices and toward a more scientific approach. It was ironic that the trauma approach had been reified as being "scientific" while the local beliefs and practices had been marginalized

as "unscientific." For one thing, the trauma scales that the team had used had not been validated in the Angolan context, thereby raising questions about their scientific soundness. In addition, a key lesson from the social sciences is that people's beliefs influence their behaviors. From a scientific standpoint, it seemed important to learn what the beliefs of Angolan children were and how those beliefs influenced the likely effectiveness of different practices. On a more mundane level, it seemed possible to systematically test the effectiveness of traditional healing practices such as cleansing rituals.

This imposition was less a product of the consultants' willful arrogance (although I have on occasion witnessed that in the field) than of power dynamics that are often invisible. In preparing for this new research, we discovered that the imposition not only was external but also had elements related to feelings of inferiority and self-silencing among the members of the Angolan team. Because this research required the use of ethnographic methodology, it was necessary to build the capacities of the Angolan team. To do the training, the Angolan team hired a distinguished ethnographer from Mozambique, which, like Angola, had been a Portuguese colony and had suffered decades of war. After the ethnographic training, the team seemed well prepared to conduct the research. Unfortunately, the researchers failed miserably in their attempt to do the ethnographic research.

Carlinda Monteiro, the technical leader of the Angolan team, perceptively analyzed the problem. The researchers, who themselves were university trained and quite Westernized in outlook, doubted the utility of traditional practices, which they regarded as backward. Carlinda realized that she and the Angolan team had, like many Angolans, internalized a sense of inferiority about their own culture. This inferiority complex was rooted in centuries of colonial domination, and it had probably been strengthened by their training in Angolan universities, which had privileged Western psychology. As a result, the Angolan team regarded traditional beliefs and practices as less useful than scientific methods and silenced themselves from expressing any support that they might have felt for traditional approaches. To correct this problem, Carlinda organized a workshop that consisted of a group reflection on why Angolans feel their culture is inferior and a process of working to understand the potential value of local beliefs and practices, without romanticizing them. With knowledge and confidence from this revised ethnographic training the researchers were able to collect useful ethnographic data that enriched their definition of outcomes to include children's spiritual well-being. They also strengthened the effectiveness of the program by referring children to traditional healers and by collaborating with traditional healers in all phases of the intervention.

Over the three years that followed, the program practitioners learned how to blend Western and traditional approaches in organizing psychosocial support for war-affected children. A key lesson they learned was that when cultural beliefs and practices are made central, local people feel respected, see the initiative as fitting their culture, and are more likely to take ownership of the program. Excited by this approach, community people mobilized others through their own indigenous networks, recruiting local helpers and activating and using practices that they deemed to be important. This process of community mobilization, although it had been externally facilitated, became in important respects internally driven and grounded in people's own sense of empowerment and agency.

These experiences taught me the value of a community-based, culturally grounded approach that emphasizes self-help, builds on the assets and resources of the community, and offers sustainable supports for war-affected children. The experiences also taught me to be comfortable in roles such as facilitator and colearner rather than "expert." In regard to evaluation and research, I learned the importance of not starting with outsider hypotheses and preconceptions about what are the most pressing concerns of children or about the best means of helping them. Instead, I needed to take an approach of grounded learning, that is, of learning and collecting data that resonate with the voices and understandings of young people and are meaningful in the local context. On a professional level, I began expanding my base of ethnographic and qualitative methodology skills, a process that continues today. I also became more skeptical about the assumption that Western psychology is universal. I learned the importance of holding this perspective in the background and focusing initially on learning and building upon local understandings. This backgrounding or bracketing was not permanent, but these Western concepts and approaches were introduced rather than imposed and in a manner that respected local knowledge.

KEY ETHICAL AND PRACTICAL CHALLENGES

In war zones, ethical and practical issues are thoroughly intertwined. For example, Afghanistan has more land mines and unexploded ordnance than any other country except Cambodia and Angola. In Afghanistan, safety and security were highly salient concerns. I faced many decisions about where to travel and what work was safe to do. Although decisions about security seemed to be mostly about practical matters of logistics and personal safety, these decisions also had significant ethical implications. For example, I often saw teams of expatriate humanitarians travel into areas that were unsafe as a result of land mines, banditry, and Taliban activity. Asked whether they had security concerns, they answered stoically that they did but that concerns about their own well-being were trumped by concerns about the ethics of denying aid to people who needed it. Although my decisions have sometimes reflected this concern, I have also tried to keep larger concerns in mind. In particular, if I (an expatriate and an American) was injured or killed while on mission, that could lead the authorities to suspend humanitarian activity in the area, thereby causing even greater denials of humanitarian aid to Afghan children and families in need. Nearly all war zones blur the boundaries between ethical and practical issues.

This blurring makes it appropriate to consider practical and ethical issues together. In the following section, I focus on a subset of issues that have proven to me to be particularly thorny and that are often not considered in traditional discussions of research ethics, which tend to focus primarily on issues of confidentiality and informed consent. Although confidentiality and informed consent are highly important, they are only a small part of a much larger array of ethical issues that are seldom discussed but that can be very significant in particular contexts.

In fact, many key ethical issues of research are highly contextual. There is enormous variability across humanitarian settings and as such, rigid assumptions that "Issue X will always be a problem" or that universalized approaches to research ethics in humanitarian contexts should be treated with caution. Issues shift and even morph according to context; the means of managing problems must be every bit as contextually sensitive as are the problems themselves. One cannot get far by assuming that an ethical challenge such as that of obtaining informed consent is roughly the same in all settings or that it can be addressed by applying a cookie-cutter solution. The primacy of context forces one into a stance of critical awareness and contextual analysis, forgoing a "one size fits all" solution or black-and-white thinking.

RAISED EXPECTATIONS

Many academic researchers work in an extractive modality in which they collect data from affected people and give little back to those from whom they collect information. The two justifications that are usually provided for this approach are that (1) the knowledge learned through research will eventually be used to benefit conflict-affected people, and (2) it is not researchers' role or responsibility to provide any aid. Many researchers regard the provision of any support as a potentially biasing factor. Concerned about ethics and reluctant to make promises they cannot fulfil, researchers typically explain at length as part of an informed consent process that they are not there to provide aid and that participants will receive no immediate benefit to themselves and their families.

Although this approach seems logical and sensitive, it does not address the dynamics of raised hope and expectations that typically arise in emergency settings. It is questionable whether affected people are in a position to understand and accept fully the scientific role of researchers. In my experience, people who are starving may understand on a cognitive level that the researchers are saying, "We do not provide aid," yet their desperate circumstances inevitably stir the fires of hope and lead them to think, "These people are in a position to help." Even if they accept that the researchers themselves will not help them and their families, they may assume that the research will soon be followed by assistance provided by others such as NGOs. In fact, this assumption has some basis in reality since most NGOs conduct assessments before they initiate programs designed to support the affected people. Moreover, outsiders are often capable of helping by virtue of the fact that they have access to transportation, which can be used to carry supplies or help carry people who need medical attention to a health post.

Unspoken norms of hospitality and situational factors also favor the development of perceptions that the outsiders will help. In countries such as Afghanistan that have very strong norms of hospitality and reciprocity, it may be understood that if I extend my hospitality to you or am willing to help you, then surely you will reciprocate by helping me. These same norms and situational pressures also complicate efforts to obtain informed consent. How can one say "No" when the cultural norms of hospitality and situational pressures such as expectations of family members may require that one say "Yes, I will talk with you." Complicating matters still further is the combined force of desperation and felt obligation to do something to help one's family. If my own family were starving or dying from treatable diseases, and no other options were available for addressing these problems, there would probably be few limits on my willingness to use hospitality, charm, and ingratiation strategies such as complicity to strengthen a relationship that I hoped would lead the outsiders to help me and my family. If those positive tactics failed, I might resort to using guilt and shaming as means of persuading outsiders to help. After extensive trust has been established, affected people in diverse contexts have told me that they use similar tactics in dealing with outsiders when the situation is very difficult. Sometimes these tactics work, thereby reinforcing the cycle.

Whatever the reason, the raised expectations occasioned by researchers' presence and activities frequently lead to subsequent frustrations and feelings of abandonment when the expectations are not met. In the 1999 crisis in East Timor, after the onslaught of the Indonesian paramilitaries and the subsequent return of displaced people to their villages, people became very frustrated with researchers who asked many questions yet did little to help. "Assessment fatigue" occurs when a camp, village, or population becomes a revolving door for researchers and practitioners who are collecting assessment data but not delivering aid. As one frustrated teenager said, "Why should we talk with people who come here and ask many questions but do nothing to help us?" Even when the frustration is not expressed, it often shades into resentment, distrust, and reduced willingness to cooperate with outsiders. These feelings are antithetical to the spirit of partnership and community empowerment that many practitioners see as fundamental for the development of effective, sustainable child protection and psychosocial support.

My preferred method of managing the problem of raised expectations has two concurrent elements, the first of which is to avoid an extractive approach. Researchers collect information that could be of use to community people, and a basic, if seldom taken, step is to feed the research findings back to communities for purposes of sharing and to obtain another check on the validity of the findings. In interagency ethnographic research on community-based child protection mechanisms I recently led in Sierra Leone, national researchers learned about local views of key risks to children and of how people typically respond to those risks. An important finding was that in response to the problem of teenage pregnancy out of wedlock, the dominant response was for the family of the pregnant girl to reach a compromise with the family of the boy who had impregnated her. Most often, a key element of the compromise was for the boy to marry the girl, regardless of the girl's wishes. When the national research team leaders fed this finding back to the participating communities, it evoked impassioned discussion by community people about the need to end such compromises. In several communities, the chiefs and local people agreed to pass and enforce new bylaws that prohibit the compromises. More than a courtesy, this feeding back of information was a stimulus for social change guided by the community.

Use of an action research approach is another useful means of avoiding a strictly extractive approach. In the aforementioned research in Sierra Leone, the ethnographic phase is part of a multiphase research approach that seeks to test ways of strengthening community-based child protection mechanisms by supporting linkages with aspects of the national child protection system, including government aspects. Communities will design and implement the interventions, thereby enabling a strong sense of community ownership while avoiding problems of imposing interventions from outside the community.

The fact that the research will benefit people living in difficult circumstances is a means of giving something back and simultaneously supporting the agency and capacities of local people.

An extractive approach may also be avoided by linking research with action or humanitarian aid in ways that are less direct than action research but that nonetheless help to meet local needs. Even amid fluid circumstances, it is often possible to follow research on the prevalence of a particular problem such as family separation with concrete, programmatic steps toward family tracing and reunification. For example, the research can be conducted for a coordination group on child protection, which includes agencies that are committed to using the data rapidly to guide programmatic support for separated children. Although researchers vary in their views of whether it is essential to link research with action, I personally view this linkage as a necessity and adhere to the ethical maxim of "no research without action." In my experience, research conducted in war zones that has no direct linkage with action often causes more harm than good.

The second, complementary element is to manage expectations right from the start. A favored way of doing this is to name the hidden expectations and power dynamics, discussing openly the unrealistic expectations that emergency affected people have had of me in other contexts and saying pointedly to affected people, "I don't have a bag of cash." This rather blunt yet honest tactic is followed by an explanation of the process one has to go through to raise funding and the uncertainties associated with it. Numerous people I have explained this to have commented that no one had told them before how the system worked. Most people have said that the approach of explaining how the system works makes them feel respected and helps to develop trust.

These two elements are an imperfect solution since some affected people may continue to harbor unrealistic expectations and to feel frustrated when I fail to meet them. Also, some researchers have commented that my approach makes their work harder since the word gets out quickly to other communities when data collection in one community has been followed by the delivery of aid. This seems to me an acceptable trade since all affected people have a right to aid. Still, it is clear there is much room for ongoing learning and development of better strategies for preventing and managing raised expectations.

EXCESSIVE TARGETING

In war zones, limited funding is available for research and for assessments and program evaluations. This limitation has often led donors to provide funding for researchers to investigate questions such as how many children have been recruited into armed forces or armed groups, how many children have been raped, or how many children have been traumatized by the armed conflict. This emphasis on specific categories of vulnerable children is owed not only to donor priorities but also to researchers' theoretical preconceptions. For example, it is natural for a trauma theorist who views PTSD as one of the most debilitating effects of war on children to want to know how many children have PTSD. Nevertheless, it is wise not to focus research, assessments, or programmatic supports exclusively on predefined categories of vulnerable people. A sounder strategy is to recognize that vulnerability is highly contextual and to learn from affected people themselves about the main sources of vulnerability and who is in the most desperate situation.

A case in point is postconflict Sierra Leone, where significant numbers of children had been recruited into armed groups such as the Revolutionary United Front (RUF) and into civilian militias (Civil Defense Units or CDFs) through which villagers attempted to protect themselves while the government was unable to protect villages. Formerly recruited children received extensive attention from researchers and practitioners in part because there was a concern that if the young people did not have appropriate support, they would not reintegrate into civilian life and might continue the war or turn to banditry and crime. Because children in armed groups are often exposed to extensive violence and killing, many analysts believed they were among the most vulnerable children and therefore were a high-priority group for research and reintegration support. In some cases, intervention research tracked the path of formerly recruited children and attempted to answer questions such as what percentage of formerly recruited children integrate successfully into civilian society and whether formerly recruited children were more likely to reintegrate if they had participated in reintegration programs organized by NGOs than if they had "spontaneously" reintegrated without NGO or government support.

This excessive targeting of formerly recruited children led to a number of problems. For one thing, the initial focus was on boys, despite the fact that large numbers of girls had also been recruited. This pattern of gender discrimination led to biased research since few researchers inquired into formerly recruited girls, and reintegration supports were extended mainly to formerly recruited boys. To address this imbalance, research focused on girls was conducted over the following years. Broadly, the results indicated that among formerly recruited children, girls had been affected at least as strongly as boys had been, and girls also carried a greater burden of stigma and had additional difficulties associated with mothering, reproductive health, and ongoing gender discrimination in the wider society. Excessive targeting of formerly recruited children also sparked a backlash and a form of reverse discrimination. Local people who had been attacked by former child soldiers began to complain that reintegration support was "blood money" that rewarded former soldiers. Former child soldiers reported that they often felt discriminated against by people who were angry that the former soldiers were dressed and fed better than most people in the village. The resulting social divisions occurred at a time when there was tremendous need for social unity and harmony.

The excessive focus on formerly recruited children was also problematic because many local people were discernibly worse off than the child soldiers who had attacked them, destroyed their homes and farms, and looted their villages. Highly vulnerable children included those who had been separated from their families, child amputees and other children with disabilities, children who lived and worked on the streets, children who engaged in dangerous labor, and children who were sexually exploited in the present environment, among others. The needs associated with these issues were enormous yet were invisible in part because they had been dwarfed by the excessive attention of the international community to former child soldiers. An important lesson, then, is that excessive targeting of research can contribute to the misguiding of humanitarian aid and become part of wider patterns of discrimination and social injustice.

NEGOTIATING CULTURE

In researching which interventions lead to positive outcomes for war-affected children, a key question is, Who defines positive outcomes? In many research projects, researchers define positive outcomes in terms of child development theory and measurement concerns. In disciplines such as psychology that seek to identify universal laws of behavior, they often use outcomes that have some claim to being generalizable across cultures. In many cases, universal human rights standards such as the United Nations Convention on the Rights of the Child (CRC) are used as benchmarks for judging the acceptability of various outcomes.

Although this approach has its merits, it often causes unintended harm by imposing on local people ideas that they regard as alien and even inappropriate. Because the imposition of outsider ideas marginalizes local understandings and practices, it often seems to local people a new form of colonialism in which those who have power seek to substitute new ideas and values for those that had existed in the population previously. Understandably, this approach frequently generates backlash since local people feel disrespected and powerless.

To guard against this problem, I have often used ethnographic and free listing methods to obtain local people's views regarding positive outcomes for children. Using a method developed by Jon Hubbard in Sierra Leone, for example, we asked representative samples of people to picture a child who was doing well and to then identify the things that told them the child was well. Often, respondents identified characteristics such as "being serious in school" and "being respectful of parents and elders" as indicators that a child is doing well. Frequency analyses of the free listing data can help to identify which outcomes are most important in the eyes of local people, and in-depth probing or additional ethnography can help to clarify the meaning and significance of the identified outcomes in the local sociocultural system.

Usually, there is partial overlap between the outcomes for children that are identified by these outsider-driven and insider-driven approaches. For example, both approaches frequently identify participation in education as a positive outcome for children, with measures of actual learning as part of the measurement strategy for that outcome. However, significant disconnection often arises between the outcomes defined by researchers and the outcomes defined by local people. For example, many researchers would not identify exposure to harsh corporal punishment as a positive outcome for children. Yet in Sierra Leone, people tend to view parental use of harsh corporal punishment as essential for the development of respect, obedience, and proper behavior. A starker example is in regard to the practice of female genital mutilation/cutting (FGM/C), which is very widespread in Sierra Leone. Most researchers from Western contexts view FGM/C as a harmful traditional practice that undermines the well-being of young women and violates their human rights. In contrast, many women in Sierra Leone view circumcision as a pathway to full status as a woman, and parents view it as necessary for ensuring the marriageability of their daughters.

Researchers and agencies differ widely in how they respond to this disconnection between local and universalized views of positive outcomes for children. Some have tended to reject local views as tainted by human rights violations and as part of the problem in promoting children's well-being. Others have tended to romanticize local views, possibly as a form of exoticism, a reaction against the arrogance of imposition, or a tendency to listen to chiefs and other voices of tradition. Both approaches, however, are simplistic as they present essentialized views of culture as static and fossilized, rather than the reality that culture is dynamic and continually evolving. Also, both approaches are stereotypical in that they present culture as either unswervingly bad or good. The "culture is the problem" view demonizes local culture and overlooks the fact that local cultures and social norms include many positive practices that support children's well-being. In Sierra Leone, for example, a powerful social norm is for parents to be responsible and to protect their young children from harm. Similarly, the "local people know best" view overlooks the fact that all cultures and societies have strengths as well as weaknesses and areas for improvement.

In responding to the disconnection between outsiders' and local peoples' views, useful steps for researchers are to engage in critical thinking, interrogate hidden assumptions, empathize with local people, and avoid imposing outside values and practices. Critical thinking helps to undermine stereotypical images and illuminate the complexity inherent in human practices, regardless of whether one agrees with those practices. Also, it is useful for the researcher to cultivate a spirit of ongoing learning about other cultures and the interplay of humanitarian work and culture. Although humanitarian work is often conceptualized in terms of "saving lives" (which is highly valued!), it is useful to think of it as a space in which indigenous values and practices meet and engage with outside values and practices. Into this space, different people – local people as well as outside humanitarians and researchers – introduce diverse potentially conflicting values, a host of hidden power dynamics, and divergent views about what should happen. To negotiate this complexity, ideally with a spirit of humility and learning and a historicized understanding of the context, strikes me as one of the greatest of all research challenges.

COORDINATION: RESEARCH, ASSESSMENT, AND RESPONSE

It is an understatement to say that coordination is the Achilles heel of the humanitarian enterprise. The challenges in coordinating psychosocial work are amplified considerably by the polarized nature of the psychosocial field among both researchers and practitioners. Broadly, there have been two camps – clinical and community-based. The clinical approach is grounded in the health system, focuses on severe mental health problems such as depression and posttraumatic stress disorder, and typically uses specialized psychiatric and psychological interventions such as counseling. The community-based approach is grounded more in social work, addresses nonclinical forms of distress such as those that arise from multiple losses or family separations, and takes a holistic approach to intervention that may include steps to reunite separated children with their families or to increase household income. The two camps are like two cultures: the members of the camps have different training, use different vocabularies, conceptualize the main problems in divergent ways, and prescribe different solutions. In most emergencies, they compete for the same scarce resources and try to convince donors that they focus on the most important problems and offer the most useful interventions.

This cleavage leaves many donors feeling uncertain about which approach to support for both research and resulting intervention, and it creates myriad problems for comprehensive assessments as well as for relief efforts. For one thing, researchers and fieldworkers in the two camps typically collect different kinds of data and tend not to coordinate their data collection with those in the other camp. As a result, it becomes difficult to construct a comprehensive strategic plan on mental health and psychosocial support for war-affected people. For example, if the only assessment information one has is the prevalence of trauma and depression issues, one will not have a complete picture of the full range of mental health and psychosocial distress since many psychosocial problems arise from being homeless, lacking a livelihood, failing to bury the dead properly, or fearing attack.

To guide donors and organize comprehensive supports, it is essential to have an integrated picture that includes the assessment information commonly collected by both camps. Yet the holistic approach that is needed often fails to materialize since members of each camp tend to use their research and assessment data to guide only their particular interventions. During the war in northern Uganda, for example, there was an abundance of community-based psychosocial programs for children. But there was nowhere to go for help when a child turned up in need of clinical support. The polarization of researchers and practitioners into camps contributes to noncomprehensive approaches that cannot possibly address the holistic needs of the affected population.

This divided field is also mirrored by separate coordination structures. In humanitarian emergencies, coordination is promoted through the cluster system, wherein a particular agency (typically a United Nations agency) plays a lead role and convenes coordination meetings and activities with NGOs and the government of the affected country. However, many holes in this system exist. Coordination groups often do not work closely with the government or local humanitarian or human rights organizations, thereby enabling the establishment of a parallel system of supports. In most emergencies, work on clinical and mental health problems is coordinated by the United Nations Health Cluster, which tends to take a medicalized approach. Research and assistance on community-based psychosocial support are coordinated by the Protection Cluster, typically through the child protection subcluster. Cross-cluster coordination is impeded by many factors, not least of which is the profound urgency of a crisis. Coordination meetings in a single cluster occupy precious time, and many researchers and practitioners are wary of spending too much time in meetings. Even if the coordinators of the separate coordination groups want to encourage cross-coordination through mechanisms such as joint meetings, they may be unable to do so because their workload is already very heavy.

In attempting to manage this problem, both personal and systemic steps are useful. Personally, one can enable coordination by working in a collaborative manner (e.g., sharing information), participating regularly in coordination meetings, and coordinating visits to camps, villages, or other sites through the coordination groups, thereby reducing problems such as duplicating efforts as well as reducing the research and assessment fatigue experienced by communities. However, such personal efforts are limited by the multitude of factors that discourage or impede coordination. For example, agencies that collect solid assessment data and keep them to themselves may thereby gain a competitive advantage over other agencies in obtaining scarce funds. Also, in many emergencies, individual psychologists with no background in humanitarian emergency response nonetheless parachute in. Blinded by the conviction that somehow they will be able to help, such individuals and the homespun organizations that support them contribute to disaster tourism and chaos, strain precious resources such as food and water, and do not coordinate in part because they do not even know about or appreciate the importance of the coordination system.

A useful strategy for helping to manage the systemic aspects of poor coordination is to develop interagency guidelines or standards that build consensus regarding coordination, define agreed upon interventions, and nurture a process of collaboration. Between 2005 and 2007, twenty-seven agencies that were part of a global UN-NGO task force developed the first consensus global guidelines for the field – the Inter-Agency Standing Committee (IASC) *Guidelines on Mental Health and Psychosocial Support*, which were published in 2007. These guidelines emphasize that the clinical and community-based approaches are complementary by situating them within an intervention pyramid that defines a comprehensive, layered system of supports. Within this framework, it is meaningless to ask which approach is more important – both are important for supporting people who have been affected in different ways. In countries such as Kenya and Colombia, I have found that the guidelines serve as a powerful tool for advocacy with various agencies and governments. After the political violence in Kenya in 2008, for example, agencies were collecting data focused mostly on trauma symptoms, and counseling was their main intervention. By asking different agencies at a mental health coordination meeting to locate their work in a particular layer of the pyramid, it became apparent to everyone that there was too much attention to trauma and counseling and not enough attention to other forms of distress (e.g., lack of access to education, which is often one of children's biggest concerns) and interventions. As a result, the group decided together to take the more comprehensive approach called for by the guidelines.

The process of developing the guidelines also contributed to improved coordination by enabling collaboration and eroding the tendencies to protect one's turf. As agency representatives worked together, they developed relationships of trust and respect, and they learned how to work together with their agency hats off. These good working relationships and habits of interagency problem solving subsequently made it easier for agencies to collaborate at field level. Although there is no silver bullet, a collaborative approach to the development and implementation of standards offers considerable hope for strengthening coordination for research and response.

IDENTITY CHALLENGES

Since graduate study, my identity has shifted away from that of researcher to that of practitioner and researcher, focused on analyzing the effectiveness of community-based psychosocial and child protection supports. The practitioner dimension is foremost since I conduct research in order to strengthen practice. Yet the interconnection between practice and research is crucial since practice without research and reflection tends to leave one ensnared by one's dogmas and preconceptions, just as research without practice tends to leave one disengaged and trapped in the ivory tower. Because of the merits of the practitioner-researcher model, I have kept one foot in academe, first at Randolph-Macon College then, beginning in 2006, at Columbia University, while keeping the other foot in the NGO world.

Pursuing this dual identity is not without challenges. The world is besieged with so many armed conflicts and other emergencies that practice has demanded the larger part of my time and energy, making it difficult to stay abreast of current research. Also, it is challenging as a practitioner-researcher to compete in the research world, which privileges the most rigorous, robust methodologies. In war zones, it is impossible to achieve the levels of control and precision that are attainable in laboratory research. Working in war zones is not the easy path toward landing major research grants and publishing in the journals that have the highest scientific credibility. In addition, there are trade-offs between the technical design of research and effective practice that can leave one questioning one's legitimacy as a researcher. For example, scientific rigor is easier to achieve using standardized questionnaires than using highly participatory, open-ended methodologies. Yet participatory approaches may be better suited for enabling the community mobilization and ownership that contribute to effective practice. I am continually negotiating these trade-offs, testing my convictions and weighing the primacy of practice against the value of scientific research.

Efforts to bridge or negotiate the worlds of practice and research are made difficult by their very different cultures and orientations. Of necessity, practitioners move fast and want answers now in order to guide the urgent action that is needed. In contrast, researchers typically work with much longer time frames in which studies might take years to complete. In addition, there are mutual suspicion and distrust between practitioners and researchers. For example, many practitioners are concerned that researchers will show up, rip children open emotionally by asking about their most horrific experiences, and leave them feeling vulnerable. Practitioners also fear that the data collected by researchers will not reflect the richness of their projects or may damage their agencies' reputation. Conversely, researchers are often concerned that practitioners are biased in their data collection since they have a vested interest in the outcomes and may be ethically lax since they are willing to use unproven interventions. Often I find myself departing from a fully integrated approach by wearing my practitioner's hat when talking with practitioners and wearing my researcher's hat when talking with researchers.

Challenges related to identity also arise from the politics of working in war zones, which include factors that are beyond one's control. When I entered Angola in 1995, the country was tense and divided, as the government controlled half the country and the opposition group, National Union for the Total Independence of Angola (UNITA), controlled the other half. Although my personal and professional identity was that of humanitarian operating with impartiality, UNITA supporters did not see it that way. For them, the fact that I had obtained my visa through the government challenged my claims of political impartiality and made me seem a potential enemy. It was a bitter if important lesson: my presence in a war zone was a political act even if I had not intended it that way. Equally political was the source of my identity papers – at the time the only way to enter Angola legally was with a government-issued visa.

The political implications of one's identity have taken on new importance since 9/11. In working in Afghanistan, my identity as an American seemed well received by most people in the northern provinces, which had been the home of the Northern Alliance, who partnered with the United States forces in fighting the Taliban in late 2001. After the United States' war and occupation in Iraq, the Taliban resurgence gained momentum, increasing the target value of humanitarians, particularly of Americans. However, for me a greater issue than personal security was whether I was causing excessive harm simply by being in Afghanistan. I had worked hard to explain to local people that my purpose in being there was strictly humanitarian. Yet the policies of the Bush administration had made humanitarian aid a handmaiden for a wider political agenda guided by a dangerous mixture of American militarism, exceptionalism, and self-interest. When donors from USAID visited the communities in which I and Afghan colleagues worked, they had a security entourage of approximately forty soldiers, hardened vehicles, and an ambulance. Such visits increasingly undermined my identity and credibility as a researcher and humanitarian practitioner. Within this shrunken humanitarian space, some villagers asked me whether I was a spy.

These and other experiences have stirred much reflection for me about which countries it is appropriate to work in and whether my presence will cause more harm than good. They have also encouraged me to try to correct the imbalance that had developed between my humanitarian work and wider peace activism. Since the early 1990s, my work has turned from peace activism through organizations such as Psychologists for Social Responsibility and the Division of Peace Psychology of the American Psychological Association toward research and humanitarian fieldwork. The demands of humanitarian work have effectively pushed my peace activism, an aspect that I consider an essential complement to socially just humanitarian work, onto the back burner. Critical reflection on how well one is achieving the necessary balance is an important companion to research and humanitarian work. Since 2005, I have worked to correct this imbalance by becoming more engaged in examining research on psychological methods of torture and efforts to end psychologists' involvement in coercive interrogations of detainees in places such as Guantanamo Bay.

On a personal level, humanitarian work has challenged my identity in a multitude of ways, some of which are subterranean and difficult to articulate. I often find myself more comfortable sitting under a tree in a remote village discussing with youth how to rebuild their lives after armed conflict than I do visiting an average shopping mall in the United States. The opulence and luxury of one's own life become starkly visible when contrasted with the unacceptable conditions many war-affected people are forced to live in. Increased awareness of this global gap in wealth and well-being has strengthened my desire to give back and to work for social justice.

More broadly, research linked to humanitarian work has heightened my sense of relationship with people in different countries and has encouraged a spirit of global interdependence and citizenship. Having had the honor of working for years with teams of talented psychosocial and child protection workers in countries such as Afghanistan, Angola, Sierra Leone, and Sri Lanka (to name only a few), I have developed close friendships forged in the fires of urgency and great need. At community level, I have been inspired by the resilience of people facing difficult circumstances and moved by people's statements that they feel comforted by knowing that outsiders care. In the process of experiencing their ways of living and accepting their hospitality, I have become more collectivist in my identity and values. My identity as an American remains strong, yet this identity is tempered with a sense of global solidarity. This is appropriate, since humanitarian work and research achieve their full potential when they are liberated from the shackles of nationalism and anchored firmly in international human rights.

BIBLIOGRAPHY

Inter-Agency Standing Committee (IASC). 2007. *IASC Guidelines on Mental Health and Psychosocial Support.* Geneva: IASC. Available at http://www.humanitarianinfo.org/iasc/pageloader.aspx?page=content-products-products&productcatid=22 (accessed August 8, 2011).

4

Researching Social Life in Protracted Exile

Experiences with Sudanese Refugees in Uganda 1996–2008

Tania Kaiser

INTRODUCTION

Commentators on conflict and forced migration have had plenty to consider in northern Uganda and its neighboring countries. As many as 1.8 million Ugandan civilians have been displaced by conflict and insecurity during the last twenty years, and hundreds of thousands of people have been forced to cross international borders in search of a place to live in peace and security. Sadly, for many, such ideal places of refuge proved few and far between.[1]

Uganda has a long history of both hosting and producing refugees. In the 1960s it offered sanctuary to southern Sudanese fleeing the conflict that erupted in Sudan in the immediate postcolonial period. This prolonged exile ended for most refugees with the signing of the 1972 Addis Ababa Agreement. But while the agreement brought an end to the conflict in Sudan, it also sowed the seeds of the second civil war, which produced vast refugee movements in the 1980s and 1990s. In the late 1980s, large numbers of southern Sudanese fled into exile in neighboring countries, some for the second or third time in their lives. As the second Sudanese civil war heated and produced extreme suffering in the lives of civilians, people escaped from different locations for diverse reasons. By the mid- to late 1990s, more than a quarter of a million southern Sudanese were refugees in Uganda. Initially accommodated in transit camps, the majority were eventually transferred to agricultural settlements, where they were allocated plots of land for farming and exhorted to aspire to self-sufficiency.

In March 1996 I set off from the United Kingdom full of ideas and half-formed plans for research in a refugee settlement in northern Uganda.

---

[1] Some have been able to return to their home country after the signing of a Comprehensive Peace Agreement (CPA) in Sudan in January 2005. The CPA provides for a referendum on secession for the south of Sudan in January 2011, and in February 2011, over 98% of Southern Sudan voted for secession.

Several months of negotiation in Oxford had led to a hard-won agreement with Oxfam Great Britain that I would carry out field research toward my doctorate in anthropology in the Ikafe Refugee Settlement in Arua District. Here, Oxfam was working hard to resettle a large population of Sudanese refugees from transit camps along the border. There was hope in the air. Not only would these refugees be moved out of congested and sometimes dangerous transit areas, they would also be allocated plots of previously unused land in their new temporary homes, which would allow them to work toward agricultural self-sufficiency. Oxfam was unusual in taking a significant interest in the internal dynamics of the refugee groups with whom it was engaging and setting out to work in a way that was to some extent consultative and participatory. The new settlement of Ikafe would be carved out from land that was bush and forest. Rather than continue with emergency programming styles and cycles, Oxfam intended to adopt a developmental approach to refugee management where possible (Neefjes 1999, Payne 1998). All of this was fascinating to me as a student of anthropology, keen to understand how displacement affected sociocultural and other dimensions of refugees' lives and how aid mechanisms intersected with the political context and with refugees' own attempts to make a present and future for themselves in challenging circumstances. I was soon to learn that carrying out research with populations of forced migrants in such a complex and contested environment would not be straightforward.

SUDAN AND ITS NEIGHBORS: CONFLICT AND FORCED MIGRATION

Uganda's own political turmoil at the end of the 1970s had caused large numbers of northern Ugandans to cross into Sudan and (then) Zaire for their own security after the fall of President Idi Amin. Many returned to Uganda when Sudan's conflict became too dangerous, and they were accompanied by Sudanese seeking refuge. Some were escaping Sudanese government forces, others the southern Sudanese People's Liberation Army (SPLA). The regional conflict complex involved, among other things, a delicate interplay of international relations whereby the Government of Uganda provided aid and assistance to the SPLA in their armed struggle against the Government of Sudan, who, in turn, supported the infamous Ugandan rebel group the Lord's Resistance Army (LRA). Similar arrangements were in place with other Ugandan rebel groups including the West Nile Bank Front (WNBF), who harried the civilian population on the west side of the River Nile in northern Uganda during the 1990s.

President Yoweri Museveni swept to power at the conclusion of a bush war that saw former president Obote ousted in 1986, but his leadership was disputed

by many – especially in northern and eastern Uganda – and his government
was not subsequently seen as representing the northern political constituency.
Numerous insurgent groups emerged to contest his government's legitimacy,
and life became difficult and dangerous across the north of the country. One
consequence was that for twenty years from the late 1980s, living as a refugee
or internally displaced person (IDP) in northern Uganda was a precarious
business. The place of refuge was frequently insecure, violent, and buffeted
by both political and military dispute and confrontation. Civilian targets were
frequently attacked and army protection was woefully inadequate. For many
years, low-level, guerrilla style conflict was the backdrop to life in much of
northern Uganda. There were regional variations, depending on the specific
area and the ways in which local conflicts and competitions played into the
wider conflict context, but forced migrants were regularly subjected to military incursions and attacks in their places of refuge, even when these locations
were supposedly being protected by Government of Uganda security forces.
Major attacks were carried out on refugee locations by the WNBF in Arua
District and surrounding areas in the mid-1990s, while the LRA carried out
innumerable ferocious ambushes and attacks on IDP and refugee locations,
camps, and settlements across northern Uganda, including a number of massacres in the Uganda-Sudan border area, and at the Achol-pii refugee settlement in 1996 and 2002, in which scores of refugees and others were killed
(Allen 2006, Finnstrom 2008, Leopold 2005, Kaiser 2000).

FROM IKAFE TO KIRYANDONGO

During a month of careful preparation in Ikafe in March 1996, I laid the
groundwork for my fieldwork by familiarizing myself with the settlement and
its personnel and learning about the fluctuating security situation and the
extent to which local rebel activity might compromise free movement and
residence in refugee locations. I identified refugee villages in which I would
work, gained permission from refugees and other stakeholders to carry out the
research, and liaised with the Oxfam research team (itself an innovation) as
to how my work could make a practical contribution to the Ikafe project, as
well as allow me to complete my doctorate. Finally, I headed back to Oxford
to complete the initial upgrade process that would allow me to embark on the
field research stage of my degree.

By September I was back in Uganda, ready to begin work, although worried about reports that the security situation in Arua had deteriorated significantly. Oxfam had already signaled their reluctance to proceed with our
arrangement on the basis that rebel activity had stepped up to a dangerous

extent. I thought they were being overcautious and while I made inquiries as to possible alternative research settings, I assumed that I would be conducting my fieldwork in Ikafe. The day after I arrived in Uganda, a WNBF rebel attack resulted in the death of a much liked and respected local government officer in Ikafe, and the injury of several other people. Over the next few weeks the situation worsened until the settlement was all but unrecognizable. Large numbers of its refugee residents had fled back to Sudan, or to urban areas or transit camps in Uganda, or to the southern parts of the settlement, perceived to be least at risk of further attack. New transfers were halted, and Oxfam's vision of a developmental settlement was shattered.

What should I do? Part of me clung to the idea that some form of circumscribed research must still be possible with the remaining refugees at Ikafe, but refugee advocacy groups, NGOs, and government officials repeated the same advice: "Find another research site." At Ikafe it was no longer possible to address the kinds of research questions I had defined. There was also the risk that my presence would create security risks for me and for the few remaining refugees and NGO staff attempting to live and work there while keeping a low profile. So, after a year spent preparing to work with the largely Western Equatorian Sudanese population at Ikafe, becoming familiar with their history and conflict background, making an attempt to learn the lingua franca, and trying to forge a working relationship with Oxfam, I found myself working in another district of Uganda. My first lesson in forced migration studies was well and truly learned: expect the unexpected and be aware that research with people whose own lives have been repeatedly subjected to upheaval and reversals means long-term planning based on an assumption of no change is likely to be wrong footed. Although I had a contingency plan, some of the research I had conceived as appropriate and relevant in the context of Ikafe required some serious rethinking when I arrived in Kiryandongo.

Kiryandongo Refugee Settlement in Masindi District was a long-standing settlement for mainly ethnic Acholi and Madi refugees from Eastern Equatoria, Sudan. It was established in 1992 and by 1996 was managed by a local Ugandan NGO. The refugees had entered Uganda in 1989 and were transferred to Kiryandongo from a camp in Kitgum District after they had been repeatedly subjected to attacks by the LRA. Kiryandongo is located south of the Victoria Nile, a boundary that had in the past acted as a natural limit to the LRA area of operation. Masindi is a relatively lush and fertile district, known for maize growing, and only a three-hour drive from the capital, Kampala. All of these characteristics made it a desirable location for Sudanese refugees who did not mind living quite far from the Sudanese border, and it was home to around fourteen thousand people for most of the 1990s and early 2000s. Not all were officially registered. Some were registered as refugees in less secure locations and had transferred illegally to Kiryandongo, to join family members or to benefit from its increased security and opportunities. Security was poor for refugees living near Gulu, Kitgum, and the border areas for much of the 1990s, and Kiryandongo looked appealingly secure and offered better income generating opportunities than many of the more remote refugee settlements.[2]

When I arrived to carry out my research in 1996, the settlement had already been in existence for four years. Many of the income generating projects implemented there in the early days of the settlement had been withdrawn by the United Nations High Commissioner for Refugees (UNHCR). The refugees subsisted on a mixture of World Food Programme (WFP) rations, crops from their own gardens, and income from small-scale economic activity, NGO incentives, and agricultural work. The settlement was laid out on a former ranching area with a series of unfenced refugee villages made up of mud and grass thatched huts and very few permanent structures (mainly schools, a health post, and offices).

Near the central market was an area devoted to various small income generating and civil society organizations including the largely defunct "Widows and Orphans Association." From their caretaker I rented a small *tukul*, or hut, conveniently located near a borehole, the market, and the school where I volunteered as an English teacher for several hours a week. What anyone thought of my presence, initially, is hard to imagine. No NGO or other institutional actors maintained an overnight presence in the settlement because of the potential security risk. With the exception of a locally hired field officer, UNHCR staff shuttled in from Kampala (if at all) or from closer field offices. There was no precedent for a foreign woman setting up house and home in the heart of the settlement. I lived alone, with neighbors who were generous and hospitable and whose lives quickly became bound up with mine. I remain in contact with many today, although few now remain in the settlement. Although I remained unaffiliated to any organization during my time at Kiryandongo – there simply was no organization there playing a comparable role to Oxfam in Ikafe – a local NGO generously provided logistical support in the early days.

My presence in the settlement had to be approved in advance with written research permission and a residence permit from various government

---

[2]   Although Uganda's refugee settlements did not allow refugees freedom of movement, in
      practice it has been relatively easy for some to (illegally) move outside the settlements or
      between settlement locations.

ministries and local authorities. I also applied for permission to stay in the settlement from the Refugee Welfare Council, the only representative body for the refugee communities. I lived in "my" tukul in the settlement from October 1996 to November 1997, returning to the United Kingdom for a period in early 1997. After this stay in Kiryandongo I maintained close contact with my refugee friends and colleagues and continued to visit the settlement in 2002, 2003, 2006, and 2008. I also carried out related research in other settlements in northern Uganda (including at Rhino Camp and Mvepi Settlements) and in refugee hosting nonsettlement areas.

WHICH RESEARCH QUESTIONS AND WHY?

Although the prospect of observing and examining the establishment of a developmental approach to refugee management by Oxfam at Ikafe had disappeared with the dispersal of the camp's inhabitants, I remained interested in both the internal dynamics of refugee communities (real or imagined) and the political and humanitarian response by governmental and aid actors. At Ikafe I had intended to consider the way in which assistance was provided, in the expectation that an anthropological analysis might generate insights to Oxfam for policy and practice. However, in Kiryandongo the "emergency" phase was over. Delivery of assistance had been scaled down and other sectors had closed in anticipation of an imminent withdrawal by UNHCR. This situation raised interesting questions of a different kind about the future of long-term settlements and about food and other forms of human security for long-term refugees. How were refugees coping? Many were no longer receiving food rations, and access to markets for crops was only possible on unfavorable terms. Refugees were increasingly expected by humanitarian actors to meet their own nonfood needs in the absence of enabling conditions. Research in Kiryandongo, informed by the background research already done for Ikafe, might reveal some useful insights into the management of similar settlements over time. How is the experience of life as a refugee subject to policies defined by economic and political considerations, as well as humanitarian ones? As the research progressed and developed, questions relating to the protection of refugees became more compelling as their suffering in Sudan and the conditions of their flight to Uganda became evident.

Working in a single location over a long period makes it possible to address a number of related research questions. An important dimension was the legal, political, and policy frameworks of refugee management in Uganda, in the context of what became a protracted refugee situation. As an anthropologist, I had interests that included the sociocultural, ritual, and political aspects of life for refugees in both camp and noncamp contexts. In general the academic literature on refugee situations has emphasized the former at the expense of the latter (with some notable recent exceptions including Horst 2006, Hammond 2004, Loizos 2008, Dudley 2010). I wanted not only to explore these two important facets of refugee life and experience in environments of ongoing uncertainty and insecurity, but also to raise questions about how issues arising for refugees from both the legal-political and the sociocultural domains intersected with each other.

In the 1990s, I explored the legal, protection, and assistance frameworks that existed for Sudanese refugees in Uganda and the extent to which these were informed by refugees' own survival strategies and mechanisms of self-protection and management. I was guided by the following questions: What were government policies governing how refugees were treated in Uganda? Were these clearly and transparently implemented by government and nongovernmental actors? Did they appear to be fair and to meet the needs of refugees? I then investigated the broadly social consequences of displacement, an area of inquiry that was at that time often relegated to the footnotes in reports and discussions of refugee well-being. What impact did conflict generated displacement have on societal forms, practices, and processes? What degree of compatibility could be observed between the support offered to refugees by humanitarian and political actors and their own efforts to respond to the challenges and opportunities of exile? My hypothesis was that the internal dynamics of refugee communities, the reasons that refugees had for acting and responding as they did to the conditions of their exile, might be imperfectly understood by refugee assistance providers and, most importantly, might also be relevant to establishing the success or failure of refugee support programs.

Refugees are often described as suffering from "cultural bereavement" (Davis 1992, Parkin 1999, Dudley 2010) when they are forced to leave their homes, and it is often assumed that they will attempt to create as close an approximation as possible of their preflight lives in exile. My research explored the extent to which refugees sought to reproduce their home lives in exile (in this following Loizos 1981). This work was predicated on the recognition that conflict and displacement and peoples' responses to these are not aberrations but are instead embedded in the social relations and histories of the people involved in them and amenable to analysis on this basis (Colson 1971, Turton 2005). The way in which displaced people respond to their experiences of conflict and forced migration is not singular but continuous with their preconflict social, political, and economic lives. As well as managing challenges to their protection, livelihoods, and family integrity, refugee actors address a range of less tangible challenges related to identity, social action, and interpersonal relationships. Their responses sometimes take material and aesthetic form, for example, in explicitly cultural, ritual, or productive activity, or may revolve around the management or reconfiguration of social relations and practices.

For example, the Acholi population in Kiryandongo had in Sudan been accustomed to carrying out much agricultural activity communally, using clan based work groups as an organizing principle. These groups not only served to meet a practical need for labor at seasons of intense agricultural activity, but also reinforced group identity and the perceived importance of clan relations. Moving to a refugee setting seriously undermined such groups since clans no longer resided together, having in many cases been allocated plots of land far away from each other. Refugees responded to this challenge creatively, by reimagining work groups and populating them with neighbors from different clans, and even different ethnicities in some cases. In this way, they protected the idea of working together and preserving important relationships through the mechanism of work groups even if they were unable to reproduce them in exactly the same form they had taken in the home context.

My work has rested on the important recognition that not everything in a refugee or refugee community's life is defined by the fact of displacement. There is a serious risk, in social science terms, of ascribing to the fact of displacement all observable social phenomena, particularly when these relate to social change. At the very least, it is crucial that we also research social practice and process in refugee settings. In order to do this, I also set out to answer questions about the domestic, familial, cultural, ritual, and interpersonal lives of the refugees at Kiryandongo. How is social and political life organized? What kinds of ritual activities take place? How has this changed in the context of exile? What perspectives are offered by members of different subgroups of the population on the kinds of changes that have been experienced? How are specific institutions and events preserved, managed, and transformed in exile? How are marriages negotiated and enacted? What kinds of funerary arrangements are in place and with what consequences for clan identity and relations? What do people joke, gossip, and listen to rumors about?

As time passed and exile became prolonged for the Sudanese, questions relating to notions of "home" and "identity" also became compelling. How do understandings of these categories change over time in the context of exile for successive generations? My field research carried out in 2006 and 2008 focused on refugees' affective relationship with physical places and on the ways that the idea of place was constructed by and for them. Not only was it important to establish how refugees themselves defined their temporary home, but also of interest were the assumptions of local hosts and government about how refugee land was allocated, imagined, and governed. Refugees do not own land and the kinds of things that they can do on and with it are consequently limited. What kinds of activities – agricultural, ritual, social, economic – can be properly carried out in which locations and why?

In summary, my research then and today assumes that the people living in refugee camps and settlements are people – and, as such, social actors – first and displaced people second. Their ways of life are likely to have been affected by their conflict experiences and displacement, but also by numerous other factors. Their experiences and responses are continuous with their preflight lives and behaviors, and their activity in exile is not just simply about survival – about some kind of refugee "bare life" – but should be investigated with reference to their aspirations, plans, and objectives for the present and future.

METHODS USED AND WHY

As an anthropologist, I have organized my field research around the basic principles of ethnography. At Kiryandongo, I immersed myself in the lives of the communities, working and interacting with many different types of people. In this and subsequent projects with refugees, Ugandan host populations, and displaced Ugandans my research has been based on participant observation and a range of complementary data collection methods. These included the collection of oral histories, written testimonies, and accounts; formal and informal interviewing techniques; group discussions and focus groups; taking photographs and employing photo elicitation techniques; recording songs and other cultural productions; and writing and drawing activities with children and young people. In all cases, care was taken to canvass the opinions of members of different groups within the population, notably people of different ages, genders, socioeconomic statuses, ethnicities, and professional groups (e.g., farmers, traders, teachers, entrepreneurs). Particular attention was paid to clan, ritual, and other leaders; opinion makers; and members of religious groups.

I have found it important to adopt different research approaches and styles depending on the particular topic and context of research. Any researcher in the domain of conflict and forced migration studies is aware that the flow of information – who controls it, who possesses it, and who seeks to share and disseminate it – is highly charged, contextually specific, and always political. Information sharing is never neutral, especially where it can increase or decrease your security, affect your capacity to generate income, and/or raise or lower your prestige in the eyes of your community. Researchers working with populations who have suffered or witnessed atrocities and who may have been forced to flee their homes under highly stressful and frightening circumstances are asking informants for much more than their time and stories when they seek out information such as personal narratives, family histories, and testimonies. Caution is required as questions about an apparently noncontentious topic may have painful resonances for individuals. In 2008 I interviewed numerous refugees about their interest or otherwise in repatriating to Sudan after the signing of the peace agreement there. For many, talking about the possibility of return brought back the pain and distress they experienced on leaving the country nearly twenty years before.

Being sensitive to atmosphere, mood, and tone when one carries out such research in refugee settings is key. Innocuous questions about apparently uncontroversial topics can unexpectedly elicit painful testimonies of individual suffering. In one case, broad queries about a woman's plans for the future led to a heartbreaking account of her desperate need to escape a situation of domestic violence. In Kiryandongo, my research was carried out as informally as possible, especially in the early period. It quickly became clear that establishing a very formal frame of inquiry worked against the generation of high-quality usable data. What this does not mean, however, is that it was in any way covert, nontransparent, or unsystematic. The early part of my research in Uganda involved a lengthy process of gaining permission and approval from all key research respondents. In addition to the required permits and permissions from the Government of Uganda, this meant meeting local expectations of courtesy and security by presenting myself to a wide range of institutions and individuals inside and outside the refugee settlement.

I was interested in the way refugees were being dealt with by governmental and aid actors, so it was important to include all relevant actors – refugees, their hosts, government officials at various levels, assistance providers, and others. Each necessitated a slightly different presentational style. Where individual refugees and local refugee groups often withdrew at the slightest sign of officialdom and formality in the research process, government representatives required a formal approach. Attempting to access a government official, especially in a context of heightened security concerns, without brandishing signed and stamped paperwork (preferably in duplicate) and employing the correct channels of entry and formal demeanor and attire was a guaranteed way to slow or sabotage the research process. Inside the settlement in the late 1990s, however, the opposite was the case. Having submitted my research proposal and plans to the settlement's Refugee Welfare Council for approval, I attended a rather intimidating Refugee General Meeting so that objections to my presence and work could be expressed by any settlement resident. Being vetted in this way by the refugee leadership made an enormous difference to the way that I was received by refugees, even by those who had not attended the meeting and had only the haziest idea of what I intended to do there.

My refugee respondents were initially reluctant to participate in formal or structured interviews. People would happily discuss their lives and histories with me in the course of an informal conversation but were intimidated and tongue-tied when I tried to formalize the event. They were aware that I was carrying out research but became uncomfortable with a structured question-answer format, which smacked of the kinds of past interviews with authorities they had found oppressive, tedious, extractive, or unfruitful. For instance, my attempts to get answers to systematic questions on the theme of refugee livelihoods were initially clearly compromised by refugees' previous experiences as respondents in needs assessment exercises – which they felt had not led to any obvious benefit for them. Over several years, the level of intimacy and trust between refugee respondents and me increased. People became willing to update me on events that had taken place in my absence and to provide analysis and interpretation very freely and openly on some subjects.

It is hard to overestimate the importance of the information economy (Marriage 2006) in a refugee setting. Rumors and counterrumors are rife, and this condition makes triangulation a crucially important research principle. One advantage of long-term research in a small number of locations was that I was able to seek confirmation and corroboration of key facts in subsequent visits to see what had changed and why.

Over time, the research context shifts. The demographic profile of refugee groups changes as the conflict evolves, and what refugees want and work toward also change. This means the research agenda must change, too, not least because respondents participate more enthusiastically when the research coincides with their own interests. It is easy to spot the research question that elicits no interest from interviewees! In 2002 I visited Kiryandongo thinking that I knew what the next phase of my research looked like, only to discover that the arrival of a large number of refugees in transit had transformed people's interests in the short term. To be true to refugees' interests meant reflecting these in my own research questions and priorities, so I incorporated new research questions about the impact of the recently arrived refugees on the existing population

Finally, a few words on my own status and situation. As a white woman living independently I was an anomaly in the refugee settlement. As one of my refugee friends put it, "Of the fourteen thousand people here, you are the only one who chose to come." Perhaps my greatest obstacle to social incorporation was that I arrived and established myself in the settlement alone. "Does your father know you are here?" was a common question, speedily followed by "No husband? No children? At your age!" from many of the women. Conversations and photos were somewhat reassuring in that they proved that I did have a family somewhere. A visit from my older sister worked wonders in positioning me as the younger sister in a family. My teacher label also acted as my name. "Lapwonye!" or "teacher!" is a friendly and respectful way of greeting a teacher in the Acholi language, and having this position and status helped to integrate me. Like many foreign female researchers, I benefited from a certain gender blindness whereby usually male leaders were willing to talk with me on the basis of my education and foreignness despite the otherwise substantial obstacle of my femaleness. Honorary male status among men was galling, but useful from a research perspective. Public, political, and economic matters tended to be addressed mainly by men in the formal and informal structures of the settlement, while domestic, livelihood, and family matters were more frequently discussed by women.

CHALLENGES TO THE RESEARCH; ETHICAL QUESTIONS AND PRACTICAL MATTERS

For researchers working with impoverished refugee groups in situations of physical insecurity, everything from their presence to what they do with finished research outputs has an ethical dimension. The temptation is to privilege one's ethical responsibilities to refugees in camps over and above those owed to other participants in the research. But one's ethical research duties extend as much to government bodies, even when they are implementing policies antithetical to one's personal views. For instance, I was at one point tempted to enter the settlement at Kiryandongo by an unofficial "back door" despite the government's temporary closure of the settlement. This posed an ethical dilemma. On the one hand, I was keen to document abuses that I was assured by refugee informants had taken place there; on the other, doing so would have been in direct contravention of my ethical responsibilities to the government as the issuer of my research permission. I did not enter, on that occasion, although these ethical concerns were admittedly not the only reason that I chose not to do so.

Impoverishment and disenfranchisement have been the norm for Sudanese refugees in Uganda, and it is often easier for a researcher to access UNHCR and other aid actors than for refugees to do so. This leads to the difficult question of how much one should become involved in advocating for individual refugees with institutional actors. Too much promotion of individual cases can lead UNHCR and NGO staff to start to avoid researchers – to the detriment of both researcher and refugees. There is also sometimes a dangerous tendency, prompted by the desire to advocate on behalf of refugee groups that one sees as poorly treated, for researchers to speak *for* rather than *about* refugee groups in public fora. This too is problematic. Researchers do not earn the right, by virtue of their presence, to represent the people with whom they carry out research. This tendency increases with distance from what Hyndman (2000) notes is a highly fetishized category, "the field."

A significant challenge is how to engage refugees in research without raising expectations unrealistically. My practice has been to convey that individuals will not benefit directly from involvement in the research process. It has been a testament to the integrity of refugee interlocutors that so many have nevertheless been willing to be involved, on the grounds that the research might be of interest or benefit to others in the future. One also has to manage economic expectations at the personal level. When I moved into the settlement it was assumed that I would hire domestic staff and many refugees applied for a nonexistent post. There were also many requests for assistance and I had to decide carefully what I could manage and justify. Over time I became better at figuring out what was culturally appropriate gift giving behavior. I did not pay research respondents, but made gifts of coffee or sugar to old people, or sodas or local beer to students or elders, respectively, when they met with me. My giving was reciprocated with gifts of prepared food (e.g., sesame paste) or garden produce. Nowadays, in my more frequent absence from the settlement, requests for help are few and far between, but when they occur they are for plane tickets or laptops, not for a few hundred shillings.

I have always been aware of the need to avoid promoting a single view of the refugees or the refugee population. Unfortunately, in policy and aid circles the notion that the portrayal of a single refugee community may be problematic, even in places like Kiryandongo, where residents are from different locations in Sudan, is treated as academic nit-picking. At the very least it is necessary to be clear about the range of views that may exist on a given topic, and to be reflexive in one's presentation so that any biases picked up from the research process are made explicit. For example, in my research the networks of people with whom I had the closest contact meant the political analysis I was exposed to was likely to be more pro-SPLA. In Kiryandongo educated people including teachers – of whom many in the settlement became my friends – took a pro-SPLA line. Less educated farmers might have had more mixed views of the rebel army, which some saw as the cause of their displacement.

Nonrefugee actors also raise many ethical dilemmas. In difficult or dangerous places, one is sometimes grateful for logistical assistance from aid personnel, and then one finds oneself criticizing their organizations in reports and articles. On one occasion I got a lift in a comfortable UNHCR vehicle, and during the conversation it dawned on the amiable protection officer that I was the person who had published a damning account of one of UNHCR's programs for Sudanese refugees. His good humor remained intact, however. In another case I struggled over whether to report that in some areas in northern Uganda, refugees were benefiting significantly from the failure of government personnel to implement the more draconian elements of government refugee policy. Worried that this would result in the end of such happy loopholes for refugees, I chose to remain largely silent. To some extent the information economy around refugee situations depends on a kind of functional ignorance among actors. Researchers gain access to privileged information and their discretion is relied on in their interactions with stakeholders. It is not just a question of what one does or does not publish – aid agency or government staff seldom read academic journals. But researchers often communicate their research findings informally, as they engage with aid and political personnel in the course of their work. Knowing what not to say in these situations becomes crucial if the interests of relatively powerless groups are to be protected.

Researchers often learn about the illicit activities of refugees, such as efforts to supplement their meager incomes or to gain access to resettlement. In Kiryandongo, as elsewhere, parents raised money for school fees by cutting and burning trees to make charcoal, in contravention of environmental protection legislation. Some refugees accessed third country resettlement programs by using fake documents or by lying about family relationships with contacts in countries like Australia and the United States. What should I have done with this information? In each of these cases I chose not to disseminate information that would have caused trouble for the refugees; I am not necessarily sure this was the right judgment. The difficulty of balancing ethical responsibilities is great in such circumstances.

Carrying out research on the conflict experiences of refugees and on their coping strategies is a sensitive matter. One has to be sure not to seek a dramatic narrative for its own sake, and lines of investigation should not be pursued if they cause pain to respondents and can be avoided by the researcher. Many refugees with whom I was working had suffered greatly in the Sudanese and Ugandan conflicts, and many seemed to be traumatized to some extent as a result. People deal with difficult experiences in different ways, but with no medical or psychiatric training I considered it unethical to ask people to give detailed accounts of terrible atrocities when I could only offer my personal sympathy in response. This kind of judgment call becomes even more pressing in research with children and other groups with particular vulnerabilities. I believe talking with children directly about conflict sensitive issues should only occur if research programs include a practical therapeutic dimension, which my projects lacked. Research engagement with children should not directly require them to touch on sensitive conflict related experiences.

Working with children reveals the ethical and practical problems associated with unequal power relations in refugee research. I have tried to be sensitive to the implications of my own economic and social status, but it is often a glaring anomaly. Need a lift from one refugee camp to another? UNHCR may be able to help – but not for your refugee friends (not covered by insurance, according to one contact). Stranded somewhere and need a permit, or accommodation, or a phone to call someone? No problem if you have easy access to government offices, to cash, and to professional networks; definitely a problem if you are a refugee illegally outside a camp with no permit and no money. It can work the other way around, of course. I have often been amazed by the resourcefulness of refugee friends traveling through dangerous places with no cash reserves, drawing on social networks to gather the information and acquire the protection to get them where they need to go.

One's status as a foreign and (relatively) wealthy researcher does not mean you can always sail through political obstacles. In general I have had comparatively little trouble in acquiring the relevant government research permissions in Uganda, but there have been exceptions. In 2002 the Government of Uganda forcibly relocated a large group of refugees from Kiryandongo Settlement to locations in northwestern Uganda (Kaiser 2005). After this reportedly brutal and terrifying event, I found my usual contacts in the ministry unaccountably unavailable when I tried to get permission to go to the settlement. No one denied me a permit; they simply made it impossible to apply for one. At the local level, too, permission was sometimes withheld for political reasons. In 1997 during the parliamentary election campaign local authorities reacted with alarm when I applied for permission (which was required even for very informal gatherings) to hold a focus group meeting in a market near the Kiryandongo Settlement at Bweyale. Permission was denied on the grounds of security, despite the fact that the topic of the proposed meeting was fairly innocuous in terms of local politics.

SECURITY RISKS AND CHALLENGES

Expatriate and elite Ugandans often questioned my judgment for living in the settlement, assuring me that I was unnecessarily risking my personal security. But I felt safe living in this small, quiet community, where the sanctions of family and social networks ensured good behavior toward a guest. I was never robbed, disturbed, or hassled to any unacceptable degree. Friends and neighbors were unfailingly kind and protective and saw me through any difficult challenges with enthusiasm. Like many researchers working with communities who have seen and suffered a lot, I recognize that my own security depended on their quick and accurate judgments and action, and on the quality of my interpersonal relationships. I felt I could trust the refugees with whom I developed substantial relationships and friendships to look out for me if the occasion demanded. When I traveled by bus through parts of the LRA operating zone or stayed overnight in camps where rebel attacks were known to take place, refugee friends were careful to include me in their sensible security plans. For example, at Achol-pii Settlement in 1997, my refugee hosts established which part of the bush was safest for us to take refuge in should the LRA put in an appearance during our stay.

The kind of research I did required close observation and engagement with sociocultural practices, reciprocity, sharing, and the development of trust and mutual learning. All this would never have been possible if I was not fully resident in the settlement. Its physical location meant Kiryandongo was not a very risky place in terms of possible rebel activity. Occasional rumors of an impending attack never amounted to anything. The benefit of being present morning, noon, and night; the effect on social relationships of being able to go to and host parties and receive hospitality, and to gossip with neighbors at the borehole at dusk was immense and contributed to the more formal aspects of the research process. I sympathized with the NGO staff who were loaded onto four-wheel drive vehicles and shipped out of the settlement at 5:00 p.m., with half that day's story and work still yet to unfold. I was glad I could stay and keep asking questions.

Security is a relative term and one's own level of risk in a generally unpredictable security environment depends on identity and reputation. In some of the places I have worked it was probably safer for me than for some of my refugee interlocutors to be there because I was perceived as an outsider who did not pose a political or other threat. On the other hand, in rebel affected areas there is sometimes a fear that a foreigner may be considered a prize worth kidnapping for the publicity this is likely to yield.[3]

In the case of the forcible relocation described previously, I was unable to obtain the required government permits to enter the settlement in the immediate aftermath. This led to ethical and practical dilemmas. At the nearby

[3] Refugees themselves can be seen as a security risk in refugee hosting areas (Loescher & Milner 2008). This has been somewhat true for the Sudanese in Uganda where civilian refugees have hosted military figures on so-called 'rest & relaxation' from the front line. However refugees were more at risk from various sources in Uganda, such as rebel attacks in their transit camps in Kitgum and Lira and attack from government forces when they resisted being moved to new locations they considered unsafe.

trading center of Bweyale I established myself in a small guesthouse and received a stream of refugee friends eager to report what had taken place. Several encouraged me to use the small back roads to bypass the main gate and government offices and enter the settlement to see the damage, and talk to witnesses and victims of the violence. Doing so would have been easy, but I realised that my refugee friends left behind when I returned to the United Kingdom, would likely be blamed and punished directly or indirectly for facilitating my visit. My own future research access would also have been seriously compromised. Instead, refugees continued to travel to me in Bweyale, where I could transcribe their accounts and pass on their reports to refugee rights organizations in Kampala. Meanwhile, a trusted and courageous refugee friend volunteered to photograph the physical evidence in the form of destroyed houses, so that I could also pass on this material.

When it came to internal violent conflict within the refugee settlement and between different ethnic groups the research problems were different. These events took place while I was in England, and the minority group who had been chased from the settlement was difficult to track down for their account of what had happened. The majority group was defensive and self-justifying, creating uncertainty about the objectivity of their accounts. A few important opinion leaders were reluctant to discuss the situation, fearing that further attention would again inflame tensions. While it was hard to draw firm conclusions about the causes and nature of the violence, it was possible to learn quite a lot about the nature of the tensions and manipulated hostility between the two groups.

Apart from these instances, I never felt that I endangered the physical security of refugee respondents by involving them in my research. This might have been different had my anthropological work been carried out in a camp closer to the border where military activity was more readily observable. Explicit policy oriented research in border camps and refugee hosting areas of northern Uganda can create risks for refugees. In order to survive, refugees are obliged to break various rules, such as accessing food rations in camps or living illegally in prohibited locations. Some refugees pretend to be Ugandan nationals in order to access employment or educational opportunities. My policy on all such questions has always been never to blow the cover of refugees and put them at risk of reprisals even if this means that my writing packs less of a punch.

CONCLUSIONS: WHAT DID I LEARN AND WAS I ABLE TO COMMUNICATE IT?

It is difficult to measure the impact of one's own work. By engaging closely with a small group of refugees over a relatively long period, I have aimed to increase our collective understanding of the complex ways in which conflict generated displacement affects individuals, families, and communities, and how refugees respond to the challenges of conflict and exile. Over the last decade or so a number of studies have explored the sociocultural, ritual, and aesthetic aspects of life for refugees and other forced migrants (Hammond 2004, Dudley 2010, Grabska 2010). My work contributes to this body of work and extends the empirical material available on the basis of which new theoretical departures may be made in an expanded domain of "forced migration studies."

I hope to prompt recognition from policy makers and aid practitioners that there are important questions remaining. For example, how do indigenous agricultural practices transform in exile, and how is this connected to the way that refugee groups conceptualize and construct notions of home and exile in settlement contexts? This has implications both for the way that agricultural extension services are offered and taken up in settlement contexts and for refugees' ability to achieve the "self-sufficiency" that aid providers want to push them toward. In another example, how are marriage and relations between married people conceived and transacted in exile, and how does this intersect with the way that well-meaning NGOs attempt to intervene in the important problem of domestic violence in the settlements? At one stage in Kiryandongo, some refugee residents were so outraged by the measures taken by a Sexual and Gender Based Violence (SGBV) program that they called for its termination. Social and cultural research is an important tool for understanding the experience of the displaced and has the potential to make a significant contribution to the efficiency and effectiveness of humanitarian responses.

Carrying out research with a refugee or other population over an extended time frame offers the possibility of reflecting on changes and transformations in a protracted refugee situation. For example, in the case of Kiryandongo a few years after the establishment of the settlement (around 2001), policies adopted there appeared relatively successful in supporting refugee livelihoods. However, by 2005 these promising results were less clear. Important policy questions about the potential shelf life of settlements like Kiryandongo might not have emerged if the research engagement had been shorter. For example, the Government of Uganda has been firmly committed for a decade or more to the idea that refugees in settlements like Kiryandongo should achieve what they call self-reliance. There have been points in the history of the settlement when this seemed to have been achieved, only for the livelihoods of refugees there to have declined again later, casting doubt on the proclaimed success of the policy.

These research lessons were not necessarily greeted with much enthusiasm by aid and policy actors in Uganda and farther afield. By actively disseminating research findings and targeting tailored research outputs to relevant institutions and organizations, it is possible to generate interest in research, but seeing policies change as a consequence is a much harder claim to make. One hopes that one's work will contribute to long-term policy transformation, but much depends on whether one's recommendations are taken up by key individuals in organizations and government bodies concerned with refugee policy and welfare. Good personal relationships with opinion makers and decision takers are an important goal of research, and, like most researchers, I have experienced successes and failures in this respect.

At one stage I had a series of off the record and unofficial interactions with a senior Kampala-based official in UNHCR, and this led me to believe that my research findings were contributing productively to UNHCR thinking and policy making. At other times, however, UNHCR personnel in Kampala simply did not want to entertain a view that complicated and contradicted their working stereotypes of refugees. Having a positive impact on government actors was a much taller order, given the multiple objectives of any government's refugee policy. Yet influencing government policy is one of the most pressing research challenges for those working with forced migrants

As informed advocates for forced migrants, researchers are able to engage seriously with particular research settings over time. While they should not aim to speak for refugees or those affected by conflict, researchers can express the concerns of such groups to the relevant organizations and institutions. Governments will frequently override the needs and desires of refugee populations; nonetheless there remains a clear need for research that makes engagement at this level possible. Over the last few years, a growing body of work has demonstrated how close, careful social and anthropological analysis in refugee situations can lead to a greater understanding of the challenges faced by refugees and the responses made by them and for them. Further work of this kind will be critical to refine and improve institutional responses to those coping with conflict and forced migration.

BIBLIOGRAPHY

Allen, Tim. 2006. *Trial justice: The international criminal court and the Lord's Resistance Army*. London: Zed Books.
Colson, Elizabeth. 1971. *The social consequences of resettlement*. Manchester: University of Manchester, The University Press.
Davis, John. 1992. The anthropology of suffering. *Journal of Refugee Studies*, 5(2): 149–61.
Dudley, Sandra. 2010. *Materialising exile: Material culture and embodied experience among the Karenni refugees in Thailand*. Oxford and London: Berghahn.

Finnstrom, Sverker. 2008. *Living with bad surroundings: War, history, and everyday moments in northern Uganda.* Durham, NC: Duke University Press.

Grabska, Katarzyna. 2010. Lost boys, invisible girls: Stories of Sudanese marriages across borders. *Gender, Place & Culture* 17: 4, 479–97.

Hammond, Laura. 2004. *This place will become home: Refugee repatriation to Ethiopia.* London: Cornell University Press.

Horst, Cindy. 2006. *Transnational nomads: How Somalis cope with refugee life in the Dadaab camps of Kenya.* Oxford and New York: Berghahn.

Hyndman, Jennifer. 2000. *Managing displacement: Refugees and the politics of humanitarianism.* Minneapolis: University of Minnesota Press.

Kaiser, Tania. 2000. Experience and consequences of insecurity in a refugee populated area in northern Uganda. *Refugee Survey Quarterly* 19: 38–53.

    2005. Participating in development? Refugee protection, politics and developmental approaches to refugee management in Uganda. *Third World Quarterly,* 26(2): 351–67.

Leopold, Mark. 2005. *Inside West Nile: Violence, history and representation on an African frontier.* Oxford: James Currey.

Loescher, Gil, James Milner, Edward Newman and Gary Troeller, eds. 2008. *Protracted refugee situations: Political, human rights and security implications.* Tokyo and New York: United Nations University Press.

Loizos, Peter. 1981. *The heart grown bitter: A chronicle of Cypriot war refugees.* Cambridge: Cambridge University Press.

    2008. *Iron in the soul: Displacement, livelihood and health in Cyprus.* Oxford and London: Berghahn.

Marriage, Zoe. 2006. *Not breaking the rules: Not playing the game: International assistance to countries at war.* London: Hurst.

Neefjes, Koos. 1999. Participatory review in chronic instability: The experience of the Ikafe refugee settlement programme, Uganda. *Humanitarian Practice Network Paper 29.* London: Overseas Development Institute.

Parkin, David. 1999. Mementoes as transitional objects in human displacement. *Journal of Material Culture,* 4(3): 303–20.

Payne, Linda. 1998. *Rebuilding communities in a refugee settlement: A casebook from Uganda.* Oxford: Oxfam.

Turton, David. 2005. The meaning of place in a world of movement: Lessons from long-term field research in southern Ethiopia. *Journal of Refugee Studies* 18: 258–80.

PART III

SAFE SPACES

Figure 5. "Highway for Peace and Unity – Inquire Within" 2002, Sri Lanka.
Photographer: Cathrine Brun

The photo was taken on one of the main checkpoints separating Liberation Tigers of Tamil Eelam (LTTE)–controlled and government–controlled areas in northern Sri Lanka, just after a cease-fire between the two parties had begun in 2002. The optimism for peace was very visible at that time, as the photo indicates. As we know, the ceasefire did not last and the area in which this check point was located experienced renewed violence and devastation in the final stages of the war that ended in 2009.

5

"I Love My Soldier"

Developing Responsible and Ethically Sound
Research Strategies in a Militarized Society

Cathrine Brun

Researchers working in difficult situations are often a self-sacrificing and even reckless lot. They work long hours, travel across insecure borders, shrug off sexual harassment and other forms of mistreatment that they would never tolerate back home, expose themselves to incurable diseases.

(Mertus 2009, 165–6)

Every time I return from Sri Lanka I am asked whether I experienced fear. Whether there was any immediate threat. My response has always been negative, "of course not": one quickly (all too quickly) adjusts to the military presence, the checkpoints, even body searches.

(Bell 2009, 87)

INTRODUCTION

"I love my soldier" was the slogan I saw on a T-shirt sold in an outlet shop in Colombo in February 2009. The slogan symbolized an increasingly militarized society and a simultaneous decline of freedom of speech and democratic institutions (de Mel 2007). The T-shirt also reflected the sense of victory among the population of southern Sri Lanka and their support for a military closer than ever to winning the war against the Liberation Tigers of Tamil Eelam (LTTE). This mood culminated in May 2009 when the president of Sri Lanka declared victory over the LTTE and people celebrated in the streets of southern Sri Lanka. Although victory was declared, the conflict has not ended.

In this chapter I offer some reflections and analysis of my research experiences and practices in a context of conflict and militarization.[1] Sri Lanka's history of conflict and militarization has created a society where the silencing

---

[1]   I write this chapter in the memory of Professor Ravindranath, who never stopped believing in academic excellence as a way of strengthening societies – even during conflict.

of the population is a common act. This creates particular challenges for how researchers conduct fieldwork, understand people's silences, or make safe spaces where people can talk and the researcher can act as a safe witness. I discuss the challenges of developing ethically sound and responsible research projects in such contexts. My ambition is not to provide a clear-cut formula of how to conduct research in a militarized society, but rather to explore the dilemmas I have encountered in a particular and changing context of conflict.

Before analyzing my fieldwork experiences, I believe it is critical to question my role both as an outsider and as a researcher who chooses to work in such environments. The tension is well captured in the two observations quoted. On the one hand, conducting research in a conflict environment can be understood as a reckless act, but, on the other hand, it is not necessarily experienced this way when in the midst of it. Perhaps, as Bell (2009) reflects, this negation of fear stems from my and other privileged researchers' origin in safe communities? In the case of Sri Lanka, however, the environment is becoming increasingly critical – even hostile – to outsiders such as aid workers and researchers, as I discuss later. My starting point is that as researchers we should not take unnecessary risks because we have a responsibility to do no harm in our research – to others and to ourselves.

Many of the ideas I introduce here are not unique to a conflict setting. The complex web of power relations embedded in a conflict environment, however, makes some of the challenges more explicit and potentially more fatal. In the chapter I show some of the ways in which I became implicated in these power relations. My research experiences do not involve research under fire. Rather I carry out research in conflict settings where I need to be careful about becoming entangled in power relations I will never fully understand.

The chapter begins by explaining what distinguishes Sri Lanka – particularly northern and eastern Sri Lanka – as a research field. I then discuss my notion of "the field" and how to formulate an ethically sound and responsible research agenda. Most of my research has been qualitative and ethnographic in its approach. I am interested in how people affected by adversities such as conflict, disasters, and displacement strategize and change their societies. I have found through years of fieldwork that understanding war related experiences often requires understanding what people do not talk openly about, and I have attempted to understand such silences in my research. In the following sections, I discuss three types of research encounters. First, I describe my attempts to create safe fieldwork spaces with young people. Second, I consider how my collaboration with local universities and local researchers is embedded in local, national, and international power relations. And finally, I discuss the act of writing the conflict and our role as witnesses and disseminators of that experience. In all these encounters, my aim is to create and maintain safe spaces for the research participants. The final section of the chapter offers some reflections on how research in militarized and violent societies can be ethically sound and responsible.

THE RESEARCH CONTEXT: MILITARIZATION AND
SILENCING IN SRI LANKA

It is through militarization that the ideology of militarism, which mediates aggressive, hyper-masculinist, militant solutions to conflict, and justifies violence and terror, is ushered into our institutions and ways of thought. Militarization, thus, occupies a structural position in societies at war because it becomes the organizational means through which the ideology of militarism as a principle of coherence is constructed. But the process itself begins before the war, for it works to lay the groundwork that justifies and legitimizes war, and lasts long after the last guns have fallen silent on the battlefield because as an ideology, militarism has seeped into our institutions and ways of thought. (de Mel 2007, 12)

Social and political violence has become a central theme in Sri Lanka's processes of change since its peaceful independence in 1948. The violence spans familial conflict, local conflicts that turn violent, communal riots, state-sponsored violence against particular groups, and the war between the state and the LTTE. While the war between the LTTE and the government is officially over, my research has explored the ways in which the ideology of militarization lives on.

Since the war started in 1983, people in northern and eastern Sri Lanka have lived with conflict, displacement, and marginalization. It is believed that more than seventy thousand people have been killed and millions displaced, often multiple times. An entire generation has suffered the loss of education and economic opportunity. I have been involved in research in Sri Lanka since 1994. The first time I visited, I did not work on conflict related issues and was hardly aware of the fact that a war was being fought in a different part of the country. I studied street vendors and family enterprises in the informal sector in Kandy, in central Sri Lanka. My research assistant at that time took me to Puttalam in northwestern Sri Lanka, where she worked as a volunteer helping the sixty thousand Muslim internally displaced persons (IDPs) who were expelled by the LTTE from the north in 1990. This visit marked the beginning of my interest in displacement and conflict. I returned in 1997 to conduct my doctoral research on local integration processes among this group and their hosts. My work has since concentrated on the effects of

the conflict and protracted displacement on young people, on nationalism,;
and on the postwar recovery process as well as the recovery process following
the 2004 Indian Ocean tsunami that devastated the war affected areas of the
Sri Lankan coastline. I have conducted fieldwork in many different parts of
the country – sometimes in the war zone, sometimes outside. I draw on two
research projects I have been involved with – one in northern and one in eastern Sri Lanka – in later sections of this chapter.

A distinguishing feature of people's lives in the north and east has been
what I call "complex citizenship." Complex citizenship refers to a situation
in which citizens lack a clear-cut relationship with the state and are forced
to relate to several governing actors (Brun 2008b). In northern and eastern
Sri Lanka, the LTTE and the Government of Sri Lanka have been the most
prominent of these governing actors, but since 2004 other armed groups –
such as the Karuna, a breakaway faction of the LTTE – have made the web
of power relations even more complex. People have had to learn to maneuver
in a situation where they cannot discern between friend and enemy. During
the war, control over territories shifted, making it necessary for people to learn
how to live with different powers successively and sometimes simultaneously.

In 1994 peace negotiations and a cease-fire seemed promising, but war
broke out again in 1995. The most durable cease-fire ran from 2002 to its official termination in 2008, although in reality, hostilities started in late 2004.
The early years of the cease-fire represented optimism and hope for personal
security. However, by 2006, Sri Lanka had one of the highest numbers of
disappearances in the world (HRW 2008). This was not the first period of
frequent disappearances. During the 1970s and 1980s, Sinhalese armed youth
insurrections were violently repressed by the government. In southern Sri
Lanka between 1987 and 1990, an estimated thirty-five thousand predomi-
nantly Sinhalese youth and men went missing (de Alwis 2009). While some
disappearances were carried out by militant Sinhala groups, the state also conducted this form of terror and violence on a coordinated and extensive scale
(de Alwis 2009). As a result, every region of Sri Lanka has been affected over
time by the violence and terror of disappearances. People have been reluctant
to take these cases to the authorities, for fear of placing themselves or the disappeared in further danger.

This reluctance to report disappearances represents only one of many ways
that people in Sri Lanka are silenced. The need to be silent has varied during
the last forty years according to the level of tension and fear in the country,
but it has endured as a strategy of survival. Silence is the act of being invisible;
it represents a fragile kind of protection. It may also be understood as empowering. Silence can also encompass the "muteness of trauma, erasure and

loss" (Lawrence 2000, 178). Silence thus takes on different forms for different purposes, a theme I will return to later.

Since the president declared victory over the LTTE in May 2009, violence has decreased, but personal security has not improved. Surveillance at checkpoints is less prominent, but state intelligence is active – one has the feeling that there are ears and eyes everywhere. Freedom of speech is therefore strongly limited. Intellectuals and journalists risk arrest or disappearance. Censorship also begets self-censorship (de Mel 2007). Not surprisingly, working with a silenced population has implications for how fieldwork can be conducted and how knowledge can be produced in the field. In conflict zones, I argue that safe spaces are necessary. But what do these safe spaces look like? Can alternative spaces for speaking – or so-called permitted spaces in Obeysekere's terms (1999) – occur in research situations, and is it possible for a researcher to be a safe witness? In order to respond to these questions, I should first clarify what I mean when I use the terms "field," "fieldwork," and "responsible research."

FIELD AND RESPONSIBLE FIELDWORK

> Much fieldwork can actually be quite painful. There is not only that sense of dislocation of values which you take for granted – which comes and goes – but also the difficulty of negotiating with people when you don't know all the small and unspoken ethical ground "rules" that make up everyday life, rules which you have arduously to construct. (Thrift 2003, 105)

I often feel like a stranger in the field, but unlike Simmel's stranger,[2] I leave. I travel between a university in Norway and the field several times every year. Unlike the people I work with in Sri Lanka, I choose when to arrive, where to go, and when to leave. My movements represent the mobility of the affluent, a stark contrast to the lives of people I interview in the conflict areas in Sri Lanka, whose movements reflect the pressures of forced displacement, deprivation, and marginalization (Brun 2008a).

I view fieldwork as a set of encounters between the researcher and research participants, often with the involvement of research assistants and other actors who function as gatekeepers and resource persons. During these encounters, hybrid forms of knowledge are coproduced by the research participants, research assistants, and researcher. Fieldwork takes place in a field, but *where* is

---

[2] Georg Simmel (1950, 402) describes the Stranger "as the wanderer who comes today and stays tomorrow." The stranger has often been interpreted in migration studies as the migrant – a marginal person – who aspires to, but is excluded from, full membership in a new group.

the field? I have talked about going to the field, being in the field, and traveling away from the field. This may give an impression that the field is represented as "over there," but it is now an accepted view that we need to question this separation in distance and time between the field and "home." Engaging in fieldwork does not only mean entering a physically designated place where another culture or society lies waiting to be observed and described, like a laboratory (Gupta and Ferguson 1997, Katz 1994). The field is a social terrain in which researchers can strengthen, through direct experience and encounters, the academic foundation of knowledge, thereby forging bonds between the academy and the world at large (Kobayashi 1994, Nast 1994). The field can be conceived as constructed through processes operating at local and nonlocal scales and is always constituted through a complex web of power relations. We are part of the field both when we conduct fieldwork and when we are away from the locations we define as our field. This has implications for how we understand our position as researchers. But we cannot ignore distance – social and geographic – when engaging with the field (Brun 2009).

A number of researchers have written extensively on the role of distance and fieldwork. Sharon Bell (2009), for example, writes about the sense of intense inclusion she developed in Sri Lanka during years of ethnographic fieldwork, in contrast with the feeling of intense exclusion she felt during times of terror, conflict, and posttsunami conditions. As a foreign researcher she has negotiated relationships and struggled to find a legitimate voice through shifting geopolitical affective and symbolic distance. She describes her earliest anthropological fieldwork experience as a time of incorporation in a rural community. This intense inclusion, however, is countered by feelings of intense exclusion experienced during times away and on visits in Sri Lanka "after the violence." The violence experienced by friends and colleagues awakened in her a sense of intense exclusion and communal indebtedness through the inability to feel and share others' pain. These feelings are quite familiar to researchers who engage with societies in conflict or struck by disasters. Dilemmas concerning our responsibilities during times of adversity when we are away are an intrinsic part of the long-term relationships we develop with people and places over years of research (Brun 2009).

Much has been said about the ethics and responsibilities in play when we engage with the distant other (Barnett and Land 2007, Carter 2007, Massey 2004, Young 2006). One argument is that we need knowledge about the distant other to be able to care and feel responsible for what is happening in distant places, and thus research in conflict areas may be understood to be necessary and justifiable. Meaningful connection with distant others should be developed through encounters and practical action (Barnett and Land 2007). Iris

Marion Young's writings are instructive for how we can develop principles for ethically sound and responsible research. Young (2006) introduces a "social connection" model of responsibility and theorizes the responsibilities that moral agents may have in relation to global processes. Young is concerned with structural inequalities – or injustices – and points to the moral obligations we have to act on such inequalities. For example, she explores how we are all implicated in the structural inequalities that enable the sweatshops and the marginalization of workers in such factories. "Responsibility" in this context does not refer to liability for wrongdoing, but rather ways in which agents carry out activities in a morally appropriate way and aim for certain outcomes. Young concludes that this responsibility is ultimately a political responsibility because it involves joining with others to organize collective action to reform unjust structures. She states that we need to make choices about *where* our actions can be most useful.

Conducting ethical research in a situation of conflict and militarization requires self-reflexivity and an understanding of our role as researchers in that field both when we are present and when we are away. It also requires reflecting on our power, privileges, and interests in that field and our collective ability to act with our partners, colleagues, and research participants in morally appropriate ways. Such ongoing reflection may move us closer to an answer as to where and in which ways our actions as researchers are most useful in a conflict situation. In the sections that follow I discuss some of the strategies that have emerged for me over years of reflection and research.

UNDERSTANDING SILENCES

We might envision the space of research as a much more varied space. We can conceive of it, not only as the space of authentic testimony ... but as a riotous theatre of transgression in which we take our role as improvisational directors both more lightly and more seriously, to create spaces from which to speak and perform the unspeakable. (Pratt 2000, 650)

In Sri Lanka, I use conventional research methods and techniques such as interviews and focus group discussions with research participants, authorities, resource persons, aid workers, and others. These conversations and interview sessions constitute the main body of knowledge I gather about the topic and are crucial in answering my research questions. In addition, I collect secondary information from various libraries, archives, institutions, and organizations and participate in as many related activities as I can access. However, I often find these well-known techniques of knowledge production insufficient in understanding how people cope with and strategize in situations of war, displacement, and disaster. I have found that the time outside interviews spent with people is as important as the formal techniques. In a militarized society, interviewing and other formal techniques of research can be inappropriate and dangerous. People may be too upset, exhausted, research-fatigued, or scared to participate in a formal interview, or they may not be in a position to do so because of security, personal problems, and work, among other reasons. In such situations, just being there, showing interest, and bearing witness have proven important for people.

"Being there" is nothing new and is a necessary condition for most ethnographic fieldwork. However, noninterview time becomes more valuable when silences dominate the way people communicate their experiences with a researcher. This is not to say that people will not *talk* in interviews. On the contrary, I find that people are quite communicative in interviews in Sri Lanka and uncomfortably accustomed to being interviewed by researchers. However, it is what people keep silent about that we need to pay attention to and seek to understand. As mentioned, these silences can have different purposes and take different forms. First of all, for protection, people are silent about their sympathies and antipathies, and they avoid speaking openly about the identity of actors behind atrocities and sometimes omit mention of atrocities they have experienced. For protection, people may also be extremely wary about recounting where they have been at different times, whom they were with, and how they got there. In other situations, people's silences represent the inability to speak of terror they have experienced because it is too painful and will recall the trauma they experienced. In other instances, silence may be a way of taking control over an interview situation and consequently be experienced as empowering. In the latter case, silence does not necessarily represent a lack of voice, but rather a space one creates for oneself, to maintain a sense of self or as a means of protest.

Understanding and recognizing these different forms of silence take time and require unconventional methodologies. They mean being open to the various ways in which people might communicate to you what they will not say. These situations have been termed "spaces of thoughtfulness," where the coproduction of knowledge takes place during dialogue and through the sharing of reflections (Thrift 2003, 114). "Hanging out" has been posed as a strategy and shorthand term for the importance of the informal and everyday nature of the interactions needed to generate information (Rodgers 2004). While this is a very gendered notion – hanging out would not be very appropriate for a woman in the Sri Lankan context – the ways in which we make these informal and noninterview spaces of thoughtfulness available are essential for understanding silences.

Long-term relations with people in the field may be one strategy to create these spaces and can be developed in at least two – often overlapping – ways. The first strategy is to stay with people in a particular location continuously over a long period. A second strategy is to keep returning to people over a longer period. "A long period" is again a vague term. In some cases, this has meant initially staying in a place over a period of more than six months and continuing to revisit an area every year after that. In other projects, I have stayed in an area for three weeks at a time but continued to visit the same people, often multiple times per year.

In my experience, the creation of such spaces has not been the result of a conscious strategy, but rather an outcome of learning the field and learning to live up to people's expectations. I spend time with people in ways that are culturally appropriate. As a friend and longtime acquaintance, I should visit people in their homes and should expect to be served tea and a meal. I make sure I have enough time to sit down with people, and then I return to see how they are faring. It is crucial that the research participants are the hosts who define the setting. The gendered aspect of such spaces often determines whether or not and to whom I have access. I have spent much time in the kitchen part of families' compounds, chatting with women of all ages during the preparation of lunch and dinner. During these sessions, the chatting might result in casual references to such past experiences as a daughter's or son's last meal before joining the LTTE, a description of an old kitchen prior to displacement, how a soldier entered the kitchen to take their food, the way they hid kitchen utensils and other valuables when they had to leave their homes, or the experience of seeing their old kitchen in ruins when returning to their homes after displacement. I gained a deeper understanding of their past and present lives from these passing references to past experiences than what I had learned from interviewing them earlier. Perhaps they had kept silent in the previous interview because they considered such details irrelevant or perhaps the subject was too painful or awkward to talk about.

Part of developing long-term relationships with people in the field has been the deepening of my understanding of the expectations people have for my participation in ceremonial functions. These events may be weddings, coming of age ceremonies, funerals, or the visits one should make in connection with religious festivals. In such situations as a female researcher in Sri Lanka, I have often experienced being treated as a man. Sometimes this is because I always visit without my family, move around on my own, and often behave more as a "man" than a "woman" according to their cultural norms. However, I often need to be in a male role in order to have access to particular interviewees. For example, some of the men in the families I am attached to who know me well introduce me to people they think would be good contacts. I have also often been placed on the men's side instead of the women's side at Muslim funerals. The first couple of times this happened, I felt awkward and miserable because I was not being treated the same as the people I was researching. However, I now consider such situations to be helpful on the whole and much less problematic than the first encounter. I found that functions, such as the funeral I mentioned, often served to strengthen or call back feelings and memories of loss, displacement, and violence. Being in attendance and showing my support during such important events have helped me to understand on a deep personal level how war and displacement have affected people's lives. My presence at such events has also frequently led people to want to tell me stories about war and displacement. What before had been silence begins to unravel as I become more integrated into the community.

MAKING SAFE SPACES

Understanding silences by making spaces of thoughtfulness is not always straightforward in a conflict related setting; multiple spaces must be established for the research participants, the research assistants, and the researchers. The following example illustrates how I negotiated safe spaces while working with young people. My research project on young people living with conflict took place from 2002 to 2004 and began when university staff I knew in Jaffna in northern Sri Lanka invited me to come to the university to interview students.[3] They helped me to contact different groups of students, and the university allowed me to use their premises for the interviews. This both facilitated and complicated the interviewing process as the university was itself a highly politicized environment. I managed by way of various contacts in the university to inform the university, the LTTE, the government, and the main student organizations about the purpose of my research. The focus of my research was presented in very general terms as being about displacement and how war related experiences affected young people in Jaffna during the cease-fire. Displacement at that time was not a very controversial issue, and among the students the university was considered a relatively safe space, although the spaces of speaking and acting were clearly dominated by the LTTE. Students

---

[3]   As a result of identity politics and politics of mobility during war, Jaffna had become an almost monoethnic Tamil community by the beginning of the cease-fire in 2002. Most interviewees in this project were therefore Tamils.

willingly participated in group discussions over the next weeks. I left it up to the students how much they wanted to talk about the current situation in the country. I never asked directly about politics but found that despite this omission, their answers touched upon nationalism, political solutions to the conflict, and how they saw their role in the conflict. However, these responses commonly reflected LTTE propaganda. Still, during these interviews, we managed to generate interesting background information about their histories and the realities of life among young people in northern Sri Lanka during war and during the cease-fire.

The early cease-fire period created a relatively safe space and people were much more open during this time than they had been during my previous research trips. It was clear, however, that people were still actively negotiating the "complex citizenship" identities I describe earlier, and they knew that what they said and did was monitored. The young people established their safe spaces by speaking in recognized and accepted language and by omitting contentious information. As a researcher I had a responsibility to recognize what they said and what they kept silent about in these interviews. This involved an in-depth understanding of the context in order to understand why they talked about events in particular ways. As an outsider, I know that I will often miss out on crucial details. Over time and through triangulation (putting together bits and pieces of information from a number of different interviews from different individuals), I have gradually learned how to read between the lines on particular topics. The youths' displacement stories offered telling details, such as where they went during their displacement and how those locations would affect their lives later. For example, there was a significant difference between being in the government controlled capital of Colombo during some of the peak displacement times and being in the LTTE controlled Vanni. This difference was often connected to class, caste, and resources. It often also signified a difference in how they were treated after the cease-fire and upon return to Jaffna. Many of those who were displaced to the Vanni did not have ID cards upon return, as they were issued special LTTE ID cards during their displacement. For young men in particular, but also for young women (the LTTE were well-known for their significant numbers of female cadres), showing a newly issued ID card at one of the many checkpoints in Jaffna told a story of being close to the LTTE. This element of risk added to the insecurity and lack of freedom of movement in day-to-day life in Jaffna.

During fieldwork with young people, I was living with my research assistant and interpreter in Jaffna. Some of the students who attended the group discussions in the university would visit our guesthouse and invite us to their homes. Others wanted to show us places they thought would be of interest to us, places that were important for them. Many had friends or people they wanted us to meet, and these encounters developed into the non-interview situations mentioned previously. These were the spaces that the university students themselves made safe. They invited us into their homes to watch videos from the war, they would chat in our vehicle – where no one else could hear us – and they would take us to places where their friend was killed or a sister was forcibly recruited by the LTTE or to places they were proud of – places that described their identities as young Sri Lankan Tamils. For them I was their witness, someone who could communicate their experiences to the outside world. They introduced me to lives and experiences I would never have understood otherwise.

These encounters happened over the course of two years of research in Jaffna. Aided by my research assistants, we developed trust with the students by keeping in touch with them while we were away. [4] The safe spaces where the silences unraveled or were explained expanded over time. We only traveled with the youngsters or went to their houses when they invited us. At that time, doing so did not create any problems. The LTTE knew we were keeping in touch with the young people. I think this was very particular to the situation of openness during the cease-fire. We were monitored but not considered a threat. I visited the LTTE and the government agent once to update them on my research and was not pushed to talk about whom I had interviewed. (They probably already knew what I was doing anyway.) *Their* way of controlling was to ask what I thought about the situation in Jaffna. I tried to be careful, diplomatic, and uncontroversial in my response – a tone I had learned from the youth we interviewed and my research assistants. The LTTE and government agents seemed interested and even asked for advice about starting youth projects and other ways of involving young people in the recovery of Jaffna. Despite these seemingly positive encounters, I was wary of continuing to move freely around with research participants, and later on when checkpoints became more hostile, I became reluctant to take research participants with me in our vehicle. The changing context on the ground caused the safe spaces we had established to shrink and become less safe.

After leaving the field, and leaving the interviewees behind, there was little I could do to make sure nothing would happen to them. At this time, contact with me as a foreign researcher and my research assistants from southern Sri Lanka was considered to be more of an asset than a problem for the people involved. My research assistants and I did our best to make the so-called power

---

[4]   I have decided not to describe the research assistants in more detail in order to protect their anonymity.

holders – the LTTE and the government – understand that we were not giving any benefits to the young people we interviewed and that we were not challenging their position as power holders in any ways.

When the war resumed in 2006, it became impossible to maintain contact with the students. In losing touch with them, I experienced the intense exclusion described by Bell (2009) earlier. However, I was able to stay in touch with my research assistants. They were also translating for other groups – both Sri Lankan and international – or had their own personal interests in collecting stories from northern Sri Lanka. We communicated with many different actors, including the LTTE or those who had close links to them. I offered my business card to them all and found that the card served to legitimize my presence. My research assistants also exchanged addresses with people we met and continued to communicate with them while on missions with other researchers, organizations, or various peace groups, even after I had stopped traveling to Jaffna. When the conflict intensified in 2006, these links became increasingly problematic. Some research participants used their connections with my research assistants to escape the conflict zone or to gain other types of assistance. The problem for the research assistants was that any contacts with people from the north could potentially be considered dangerous. In some instances, former research assistants were pressured into assisting militant groups. *Their* closeness to the field meant that I and others who had employed them to work in the conflict zone and their own work in the north had placed them in danger. The safe spaces that we had jointly developed for the research participants in Sri Lanka were challenged and turned into spaces of insecurity for the research assistants.

Safe spaces of research must also include the researcher. My status as a researcher is substantially different from that of many other outsiders, such as aid workers. As a researcher, working either alone or with local institutions, I am not part of the security regimes of the humanitarian agencies present in the conflict zones. Although I inform my embassy that I am in the country and about to travel to the conflict zone, I do not report to the embassy on a regular basis. I move freely around, on the basis of the advice of my local colleagues, friends, and research participants. I stay in local guesthouses with international staff from humanitarian agencies, who, in contrast, report their whereabouts every day at a particular time to a security office in the capital. They cannot go out of the guesthouse area without their driver and the agency's official vehicle. I often find that humanitarian agency staff perceive the situation in the area as more dangerous than I do. This is not without reason – aid workers have been targeted with fatal consequences and the resources understood to be attached to an aid worker are far greater than those of a researcher.

While I recognize that we researchers have much to learn from the various security guidelines provided by humanitarian agencies, I also think that as researchers with ethnographic field experience, we have something to teach our colleagues in the humanitarian agencies. First, their security measures are often detached from the local context. They have no possibilities of just being there – hanging out – and trying to grasp the everyday experiences of conflict and displacement as well as the ways in which local people address security challenges in the area. Second, their lack of ethnographic experience limits their understanding of the complex power relations that are being played out on the ground, and the ways in which we become a part of those relations when we are in a militarized area.

SHARING RESPONSIBILITIES, DEVELOPING INSTITUTIONAL COLLABORATION

With time, my responsibilities in the field have changed. As I have conducted research in Sri Lanka since 1994, formalizing relationships with institutions there seemed to be a natural progression. First, this took place by way of action research through collaboration between colleagues at the Norwegian University of Science and Technology (NTNU) and a Scandinavian NGO on housing and livelihoods reconstruction after the Indian Ocean tsunami (Brun 2009, Brun and Lund 2010). Second, and as a result of the post-tsunami work, we collaborated with three Sri Lankan universities through a NORAD/ Norwegian Centre for International Cooperation in Higher Education–funded project on recovery, reconciliation, and strengthening of collaboration across the conflict lines.[5] The university collaboration has made visible a number of challenges related to working with institutions in a militarized society.

Sri Lankan universities in the war zone have lived through difficult times. Despite the many interruptions caused by war, faculty and staff have managed to keep them running. This has been beneficial for my work, as researchers based in these universities have enabled my access to the field. It is, however, important to distinguish between collaboration with individual researchers and institutional collaboration. The latter represents a different set of power relations at the local, national, and global levels. Universities in Sri Lanka – like other local and national government institutions – are heavily politicized. The president of Sri Lanka appoints the vice chancellor, and it is difficult to

---

5   The project is a collaboration of Eastern University, South Eastern University, University of Peradeniya, and NTNU and runs from 2007 till 2011.

achieve the highest position of the university unless the political and military actors in the area approve the appointment. It is common to find these actors present in senate meetings or other institutional bodies of the university. Working with universities in such circumstances can result in personal and professional dilemmas both ethical and practical. It can mean supporting actors one would prefer not to support and being used by these actors for their benefit. I decided to continue seeking advice and guidance from my colleagues in the university, although I cannot be certain I am avoiding all the pitfalls. For instance, I do not have control over appointments in the project, and some may use their positions in the project to gain political influence in the university and outside.

This collaboration with the university was marked in the beginning by the most difficult incident I have experienced as a researcher and project coordinator. In December 2006, Professor S. Ravindranath, a founding member of the collaboration, a good colleague, an eminent academic, and the vice chancellor of the Eastern University of Sri Lanka, was abducted by an unknown group in broad daylight in central Colombo on his way back from a meeting for the Association for the Advancement of Science. He has never been found. There had been abductions in the university before, and Professor Ravindranath had received threats. Despite all this, the disappearance was a shock for his family, friends, and colleagues. Much speculation and discussion have taken place about the unfolding of the events that led to his disappearance. I will not touch on these here. While our collaboration was probably not the reason for the disappearance, the incident shows the ways in which our projects become implicated in the complex relations of a society in conflict. This incident also heightened the sense of insecurity among the members of the project. As a result, we have had to negotiate security in many different ways during the first three years of the project.

We decided to put fieldwork on hold for two years after Ravi's disappearance. The situation in eastern Sri Lanka was in flux. When the fighting ended in June 2007, there was no longer a war, but peace was not established.[6] Unidentified armed groups were entering people's homes and demanding money at gunpoint. At the same time, political violence was taking place, and it was difficult to know whether a violent incident was a criminal or a political act or a combination. The unidentified armed groups, for example, were often men with face masks and weapons who would travel around on motorbikes without number plates. Their presence created much anxiety and

---

[6] Government forces regained control over the last territories in eastern Sri Lanka in June 2007, and the fighting continued in northern Sri Lanka up to May 2009.

speculation about their identity, as they seemed to travel freely through the military and militant checkpoints in the area. Under these circumstances, people – those in the project and potential research participants – expressed a very high sense of insecurity. To be seen with a notebook or even to enter people's homes could be a potential danger both for the people we wanted to interview and for us as researchers. There were also concerns about traveling to the conflict area based upon the researchers' origins (inside or outside the conflict zone, Sri Lanka or Norway) and/or to which ethnic group they belonged. In this situation, we could not afford to take chances. We kept fieldwork on hold, while continuing to meet and develop our research project in other ways – through academic discussions, by developing a master's degree, and through engaging in literature reviews. Our meetings took place in the universities in the field area and outside. We found that visiting the field area without conducting fieldwork was a way we could maintain research relationships and gain a better understanding of what it means to live in a militarized society. The collaboration and our activities – while not traditional fieldwork methods – were appropriate and realistic techniques that allowed us to maintain a presence in the conflict zone and to witness the violence.

From late 2008 security conditions improved, and fieldwork resumed in 2009 after a monitoring process involving an internal workshop where potential risks and their consequences were discussed. This workshop gave researchers a better understanding of the risks and how to deal with or avoid them. It was also quite useful for differentiating between real risks and perceived risks, which varied according to the social and geographical location of the researchers. This monitoring has continued in the form of communication with colleagues and researchers located in the field and the assessment of different types of risks and their consequences for individual researchers.

Just as our research participants do, the researchers in Sri Lanka use silence as a survival strategy. Certain topics cannot be discussed, and this affects both the formation of the larger research questions as well as the interview protocol. Similarly, the silences and self-censorship continue to be prevalent to some extent within the project group itself. In the autumn of 2009, the project group met in Norway for workshops, research seminars, and discussions. During the course of the events, which were all privately held, internal seminars, or seminars for specially invited researchers, it became clear that the Sri Lankan Tamil diaspora environment in Norway knew in detail our plans for the research meeting and our discussions. In traveling away from the field, we had taken the field with us.

BEARING WITNESS, DISSEMINATING CONFLICT,
RESPECTING SILENCE

You will learn to be obedient,
obedient and subservient.
And you will learn to use the Language [Afrikaans],
you will use it subserviently

(Breyten Breytenbach in Coetzee 1996, 225)

The poem quoted was written by the poet, writer, and activist Breyten Breytenbach during his imprisonment in South Africa. He was allowed to continue to write in prison subject to various conditions, knowing that his enemy was reading over his shoulders. The poem, which is said to be "double-voiced" (Bakhtin in Coetzee 1996), uses the language of the enemy for his own purpose. Many authors have risked their lives to challenge the restrictions of speech in militarized societies. For researchers in conflict zones, as I see it, the challenge is to find safe spaces to write from and within. Control over knowledge production, information, and news is a part of everyday life in Sri Lanka. Self-censorship is one way to conform and be obedient in our writing. How can we balance safe writing and the primacy of security with the need to inform people outside the conflict zone? Is it possible to bear witness and disseminate the experiences of the conflict but still respect the silences? There are deep-seated dilemmas involved in working with Sri Lankan colleagues and interviewees while respecting their silences. The dilemmas are related to institutional and funding demands for publishing. We have to acknowledge that even when publishing in academic journals we are still in the field, we are still connected with the field, and our actions and writing may place people in danger. Writing requires what Malkki (1997, 94) describes as "a form of caring vigilance."

There are many other venues besides academic journals where I disseminate my research – although they are not viewed as having academic merit. For example, local stakeholders are genuinely interested in my research and want to discuss new ideas. Even government officials and militant groups are interested in discussing, learning, and giving me advice. There are also many organizations and institutions outside the conflict area that are interested in my findings. Collaboration with an organization can have an impact beyond what I can do alone as a researcher and potentially change organizational practices (see Brun and Lund 2010). Teaching is also a major channel for dissemination; it is vital to develop degrees and reading material that can be used by universities in the areas where research has been conducted. Libraries have suffered greatly from the scarcity of resources during the conflict. In some cases they have been destroyed, as is the case with the Jaffna public library. In the context of Sri Lanka, strengthening the universities is clearly a most important strategy for moving research into policy; our colleagues in the universities in Sri Lanka communicate frequently with policy makers and government agents through various dialogue forums, as advisers and knowledge providers. By writing and disseminating our research in different ways in the field area and outside we take responsibility as researchers. As academics, we can bear witness to what is happening in a situation of war in more than one arena; we are not limited to the traditional academic fora.

REFLECTIONS ON RESPONSIBLE RESEARCH IN A MILITARIZED SOCIETY

We bear responsibility because we are part of the process. (Young 2006, 119)

Ethically sound and responsible research in militarized societies is about respecting silences and making safe spaces where research can take place. Respecting silences and making safe spaces means that sometimes "traditional" fieldwork is not possible. Sometimes one can still travel to the field, still be there as witness. However, sometimes, we also need to acknowledge that we cannot travel to the field – that the best safe space we can make is staying away and writing and disseminating from a distance. In any case, conducting research in a conflict setting or a militarized society requires knowledge of the field, good colleagues and resource persons in the field, self-reflexivity, and attentiveness to a potentially rapidly changing context.

To do ethically sound and responsible research we therefore need to learn from the field. The most important way of learning the field and learning how to be there in a conflict setting is through the research participants. By understanding – by interviewing and by being there – how people have maneuvered their lives through war and displacement, how they speak, what they keep silent about, and how they communicate the unspeakable we as researchers can also be able to understand how to make safe research spaces. But how can we do that from the beginning – before we have learned the field? Does it mean we cannot research a conflict context that is unknown to us? Unless we conduct research in partnership with others who do know the field there are many reasons for being careful. However, this is not an easy question even for those who do know a research setting because the field is constantly changing. As I have shown, the safe spaces established during fieldwork in Sri Lanka were not isolated and unassailable islands. They were established in the midst of the complex power relations and the dangerous field of a militarized society and they changed all the time. As researchers engaging with militarized societies, we continuously need to reflect on our power, privileges, and interests in the field and our collective ability to act with our partners, colleagues, and research participants to create safe spaces for gaining and disseminating knowledge. We must continue to question whether ethically sound and responsible research can be undertaken, and if we cannot be there, more reflection is needed on how and whether we can make a difference from a distance.

BIBLIOGRAPHY

Barnett, Clive and David Land. 2007. Geographies of generosity: Beyond the "moral turn." *Geoforum* 38(6): 1065–75.
Bell, Sharon. 2009. The distance of a shout. In *Spatialising Politics: Culture and geography in postcolonial Sri Lanka*, ed. C. Brun and T. Jazeel, 71–99. New Delhi: Sage.
Brun, C. 2008a. *Finding a place: Local integration and protracted displacement in Sri Lanka*. Colombo: Social Scientists Association.
    2008b. Birds of Freedom: Young people, LTTE and representations of gender, nationalism and governance in northern Sri Lanka. *Critical Asian Studies* 40(3): 399–422.
    2009. A geographers' imperative? Research and action in the aftermath of disaster. *Geographical Journal* 175(3): 196–207.
Brun, C. and R. Lund. 2010. Decolonising practices or just another spectacle of researcher-practitioner collaboration. *Development in Practice* 20(7): 812–26.
Carter, Sean. 2007. Mobilising generosity, framing geopolitics: Narrating crisis in the homeland through diasporic media. *Geoforum* 38(6): 1103–12.
Coetzee, John Maxwell. 1996. *Giving offence: Essays on censorship*. Chicago: University of Chicago Press.
de Alwis, Malathi. 2009. "Disappearance" and "Displacement" in Sri Lanka. *Journal of Refugee Studies* 22(3): 378–91
de Mel, Neloufer. 2007. *Militarizing Sri Lanka: Popular culture, memory and narrative in the armed conflict*. New Delhi: Sage.
Goodhand, Jonathan. 2000. Research in conflict zones: ethics and accountability. *Forced Migration Review* 8: 12–15.
Gupta, A. and J. Ferguson. 1997. Discipline and practice: "The field" as site, method, and location in anthropology. In *Anthropological Locations: Boundaries and Grounds of a Field Science*, ed. A. Gupta and J. Ferguson, 1–46. Berkeley: University of California Press.
HRW. 2008. *Recurring nightmare: State responsibility for "disappearances" and abductions in Sri Lanka*. Human Rights Watch March 2008. Available at http://www.hrw.org/en/reports/2008/08/27/recurring-nightmare (accessed January 15, 2010).
Katz, Cindi. 1994. Playing the field: Questions of fieldwork in geography. *Professional Geographer* 46(1): 67–73.

Cathrine Brun

Kobayashi, Audrey. 1994. Coloring the field: Gender, "race," and the politics of field-work. *Professional Geographer* 46(1): 73–80.

Lawrence, P. 2000. Violence, suffering, amman: The work of oracles in Sri Lanka's eastern war zone. In *Violence and subjectivity*, eds. V. Das, A. Kleinman, M. Ramphele, and P. Reynolds, 171–204. Berkeley: University of California Press.

Malkki, Liisa. 1997. News and culture: Transitory phenomena and the fieldwork tradition. In *Anthropological locations: Boundaries and grounds of a field science*, eds. A. Gupta and J. Ferguson, 86–101. Berkeley: University of California Press.

Massey, Douglas. 2004. Geographies of responsibility. *Geografiska Annaler* 86B(1): 5–18.

Mertus, Julie. 2009. Maintenance of personal security: Ethical and operational issues. In *Surviving field research: Working in violent and difficult situations*, eds. C. L. Sriram, J. C. King, J. A. Mertus, O. Martin-Ortega, and J. Herman, 165–76. London: Routledge.

Nast, Heidi J. 1994. Opening remarks on "women in the field." *Professional Geographer* 46(1): 54–66.

Obeysekere, Ranjini. 1999. *Sri Lankan theater in a time of terror: Political satire in a permitted space*. London: Sage.

Pratt, Geraldine. 2000. Research performances: *Environment and planning D: Society and space* 18 (5): 639 – 651.

Rodgers, Graeme. 2004. "Hanging out" with forced migrants: Methodological and ethical challenges. *Forced Migration Review* 21: 48–49.

Simmel, Georg. 1950. The stranger. In *The sociology of Georg Simmel* by Kurt H. Wolff, 402–8. New York: Free Press.

Sluka, Jeffrey. 1995. Reflections on managing danger in fieldwork: Dangerous anthropology in Belfast. In *Fieldwork under fire: Contemporary studies of violence and survival*, eds. C. Nordstrom and A. C. G. M. Robben, 276–94. Berkeley: University of California Press.

Thrift, Nigel. 2003. Practicing ethics. In *Using social theory: Thinking through research*, ed. M. Pryke, G. Rose, and S. Whatmore, 105–121. London: Sage.

Young, Iris Marion. 2006. Responsibility and global justice: A social connection model. *Social Philosophy and Policy* 23(1): 102–30.

6

Power Dynamics and the Politics of Fieldwork under Sudan's Prolonged Conflicts

Jok Madut Jok

Sudan, like many African countries, has been ravaged by prolonged wars since independence. War was the most important subject of my study when I conducted research for my doctorate in anthropology in South Sudan (1993–5), yet it was a subject that was both poorly understood and extremely complex. There existed varied and poor analyses of war-induced shifts in the social order of Sudan, yet few studies accurately traced the historical trajectory of the root causes of the wars in Sudan (for a notable exception see Johnson 2003). Little attention was paid to the effects of food insecurity, poor health, and destruction of infrastructure in people's everyday lives and how these upheavals in turn became factors in the next phase of the war.

For me as a researcher and an insider, understanding these rapidly changing social systems was crucial for the design of culturally appropriate humanitarian and human rights interventions. Yet obtaining this information was also extremely daunting because of the complex and multilayered nature of war zones. Since the early 1990s, my fieldwork in South Sudan has included ethnographies of political violence, slavery, and the racial and religious bases of Sudan's political violence. Research in South Sudan then and now involves security risks, issues of access, and logistical challenges. It also entails ethical dilemmas, given that the subject matter includes war-induced poverty, hunger, dying, gender-based sexual violence, and power-based sexual blackmail.[1] My experiences have taught me that issues of gender inequality, militarism, reproductive health, and overall family health are central to building an equitable society, and as such they remain touchstones for my research. In this chapter, I explore how such issues can be studied in war zones when one is

---

[1] Sexual blackmail was observed to occur over the distribution of humanitarian relief items, where some men in charge of such distribution might demand sex with desperately poor women in exchange for these supplies.

both an insider and an outsider in a complex web of politics, ethical dilemmas, logistical challenges, and security risks.

I grew up in the part of South Sudan I knew as Pan Muonyjang, but left the country in the midst of the second round of Sudan's civil wars. Like so many of my male Jieng (Dinka) age mates, I went abroad in search of education at the age of eighteen.[2] Through a combination of luck, audacity, random applications for scholarships, and encounters with generous people, I enrolled in a university in Egypt and subsequently moved to the United States.[3] When I returned home for the first time after more than ten years away, it was to a war-provoked famine.

The war in my country was rooted in multitude of factors, including the colonial legacy, Islamic radicalism in the north, and aspirations for independence in the south (Hutchinson 1996, Johnson 2003). The round of conflict I grew up in and returned to (1983–2005) had created the expectation in South Sudan that every able-bodied man would join either the freedom fight or the Sudanese army. I arrived – young, strong, and educated – just the kind of person the opposition Sudan Peoples Liberation Army (SPLA) expected to recruit. Local SPLA leaders viewed me simultaneously with suspicion as to my motivations for return and desire to recruit me. I was educated and therefore expected to be politically aware and to understand the importance of joining the opposition against the north. Yet, I had been absent for a number of years, and my loyalties were unclear. On top of this, I arrived with the logistical support of an aid agency, further complicating my identity. Prominent people in the community recognized my family name and verified that I was indeed one of their own. But the SPLA authorities treated my political views, loyalties, and reasons for return as cause for suspicion. Civilian leaders were reluctant to introduce me to the rebel commander, lest they taint their own image or risk their lives.

The only people who could persuade the rebel commander to suspend his suspicions were the foreign aid workers I had accompanied to Sudan. The British director of the NGO who had flown in with me took me to the rebel

---

[2]   The members of the Sudanese ethnic nation, known as the Dinka, do not actually call themselves Dinka, but rather Muonyjang or Jieng. The origins of the term "Dinka" are not well known, but it is surely a foreign term, possibly a mispronunciation of something one person may have uttered at the time of early contact with outsiders.

[3]   Such opportunities were not very common and proved to be even harder for women, whose mobility is greatly restricted if they are not traveling with their families.

commander and introduced me, explaining my double role as researcher and relief worker. The irony was palpable. I was supposed to be a guide for the British aid director, helping him to navigate the cultural complexities of the war, local traditions, and humanitarian aid. Instead, I needed a foreigner to provide me with introductions to my own people! The elite of my own community viewed my foreign friends as more believable and trustworthy than a native son. I came to call this, in jest, the *khawaja* edge, the advantage of being in the company of white people.[4]

It was in vogue in the 1980s to speak of an "African" or "indigenous" anthropology, one where former subjects of anthropology in the developing countries were beginning to appropriate and own anthropology as a method of inquiry and free it from its historical burden of being rooted in imperialism and colonialism (Mafeje 1992, 1993, 1996). This was all very interesting as a theoretical discussion. But my encounters in the field suggested that anthropologists from the global south cannot really succeed in domesticating anthropology (Mafeje 1986). Because of historical power dynamics between researchers from the global north and their research subjects in the developing world, a history that dates back to colonial times, the cold war geopolitics, and the current globalization in which Africa remains on the periphery, anthropology will remain a Western monopoly – essentially a method of knowledge acquisition concerning societies in the global south (Smith 1999). Furthermore, Western aid and development workers have gained power over the aid recipients, that is, the local population, especially in areas of material deprivation like South Sudan. These power structures mean indigenous anthropologists are at a great disadvantage, as the impoverished people in the developing world increasingly view aid providers as more influential than researchers. So my euphoria about becoming researcher and subject at the same time was short-lived. I had imagined that the community I was going to study would view a researcher with my background as more capable of accurate translation of their culture. However, some of them saw me as subordinate to my European friends, who, in the eyes of the local elite, occupied the position of power, not the least because they controlled relief items that everyone wanted and needed.

My first day back was one of truly mixed feelings. I felt great joy upon returning home, receiving welcome and witnessing that life had continued despite many years of suffering. But I could not stop making comparisons between the homeland I knew as a child and the one I had returned to as an adult. The mental images I had of small children running across the long grasses of the

---

4 The word *khawaja* is a Sudanese colloquial term for foreigner, mostly referring to a white person.

savannah and the open woodland to attend school early in the morning were now replaced by the reality of malnourished children lined up in front of therapeutic feeding centers waiting for their meager rations. My mental picture of women singing as they worked in their fields was now replaced by frail women climbing and cutting down tree branches in order to pick the leaves for a day's meal. These stark images of conflict and famine were powerful reminders of the remarkable changes that had occurred in social networks and social expectations, changes that had profoundly influenced the Jiengs' long-term coping strategies.[5] The Dinkaland I remembered no longer existed.

As I interacted with people, the most noticeable changes were shifts in gendered and generational linguistic markers. Certain manners of speech, semantics, and vocabulary had previously been used only between individuals of one age set or between members of the same sex. The changes in these speech patterns suggested the emergence of new kinds of relationships between men and women and between adults and children. It seemed that economic and political pressures had influenced Jieng institutions, which explained why my impressions of Jieng family life I was encountering differed greatly from my childhood days. Cultural arrangements that had historically functioned to govern economic, power, and gender relationships between individuals and among communities appeared to have been modified. These observations led me to focus my doctoral research on the shift in gender relations under the weight of the protracted conflicts in Sudan. I was particularly interested in sexuality, sexual violence, and reproductive health as the intersecting sites where gender socialization and its everyday dynamics play themselves out.

In order to understand this altered world, I decided to use cultural dialogues as a point of entry. An ethnography of dialogue would be a product not only of the interactions between the anthropologist and his informants, but of people's interpretive strategies. What were the content and purpose of interactions between men and women, children and adults, soldiers and civilians, and locals and outsiders?

My interview questions were designed to explore how a person in Jieng culture comes to occupy a particular status or image both in his or her own eyes and from the perspective of others. These questions had to be phrased appropriately to fit the nature of the subject matter, as well as the gender and the age of the individual being interviewed. The process of recruiting informants provided unexpected openings into understanding status. For example, when community elders advised me not to speak to a particular person because he

---

5   The words "Jieng" and "Muonjang" are used here interchangeably, as these are the words the "Dinka" know themselves by.

or she did not present a positive image of the society, this cultural "deviance" afforded me opportunities to investigate how a person gains that status. My key informants were recruited primarily through snowball sampling. Women with traditional expertise in health issues, especially obstetrics and/or sexually transmitted diseases, were particularly helpful in recommending key study participants.

My informants included tribal chiefs, military men, civil servants, farmers, traditional birth attendants and other health care workers, sex workers, women who had dealt with abortions, and married women and girls who had experience with sexually transmitted infections. There were many challenges to pursuing my research agenda in the context of war. The most immediate hurdle was the power dynamic between a native son who returned as a social science researcher and the community leaders. The long-term challenge, however, was developing rapport with women informants, which took me a full year. This rapport was achieved through a careful dance involving time, confessions on my side about the motives for doing this fieldwork, and a deepening understanding on their side about what they might gain from the results of this research. These hard won relationships supported my later research on the militarization of ethnic identities, slavery, and sexual violence in the course of my research over the next ten years of the war. During these field trips the results of earlier fieldwork were shared, debated, and applied in the search for appropriate humanitarian action. The deepening of these relationships and continued engagement with the first field site were central to the success of all my following fieldwork during conflict.

WAR, POWER RELATIONS, AND FIELDWORK

The basic requirements of fieldwork in remote places in the developing world range from minute details such as vaccinations and visas, to the ethics of interaction with the host community and state authorities. Fieldwork requires adapting and honing interviewing techniques, such as how far to dig into personal lives and how much information can be revealed without endangering the participant's positive image (Armbruster 2008, de Laine 2000). These are key issues for any fieldwork, but they raise particularly complex concerns in a conflict setting, especially if the subject matter is related to the politics of the war and how it is lived and experienced day to day. Notably, social systems are in flux during war, and previous studies may not adequately guide the new researcher.

Among the Jieng the challenges of studying sexuality and reproduction are vast, especially as an insider asking questions and particularly as these issues relate to war-driven sexual violence. For one thing, as an insider, I am assumed to know the answers already. There exists an etiquette of respectful restraint that a "young man" must exercise when talking to women, especially married ones, as they are normally considered one's "mothers."[6] Why would I wish to transgress such rules? I was also aware that my would-be informants might wonder why, of all the burning issues related to war, I would choose to ask them about sexuality. Above all, I was conscious of Jieng structures of femininity, masculinity, and the strict gender division of roles, including the use of gendered language to address certain topics. I knew that gender constructs dictated what questions I – a Jieng man socialized to fit a certain image –could and could not ask. I also expected that men would have a derisive response to my suggestions that men and women experience war differently. Despite these trepidations, I remained convinced that examining sexuality and reproduction would provide a window into the war-induced changes in social order, of which there were many.

Violence was reproduced within communities and families, and I could see this in the ways young men had become conditioned to violence over a long period. Women were assuming more responsibilities as men left to take up their positions in war, particularly by upholding the "reproductive front."[7] Alcohol consumption had increased among men as disastrous food deficits threatened norms of sharing. I was interested in understanding how the shifts in sexual relations could shed light on these new dynamics. But sex, like death, is also a topic the Jieng will not discuss openly, and the vocabulary of sexual relations is metaphorical, requiring intimate grasp of the society's ethos and idioms in order to discuss it at all.

The lens of cultural models established by earlier anthropological studies is not useful for studying the reconfiguration of gender relations, gender-based violence, and reproductive health during war (Nordstrom and Robben 1996, Hutchinson 1996). Hunger and starvation do not lend themselves to "participant observation" – the hallmark of anthropology. For example,

---

6   In the Jieng order of all things social, a young unmarried man considers any married woman as a "mother," which really means a potential mother-in-law, and one is expected to behave in a certain prescribed manner around her. One is also expected to avoid direct contact without proper announcement that one is approaching. Language, manners, and appropriate terms of address all have to be considered in the interactions between men and women.

7   "Reproductive front" was a phrase commonly used throughout the war to refer to women's responsibility of contributing to the liberation struggle through frequent childbirth. As men wished to have many children, in case they perished in war, and as military leaders began to reason that higher fertility would compensate for war-induced high mortality, pressure to produce as many children as possible became a national decision, as opposed to a family decision.

a woman who was widowed or separated from her family, displaced, and dispossessed by war might become so desperate that she could be pressured into providing sexual services in exchange for food in order to feed her children. She would be stripped of her ability to maintain dignity. In a society that places a high premium on modesty and chastity, how a woman arrives at such a heart-wrenching choice is a story as difficult to tease out and record as it is challenging to guard so that the woman is not further victimized through public shaming.

Likewise, sex and sexual violence do not readily lend themselves to observation, and it is extremely difficult to gain accurate information through traditional interviews. The victims are too distressed or reluctant to speak of their experiences. The perpetrators are not easy to track down; nor are they willing to admit to their actions. I found that victims of sexual violence who decided to press charges were so humiliated by the justice system that they preferred to suffer in silence rather than be made to relive their horrors in a system that would not grant them remedy or restitution. Medical services that could be called upon to corroborate a rape case were inadequate, even if the justice system showed interest. It was during a research project many years later that I came to realize that without cooperation among medical personnel, police, and court officials, it is nearly impossible for victims of sexual violence to get justice. Researchers cannot claim to have a full picture about how and why war seems to affect women much more than men without investigating such structural factors. While some issues can only be comprehended after the fact, in a postwar environment, I have also learned the importance of investigating events as they unfold. The passage of time leads to memory lapse, the emergence of other more important problems, and the desire to sweep the wartime atrocities under the rug in the interest of focusing on the end-of-the-war euphoria. The researcher has to be trusted by victims and perpetrators, a rather fantastic expectation.

IDENTITY AND ACCESS

I inhabit a rather peculiar position as an indigenous researcher asking about intimate aspects of people's lives. There are certain questions that people feel obliged to answer only if they are asked by a foreign aid worker or researcher but are considered strange if they are from a local, someone who is supposed to know the answers. If I emphasized my independence of my foreign friends, the suspicion of the opposition army leaders could be detrimental to my physical well-being, or, at the very least, my ability to conduct my research. But by too closely associating with them, I risked appearing to have rejected my place among my people. One of the characteristics that separated me from foreign anthropologists or foreign aid workers was the assumption by local people that I did not possess material "stuff," and I was thought to have less money than my foreign colleagues. These power relations revealed themselves in ways that were sad and sometimes comical. For example, in my double role as an aid worker, people would bypass me to consult with foreign aid workers, even in circumstances in which I was more senior. They reasoned that a local Jieng could not possibly be higher in rank than a white person.

South Sudan in the 1990s was extremely hard to enter from outside the country. To get to one's field site in the middle of the war was logistically near-impossible without the help of either the aid agencies or the armed forces of one of the warring parties. If I went with the military or armed opposition group, they would scrutinize every step I took and the civilians would not talk to me out of fear. If I went with an aid agency (the option for journalists, human rights agents, and researchers of all kinds), the line separating my role as a researcher and as an aid worker was blurry. One's role as a potential source of aid supplies would override the role as a researcher, and that would cause people not to talk to you truthfully since humanitarian aid distribution is often fraught with the recipients' wish to inflate their level of need and conceal their real socioeconomic status.[8] For example, some individuals who had cultivated acquaintance with me through my research approached me with hopes that I would sneak relief items to them behind the backs of foreign aid workers. To favor them with relief items might have won me their support for my research project. Yet this would have amounted to bribing my informants. But to object to their requests risked antagonizing them and imperiling the friendship and trust that were so crucial to my research project. The solution to these dilemmas was something that I could only learn over time as I tried to negotiate my relationships with the various groups while keeping focused on my research agenda.

These difficult encounters did not mean that I could not be a good anthropologist. It just meant that I had to negotiate my relationships with

---

[8] Because of the philosophy of humanitarian aid, one that is rooted in the ideas of the welfare state of the Western countries and based on targeting specific people for assistance, the practice has been that an aid agency has to establish the basis on which aid supplies are given to a particular person or family; these bases usually include socioeconomic status and war-related dispossession, i.e., how poor one is. Because the idea of targeting specific individuals is such a foreign concept, a necessary one of course as aid cannot possibly reach everyone in the war-stricken country, aid recipients have to lie about their status and label themselves as "poor," something they do with a sense of shame and humiliation, and the presence of a humanitarian aid worker who is also a researcher and a local makes that sense of humiliation all the more pronounced. For further details on this issue see Jok Madut Jok (1996).

the informants, the community, aid groups, the military, and insurgent authorities in ways that were completely different from what I had learned in my field methods class. I came to realize that being an insider, fluent in the field language and familiar with the basic structures of this society, contrary to my assumptions, did not necessarily grant me many advantages. As a native researcher, I lacked the privilege of being considered ignorant and forgivable for asking absurd questions. Being able to ask stupid questions and expect brilliant answers is the stuff good anthropological research is made of, the edge that an outsider researcher has over an insider. Learning about a new culture is more or less like a child's learning a language. Outside researchers who make mistakes in their encounters with the locals may receive corrections and offers of guidance. As a local, not only did I get no such assistance, I was reprimanded!

I had to claim ignorance when I was caught asking questions I should not have asked. I blamed such ignorance on my long absence from home; I had forgotten certain cultural givens. I found myself having to claim memory lapse about my own culture as the way to persuade my informants to indulge my questions.[9]

ETHICAL ISSUES: PARTICIPANT BENEFITS

Those who have conducted both ethnographic research and needs assessments during war and famine realize that they cannot overemphasize the importance of clearly distinguishing between the two, particularly in terms of what one tells informants about the project. Many communities living in war zones have been studied over and over again in an effort to assess their humanitarian needs, to map out the level of poverty, and to document wealth disparities, coping strategies, and ethics of sharing, all with an eye to efficient and targeted distribution of relief goods. The result has been that needs assessments have, by and large, given some communities and individuals false hopes that some benefits will accrue from their participation in the research. As people grow to realize that frequent assessment missions do not necessarily yield aid, they dislike being overresearched (Jok 1996). A researcher who is conducting long-term ethnographic research must establish realistic expectations from

[9] Many others, including Soraya Altorki and Camillia F. El-Soh (1988), had similar encounters. As an Arab woman, Altorki, who had gone to conduct fieldwork in her native Saudi Arabia, was confronted with questions of why she needed to study her own people. While most Western women generally had easier access to their field settings in the Middle East, she had to conform to a variety of restrictions that were not applied to Western women anthropologists.

the outset. Study participants should be made aware of these dynamics. The responsibility to safeguard the interests of one's research subjects and adhere to the ethics of research falls squarely on the researcher.

My plan to focus on sex, the social order, and reproductive health was considered marginal by many men in light of urgent issues such as the politics of liberation, food deficits, and the role of the international humanitarian community. I came to view skepticism from the local leaders as an opportunity for a dialectical engagement as well as a hurdle. I agreed with them that war and its immediate health consequences were worthy of research, and in discussion I pointed out that these were exactly the issues I wanted to study, but from a different angle than they might expect.

The rush to blame the conflict for every social ill blinded the leaders to the possibility that the war exacerbated women's suffering because of static sociocultural practices. The usual gender divides were being applied in a completely changed environment, as if the social order produced by the war situation did not require a change in these gendered attitudes. There was general awareness about changes in women's situation, but their voices were still being deliberately excluded in planning and sustaining the revolution, as they were simply assigned their "revolutionary roles," such as motherhood and support services for the men. Motherhood had become political and was emphasized as part of the struggle, in terms of both care for children in the absence of men and frequent childbirth. In my dialogue with the community leaders, I wanted to spur the local authorities to take a careful look at war-related violence as being fueled by inherent gendered "traditions," as well as by the war. How is the impact of war tied to one's gender, social status, or access to guns? Where is the line between wartime and peacetime gendered violence?

I was finally able to justify my research by calling attention to the dire state of maternal and infant health. Sudan has among the world's highest maternal and infant mortality rates, which exist in a deadly relationship. The higher the infant mortality, the more pressure there is on women to bear children, putting both mothers and children at a further risk, especially given that South Sudan has the world's lowest number of doctors per patient. Women are seen as appendages to their menfolk, an attitude that underlies men's sense of entitlement to their sexual availability. Should the woman try to assert any sexual autonomy, domestic violence is often the result. Such attitudes and their negative consequences for women's health are built upon a social order that assigns different values for boys and girls. For example, there is emphasis on investment in male children in such areas as education, while young girls are destined for early marriage and early motherhood.

GENDER, AGE, AND WHAT QUESTIONS TO ASK

I found anthropological fieldwork methods to be well suited to address these sensitive issues because of the intensive fieldwork methods and relationships created. I examined the behavior of young military men as members of a social group, with responsibilities and obligations, and related this behavior to the tension between their gender socialization as males and the demands of their new roles as liberators. More often than not, the members of insurgent groups who engaged in violent actions, including the reproduction of violence within their own families, are also integral to the community under study, and they straddle military and civilian lives. Thus a military man in the context of a civil war is a liberation fighter *and* a civilian, if sometimes more one than the other. Understanding these men's perspective on their own behaviors is as crucial as hearing and recording the women's war experience.

I was profoundly impressed by the openness of women – who were in essence my "mothers" in the Jieng scheme of relationships – about such culturally sensitive issues as sexual relations and reproductive matters. It took me a long time to establish rapport with the women, but once I was accepted, I was touched by the willingness of Jieng women to trust my representation of their worldview and discourse. I needed them to help me to understand and explore my research questions, and they were interested to have me hear their stories of living in war. As they opened up to me, I learned that few people in the aid world seemed interested in hearing their stories or recording or using their narratives as a basis for improving interpersonal relations and effective aid delivery. My informants were willing to grant that life under chronic violence was a mystery and that my research might help their communities come to terms with the realities of war-induced social change. For them, the waning norms of sharing, aid agencies' insistence on "targeting," actions of armed men, increasing numbers of miscarriages, increasing infertility, abandonment of children by parents, absence of the state, and the generalized violence were all experiences that contradicted life as they had known it.

I tried to remain vigilant of my responsibility to respect the boundaries between public and private discourse about sexuality, rape, sexually transmitted diseases, unwanted pregnancies, abortion, childbirth and child rearing, gender relations, age relations, and civilian-military relations. I paid careful attention to the sorts of things that people said in one-on-one conversations and what they were willing to say in group interviews. In focus group discussions, people might be speaking about their own experiences but were quick to attribute them to an imaginary "friend" or "colleague." In such cases, I would refrain from probing further in public as to the identity of these friends and colleagues. Their stories described a society in turmoil and were to form the building blocks of my research. I was aware of both the risk and the suspicion that this project – run by a man about matters private to women – could rob them of their discourse, their own voices. Some brave women even made remarks to me during the interviews or focus groups whether my questions were an attempt to steal "women's secrets." One woman suggested that one of the few areas of social relations that women have control over is reproductive issues, which may sometimes involve a woman's acting weak and helpless, and if men begin to probe into these few areas that "we still keep under cover, we will have nothing left to call ourselves women by." To this day, I cannot say that I have successfully safeguarded against these risks, but offer the only consolation I can: that I was constantly aware of the possibility that women's voices could be hijacked and did my best to minimize that possibility.

In the history of anthropology in South Sudan, women's voices were not heard in the earliest ethnographies, a result of the unquestioning acceptance of gender hierarchies within the societies being studied as well as the assumptions held by the male researchers themselves. My fears that my own research could add to that oppressive history led me to seek a sample that represented all sectors of the society, including men and women, youth and older people, people within a variety of professions and a range of marital statuses. But it quickly became clear that it was not only anthropologists who had neglected what women had to say about their own culture and society. In response to my research questions, a variety of male figures of authority made remarks that were specifically meant to suppress women's commentary on their daily lives and on the society in general. For example, some types of women were quickly pointed out to me as "bad women," whose views I was asked to exclude from the research findings because they would "tarnish the reputation of our community." Divorced women or women whose husbands had abandoned them during flight from conflicts and women who were living in the displaced persons' camps were all typed as people whose lives contradicted the image some community leaders wanted to project about their society.

But of course it was such attempts to muzzle the voices of certain members of the community or render them invisible that would make a social scientist more curious as to how each member of society earns his or her reputation, positive or negative. I wanted to know how someone becomes a "bad woman." I eventually found a few women who were willing to explain to me what it means to be a bad woman. I found them through a connection they all had to one particular woman who made beer in the market. She was the central figure in that circle of supposedly dubious women in town. She made jokes about this labeling and how it revealed the hypocrisy of the so-called male leaders, yet at the same time provided an environment of safety for the outcasts of the market. This phrase "bad woman" was applied to any woman whose social life, occupation, and behavior (whether based on rumor or fact) were considered unacceptable. Known sex workers, unmarried women living alone, and women often seen in the company of different men, all fit the image of bad women. But since Sudan in the 1990s was home to the world's largest population of internally displaced persons (IDPs), this definition would make millions of women bad women, as the majority of Sudan's IDPs were women. And the labeling of some women as bad was certainly contested. As one of my informants explained, "If any one of us women in this market was considered a bad woman, it would mean that we are all bad women ... we do the same odd jobs to feed our children, and on that basis alone, a chief's wife or the wife of the commander is no more honorable than any of us."

SEAMLESS TECHNIQUES TO INVOLVE WOMEN

A most common critique of the earlier anthropological scholarship of Sudan that I mentioned earlier is its supposed disinterest in gender relations. In this earlier scholarship of Sudan, women and their position in society, their roles in everyday life, and their voices in the ethnography are noticeably missing. In classic works such as Evan-Pritchard's *The Nuer* (1940) or Lienhardt's *Divinity and Experience* (1961), the Nuer and the Jieng became celebrities of the anthropological literature, mainly for their supposed warlike traditions, their seemingly chaotic political structures, and their spiritual leaders who were assumed to have significant powers over their people. Even in situations where polygyny, a system that intrinsically concerns women's status, was addressed, it was described from the perspective of the men as a symbol of male political and social status (Evans-Pritchard 1951, Lienhardt 1963). There was little mention of how such institutions subjugated women or how women may at times have used them to their own advantage while projecting an image of submissiveness. In other words, how women and men in these societies negotiated these power relations supposedly was, according to these earlier anthropologists, not part of the analytical scheme of their culture.

When I became familiar with these works as an undergraduate student, this lacuna in the literature was noticeable and intriguing to me. But now, during my own fieldwork, I had the opportunity to find out how such a glaring gap was left by anthropology's pioneers who had done so much to make our discipline what it is today.[10] When I called upon a household in the interest of

---

[10] It is important to acknowledge here that there is a serious attempt by a younger generation of anthropologist to bridge this gap. The work of Sharon Hutchinson (1996) and Diana Shandy (2007) with the Nuer, which addresses these historical gaps, is worth noting.

engaging both men and women in a conversation, the woman often deferred
to the man. Sometimes she even denigrated herself by remarking that I should
just speak to "the man of the house because I am only a woman and I know
nothing." I often obliged and excused the woman to leave the room but would
search her out for an interview a different time at another location. Research
that seriously engages and involves women requires a conscious decision to
go beyond the usual interviewing opportunities. Rural Sudanese women are
always very busy and cannot afford to sit down with a researcher for hours on
end. One way to resolve this issue was to be considerate of women's chores and
to follow them to their farms or water points or areas for collecting firewood.
I found it important to engage my women informants without creating clashes
in the household, as men might be unhappy with women talking to me without their permission. I would explain to the men the importance of talking
to women about their work. I found that women would try to minimize conflict with the men by appearing weak, so it was useful at times to seek men's
approval by downplaying the interviews as a conversation about the "usual
problems of women." My follow-up interviews gave the women the opportunity to offer their opinion on the same issues in a safe and separate space.

CONCLUSION: MAKING THE WORK MATTER
TO LOCAL POPULATIONS

It has been nearly fifteen years since I carried out the dissertation research
that I discuss earlier, and it is refreshing that the recent generation of anthropologists has been addressing the gaps I saw then (Hutchinson 1996, Shandy
2007). In my further research, I conducted a joint field project with Sharon
Hutchinson that sought to understand the volatile relations between the Jieng
and the Nuer (*Naath*) and the militarization of these relations by their political leaders as they struggled for control of power in South Sudan. This project restored my hope in anthropology. Our twin projects, Hutchinson on the
Nuer side and I on the Jieng side, focused on the perceptions that one group
holds about the other. Our findings showed that the violent conflicts between
the two groups from 1991 to 1999, though depicted in journalistic accounts as
a manifestation of primordial hatreds, were indeed "wars of the educated,"
meaning that they were fanned by political elites to their own short-term political ends (Jok and Hutchinson 1999). This research for me was a major break-
through in making ethnography immediately useful for the people studied.

I have grappled extensively with the question of the value of ethnographic
research for the participants of the study. Much of my work has been conducted
with communities whose survival was at stake; that circumstance raised the

hope that my research could lead to solutions for some of the community's immediate problems of health care, nutrition, and violence. How anthropologists understand and approach the dilemma of how to contribute to solutions and what obligations we have to our informants is one of the primary ethical challenges the discipline must confront head on. Without any conception as to the solution, anthropology will become ever more questionable as a human science.

One of the most frustrating aspects of conducting fieldwork in the global south from a base in the global north is the question of how the people studied obtain access to the findings and whether or not they have any opportunity to comment on the results of the study. I had been asked very often during fieldwork whether "we will be able to read about ourselves in a book." While educated Jieng could read and debate my findings, those I interviewed and studied were from rural communities where the level of literacy was quite low, standing at a pathetic 2.5 percent for women. So the people whose comments would have been of most use and interest to me were the individuals most difficult to reach with written text. I tried to mitigate this situation by holding meetings with my informants on several subsequent trips to the original field site. I thought that this would be an opportunity to share with them my work. However joyous and rather comical it was, reading sections of my dissertation to them did not really afford them ample opportunity to comment.

My other concern is whether or not the findings could be applied to service or development programs that positively affect people's lives. My research was conducted under desperate circumstances, where war had dispossessed and displaced the people and had destroyed their assets – the need for improved humanitarian services was paramount. A massive humanitarian response to these crises had been launched – Operation Lifeline Sudan – an operation that later became the developing world's biggest, most expensive, and longest-running relief effort.[11] These two realities, for me, meant that if these humanitarian efforts were to be meaningful and to save lives and preserve the dignity of the recipients, affected communities must be correctly understood, and aid should be provided to them with humility and respect for their humanity. As a result of this concern, I shifted gears to focus my ethnographic work on humanitarian assistance. I believe that if anthropology does not offer something of value to the study subjects, the power dynamics that I have discussed

---

[11] This was to be known as Operation Lifeline Sudan (OLS). Led by the United Nations, it included more than forty nongovernmental organizations and thousands of expatriate workers from Europe, North America, and East Africa.

between study participants and the anthropologist, and between researchers from the global north and native researchers, will remain lopsided.

Anthropologists will continue to collect data, return home, and build careers as scholars or practitioners with very little to offer the people studied. The least we can do is to acknowledge that and drop the pretence of working on behalf of our study subjects, so that on the odd occasion that anthropological findings lead to policies or actions that positively affect peoples' lives, we can rejoice while remaining humble. While my publications may or may not directly affect the lives of the people in my research, acting on my knowledge gained from the research can. To this end, I started a primary school in Warrap State, South Sudan, that is focused on offering young women an opportunity to be primary decision makers over their lives. With education, girls are able to delay marriage, delay childbirth, learn how to be better mothers when they do become mothers, gain sexual autonomy so as to safeguard their sexual health, and learn the best ways to space their children. My vision is that a community with educated girls and women will be a healthier community over all, with adequate knowledge of hygiene, proper nutrition, good levels of child immunization, and HIV/AIDS awareness. To achieve this, the ultimate goal of the school is to create a midwifery high school and train young women in community health. We have already made significant inroads toward this goal.

BIBLIOGRAPHY

Altorki, Soraya and Camillia F. El-Soh. 1988. *Arab women in the field: Studying your own society.* Syracuse, NY: Syracuse University Press.

Armbruster, Heidi and Anna Laerke, eds. 2008. *Taking sides: ethics, politics, and fieldwork in anthropology.* New York: Berghahn.

de Laine, Marlene. 2000. *Fieldwork, participation and practice: Ethics and dilemmas in qualitative research.* London: Sage.

Evans-Pritchard, E. E. 1940. *The Nuer: A description of the modes of livelihood and political institutions of a Nilotic people.* Oxford: Clarendon Press.

1951. *Kinship and marriage among the Nuer.* Oxford: Clarendon Press.

Hutchinson, Sharon. 1996. *Nuer dilemmas: Coping with money, war, and the state.* Berkeley: University of California Press.

Johnson, Douglas. 2003. *The root causes of Sudan's civil wars.* Bloomington: Indiana University Press.

Jok, Jok Madut. 1996. Information exchange in the disaster zone: Interaction between aid workers and recipients in south Sudan. *Disasters* 20(3): 206–15.

Jok, Jok Madut and Sharon E. Hutchinson. 1999. Sudan's prolonged second civil war and the militarization of Nuer and Dinka ethnic identities. *African Studies Review* 42(2): 125–45.

Lienhardt, Godfrey. 1961. *Divinity and experience: Religion of the Dinka.* Oxford: Clarendon Press.

Lienhardt, Godfrey 1963. Dinka representation of the relations between the sexes. In *Studies of Kinship and Marriage*, ed. Shapera. Royal Anthropological Institute Occasional Papers No. 16.1: 79–92. London: Royal Anthropological Institute.

Mafeje, Archie. 1986. *Studies in imperialism: A discourse in methodology, research methods and techniques*. University of Zimbabwe, Departments of Economics, Law and Political and Administrative Studies.

1992. *In search of an alternative: A collection of essays on revolutionary theory and politics*. Southern Africa political economy series. Harare: SAPES.

1993. *African philosophical projections and proposals for the indigenisation of political and intellectual discourse*. Issue 7 of Southern Africa political economy series. Harare: SAPES.

1996. *Anthropology and independent Africans: Suicide or end of an era?* Monograph Series, Codesria.

Nordstrom, Caroline and Antonius C. G. M. Robben, ed. 1996. *Fieldwork under fire: Contemporary studies of violence and culture*. Berkeley and Los Angeles: University of California Press.

Shandy, Dianna. 2007. *Nuer-American passages: Globalizing Sudanese migration*. Gainesville: University Press of Florida.

Smith, Linda T. 1999. *Decolonizing methodologies: Research and indigenous peoples*. London: Zed Books.

PART IV

TRUST

Figure 6. "Prayer Beads" October 2003, Baghdad, Iraq.
Photographer: Molly Bingham

"The Teacher," one of the individuals we interviewed multiple times for our reporting, was actively involved in weapons acquisition for a resistance group. Here, along the banks of the Tigris River in Baghdad, he talks about honor and dignity, the Iraqi notion of *Ghira*.

7

Reporting the Story

Thoughts for Reporting on Violent Groups in a Turbulent Environment

Molly Bingham and Steve Connors

Introduction

We are photojournalists who between us have thirty years of experience covering conflict. As we have done in other conflicts during our careers, we were working as freelancers for mainstream Western news organizations in Baghdad after the fall of the country to U.S. and British forces in April 2003. Over the course of our reporting during those early months, we noted an increasing number of small-scale attacks on the coalition forces. Our awareness of and interest in them were heightened by a chance meeting with a man who identified himself as being involved in such violence. We began to wonder what lay behind these attacks. Throughout our lives, our work in different ways has revolved around two general questions: What it is that drives human beings to pick up weapons to express themselves? And what kind of result does that decision bring? We stayed in Iraq for a total of fourteen months, ten of which – August 2003 until June 2004 – were spent reporting on the Iraqi resistance to the U.S. led occupation, trying to answer those questions and the hundreds more that emerged in the process. We did not know what we would find when we started and we did not fully understand what we had until we stopped. This chapter outlines how we came across the story, how we chose to cover it, how we dealt with the complexities and choices along the way, as well as some of our findings.

A Brief Context

In the last seven thousand years, the region that now encompasses modern-day Iraq has repeatedly been subjected to invasion and conquest, suffering greatly as the arena in which empires fought out their regional rivalries – at times with near-genocidal viciousness. From the Sumerians to the British, through Alexander, Cyrus the Great, Genghis and Hulagu Khan, Iraq has a long and bitter history of foreign interference from which it only emerged as a fully independent state in 1958. Unsurprisingly, the people of the region have an equally long but lesser known history of uprising, rebellion, and revolution.

In the past few years it has become fashionable among Western commentators, policy influencers, and journalists to speak of Iraq as a nation "cobbled together" by the British from three Ottoman provinces at the end of World War I. This conviction has been put forward mostly in support of partitioning the country in the aftermath of the 2003 invasion but – beyond Western notions of the primacy of the nation-state – has little in the way of historical underpinnings. Leaving aside Ottoman era documentary references to the "Iraq region," etymological studies of the word "Iraq" tell a very different story. The Arabic term "the land of Iraq" (meaning *the fertile* or *deep rooted*) has been used since before the sixth century. Some studies trace the origins of the word back as far as the Sumerian period of the fourth millennium B.C. This is the land where, in their minds and in their souls, Iraqis have always lived and continue to live.

Iraqis are taught about their part in this long history throughout their grade and high-school education. That story is one of opposition and resistance to foreign rule. The story has its heroes – such as Sheikh Dhari, who killed a British army officer, Lt. Col. Gerald Leachman, in Fallujah in 1920. In present-day Iraq, Sheikh Harith al Dhari continues to follow in the footsteps of his celebrated grandfather. The story also has its traitors, among them the abu Risha clan, who were forever shamed by their collaboration with the Ottomans against their own people. One of the latter-day leaders of the clan, Abdul Sattar abu Risha, a founder of the 2007 "Anbar Awakening," publicly met with U.S. President George W. Bush and was killed within days of the meeting.

When we began the reporting for *Meeting Resistance* in August 2003, Iraq had just entered a period of chaos and upheaval. The war and its aftermath served to diminish, sour, and destroy the lives of millions of its citizens, leaving a lasting legacy of animosity and a slew of generational consequences. The invasion of the country had led to the overthrow of Iraq's president of twenty-four years, Saddam Hussein. The toppling of his regime was followed by widespread looting of the presidential palaces and almost every public building in Baghdad and other cities. With the notable exceptions of the heavily guarded oil and finance ministries, U.S. troops stood by and watched, or refused to provide protection, as the nuts and bolts of the nation's bureaucratic and cultural infrastructure – including the National Museum with its irreplaceable ancient treasures – were systematically and literally dismantled before their eyes.[1] While Iraqis were rightly shocked and disgusted at this failure to value and protect their property and heritage, some of their new American governors were pleased that they could so easily begin again: not to rebuild, but to remake Iraq.[2]

Iraqis were shaken to the core by the unfamiliar chaos that suddenly engulfed them. And they were shocked by the callousness with which their misfortune was viewed in faraway Washington when U.S. Defense Secretary Donald Rumsfeld responded to a journalist's question about the widespread looting with "Freedom is untidy" and "Stuff happens." The U.S. government had a mandatory responsibility to administer the country, but as far as most Iraqis could tell, their management style involved doing little that improved the daily realities for the Iraqi population.

With the exception of the followers of the young Shi'ite cleric Moqtada al Sadr, who mobilized social support services for the vulnerable and ensured the safety and administration of the hospitals, there was virtually no political organization in the country in those early months. Saddam Hussein had brutally suppressed any form of political structure outside the ruling Ba'ath Party, seeing it as a threat to his own power. With little experience of creating a political framework and with all they had known and depended on collapsing around them, the Iraqis were in no position to shape events. There was a major power vacuum that no Iraqi individual or entity was in a position to fill. Iraqi society was suddenly subjected to a tidal wave of unprecedented competing forces with diverse agendas and objectives. These took the form of financial, social, political, and oil interests; nongovernmental organizations (NGOs); and returning exiles. The Iraqi population lacked the tools and structures to understand or manage this influx, making it – at least temporarily – vulnerable to the will of these external forces.

On July 13 Ambassador Paul Bremer, the head of the Coalition Provisional Authority of Iraq (CPA), appointed – using strict but inappropriate ethnic and sectarian quotas – an Iraqi "Governing Council" of leaders who would put an Iraqi face on the administration of the country.[3] Bremer showed little regard for how the Iraqi people themselves would consider these appointments. Indeed,

[1] As reported in a United Press International (UPI) analysis of the incident, although the reported losses from the museum remain the subject of controversy, the allegation that U.S. troops refused to prevent the looting of the museum is not in dispute (Bloom 2003).

[2] One American charged with running the Iraqi education system told the *Washington Post* reporter Rajiv Chandrasekaran that he regarded the looting as an "opportunity to make a clean start" (Chandrasekaran 2006, 187).

[3] L. Paul Bremer replaced Jay Garner in May 2003, becoming the U.S. administrator of the Coalition Provisional Authority of Iraq, a title he retained until he departed the country on June 28, 2004.

most of the appointees were returning exiles, many of whom had not set foot in the country for decades. Because they had not experienced the hardship of those years of war and sanctions, these exiles broadly lacked legitimacy as leaders in the eyes of the Iraqi population.

One key group of exiles that particularly lacked legitimacy in the minds of many Iraqis were the Shi'ite, Supreme Council for Islamic Revolution in Iraq (SCIRI) and their militia, the Badr Corps (later to become Badr Organization).[4] SCIRI had been waiting in the wings in Iran for more than twenty years, enjoying considerable support from the Iranian revolutionary government of Ayatollah Khomeini and his successors. As a political entity that opposed Saddam Hussein's leadership in Iraq they also eventually garnered financial and political support from the U.S. government. The SCIRI leadership had sworn allegiance to the Iranian regime and its distinct system of Islamic jurisprudence – a system that contradicts the practices of the Shi'a of Iraq. Moreover, the party's military wing, the Badr Corps, which had been created and trained by Iran's Revolutionary Guard, had fought against Iraq during the Iran-Iraq war of the 1980s. In alliance with the Kurdish political parties and their Peshmerga militia – and with the blessing of the U.S. government – SCIRI and Badr would go on to dominate the Iraqi political scene largely through their standing, well-trained militias and their control of the vital interior and finance ministries. This grip on the essential levers of power would remain with SCIRI for the next five years and beyond.

These Iraqi exiles had nurtured deep relationships with the U.S. government while opposing Saddam Hussein through the 1980s and 1990s. Their efforts paid off during the 2003 invasion, as U.S. political leaders looked to Iraqis who were "known" rather than those who had remained in Iraq. The U.S. political structure viewed any Iraqi with the capacity for leadership who had remained in the country as complicit with Saddam's regime and its "Ba'athist" ideology, and hence as illegitimate. They failed to recognize any nuances in the alliances or strengths of those Iraqis who had stayed in the country. At a critical time in Iraq's history, these leaders who had remained in Iraq through its hardships knew and understood the sentiments of their people, a mastery of the Iraqi psyche that many exiles lacked.

As the exile groups consolidated their power, the everyday living conditions of ordinary Iraqis continued to deteriorate. Bremer had also – among his first acts in office – enacted policies that would dismantle the Iraqi army and purge the country's bureaucracy of members of the former Ba'ath Party of Saddam

---

4   SCIRI later changed its name to the Islamic Supreme Council of Iraq (ISCI), having decided the events of 2003 constituted their revolution.

Hussein. The ministries and public utilities were now denied the experience of people who had run them for many years. The Americans sent to replace them often had limited qualifications. With hardly any electricity and a collapsed logistics network, the country was grinding to a halt. To add to these infrastructure problems, educated secular nationalists were targeted for assassination, driving highly valued professionals out of the country in fear of their lives. The culprits were believed by many to be the Badr Corps. Regardless of who was responsible for the assassinations, the result was the same. By the end of 2003 Iraq's professional class of doctors, dentists, teachers, university professors, and pilots were all leaving in droves. This targeted and escalating, wider violence was driving out well-educated Iraqis, who were generally more secular, stripping the country of its most valuable human resources. In doing so it effectively severed the intellectual head from a nascent nationalist political body that could have unified the Iraqi population under a more secular political construct.

American troops on the street and in their bases were becoming the targets of niggling but persistent attacks. During the summer of 2003 the United States was working furiously to broaden the coalition and hence the political and military responsibility for Iraq's future. An appeal to the Indian government for seventeen thousand peacekeeping troops was rejected by the Indian parliament, who had not forgotten the country's tragic involvement in Iraq during World War I and the Iraqi uprising of 1920/21, when tens of thousands of young Indian men were killed in Iraq; the parliament refused to add to that total. In August 2003 U.S. Secretary of State Colin Powell began drafting a resolution requesting a UN-mandated – but U.S.-commanded – international peacekeeping force that would free up American combat divisions. The resolution, which had little chance of passing a Security Council vote, was thwarted by the tragic events of August 19, 2003, when a massive truck bomb exploded outside the UN headquarters, killing twenty-two people, including the UN's special representative in Iraq, Sergio Vieira de Mello (BBC 2003). Although blame for the attack ultimately settled on Al Qaeda in Iraq, there is little publicly available evidence that they were even active in the country at that time. Whoever ordered the bombing and whatever their intent, the practical consequence of the attack was that the United States was stuck with the responsibility of administering and policing an increasingly ungovernable country.

As journalists we were often as lost in this sea of dramatic change as the Iraqis themselves. As strangers to the country who did not speak the language we had only a minimal understanding of how the society was structured. Much of the accepted expertise on Iraq before the invasion – heard and read by journalists as the foundation of their reporting – turned out to be considerably wide of the mark. Many of the sources and commentators on Iraq that journalists and authors relied upon for their research were exiles with significant political and social agendas. What we really needed to know we learned and understood as we went by asking questions of all varieties of Iraqis and listening intently to their answers. For months we went to bed feeling that each day had been worse than the one before, but unable to imagine how it might be worse tomorrow. However, with every passing week, we would learn ways it could indeed become worse. Over the fourteen months we reported in Iraq we witnessed the shredding of Iraqi society, the tragedy and pain that accompany war.

Throughout this chapter we use the word "resistance" rather than "insurgency," and much careful thought has gone into that choice of terminology. An insurgency is defined by the *Merriam-Webster Dictionary* as "a condition of revolt against an existing government that is less than an organized revolution and that is not recognized as belligerency." In 2003, when we began the reporting on this project, Iraq had no legally constituted government – it had a "Governing Council" appointed by Ambassador Bremer. We believe that the term "resistance" accurately characterizes the motivational drives of the people we interviewed for the project. They were Iraqis resisting the occupation of their country by foreign troops and believed they had a right to do so in defense of their self-determination. In Karma Nabulsi's *Traditions of War*, the author clearly lays out that whether or not that right is enshrined in international law has remained a subject for debate for more than a century (Nabulsi 1999). The facts from the ground – revealed by U.S. Department of Defense quarterly reports to Congress – demonstrate the focus and force with which Iraqis were resisting occupation: as can be seen from the annotated chart on our Web site, the majority of significant attacks – 73 percent averaged between 2003 and 2008 – targeted the U.S.-led foreign forces in Iraq, not the "Governing Council" or the government elected in 2005 under occupation (*Meeting Resistance* 2008, US.GAO 2008, 12).[5] The majority of violent energy, resources, weaponry, planning, and strategy were directed at the U.S. military and its allies that occupied Iraq. It is also worth noting that no matter whether the levels of violence in Iraq went up or down between 2003 and 2008, the percentage of the attacks targeting U.S. troops remained stubbornly consistent at roughly 73 percent.

We are often asked about the civilian casualties of violence and bombings in Iraq – who was targeting civilians? It is a good and appropriate question.

---

[5] The methods used to cite attacks were changed by the United States Department of Defense in 2008, making the ongoing analysis of the information described earlier impossible.

No resistance to foreign occupation, which necessarily relies on the support and cooperation of the population, could survive if they were understood to be attacking their own people. There have been at least two concurrent wars in Iraq since 2003. The first is the one we documented, the resistance to occupation, which exhibited the majority of the violence and energy and was widely supported by the public. The second was a civil war – a fierce struggle over Iraq's political future. In addition to those two, there have been regional and international struggles that are difficult to distinguish from Iraq's internal battles.

The civil war was a struggle between two sides, the "nationalists" – those who wanted to keep Iraq's oil public and maintain a strong central government and a single Iraqi identity – and, on the other side, the "partitionists" – those who sought to privatize Iraq's oil wealth, create strong regional governments, and potentially split the country into three parts. The civil war involved inter-ethnic and intersectarian fighting as well as significant intrasect violence. Sunni and Shi'a were on both sides of the civil war – so descriptions of the conflict as the unavoidable realization of "ancient sectarian hatreds" are mis-leading.[6] On the Shi'a side, the intrasect violence played out in the very real enmities among different Shi'a factions. Theological differences within Shi'a Islam exist regarding how to determine the rightful inheritor of secular power. These political and social disagreements within Shi'a Islam were being played out in the mosques, hospitals, and political corridors and through the orga-nized violence on the streets of Iraq.

Throughout all this mayhem, polling carried out on behalf of the BBC and others consistently revealed that the Arab population of Iraq held strong nationalist convictions and were highly supportive of the nationalist agenda, including violent resistance to the occupation (BBC 2007). In this context, the most brutal strategy of the civil war was pursued by those seeking to divide Iraq by breaking the delicate family, social, and tribal bonds that held the country together. They attempted to achieve division by attacking civilians and blaming other factions of Iraqi society. While that divisive strategy ulti-mately failed, it led to the death and maiming of tens of thousands of Iraqis.

Throughout the Iraqi civil war, the United States both ideologically and militarily supported the partitionist agenda of an Iraqi political elite who had spent many years in exile, returning to seize power in 2003. Perhaps expressly in reaction to the nationalist sentiments of the Iraqi population, the United

---

[6] According to an article published by the *Washington Post*, Iraqi sociologists estimate that one-third of marriages in prewar Iraq were mixed (Raghavan 2007), while Islam Online reports a continuation of intersect marriage even at the height of the civil war (Hassan 2007).

Figure 7. "Riding Patriotic" April 2004, Baghdad, Iraq.
Photographer: Molly Bingham

In April 2004 Iraq was getting exceptionally violent and complicated. The United States had shut down Moktada Sadr's newspaper and was making incursions into Sadr City most nights and facing significant attacks. At the same time, there was a powerful U.S. response to the killing of contractors and the hanging of their bodies from a bridge in Falluja. Falluja was surrounded by U.S. soldiers, significant airpower was being used, and the city and civilian population were suffering real damage. Here, a truck loaded with medical and food relief supplies donated by both Sunni and Shia for the citizens of Falluja is loaded in front of the Abu Hanifeh Mosque in the Adhamiya district of Baghdad. The Iraqi flag is flown as a symbol of unity and sympathy for the people of Falluja.

States doggedly pursued a policy of decentralizing political power in Iraq. Ultimately, the U.S. policies in Iraq ended up supporting political parties and their militias who had long enjoyed Iranian support. The stated long-term objectives of these parties included the formation of a breakaway region made up of Iraq's nine southern provinces that would be closely aligned with Iran. As an additional irony, the other beneficiary of this U.S. policy was the Islamic State of Iraq, the Al Qaeda in Iraq umbrella group, who hoped to create a government in the center of the country modeled on the Constitution of Medina, the Prophet Muhammad's first legal document, also called a Caliphate. This aspiration to establish religious rule was even less popular with the Iraqi population than the occupying forces. By conflating all violence under the single heading of insurgency, this inaccurate description has been effectively used to confuse Americans by obfuscating the real cause of the majority of the violence: the occupation itself.

How *Meeting Resistance* Came About

From April to June of 2003 we were in Iraq working as photojournalists for various news outlets including the *New York Times*, the *Guardian*, the London *Times*, *Newsweek*, and the *Observer* of London. These assignments took us around the country on separate reporting projects. We saw many aspects of what was happening, listening to many Iraqis describe their experiences during the invasion and fall of the country as well as their thoughts on the events of the day. During those months after the fall of Baghdad on April 9, 2003, we were doing what we have done professionally for a combined thirty years – covering conflict. We were focused on telling stories, learning in order to understand better the unfolding situation, and considering how it might be told to the audiences of the Western media organizations.

As with many of the better stories in our careers, we stumbled upon the seeds of our *Meeting Resistance* project through a chance meeting. In early May 2003 Molly was on a day-long assignment in Baghdad for the London *Sunday Telegraph* photographing the last places Saddam Hussein had been seen before disappearing during the invasion of Iraq. The story took her to a tea shop and mosque in the Adhamiya district of Baghdad. While she was photographing the mosque, an Iraqi gentleman approached Molly and her translator, politely offering to show her around the mosque and its grounds. Iraqis take great pride in their hospitality, and it is considered a point of honor to welcome visitors.

After an hour-long conversation with the gentleman, Molly and her translator headed back to the hotel across town. During that ride, Molly's translator told her that the man had related something astonishing while they were chatting in Arabic after Molly had gotten in the car: he had identified himself as part of the *muqawama*, or "resistance." At that time there had only been sporadic attacks on U.S. troops in and around Baghdad. The attacks were poorly organized and described by one American commander in an Associated Press report as being "militarily insignificant" (*USA Today* 2003). A hand grenade would be lobbed into a U.S. vehicle or a few armed men would step out of a side street to fire on a passing U.S. military convoy. The idea that people were identifying themselves as being part of a movement, a "resistance," grabbed Molly's attention right away.

That man's simple statement triggered a series of questions that we discussed for hours that night. Is there a real, organized resistance? Are they remnants of Iraq's military? If so, why are their tactics during attacks – in Steve's opinion – so poor? Who is shooting at the foreign soldiers? And why? How well are they organized? What is their objective? How might they develop or change over time? What is their motivation? What are their beliefs? In short – who are they? What is it that drives human beings to pick up weapons to express themselves? What kind of result does that decision bring?

These were the kinds of questions that had engaged Molly for almost a decade. Her journalistic work in Rwanda, Burundi, Zaire, Gaza, and Afghanistan had given her experience covering conflict and rebel movements, but never the in-depth, up-close look at one movement from inception. For Steve, this was the culmination of understanding conflict through two different careers: he had covered ten wars as a journalist and had served nine years in the British Army including almost four years in Northern Ireland. His experience of insurgencies, resistance, and war was personal as well as professional.

If a resistance to occupation was indeed emerging in Iraq, we agreed that it was one of the most important stories any journalist could cover. As we would come to learn during the coming ten months of reporting, occupation and resistance are deeply entrenched components of the Iraqi identity and an integral aspect of the national narrative. The meeting with the man in the mosque had a profound impact on us and the way we were thinking. It caused us to look at the ongoing events differently, seeing the conflict through a new framework that recognized the Iraqis as active participants. We decided to poke around the edges to determine whether this one-off comment by one man was worth further investigating as a full-fledged story. In late May and early June of 2003 we spent a few afternoons sitting in the tea shops of Adhamiya, the same neighborhood where Molly had met the Iraqi man who had identified himself as part of the "resistance." We asked people about these sporadic attacks. Who did they think was responsible for them and what was their objective? Did they condone them or not? If so, why? Might they decide to become involved themselves? We learned that this violence was in the forefront of Iraqis' minds and that the notion of resistance was increasingly a topic of their conversation in a way it was not among the Westerners we spoke to or read. We decided to pursue it as a story.

Outside Looking In

We also began noting the language used by the U.S. military and political leaders (and repeated in the Western press) to describe the people responsible for attacking U.S. troops in Iraq: "Saddam loyalists," "dead-enders," "Ba'athist die-hards," "common criminals," "foreign fighters," "religious extremists," and later, "Al Qaeda." We did not know whether those descriptions were accurate or not. However, it was clear that they originated from U.S. military, diplomatic, and political individuals, not the fighters – Iraqi or foreign – themselves. Journalistically, it was critical to seek out primary sources, namely, the fighters who were actually involved. Talking directly to them would reveal who they were and what motivated them. We believed that our findings would be a cornerstone of a broader story of Iraq that was unfolding.

However, because we had each worked almost three months of extremely long days in searing temperatures, under very trying physical and emotional conditions, we were both exhausted and needed to take a break.[7] Molly had not really rested after being through a harrowing experience when she was accused of being a spy and thrown in prison by Saddam's security services during the invasion of Iraq.[8] And Steve had been working in Afghanistan for fifteen months straight before going to Iraq. It made no sense to start a challenging project when we were already so worn down. We left Iraq for six weeks to rest, reorganize, and regroup, planning to return refreshed in early August to begin working on this resistance story.

Although this was a story that we felt would benefit from our working together as a team, we recognized that for both of us to work on this project as photojournalists made no sense. First of all, it was not a visually led story – meaning it was not something you could tell as a picture story alone. Second, if we both shot it as photojournalists, we would be competing against each other for publication, and that would not support us working as a team. It would also require a writer to do reporting at some point, and that would make us dependent on a third team member to catch up or discover what we had already learned. We

---

7   For example, Molly worked for almost a month on daily assignments for the *New York Times* during May 2003, and those assignments required her to be at the *Times* office for an 8:00 a.m. briefing. She would rarely get her "goodnight" – the indication that the picture desk in New York had received all of her pictures and their questions were satisfied – until 2:00 a.m. A few hours' sleep and get up and do it again.
8   Molly was arrested by Saddam's feared "Mukhabarat" intelligence services in the early hours of March 25, 2003, and taken to Abu Ghraib with four other Westerners. They were all accused of spying, interrogated, and held in solitary confinement. To their (and their families') relief they were released (and deported) unharmed to Amman, Jordan, on April 2, 2003. Molly returned to Iraq less than three weeks later.

had both wanted to branch out journalistically – to develop professionally – and so we agreed we would each be responsible for different media iterations of the reporting. While we coreported the story, Molly photographed and took the notes necessary to write it for a print version while Steve worked in video, generating all of the footage required to build what later became a film. Owning the iteration in print or film gave each of us the capacity to control the editorial perspective in the telling of what we learned.

Rolling with the Punches – Being Flexible in Approach and Planning

We initially envisioned this project as a six-week reporting trip: three weeks moving around the country, finding and interviewing people involved on the Iraqi side, and then three weeks embedded with U.S. soldiers hearing their perspectives on who was attacking them and why. That would have book-ended project nicely, but it did not work out that way.

Once we were back in Baghdad in August 2003, our first step was to talk with the translator Molly had been working with and see whether she was willing to work with us on this project. From here on we will refer to our translator – or "fixer" – as "Amina," which is not her real name. Molly had been working with her for nearly three months before leaving in June, and they had a good working relationship. But this project was something different and required us all to think carefully about how we would proceed. Over several long conversations with Amina, Molly laid out our professional and personal histories. Most importantly Molly reassured Amina that we were not spies, that we were genuinely interested in what we would find, and that we did not have a preconceived idea of what kind of story we would tell. Amina's experiences working with Molly – witnessing Molly's reactions to events and people – combined with our conversations led Amina to agree to work with us on the project.

These intense conversations were an early indication of just how serious a situation we were walking into. As the Iraqi on our team, Amina was naturally the one our subjects would question to establish our bona fides. She would need to vouch for us, and be comfortable in doing so, as we went forward. We were trusting that she could fairly and honestly represent us – and be intelligent about what she said when we were not part of the conversation. On her end, she was trusting that we would not act in a way that would put her in additional danger or break any commitments we made in the process. We were relying on each other and each of us was literally being asked to trust the others with our lives.

We understood that this was a serious and dangerous project when we began, but over time we realized that those early conversations with Amina, as well as the trust and mutual respect among us, were essential to the success of the project. We were in fact a team. Each of us contributed a different and complementary skill set and that balance moved us forward. Inevitably, at some point during our initial encounters with the individuals who would become our sources, each person would turn to Amina and an untranslated Arabic conversation would ensue. As she would tell us later, the exchange always revolved around her integrity, our integrity, and whether she would "vouch" for us as being journalists, truly interested in understanding what we had described. Our relationship with Amina and her conviction in talking *about* us with our subjects were key components of how and why the project worked. Amina agreed to work on the project with one caveat. She would work with us to find individuals who would go on camera and be interviewed, but she would not conduct the interviews. She felt that it was too dangerous to be that deeply involved and we agreed with her assessment. With Amina onboard, we headed across town to Adhamiya in the hope that we could find the man Molly had met at the mosque in May. We were lucky and by chance found him there. After a lengthy conversation where Amina explained to him what we wanted to do – vouching for our journalistic and personal integrity – he agreed to be interviewed on camera.

Our first few weeks of reporting set us on a steep learning curve that also required us to rethink our original game plan. We went every day to the tea shops of Adhamiya, sitting and chatting with anyone who would strike up a conversation or play backgammon. Eventually we turned the conversation to the subject of resistance. After several interviews with the man Molly had met at the mosque – whom we now called "The Teacher" – we encountered another man in the same neighborhood, who also agreed to be interviewed. What began to emerge through these first encounters was a picture of a nascent, but still fragmentary movement. We learned that individuals were organized into small cells with some cells connected to each other, but there was no central command or control mechanism. Even in their disparate cells, they were more highly organized – and covert – than we had suspected that they would be when we had initially conceived of how to cover the story. And within weeks of beginning the project one point was abundantly clear: the resistance was rapidly growing, adapting, and evolving.

Because of what we learned in our initial interviews, very little of our original plan survived contact with reality. We swiftly recognized that because of their covert cell structure our idea of traveling around the country to interview fighters was not feasible. We simply would not be able to find, gain access, and trust and conduct multiple interviews with individuals in multiple locations. Simultaneously we began to recognize that as far as the resistance was concerned, Adhamiya was a hub of activity. Through our conversations we came to understand that because of the family and tribal ties of each individual, the cells and small groups in Adhamiya had ties with other cells in different parts of Baghdad and the provinces. These connections provided them the contacts to develop networks of groups and to share resources, expertise, and occasionally manpower among them. Because of these vibrant social connections running through Iraqi society, what we were discovering in Adhamiya was a good indicator of what was happening in the broader context. We had managed to find two sources quickly in Adhamiya, and we revamped our plan to focus on that single area as a way to study the phenomena of the nascent resistance movement.

There was another aspect of the plan we had to change. We abandoned the idea of embedding with U.S. troops. Those first few interviews taught us that the Iraqi groups had already set up a sophisticated network of spotters reporting the comings and goings at the U.S. bases. For us to be seen entering or leaving a base – or for us even to engage in conversation with the U.S. military on the street in Adhamiya – would raise questions about our identity and motives. Were we truly journalists? Or were we spies? If we were perceived to be spies, at best our access would end. At worst we – Amina, our Iraqi driver, Steve, and Molly – could all be killed by our own sources. One other reason we were comfortable dropping the idea of embedding with the U.S. troops was that dozens of news crews and independent filmmakers were covering that angle of the story. We trusted that the American experience in Baghdad would be well told by those teams of journalists. In addition, we noticed that there did not seem to be any other Western media focusing on the resistance. We expected stories to pop up any day in the press quoting Iraqis involved in attacks as sources, but nothing of any substance appeared. There were a handful of articles about small groups of young men revealing information about attacking American forces, but the stories did not extend beyond the superficial. There was no serious attempt to explore and understand the other side. We understood that our access was unique. So we decided to keep working on it until it seemed that we hit a natural stopping point.

PART II: GOING ABOUT IT – ACCESS AND METHODOLOGY

As is common in many countries in extreme crisis, crossing Iraq's border was remarkably easy from the day Baghdad fell through when we left in June of 2004. There was no visa process because there were no government to speak of and hardly any border control during most of our work. Getting into Iraq physically was the easiest part of the story. Getting access to those we wanted to talk to was more of a challenge. We began this project in August 2003 when the resistance was just getting started. Our early relationship building gave us a foot in the door during an intense period of evolving and shifting allegiances within the Iraqi social structures. As the months passed it became difficult to maintain contact with those we had met early on and almost impossible to establish new contacts that were willing to be interviewed on camera.

Getting early access is common to successful reporting in many conflicts, and our August 2003 start had an enormous impact on the success of our project. First, we benefited from the resistance's lack of structure and development beyond the cellular level. Individuals were able to make decisions for themselves. Generally, emerging organizations or movements are often flattered to be reported on, and it is useful to have developed these relationships before "press relations" become a factor as the groups evolve. However, that window of time between a movement's origin and when it develops a sense of the need to convey a "message" is shrinking as the world is increasingly digitally connected and hence aware of other "messaging" efforts. They are savvier about public relations and more quickly recognize the importance of managing their image. Hence today, militant groups or governments will move quickly to control access and the flow of information. For journalists, this means more bureaucratic hoops to jump through that can hinder your access and slow you down.

Access: Letting Our Sources Find Us

There is a lot to be said for patience and perseverance, even stubbornness, when evaluating the success of this project. A daily presence and the ability to invest lots of time can be critical. We went almost every day to Adhamiya and spent an enormous amount of time in tea shops listening, over and over, to people telling the same story of the battle of Adhamiya, about the hardship of sanctions, and of their frustration with the occupation.[9] It is the habit for most Iraqi men to stop into their local tea shop after prayer or at the end of the day to catch up on the news. At first we felt we were wasting our time. But gradually we realized that this was the only way we would be able to find subjects for our reporting. It allowed them *to approach us* on their terms and in their environment. Often, just as we were getting up to leave, someone would approach Amina asking her about us, who we were and why we were in the neighborhood so often.[10]

---

[9] Adhamiya was one of the few neighborhoods in Baghdad that violently resisted the entrance of American forces.

[10] While women do not typically frequent the tea shops, Amina was recognized by the men there as working with us and facilitating our research and was as such welcomed by both customers and proprietors.

This is where Amina's work was particularly critical. She would engage in polite conversation with the person, exploring in a culturally acceptable way whether or not he might be involved in the resistance. We hung back, allowing her to have these conversations off to the side. If it seemed he was directly involved in the resistance, Amina would explain what we were doing, vouch for our credibility, and ask whether that person might be willing to be interviewed on camera. At that point many people demurred. We talked to more than forty people over the course of the reporting; most refused to be formally interviewed on camera. These conversations were still useful, however, as they broadened our knowledge of the overall situation. This knowledge – combined with our formal on-camera interviews and publicly available information – informed and shaped the questions we posed to those who did agree to on camera interviews. The time-consuming trudges across town and the days spent sitting in tea shops playing backgammon, drinking tea, and chatting sometimes seemed endless. However, the moment the effort delivered another subject we were thrilled and felt that it was well worth the time. We also did our best to keep appointments, not to be late, and never to surprise our sources by including another individual.

We should underscore that Amina was not sent out to find people, whom we then interviewed. It would have been too dangerous for her if she seemed to be "fishing" for resistance members. It would have subjected her to suspicions of being a U.S. military or Iraqi government informant. As much as we trusted her honesty, it also would have left us – and the project – vulnerable to questions about the veracity of the information we were collecting and how we had really found the subjects of our reporting. There are stories that abound of fixers who wish to please their employers, or who merely cut corners for the sake of saving time, and if they cannot or do not want to find the real thing find a cousin or friend to pose as what the journalist wants. Obviously, we wanted to take every step we could to minimize any chance of this kind of challenge to the credibility of our reporting. In the end cutting corners like these can at best be an abdication of journalistic responsibility and at worse turn into real security problems. Time is precious, indeed. But it is also a quality investment in any reporting project. Short cuts are usually exactly that and only serve to diminish the overall quality and integrity of the project.

It is only in retrospect that we have recognized how important this passive process of finding sources was for our relationships with them. The individuals who agreed to be interviewed on camera were empowered in the relationship because they had approached us, not vice versa. As a result, they did not feel that they had been singled out by us or pressured into doing something. It was less likely for them to find an easy way to blame us should something go wrong and seems to have improved our security prospects in the process. We also had a few false starts. There were several people who initially agreed but stepped back when the time came to be interviewed. One man declined because he realized that his voice would be recognized by enough people to make him too vulnerable. Another individual, whom we called "The Soldier," began asking for money after we had completed three interviews with him. He insisted even after we explained that we could not pay him for his time or his information.[11] We did not pursue interviewing him further and removed everything we had learned from him from our cross-referenced information matrix.[12]

Methodology: Interview Process, Technique, and Strategy

There are some general interview techniques that can be helpful to remember that revolve around natural human social skills and how to use them. It is worth considering what questions should never be asked of a source, even though it may be useful to know the answer. It is also important to consider when it is to your benefit to be silent. Uncomfortable pauses in conversation are gaps that we as human beings often rush to fill. An interviewer can constructively use an uncomfortable pause because often the source will fill that space with more information.

We have found that it is not necessary to prove your knowledge to your source; in fact, treating your source as someone who is teaching you about the topic can be useful. Often, simpler, clearer explanations will be delivered if you seem to know very little about the topic. However, if there is a shared experience in some aspect of the topic, an interview can become more of a conversation between peers, which may be useful, depending upon the ultimate objectives. The weakness of this approach is that a lot can be left unsaid, as the speaker will presume that the other (and hence the audience who will ultimately be reading or listening) knows what he means. If taking this "peer" approach, it is smart to introduce questions at reasonable points in the conversation that will bring out meaning and provide clarity for an audience that may not have much knowledge on the subject.

Over our ten months we conducted multiple on-camera interviews with twelve individuals. Because of the way we found our sources, we were able to have less formal conversations with several dozen more. Understanding

---

[11] Later in the chapter, in the "Ethics" section, we will address ethical issues including the idea of paying sources for information.
[12] We describe our matrix later in the section subtitled "Cross-Referencing."

how each individual was unique and what all shared in common was a key aspect of understanding their individual roles within a larger framework and the movement itself. "The Syrian," in his early twenties, was probably the youngest while "The Traveler," who was in his mid-fifties, was the oldest. We formally interviewed one woman, "The Wife," who talked about the role that she played in the resistance. "The Syrian," the one foreigner we interviewed, described his choice to fight against the occupation of Iraq. Some sources had families; some had jobs. Socially speaking, all of them were working- or middle-class, though some had had significant education or training.

Expressing a real interest in your sources as individuals, developing a full understanding of their personal history and narrative, fleshing out what really motivates them and why build a strong base for further conversation. They can also create the context that is critical to understanding your specific topic. These first hours of conversation can determine the tone of the ongoing relationship. We explained to those we met, and Amina reinforced, that we were journalists seeking to understand the attacks on U.S. and foreign troops in Iraq that were occurring. We were only interested in interviewing people who were actively involved in that violence. Once we had established that a source was willing to go on camera we would set an appointment for an interview.

We spent hours during the first interview asking the sources about their lives – intentionally avoiding any direct questions about involvement in the resistance until the end of the conversation, or even the next meeting. Those initial interviews often lasted four hours as we asked questions about their parents, education, military service (mandatory for all Iraqis under Saddam), and, if they had evaded service, how they had done so. We asked about their families, their marriages, their work, their friends, and what inspired them to be who they are. Who had influenced them in their lives? What role did religion play in their family when they were growing up? Had they ever traveled outside Iraq? We sought to develop a comprehensive picture of each individual's social, political, religious, and educational background.

We genuinely wanted to understand the answers to these questions. But this discretion served another purpose that we only realized once we were deep into the reporting. By investing so much time in understanding them as individuals they felt "known" and grasped that we really were interested in them as real people, not cartoon characters of a movement we had already decided how we were going to describe. It was clear to them that we were learning, and that we were open to understanding. That time invested had its rewards in the confidence it engendered in the relationship – to the extent that confidence was possible at all – and reassured them that we were in fact journalists, not spies. Ultimately, it played an important, but unquantifiable, role in our security, an issue we explore later in more detail.

When the opportunity arose to meet them again – as it did for most of the subjects – we could begin to ask more current questions: Where were they during the invasion of Iraq in 2003? When had they begun to get involved in the resistance? How had they understood it to evolve? And then later we would move to more specific questions: What was their skill? What did they contribute to their group? What kinds of people were in the group with them? How did their group come together? Who played supportive roles? Did they feel that they had public support, and how were they aware of it? And, most importantly, what motivated each of them to take up (or provide support to those who took up) arms?

Because of our lengthy conversations about their past, during these later interviews we felt more confident in pressing for an answer on a topic we thought was important and we did not shy away from asking our sources hard questions. But, of course, there are good ways and less than constructive ways to ask challenging questions. We tried to work the hardest questions into the thread of a conversation, so they sounded more a part of the flow of conversation and less clearly like fishing for specific information. Sometimes we got such cagey or inscrutable, evasive answers, that we would continue to push on that issue until we felt we had something we could understand and use – or that it was truly dangerous to keep asking. We often pushed for a clearer answer by explaining we needed it "for the film." We followed the same line of questioning for each source because we sought to understand whether there were similarities among them or whether each one's path to and motivation for joining the resistance was unique. For security reasons we did not ask them direct questions about their groups, but our sources often revealed operational details that were useful to our understanding of their cell, individual power, or status within the resistance movement as it developed.

As expected, our sources insisted that we conceal their identity on camera and we complied. They were particularly concerned with their faces being shown, and Steve developed an in-camera technique that would allow the shape and movement of the figure to be seen without revealing anything identifiable about them. They always checked that Steve had kept his word. All sources, in their own way, expressed that they held us responsible for their security. This played a significant role in how we conducted the interviews and security decisions we made about how to conduct the project. We were surprised that most of our sources insisted that we choose the interview location. This was a real challenge for us. We did not want to use the same location too many times or with different individuals, lest we draw attention to ourselves. We spent significant time considering the best kinds of environment and scouting locations that met those criteria.

We finished our reporting at the end of May 2004. We worked solely on this story for ten months. It can be difficult to know when to stop, when you have enough information. There were weeks, sometimes even a month when we made little progress and became very frustrated. But there were times when things moved quickly, and our interviews, events, and the story were coming together as a coherent narrative even as the situation continued to evolve. We believed our efforts had given us a clear understanding of the first year after the invasion from the perspective of the Iraqis who were involved in the violence. But our decision to stop was also motivated by the effects of the increasingly fluid and dangerous conditions on the ground. The reality was that our sources were fading away. Some had literally disappeared; we didn't know whether they had been arrested, had been killed, or simply didn't want to talk with us anymore. Some were more direct and explained that, given the circumstances, they could no longer meet with us. Because of the security situation we believed it impossible to cultivate new sources, so we called the project to a halt.

After spending nearly every day for ten months in Adhamiya's tea shops, conducting forty hours of interviews, cross-referencing that information with other things we heard, learned, or witnessed and other data in the public domain (media, reports, NGO reports, etc.), our overall findings are almost disturbingly simple. Behind the attacks on U.S. and Coalition Forces, we found a nationalist movement, indigenous to the country, that enjoys strong public support for their effort to expel the foreign troops from their soil – or at least make it very costly for them to remain.

Our reporting was published as the story "Ordinary Warriors" in *Vanity Fair* (Bingham 2004). The footage became *Meeting Resistance*, a feature-length documentary film (*Meeting Resistance* 2007). The film also revealed to what extent resistance is part of the Iraqi identity and history. While the Western press and military spokespeople blamed external influences, we had been learning about an Iraqi-grown resistance movement. It was not until we released the film and traveled to showings that we articulated our findings: throughout history and around the world there have been occupations and resistance to those occupations. *Meeting Resistance* is an updated study of the human condition under occupation.

Methodology: Reflecting on Blind Spots and Prejudices

Two major aspects of our approach to the reporting were critical to both successfully carrying it out and surviving. The first aspect was to know ourselves and be clear about how others would see us. The reality was that we are British and American nationals – the two countries with the largest number of troops involved in the Iraqi invasion – seeking to speak to individuals attacking soldiers belonging to those nations' armies. To the casual inquirer on the street Amina often described Molly as French (a language she can speak passably). But once we sat down to do our first interview with a source, Molly initiated a conversation about the fact that she was American, explaining that she wanted to be sure there was no confusion on the issue. We were asking these individuals to reveal volumes of data about themselves to us that would ultimately make them vulnerable. Demonstrating our own honesty and integrity with them up front was a critical aspect of our relationships.

Part of knowing ourselves was recognizing that our perspectives, opinions, and sensibilities have been developed through our individual experiences and cultures. We were careful to remind ourselves regularly that we were visitors in their community. Just like ours, the Iraqis' perspectives and beliefs had been shaped by their individual experiences and culture. Their perspectives were just as valuable and valid to them as ours were to us. We approached the story and the individuals we met every day with the attitude and recognition that we were there to listen with open ears and open minds. Our honesty with our sources and our clear openness to their experiences built the limited relationships that allowed us to interact with them during our interviews. Another aspect of this approach was taking the time to reflect on and discuss our preconceived notions, our prejudices, and the blind spots that they created. We were willing to acknowledge that as we learned about the players through the multiple interviews, our image of them would change and could become flawed or inaccurate. Our willingness and ability to talk with each other openly about our perspectives and assumptions allowed us to more readily identify things we might not see or consider.

For example, Amina came to Molly twice during the fall of 2003 and talked to her about the high level of chatter on the streets about Iraqis being tortured at Abu Ghraib. The second time, talking with Molly as a friend, an American, Amina asked her, "Do you really think Americans would do such things?" Molly answered that she did not. When the photographs and story of Abu Ghraib broke in the press, Molly apologized to Amina. Molly also realized that her entire concept of what America would and would not do, what America was and was not, needed to be reevaluated. The fact that she could not imagine that Americans might torture Iraqis was a blind spot, something she had not considered possible because of her belief in her country and its purported values.

Another example was our surprise at how much the Iraqis knew about the outside world, including American and British history. In our first interview, "The Teacher" referenced the methodology of the IRA and Hamas when discussing how his group had organized their cell structures. This was a man who had little reason to have encountered this kind of information in his daily life, but clearly people in his small group had understood the important security benefits of adopting these methods. Iraq had mandatory military service and had experienced hundreds of years of foreign influence; Iraqis understand the outside world much better than the outside world likely understands them. We should not have been so surprised to hear him fluidly discussing topics like the security value of an IRA cell structure. Working in a team made this discussion an ongoing process. The two of us had different responses to what we saw, heard, and learned. Recognizing these differences forced us continually to debrief our thought process, assumptions, and blind spots, building what we believe was an ultimately much sounder reporting process.

We had significant experience working around the world – from Central Africa to the former Yugoslavia, Russia, Chechnya, Israel, Gaza, and Afghanistan – but we had comparatively limited knowledge of Iraq prior to 2003. The assumption of many Western journalists was that Iraqis were secular, as the state was often described as the most secular in the Middle East. What we found was a more nuanced situation: whether an individual had secular inclinations or not, Islam meaningfully underpinned Iraq's social structure.

Methodology: Compartmentalization

In order to keep our relationship with each individual as clear of influence from others as possible we decided to keep the individuals we interviewed compartmentalized from each other. We never mentioned or described the other people we were talking to – although we used what we had learned from each to inform our questions. We also did not ask an individual to introduce us to his "cell" or "group" as we figured that would only produce a group conversation about what should be said. By speaking to them in an isolated context we believed we would get a more genuine, natural response from our sources. As far as we knew, only two of our interviewees were actually connected to each other. But one day we were filming b-roll (the supporting, cutaway images in any film project) on a street in Adhamiya and saw one of our interviewees seemingly giving orders to another. They both saw us but neither acknowledged us and we did not acknowledge them.

Another source, "The Lieutenant," once saw us in a car in Adhamiya with "The Soldier," the individual we had to cut from the research because he was asking for money. He asked us why we were talking with "The Soldier" and told us that his group had "The Soldier" under surveillance because they suspected that he was working for the Americans as an informant. In this small neighborhood in which most people knew each other on sight if not personally, as the players got to know one another it was not always in a spirit of friendship and cooperation.

Over time we were able to build a narrative database of information, triangulating our accumulated data about group size, motivation, personal backgrounds, funding, weapons sources, tactics, and attacks. We collected all of the information that we could – from our own interviews and conversations, violent incidents, and media reports – in the effort to deepen our insight into an opaque situation. The foundation of our understanding was built from multiple sources. Every piece of information in the film was confirmed by at least one other source, usually two, with the exception of personal details about those we interviewed, which we were not able to verify independently.

For example, "The Teacher" identified himself as a weapons procurer for what he described as a small Islamist group. In one of our first interviews with him he told us he had been ordered to find Strela antiaircraft missiles. More than a month later we heard from "The Lieutenant" that his group had recently received some Strelas and was beginning to work out strategies for using them. Two months after that "The Warrior" told us that his group had used them to good effect. Interestingly he was not boasting about shooting down helicopters. Once the Americans understood that his fighters had Strelas, the helicopters stayed out of the way until it was time to collect the American wounded after the fighting was over. Hence it helped his group fight on the ground against American troops without having to worry about an air assault as well.

The other component that was important in this process was interviewing the same sources repeatedly. As the resistance evolved and the social, political, and security environment in Iraq changed over the first year, we were able to understand how these individuals' perspectives were changing. We could also see how the groups and their capacities were developing in response to these rapid societal and political shifts. A one-off interview could give us some information, but only repeated encounters could allow for a meaningful grasp of the kind of rapid, organic transformation occurring in Iraq's resistance movement during 2003 and 2004.

This information and our tapes were secured in the only ways we could. Most of the "triangulation" was being done in our heads until it became too complicated and we had to write it down, creating a matrix of the groups, individuals, and what we had learned from each and which information was double or triple sourced. When it came to editing the film we created a simple, searchable database from the transcripts. We did not seek further outside confirmation of our data because confirmation from multiple sources was built into our process. While we were filming, tapes were sporadically sent out and remained in a box outside the country.

METHODOLOGY: CREDIBILITY

We cannot overemphasize the pivotal role played by Amina in our initial encounters with those who were sources for the project. As a well-educated Iraqi, and one who is well versed in the Quran, she commanded respect from others.[13] Her endorsement of us as journalists and willingness to attest to the fact that we were not spies were crucial to the project. Though Amina is Sunni, her profound knowledge of her faith and her society gave her powerful and persuasive social skills with other Iraqis, Sunni or Shi'a. She understood how important it was not to push our sources for what we needed, but to allow them to think that they had had an idea or made a suggestion themselves. In a community that had become highly suspicious and where allegiances and alliances were frequently shifting, we are certain that her testimony played a crucial role in why we survived the project. She also helped us to navigate the cultural nuances of approaching and engaging the people we were to meet, even advising on what questions to ask and how to phrase them.

Many Westerners ask what it was like to work with an Iraqi woman as our translator, what it was like for Molly working as a woman in Iraq, and whether having a gender mix on our team impacted our work. The answers are that certainly the gender dynamic impacts any reporting project to a certain extent. But it is almost impossible to know exactly how – or whether – the project would have been different with a different combination of genders. While Amina was critical to our team, in our mind her contribution had little to do with her gender. We relied on her sense of honor, dignity, and knowledge and skillful social navigation of her own culture. Molly often conducted the interviews since Steve was busy managing the camera work – ensuring that the sources' faces remained out of focus during a long interview. Molly was

[13] It is interesting to note that many middle-class Iraqi women like Amina were encouraged to attend school and establish professional lives under the socialist ideology of Saddam Hussein's Ba'ath Party. The mothers of many of her peers were illiterate – a tremendous social shift in a single generation.

treated with respect and granted every intellectual and social courtesy that Steve was. We found the Western perception that Iraqi men have antiquated attitudes regarding women to be more myth than reality – at least as demonstrated by the social behavior of those we interacted with most.

Although we were only able to interview one woman active in the resistance on camera, "The Wife," we talked to roughly a dozen women more generally about women's role in the resistance. It was clear that the men are only able to fight because the women are there, taking care of the rest of life's concerns. "The Imam" who appears in the film talked about the broader meaning of jihad as a struggle, or an exertion of effort. He pointed out that no matter what form an individual's effort takes, he or she can be said to be participating in the larger jihad. For example, if a young boy carries messages for a cell of fighters, he is participating. If a doctor helps treat injured fighters, she is participating. A wealthy businessman who donates money to a fighting group is considered to be participating. If a woman provides a meal for her sons and husband who are fighting, she is participating in the struggle. Or if she carries weapons under her *abaya*, as "The Wife" describes doing in the film, she too is participating. So, the entire notion of "fighting" in Iraq is a broad one, meaning that effort is being exerted, and as long as you are exerting effort in an appropriate way for who you are and what you are good at, then you are equally recognized as a critical component of the jihad. You are recognized by the community and, according to "The Imam," by God, as being on jihad, and hence, rewarded with heaven upon your death. While men were indeed participating in most of the literal combat, they recognized and respected the contribution made in many ways by all members of society. The whole society is involved in small ways, and the fighters are not separate from the community – they are of it.

Finally, women played a role in influencing the men to fight. Iraqi culture values honor and, by extension, often upholds the moral code by the use of shame. Women were an important and enthusiastic part of that mechanism, provoking and inciting the men into preserving the reputation of the family, tribe, and nation by joining the fight. The men, in turn, would feel it necessary to rise to the occasion. In one interview "The Warrior" described going out to an operation in Diyalah province north of Baghdad. As the men left the village they had used as a base the village's women ululated, scattering water on the ground behind the men who went to fight.[14]

---

[14] Although ululation is often regarded as a sign of grief, it is also used by women as a celebratory expression. In Iraqi tradition – a desert culture – the scattering of water is a way of expressing the preciousness to you of the departing individuals.

Once we had come to understand the Iraqi social interpretation of jihad, the U.S. military concept that fighters or "bad guys" could be isolated from the community no longer made sense. We found that the U.S. military and political leaders' descriptions of these fighters as fringe elements of Iraqi society ("criminals," "dead-enders," "Ba'athist die-hards," "religious extremists") or outsiders holding the Iraqis hostage ("foreign fighters" or "Al Qaeda") erroneously conveyed a message to the U.S. public and others that these were marginal elements who could and should be isolated from the broader society. It also implied that those attacking Coalition Forces did not enjoy the support of the Iraqi public. This linguistic strategy was used to justify the "elimination" of these violent elements by any means. The U.S. military talked about "Clear, Hold and Build." When fighting against the people of a community the only way to "clear" that space is by moving or killing the population. What is left is a depopulated area that can be "held." As the population returns to their homes there is an effort to "build." Since the Iraqi fighters and community are fundamentally one and the same, unless something about the occupying force has significantly changed, this strategy would regularly deliver the U.S. forces back to square one with elements of the population attacking them.

Methodology: Processing Interviews and Working in a Foreign Language

As we mentioned earlier, Amina did not conduct interviews with us, but she and Molly closely translated and transcribed every minute of tape together. The resulting transcripts could then be analyzed for information and new ideas. Iraq was clearly a society undergoing significant change and the resistance was rapidly developing. Having Amina's participation in interpreting and understanding what we were learning from our sources was of great importance, as was transcribing the tapes as quickly as possible.

Transcribing our interviews quickly was critical for two reasons. First, we found many differences between what we had understood had been said during an interview – usually paraphrased by a translator brought along by our source – and what Amina told us was actually said on tape.[15] Second, what we thought we heard or understood people to be saying was often different from what they actually said or meant upon closer scrutiny with the luxury of replaying and listening multiple times. Of course, any notes taken at the

---

[15] As we explained earlier in "Rolling with the Punches – Being Flexible in Approach and Planning," Amina did not conduct the interviews with us because we agreed it was too dangerous to do so. Our sources were asked to bring someone they trusted to act as a translator.

time of the interview would be equally flawed. Both of these realities are important hurdles to overcome –while we were still in the field, not when we were back in our office and realized that we did not have on tape what we thought we had.

The details and nuance in the recordings helped us carefully plan our questions for further interviews with that individual and for our other sources. There were consequences when, because of time constraints, we were not able to translate a whole interview between conversations. Building time into our schedule to ensure we went to each interview fully informed would have saved us a great deal in both time and exposure to the further risk of needing another interview to cover issues we should have been able to address in the last one. Before we conducted each interview we discussed what we were trying to understand, what gaps in our knowledge we needed to fill, and how to sequence a series of questions to get what we needed. As Steve was filming, Molly generally ran the interviews. However, during breaks Steve would often be able to point out pieces that had been overlooked or had not come across clearly. The differentiation in roles allowed Steve to raise a slightly separate issue in a seemingly innocuous way, often netting us important and interesting responses. For us, it was a reassuring way to work.

Working in translation presents many challenges. In addition to issues of comprehension, the interpretive process doubles interview time and definitely increases the cost and length of any significant project. That said, working with a very good interpreter has benefits. Knowing we would be retranslating our on-camera interviews later with Amina gave us the freedom to worry less about exactly what was said and focus more on observing and interacting with our sources. Though Molly clearly did not understand everything that was being said (she picked up a smattering of Arabic during our work) she would look at and encourage the speaker, making eye contact and reacting as he spoke. This came naturally to her, but if she had been working in English she likely would have had her head down taking notes. In this case, she only had to take notes when the interpreter spoke; that gave her the opportunity to establish direct contact with the subject. In addition, the interpretive process required between each question and answer slows the process, allowing both the interviewers and interviewee time to reflect on what is asked and what has been said in a way that can be advantageous, and even a bit relaxing.

Methodology: Teams

We have already discussed some of the advantages to working in teams, and this project was likely successful because we worked as a small team. Having just three people, we were always able to check our instincts about a person or situation. On this particular project it would have been impossible to try to work with a larger crew. To have a reporter, producer, cinematographer, sound engineer, and translator in one interview on a story with so many delicate security and secrecy requirements would not be feasible. Additionally, having Amina as a true member of the team meant that she was always raising issues and reactions to people and events from a different perspective that we often had not considered. Steve and Molly's social and experiential skill sets complemented each other well when navigating frustrating times in the project, analyzing data and managing the relationships with the sources. There are always times in a long project when you get fed up, annoyed, or just tired and overwhelmed. Being part of a team meant that we always had support available when it was needed.

Because of our varied professional experiences covering different kinds of conflicts in different parts of the world and cultures, we were constantly discussing how this project compared to our previous experiences. We have very different personal styles that, while not specifically gender based, helped us as a team during interviews. Molly has a more openly curious, empathetic nature, but she also has a real interest in ensuring she understands the details. In one conversation with "The Traveler" Molly could not grasp his explanation – even after several attempts – and "The Traveler" was becoming annoyed. Steve interjected a humorous comment that defused the situation through laughter. Working alone, that kind of intervention is less likely. Steve relates to individuals on a more intellectualized plane, and that connection with some sources was rewarding as Steve could engage them in conversation in a different way about their experiences. Ultimately, our very different but complementary emotional intelligences and social skills were a tremendous advantage during the project.

Working in a team ensured that through conversation we discovered each other's blind spots. Since we did not discuss the project openly with anyone else it was vital that we were able to have lengthy discussions about how we had understood something or which direction we should go in next. We were pretty sure that our hotel room could be tapped. This was not just paranoia – the hotel had been the home of UN weapons inspectors before the war, and the former regime must surely have wired the place for intelligence collection. We would go for long walks and discuss the most sensitive aspects of the story during that time. Finally, we would be remiss if we did not mention the importance of a reliable, responsible, and trustworthy driver. Our driver, "Mohammed," had an excellent knowledge of Baghdad, a sense for when and where trouble was brewing, and unflappableness when events turned hairy.

It also turned out he had professional driving experience – a real plus in a conflict zone, where an unskilled driver can be a huge liability.

For example, the night that the capture of Saddam Hussein was announced, we attended a rowdy antioccupation demonstration in Adhamiya. There was a great deal of anger and even more gunfire as young, Kalashnikov-toting youths vented with their trigger fingers. The same incident was described by an embedded *Time* magazine journalist in the nearby U.S. base as "celebratory gunfire"– proof, if it was needed, of the limitations of embedded journalism (Ratnesar et al. 2003). We walked with the demonstration for a couple of miles but when it was time to leave – before the interior ministry police arrived – "Mohammed" was right there with the car, ready to drive us out. On our way home that night – and on some other evenings as well – we could hear gunfire as we approached an intersection. "Mohammed" always drove with his window cracked and never played music so he could hear the street around him, a sign of his professionalism. That night he slowed short of the intersection and listened, establishing the distance and direction of the gunfire, before moving quickly across. An untrained driver would not have known what to do. We were both impressed and comfortable with him at the wheel.

PART III: GOING ABOUT IT – SECURITY AND ETHICS

There is something ironic about going to a war and becoming overly concerned with security. It may seem obvious to say so, but a war is a very dangerous place to be. Risk can be mitigated but it cannot be eliminated. That is not to say it should be taken lightly, but these are concerns that should be thought through as fully as possible before the decision is made to go to an area where there is active conflict. It is easy to adopt the self-delusion that the war is happening to others and that it will not impact me. But going to the war removes all choice in the matter. Unfortunately, even when we are lucky enough to leave a war physically unharmed the experience will leave even the most hardy of us marked, both mentally and emotionally. It is possible never to see any actual "combat" but be powerfully affected by the sight and stories of those who flee. As journalists who have been to war many times we can attest to those truths.

Security is always a major concern in conflict zones and each place has its own idiosyncrasies that need to be understood and addressed. However, it is quite rare to be working on a journalistic project that has a number of its own intrinsic security challenges. This was one such story and we will lay out those problems first before moving on to the more general, universal issues.

Security: Nationality and Your Digital Profile

A relatively new consideration when working in conflict is the existence of a digital profile. As we mentioned earlier, we learned in the first few interviews that some resistance groups were watching the U.S. bases. During the first week that we began interviewing "The Teacher," Molly had spent several days in the Green Zone on assignment for *Newsweek*. She was documenting a day in the life of Bernard Kerik, the former commissioner of the New York Police Department, who had been appointed Interim Coalition Provisional Authority (CPA) interior minister and was responsible for Iraq's security. She had driven around town in his convoy and gone in and out of the Green Zone numerous times.

We soon realized that this kind of behavior was just short of suicidal. Should one of our sources believe that we were not journalists, but some kind of agents, it was unlikely there would be an opportunity to explain. And even if there were time, the fact that she had been working on a story on Kerik, given his position in the CPA, might have only served as further evidence in their minds that she was an informant. Molly needed to wrap up the Kerik story, but before she did so, she began clearing or swapping her camera cards in the event an interviewee decided to ask to look through her pictures the way they often checked Steve's video. Having photos of Kerik, the acting interior minister, on her camera memory cards would have been disastrous. Of course, Molly never mentioned to any of our sources that she was working on a project on the U.S.-appointed interior minister. Nor did she mention the resistance project to Kerik. We should have understood and considered that these groups would be watching the U.S. bases from the outset and in retrospect feel fortunate that we did not have to face the consequences of this blunder. Had *Newsweek* run the profile of Kerik while we were working on our resistance project and someone in Adhamiya had drawn the connection between Molly's photographs in the magazine and her work in the neighborhood we could have been killed.

It is also worth noting that it is common these days for your subjects to Google you if they have Internet access. We did not face that concern when we started, as Internet access had been tightly restricted under Saddam and it was some months before it was widely available, but that is rarely the case anymore. The places you have worked, the kind of projects you have embraced, and your professional track record can be a benefit or a hindrance in any given project. But either way you need to know what they will find and consider how that could impact your safety. For journalists who are often publishing daily or weekly, this is obviously an ongoing concern. If it can be ascertained by

Googling you that you have a military background, have worked on projects with a government or military, or have a security clearance, those facts will be viewed as suspicious by individuals who may not fully understand the context in which such work was done.

In a number of abduction cases involving journalists in both Iraq and Afghanistan, militants have searched the Internet to verify whether or not the individual is a journalist. It can be helpful to be an independent journalist, for you will not be blamed for your colleagues' reporting published by your news organization. But the lack of affiliation on a project like ours can also be complicated securitywise in that our subjects could not confirm that we worked for a specific news outlet. In other words, they could continue to suspect we were actually government agents. We countered that in many ways, mostly by acting like and asking the questions that journalists – not intelligence agents – ask and not interacting with U.S. military personnel. Most importantly, perhaps, we showed up almost every day in the neighborhood – something people who are informing on individuals in a tight community likely would not do.

What your digital profile reveals is probably less problematic for journalists than those who work in other fields. With humanitarian aid becoming increasingly militarized and academic institutions becoming ever more willing to work on joint projects with defense departments, researchers, NGOs, and academics are extremely vulnerable to anyone with access to the Internet.[16]

Security: Managing Interaction and Interview Security

People who have read the *Vanity Fair* article or seen *Meeting Resistance* often ask how we managed to gain the trust of our sources and how we were able to guarantee our safety while we worked. The reality is that we were not safe. And trust is much too strong a word to describe the human interaction that allowed us all to be in the same space and talk over the months we conducted our reporting. We were always walking a fine line. We were never completely positive that when we went off to an interview we would go back to the hotel that night.

By the time we ended our first interview, each source felt well understood and known as an individual. We demonstrated our willingness to invest the time to develop a complete picture of all of them and through them the movement they were participating in. That time invested had its rewards

---

[16] As reported by Oxfam, aid and development are increasingly drawn into the fold of an overall counterinsurgency effort. This is especially observable in Afghanistan, where the U.S. military formally regards aid as a "weapons system" (Jackson 2010).

in the confidence it engendered in the relationship – to the extent that that confidence was possible at all – and reassured them that we were in fact journalists, not spies. Had any one of our sources truly believed for a moment that we were spies we would have been in real danger.

That time investment also allowed us to ask about their participation in the resistance. We generally framed our questions in the present and the past. Questions we asked that involved the future were not tactical, but strategic in nature: questions that would tell us what they were thinking and feeling, and what was changing, but not exactly how that might be manifested. If not carefully tended, conversations about the future can cause the source to express an opinion rather than reveal useful, factual information.

We studiously avoided asking any kind of operational questions, such as, How many individuals are in your group? Where do you operate from? Where do you sleep at night? What is your next planned attack? Where and when? This kind of information is tactical and would serve little purpose in painting the big picture of a movement, especially when the attacks on U.S. soldiers are in the press for the public to see every day. Such questions would also raise suspicion about our being spies. Instead, we preferred information about their motivation and the human condition, information we believe is timeless and remains relevant not only for the duration of the war but over generations. Conversely, details about military planning and structure can quickly become irrelevant. We never approached these delicate topics directly. And some topics – such as the location of an upcoming attack – were details we specifically asked not to be told because that information presented professional and legal dangers. However, in the stream of conversation some individuals revealed information about the makeup of their group or other telling details of how the group functioned. For example, in response to a vague question about how he would "describe" his group "The Lieutenant" told us how many people were in it and other operational information as part of explaining his involvement.

There were components of the reporting process that we had not expected would become our responsibility. For example, almost all of our sources asked us to suggest locations to meet for our interviews. We spent time discussing the types of places where they and we would feel safest and scouted those locations. We also assumed that if they were in a familiar environment and could see their surroundings for some distance they would feel more comfortable. Most often we chose a public place where we could easily be seen by passersby, but not be overheard. We filmed on the embankment of the Tigris, in tea shops during off-hours, in the shade of a tree in an underused park in the middle of the day, and only twice inside a building. One of the few times we did choose the location "The Soldier" showed up for our second interview with a few men he described as "friends." In order to go to a site he had picked for our interview he separated us, putting Steve and Molly in different cars. We were both very much aware that this situation had the potential to turn out badly. They had weapons in the cars – a clear sign of who was in control of this particular exchange. That was one of the most overtly scary moments of the reporting, but there were other times too. After that we happily assumed the burden of suggesting interview locations.

All sources also made it clear that they were – unreasonably in our opinion – holding us responsible for their security. Obviously, this was not a responsibility we could take, given that there were powerful U.S. government and Iraqi organizations looking for them. We always countered that because they were being sought by the U.S. military and others we could not be responsible for their security. We took the security precaution of concealing their faces because it was the only condition under which we would be allowed to interview them on camera. But because they held us responsible for their security, there were a handful of other security precautions we took that were designed to protect us – not them.

We specifically wanted to build a buffer between our sources and us as a team. The goal was to make it clear to them that we had limited information about them, making it very difficult for us to turn them in to Iraqi or American security forces. We achieved that by doing the following three things. First, we did not ask or want to know their real names. Early in the first interview we would settle on a mutually agreed upon nickname that was somehow appropriate to who they are as people. This is why they carry iconographic titles in the article and film. Second, we never went home with them, though it is powerful Arab cultural tradition to invite and host guests in your home. We felt that meeting their families and knowing where they lived would undermine the key component of our security plan – that we had limited information about them. Third, we had no way to reach them – no cell phones or e-mail addresses – we found them each time by finding them – or their finding us – in the neighborhood. While an affinity naturally develops for people that you come to understand profoundly, we never lost sight of the fact that these individuals were involved in a brutal and violent campaign and that it was not in any way our responsibility or aspiration to protect them or show them in a flattering light. When we left the country we left with no way to contact them – no names, addresses, e-mail addresses, or cell phone numbers. Hence, Molly's writing of the story for *Vanity Fair* and the cutting and public screenings of the film *Meeting Resistance* have all occurred without any interaction with our sources.

It can be difficult to know when to stop or even when you have enough information. In some cases, like ours, the decision can be made for you. In March, April, and May 2004 a convergence of events caused a major shift in the mood of the Iraqi people and fundamentally impacted our ability to work. First, four Blackwater Security contractors were killed and their bodies dragged through the streets of Fallujah. The American military response was a full-out assault on Fallujah, causing hundreds of civilian deaths and major physical damage to the city.[17] The response was widely considered by Iraqis to be disproportionate and illegal – unifying them in their deepening contempt for the U.S. occupation.

Second, the Coalition Provisional Authority ordered the closure of Moqtada al Sadr's newspaper and arrested one of his senior lieutenants for the murder of a rival cleric in 2003. Sadr's militia, the Mahdi Army, responded by attacking a convoy passing through Sadr City, killing eight U.S. soldiers. The subsequent American retaliation included deploying tanks and helicopter gunships to the area, and running street battles between the U.S. military and the Mahdi Army occurred in Sadr City for the next four to five nights. The heavily urban area of Sadr City suffered significant civilian deaths and injuries (Oliver and Wright 2004).

Third, photographic evidence emerged confirming what the families of Iraqi prisoners had been saying for months – that Iraqis were being killed, tortured, and sexually humiliated by Americans at Abu Ghraib prison.[18] Within days, what had been a tense time on the streets of Baghdad turned palpably unsafe. The invasion, overthrow of the government, and occupation

[17] There was a second assault on Fallujah in the fall of 2004 to finish what the U.S. military felt had been left undone. The city was practically flattened, leaving 80 percent of buildings unfit for occupation. Estimates of civilian casualties in the two assaults vary between 1,000 and 6,000. As usual in this battle of narratives, accurate figures are impossible to come by with most U.S. media sources being unwilling to accept figures from the Red Cross and Iraqi medical personnel inside the city. The U.S. Pentagon was willing only to give estimates of "insurgents" the military claims to have killed. The British-based *Iraq Body Count*, which estimates casualties using a conservative method of cross-referencing news reports, evaluated the civilian death toll for the April 2003 assault at 616 (Iraq Body Count 2004). During the November offensive the U.S. military was more proficient at controlling alternative sources of information by seizing control of the hospitals and medical clinics as a primary objective and excluding journalists from the city (Oppel 2004).

[18] Many journalists – including us – working in Baghdad in the fall of 2003 heard that there was talk on the streets of Americans' torturing Iraqis in Abu Ghraib. Twice Amina approached us during late 2003 to tell us about what people were saying about this topic. But because we were deeply immersed in the resistance project we chose not to pursue the torture story. We also were sure someone else would. The story eventually broke in the *New Yorker* (Hersh 2004).

of Iraq had been one thing. But for Americans, with promises of freedom and democracy, to be proved to be torturing prisoners in Abu Ghraib made a deep impression on most Iraqis. Because the UN and Western nations had allowed and enabled the invasion and occupation of Iraq, the Iraqis, quite understandably, held all Westerners responsible for the torture of their countrymen.

A fourth insidious factor had served for months to ramp up the tension and suspicion on the street. The American military had been giving rewards to Iraqis who acted as informants, willing to reveal information about individuals involved in attacks on American troops. As Iraqis raked in cash for their tips on neighbors, acquaintances, and family members – sometimes false tips just to collect the reward or take revenge on a personal enemy – levels of suspicion about informants rose and the extrajudicial killing of suspected spies by Iraqi resistance groups reached unprecedented levels. This American-created informant system caused divisions within and among families, tribes, and sects, turning the natural social fissures in Iraqi society into chasms.

Together, these events catalyzed Iraqi society into a violent and destructive seizure. Iraqi rejection of the occupation and support for the resistance increased at the same time that actions by the Americans and other forces were pushing Iraq toward a civil war. In either case, foreigners were not seen as innocent bystanders. It became dangerous for Iraqis to speak to or associate with Westerners. Even journalists who had covered Iraq since long before the 2003 invasion had to find ways to meet discreetly – if they could meet at all – with people with whom they had had long and trusting relationships.

We also recognized that from our sources' perspective the dynamic had shifted. When we began reporting in August 2003 our sources were members of cells, some of whom were connected to small but autonomous groups. All individuals had the discretion to make their own decisions about talking with us. Over the course of our reporting, those small groups coalesced into larger entities that coordinated and shared information, resources, and funding. In short, something more like a command structure had developed, and our sources now had to inform and get permission from a superior to talk with us. For all Iraqis, talking with Westerners or any journalist was seen in an increasingly negative light. For Iraqis who were consuming Western media there was a sense that the foreign press in Iraq had chosen a side, and it was not theirs. Additionally, our subjects were under increasing pressure – whether specifically from their commander or the general social pressure based on events in the country. As a consequence, some of our sources just faded away and could not be found while others were clearer about not being able to meet with us.

During our last interview with "The Teacher" he said, "There are spies everywhere – I've begun to suspect everyone ... even you!" He then added, "Even myself!" clarifying that he meant he had begun to doubt even his own capacity to judge who is a spy. His nerves were frayed and he was clearly telling us that he felt it was too dangerous to continue to meet. Afterward, Molly, Steve, and Amina discussed the way the interview had unfolded, and we agreed that it would be imprudent to meet with him again. And we did not. The last interview we conducted was in May 2004 with "The Warrior." He was well respected by both his group and his commander, who trusted him with increasing responsibilities and allowed him a high degree of operational autonomy. Just days before an interview, "The Warrior's" group was ambushed by U.S. troops as they were picking up a cache of weapons. Besides the loss of valuable resources, a number of his men were wounded as they made their escape. "The Warrior's" commander blamed the incident on his contact with us and ordered him to sever the connection or face death.

Largely because of our relationship with him and the security precautions we described earlier, "The Warrior" never blamed us, sure we could not have known about the weapons cache. In spite of his commander's order to sever his ties with us, "The Warrior" kept our scheduled meeting. He talked about the consequences of the Abu Ghraib revelations, how the "gloves would now come off" and the resistance would treat Americans in the "filthy and despicable ways" the Americans had treated Iraqis. He hinted that taking Westerners hostage could become a tactic.[19] The message he was giving us was clear. It was time to say good-bye. The tenor on the street had irrevocably changed. We had to take that vague but palpable reality into consideration as part of our security assessment. It was necessary to consider and respect how events were changing the environment and impacted our security, our presence in Iraq, our reporting, our relationships with our sources, and their perception of us. Our ability to access our sources was coming to an end. It was clear to us that initiating new relationships in this environment was all but impossible. We packed up our gear and headed for home.

[19] Nicholas Berg was kidnapped in April 2004 in Iraq and his body was found on May 8, 2004. He had been decapitated and a grisly video of his execution was publicly released (Dao et al. 2004).

Figure 8. "US Go Home" November 2003, Baghdad, Iraq.
Photographer: Molly Bingham

We spent a lot of time in Adhamiya waiting. Waiting for a contact to show up, or waiting to see someone we knew. On this day we were waiting for "The Traveller" to show up along the corniche of the Tigris River. A pick-up game of soccer was happening as a group of boys played against this wall. I was struck by the graffiti in English that had begun to appear around Adhamiya, and realized this neatly encapsulated the feelings we were hearing expressed by those we spoke to who spoke to us. Daily life went on. But the message being sent was, "Go home."

Security: Public Knowledge of the Project

We decided very early on that we would not discuss what we were working on outside our small three-person team. We made few exceptions to that rule. There were three other journalists whom we knew and trusted, and we used them as sounding boards to check our thinking on some aspects of the project, lest we lose our critical edge and perspective over the ten months of work. But in the casual beer or dinner banter among a group of journalists at night we never revealed our project. Instead we developed a boringly opaque thread that vaguely addressed "clashes of culture" between Western and Arab sensibilities. That inevitably successfully drove our dinner companions to change the subject or turn to speak to the person on their other side in hope of a better story.

At no time did we mention the project in emails or when speaking on the phone. Whenever it was necessary to do so we used vague language without obvious trigger words. The names we had given our subjects were useful here. We feared that should the U.S. military or some other government agency find that we had contacts to resistance fighters we might be followed with one of the two following consequences:. The people we were interviewing could either be arrested or killed – and we might then be held accountable by their group and possibly killed. Or we could be killed with them as American soldiers followed us to an interview and attacked the site in order to eliminate some "Al Qaeda" or "Ba'athist terrorists." We did not want to become a footnote on that story – "two Western journalists interviewing the fighters were killed in the attack." Our fears, it seems, were well founded. ABC News broke a story in 2008, sourcing two named National Security Agency (NSA) military intercept officers who had listened to calls between 2003 and 2007 from journalists and aid workers in Iraq home to their families (Ross, Walter, and Schechter 2008).

Security and Ethics: Look and Act Like What You Are

During the time that we were reporting the story we stuck to our regular Iraqi car, our Iraqi driver, no weapons, no bulletproof vests, and only a commercially available radio scanner, which we used to listen to other news organizations and pick up where attacks had happened.[20] We left this in the car whenever we went to Adhamiya, and if we were going to meet one of our subjects we often left our mobile phones with it.[21] Yes, we were more vulnerable, perhaps. But we saw that vulnerability as a security strength rather than a liability.

We did not present ourselves as potential targets or, for that matter, particularly valuable potential hostages. We did not have an expensive armored car or high-tech communications equipment. We looked and behaved like exactly what we were – a couple of Western journalists. We wore regular clothes, jeans and shirts, and Molly wore loose fitting linen tunics. We did not wear the wraparound sunglasses fashionable with intelligence, military, and private

---

[20] Molly often kept a bulletproof vest in the trunk of the car. But it is worth noting that its outer sheath was a brick red color. We advise against getting a camouflage, tan, or even blue vest as it can appear to be military or police issue.

[21] We would leave our mobile phones behind or even disconnect the batteries from the phones because mobile phones check in with local cell towers frequently. Intelligence services that have access to that information can deduce your location within an accuracy of several yards. Hence, leaving our phones behind and/or disconnecting them was an added precaution to limit our security exposure if we were in fact being tracked by the U.S. or Iraqi security or intelligence services. Cell phone locations, once identified, can be used to communicate grid coordinates for an air strike or other weapon.

contractors. Nor did we wear anything that could be viewed as military issue:; no cargo pants, no camouflage, no military issue T-shirts, no T-shirts with any writing on them, no desert boots, no "high and tight" haircuts. In the spring of 2003 Richard Wild, a twenty-four year-old independent British cameraman, was killed by a bullet to the head at point blank range as he stood in a crowd of Iraqis near the national museum. It is possible that he was mistaken for a member of the U.S. military or intelligence since he clearly looked American, had close-cropped blond hair, and was wearing khaki pants. We also took note of the fact that – as the *Independent* reported – he was not carrying his camera when he was killed (Akbar 2003).

It should go without saying – but unfortunately that is no longer the case – that, for ethical reasons, we were unarmed. The ethics of being unarmed are simple. Journalists are not soldiers. They are going to conduct interviews, not kill people. Weapons belong in interrogations but have no place in interviews conducted by mutual consent, as they powerfully change the dynamic of exchange. Being armed indicates that you are a participant in the violence, in one way or another, on one side or another. It automatically affects the public's or source's perception of you in a way that cannot be redeemed. There is general agreement among war reporters that when you really need a weapon, there will be plenty lying around. Steve and various colleagues of ours who have found themselves in those situations can attest to its veracity. Finally, while carrying a weapon may afford a certain sense of security, that is all it does. As any policeman or soldier would affirm, a weapon is only of use if the person carrying it has it ready for use and is ready to use it.

In the mid-1990s media companies – driven, at least in part, by requirements placed on them by insurers – began buying or renting armored cars for their correspondents and sending journalists on "Hostile Environment" courses, usually run by British, Australian, or South African former special forces soldiers. By 2001 journalists in Afghanistan affiliated with large media companies were more commonly using security teams. Those security teams quickly became an integral and influential part of many TV and newspaper bureaus, often dramatically affecting how stories could be covered. Additionally, this kind of protection is prohibitively expensive for all but the largest corporations.

The restrictive impact on journalism is not the only reason we see the trend in a negative light. First, being surrounded by a security detail puts an added – and often threatening – layer between a journalist and her source. There is no way this situation cannot dramatically and negatively affect the intimacy and human connection that are often required for the best and most sensitive kinds of reporting. Second, security teams can tightly curtail the amount of time the journalist is able to spend at any one site that is not viewed by the security team as a secure zone. Having an important or intense conversation cut short by your security team is at best frustrating and at worst inhibiting to good journalistic work. Third, whole areas are often put on "no go" lists – often the very places where events are unfolding that journalists feel they should witness and report. One television journalist recounted to us how his security team told him that if he went to a place they had put on their no go list and was injured or killed they would have to report to the insurance company that he had disregarded their counsel. That might mean that the insurance payments to support his family during his recovery or after his death might not be paid.

The use of security teams by journalism organizations impacts the safety of all journalists by blurring the roles of journalists with other entities and agencies that have different missions. American and Coalition intelligence, special forces and private contractors, as well as the U.S. Government players, like Bernard Kerik – viewed by our subjects as high value targets – traveled the streets of Baghdad in armored SUVs with big antennas springing from their roofs and armed guards speaking into walkie-talkies and sporting earpieces. When journalists or aid workers appear indistinguishable from intelligence or military elements to the innocent bystander – the Iraqi on the street, or, more dangerously, the Iraqi looking for a target – they are quickly seen by Iraqis as part of the problem. Blurring of the lines between journalists, NGOs, civilians, and the war machine has proved more and more deadly for journalists. Sadly, because of the investment in equipment it also gives the impression that journalists are a valuable commodity that can be traded for large sums of money.

The engagement of security teams to attempt to improve journalists' security has had a cost for the quality of the work journalists generate and actually seems to have increased the vulnerability of those it is supposed to protect. And it has definitely increased the vulnerability of those journalists who choose not to – or cannot afford to – engage security teams. That said, we also acknowledge that the rules of the game have changed. Journalists are no longer treated as the impartial observers they were once perceived to be, able to cross lines and tell stories from all sides of a conflict with a level of freedom of movement and lack of fear of kidnapping or execution.

Many journalists choose to embed with military units, and embedding has its value. It can be a revealing way to access a conflict as long as journalists retain the perspective and understanding that they are seeing a fight from one belligerent's perspective. But it should not be viewed as safer. The reality is that journalists embedded with U.S. forces have joined the biggest target in town – albeit with the most firepower – and that should be considered. However, the embedding process has other dangers, including the risk that journalists become emotionally and intellectually embedded with one side of a conflict, making it difficult for them to understand or represent any other perspective. Journalists' responsibility to their audience and to history can easily be compromised if they fall prey to this trap. The embedding of journalists as used during the Iraq war effectively utilized independent media to define and tell the story via one perspective – that of the invading forces – while disregarding or delegitimizing any information beyond that narrow purview. The U.S. Defense Department regards the process of embedding journalists during the Iraq war as one of the war planning's most successful elements, and it is considered a significant PSYOPS (psychological operations) victory.

Security: Each Place Is Different and Filming in Conflict Zones

Each conflict has its own security peculiarities and Iraq certainly added some new ones. Iraqis and journalists had to learn very quickly – and for many of the civilians, lessons were learned the hard way – that military checkpoints and U.S. military convoys were to be approached very carefully, if at all. Failing to see a checkpoint in the dark or driving too close to a convoy on the highway often led U.S. troops to open fire without adequate warning, killing and/or wounding the occupants. Whole families were killed in this way, their deaths being justified by the soldiers' belief that a suicide bomber could be attacking them. Even those we would think immune to this kind of action fell victim to it in Iraq. According to an article in the *Independent*, in September 2003, thirty-six-year-old Saad Mohamed Sultan, a translator for an Italian diplomat, was killed by a single shot from an American soldier as the car he was in overtook a U.S. military convoy. The diplomat, Pietro Cardone, and his wife were sitting in the back seat (Fisk 2003).

   As a result of these types of incidents we were very careful around U.S. troop locations, approaching any checkpoints very slowly and ensuring that we looked out for and understood hand signals. In the dark we dimmed our headlights so as not to blind the soldiers on the checkpoint. If we came upon a convoy we stayed well back from the rear vehicle or sometimes stopped altogether until we considered it safe to continue. Being alongside military vehicles in a traffic jam in the center of town had its own problems. The Iraqis were conducting a guerrilla war, which sometimes meant hitting targets of opportunity or using improvised explosive devices (IEDs) in the road. To avoid being caught up in such an attack we would – if possible – pull over and let the U.S. military or government convoy, the more likely target, pass. According to "The Lieutenant," on the evening we met, he and members of his group were lying in wait for an opportunity to attack a unit of American soldiers in Adhamiya. Their efforts were frustrated by our presence as we stood near the American Humvees. Interestingly, a few local men had just appeared shooing off the children in preparation for the attack, but as the children left, so did the Americans.

Journalists – especially television cameramen – were not immune to an instant escalation of force by U.S. soldiers. A number of them have been shot in Iraq with subsequent inquiries revealing that the U.S. soldiers concerned did not know the difference between a television camera and a rocket propelled grenade (RPG) launcher.[22] Steve rarely filmed U.S. troops on the street, and if he did, it was with the camera on a tripod, making it all the more obvious that he was filming, not about to fire an RPG.

There were other times when trying to use a camera was dangerous. We covered the funeral of a resistance fighter and – give or take a little jostling – had no problems even though some of the men in attendance were armed. A few weeks later we saw another funeral heading for what was known as the martyrs' cemetery in Adhamiya. When we noticed that some of the gunmen were not hiding their faces, we decided not to lift our cameras. A Lebanese cameraman nearby – probably with years of experience working with Palestinians – was less cautious and was badly beaten for his poor judgment. He was lucky not to be shot. We continued to watch but kept our cameras at our sides and melted back from the front row of observers lining the streets.

It can be hard to know when to start filming or taking still images on a street when something is happening. If everyone is feeling threatened and concerned with getting to safety, it is likely that few people are going to be worried about being filmed. But if the environment is calmer, like the second funeral described, noticing the environment and making a judgment call are important. You may start to take pictures and someone you are filming will turn away or leave. That is OK. Not everyone wants to be photographed. If you keep filming or photographing someone who clearly knows you are there and yet continues to ignore you, the person is tacitly accepting your actions. Of course, this does not apply if you are filming from a great distance or covertly. People often ask, "How do you know when it's OK to film?" The answer is that it is OK to film or take pictures unless someone stops you. And if someone stops you, you can try to reason with him or her or simply move to another area of the crowd and try again. People who do not want to be filmed or photographed rarely change their mind, so it is generally a better rule not to get into a dispute, but to respect their choice and move on.

In April 2004, on the first anniversary of the fall of Baghdad, there was significant fighting in Adhamiya. We found out about it and went over to the neighborhood and probed at the edges of the fighting to see whether we could

---

[22] A Reuters cameraman was killed by U.S. soldiers in August 2003 at Abu Ghraib. As can be seen in reporting of the incident by the *Guardian*, other journalists on the scene insisted that the soldiers must have recognized he was in fact a journalist (Wilson 2003).

get in, find someone we knew, or get some footage of the fighting. We ended up stuck a few blocks away from where the action was taking place, but the sounds of gunfire and the circling helicopter gunships indicated nothing had cooled down. We were standing in an empty street with a few Iraqis nearby who were held up by the fighting as they had been going about their day, and several residents standing in their doorways listening to the ongoing battle. At that moment an American military patrol began crossing the street at the next intersection, about fifty yards away. Steve was on his knees filming them and I was standing behind him with my knees in his back, also photographing them.

The soldiers at first did not notice us, but once we were spotted the unit stopped crossing the exposed street. One soldier then stepped out from his cover and looked at us through the scope on his rifle. Molly held her camera gear up in the air over her head so they would clearly see that we were Westerners and journalists with cameras, not weapons. Steve continued to film in the same position. The same soldier stepped out again and sighted his rifle right at us: Steve filming and Molly looking through her long lens photographing the soldier as he squeezed off a single shot. As we realized he was going to shoot we stayed put. Molly did not have a rational process except that if we were going to be shot at, moving at that point did not seem to alleviate the danger. Steve later pointed out that if the soldier's intent was to fire a warning shot (as it turns out it was) and we had moved, we could have just as easily moved into the bullet as away from it. What we did not know at the moment was whether he intended to fire a warning shot or unload a clip of bullets at us. We made the right choice, but it would have been easy to make the wrong one.

The footage is in the final cut of *Meeting Resistance* and was one of the more frightening moments of making the film. Interestingly, all of the Iraqis who had been standing near by but not armed and not visible to the U.S. soldiers were shocked to see that the U.S. military had fired on what were clearly two Western journalists. The only benefit of the event for us was that people on the streets saw that we were just as vulnerable to the bullet of a U.S. soldier as the Iraqis were – and that being Western gave us little protection. We could highlight many potential dangers, some of which can be identified and either avoided or planned for. However, most dangers come out of nowhere and require a response that may be neither particularly rational nor well thought out. Over the years we have relied on instinct to deal with such circumstances. However, we both readily admit that it can be very difficult to distinguish between the incredibly natural and appropriate fears that are part of being in a dangerous environment working on a dangerous project and the kind of fear triggered by an instinct that something feels wrong. If you are sensing that the location or people you are with are dangerous, your instinct could be right.

Your eyes see detail that your brain does not rationally process, but your gut understands as danger. You could be wrong, but if the anxiety is distracting to your work you may as well change your location. Ultimately, if you cannot comfort yourself into calmly going forward with something, it just may be time to stop or pause working on that project. Each of us has a threshold for risk (and what we consider worth taking the risk for) depending upon our individual makeup, experiences, and personal lives.[23]

What worked for us is not necessarily what will work for others in a different situation, or even a similar situation in a different place or time. Experience is the best way to learn how to do this work. And that experience must be gained over time. We would not recommend that individuals with no experience of working in armed conflicts jump into a project like the one we attempted, and even experienced journalists who have covered war for a long time make mistakes, have errors in judgment, or are just plain unlucky. Ultimately, if you do not believe in what you are doing enough to take a calculated risk, then you probably just should not pursue the project. If you cannot find a way to do it that sufficiently reassures you that you, the people helping you, and sources will not get killed, injured, or kidnapped because of your work, you should not do it.

Security: Those Who Remain

As journalists living elsewhere, we can always go home. But the people who have helped us along the way, whether it was Amina or our driver or perhaps just the kind man in the tea shop who would always welcome us in peace – they must remain behind, continuing to face the dangers we have left. We must be mindful that their interaction or association with us may leave them vulnerable. We know that the way we work leaves a lasting legacy for those people and is something we must always factor into our security considerations. We have few ways to resolve this problem, and those we have seem woefully inadequate. Just behaving decently toward the people we deal with each day is essential.

Many journalists, particularly photojournalists, including us, leave our fixers behind in a safe place if we are going into a very dangerous situation. Unfortunately, in Iraq many translators and fixers have been killed doing their work, most often when they were not with their employers; journalists can

---

[23] When asked by people who want to start covering conflict we often suggest that they find an experienced conflict journalist whom they can learn from in the field. In a dynamic, changing environment we think it is the best way to learn how to manage the various issues that arise working in a dangerous place or on a dangerous project.

only make every effort not to add unnecessarily to the danger of living in a volatile society and time. It is important not to pressure people to do something they feel is too dangerous. They know their culture and country and the people they continue to live with after we leave. If they say they cannot do something, it is simply necessary to find another way to accomplish it or abandon attempting it.

As journalists or researchers, we must do all that we reasonably can to ensure people who work with us are not harmed while we are working with them or after we leave. It must be a part of strategic thinking about the process of doing the work – not an afterthought. We sometimes have to make decisions for them, as we may have a perspective on events unfolding that they have not considered. For example, we advised Amina not to put her name on our film when we were completing the work. Iraq's instability made it too unclear whether she would be exposing herself to more danger if she did so. When we raised it with her it was not even something she had considered, but she ultimately agreed. Sometimes thinking through longer-term consequences with them can facilitate their managing their own safety better.

Ethics: The Whole Team Abides by the Rules

In journalism there should be no exchange of money or promises of support or assistance in exchange for interviews, access, or information. This can be hard to resist but failing to adhere to this practice will always result in corrupted and unreliable information. We have mentioned "The Soldier" who began demanding money from us after we had already completed a few interviews. From that point on we could no longer trust that the information he had given us was factual, let alone accurate, and removed everything he had told us from our final work. A financial or other significant transaction corrupts the motivation of your sources. They may choose to continue to meet you because you pay them – and tell you a lot of poppycock to get some money. Or they may begin telling you what they think that you want to hear simply to keep receiving some financial or other benefit. It will always be problematic if money or favors are involved.

It is worth pointing out that most intelligence agencies use networks of "informants" who are paid to deliver information to their "handlers." These relationships can go disastrously wrong and stories line the histories of intelligence agencies where double agents exist or the information that has been passed has been flawed or corrupted. It is worth revisiting the idea of acting like what you are. Journalists do not pay people for information; intelligence agencies do. On a project like *Meeting Resistance* we had to ensure there were no mixed messages in our approach, and offering to pay for information certainly would have made us look more like intelligence operatives.

We also made sure that our translator and driver understood and agreed to abide by these rules. It is not all right for journalists to say, "I've never paid anyone for an interview" but to have approved their fixer's doing so on their behalf, or turned a blind eye when they knew it was happening. In some cultures this can be a difficult concept for people. What is corruption to us is simply a way of getting things done elsewhere – and conversely our own everyday ways are often looked at unfavorably. However, apart from our ethical issues it is also a reality that there are potential security implications for us all when people working for us become embroiled in unethical practices. That said, we must add that basic human compassion should not be ignored. We believe that it is not a corruption of your data or research, for example, to give a candy bar or hard to find fruit as a treat once to the child of one of your sources. That is a human kindness, a gift, a surprise, and neither expected, continuous, nor agreed upon before.

Ethics: Getting Involved

For a journalist, judging when to become directly involved in a humanitarian situation – or when to intervene to help an individual in peril – is a tricky situation for which no rules can be laid down and all individuals need to navigate on their own.

Generally speaking, journalists are free to do whatever they like after their story is filed. They may choose to do whatever they think is right *before* the story is filed if the circumstances demand it. Real life does not always offer us the luxury of time to respond thoughtfully to incidents. Generally, each journalist as a human being must quickly work a calculus of factors to determine whether, when, and how to intervene on someone's behalf and whether that intervention will be effective. Our rule is that each situation must be judged on its own merits. Only you can weigh the nuances of any given situation and decide what is right within the broader context of events. Can you, should you, help a family evacuate from an area you know they are in dire danger of dying in if they stay? Only you will have to live with the consequences of attempting to intervene – or not – for the rest of your life. Intervention is tricky, and the decision about what to do is a personal choice that you have to make alone. Once you are involved, you are bound to people's future in a way you are not if you remain aside. Intervening can both fail to protect the individual you intend to help and put you directly in danger.

There is a well-known story about Kevin Carter, who photographed a starving child with a vulture in the background in Sudan during the 1993 famine. The accusations of inaction heaped upon Kevin for not helping that individual child played a role in his suicide some years later after winning numerous awards for the photograph. What those who criticized him did not know was the context in which the photo was taken. The child's mother was only yards away, waiting for food being distributed by the UN from the air-craft on which Carter had arrived. The vulture flew away before he had even finished photographing the child. The worldwide publication of that image and others that were taken of the famine helped mobilize global public sup-port to save tens of thousands of starving children in Sudan. Kevin had not intervened on that child's behalf because he perceived intervention as unnec-essary and he recognized the power of the images he would make might help mobilize the public.

For journalism – particularly covering militant aspects of human behav-ior – it is critical that you not have a vested interest in the outcome of the con-flict or how what you reveal impacts your military subjects – beyond the basic humanity regarding their survival. Professional journalists must be able to remain apart from what they cover – yet remain human in their grasp and empathy for others' experiences and problems. Journalism's power is revealing events through broad publication to a global audience that otherwise would not be aware of them. The public is then able to grasp the implications of events and choose what action or pressure to apply to effect change.

Ethics: Going Public

After ten months of reporting we concluded that the Iraqi resistance was indig-enous to the country – not driven by outsiders – and that it was popularly sup-ported, composed of nationalists, secular people, and religious people. It was not run by Saddam loyalists. The people we interviewed were not criminals. On the contrary, they were often respected members of their communities, family men sometimes holding down jobs while also active in the resistance. Our findings profoundly challenged and complicated the dominant American narrative of the conflict in Iraq. We had not set out to dispute the occupation's official version of events, but in the end, we found there was no evidence on the ground to support it.

In 2006 the National Intelligence Council director (the individual respon-sible for coordinating the sixteen U.S. intelligence communities) discussed the contents of the October 2003 National Intelligence Estimate on Iraq that he delivered to the White House at that time. His summary of that report, described in an interview with *McClatchy Newspapers*, noted that the intelligence community had reached the conclusion that the resistance in Iraq was indigenous to the society, with "deep local roots," and was motivated by "deep grievances including the presence of U.S. troops" (Strobel and Landay 2006). The U.S. intelligence community knew what we knew, almost exactly when we knew it in 2003. But the decision was made to suppress that kind of information about the war and not to acknowledge that our greatest challenge in Iraq was a homegrown, locally supported resistance to occupation.

Returning from Iraq we encountered a skeptical response to our work from some in the professional journalism community: these were not the questions to ask nor a community that we should seek to understand. There was also a certain amount of suspicion about how and why we had been able to gain access to a community that others had not. More than once we were encouraged to make the film more about ourselves, because it would be easier for a Western audience to identify with us as they followed our relationship – we are a couple as well as a reporting team. We rejected this option because we believed that in this scenario the Iraqis would become little more than bit players in our romantic story. A senior producer at one U.S. network commented, "This is amazing work – but I can't put it in front of my audience." This sort of response was not just confined to the United States; a senior BBC executive, after describing a short teaser cut of the film as "outstanding work," passed us on to a senior producer. After several weeks of silence Steve reached the producer, who told him that they would not even contemplate running the film because it "goes against what our politicians are saying."

Whichever way we looked, we seemed to have little choice but to finish the film ourselves and release it independently, without the backing of a large production company or documentary outlet to cover the considerable costs of producing and launching a film. We are deeply wed to our standards of good journalism and did not want to make an advocacy film. Nor did we want to be in the film ourselves because we felt it was both inappropriate and unnecessary. *Meeting Resistance* allows the viewers to consider the information presented in its complexity and draw their own conclusions. We feel strongly that the film stands as a unique document of what has happened in Iraq, with original, critical sources discussing their own lives and worlds. *Meeting Resistance* was released in theaters in 2007 followed by a DVD release in 2008. Although it was well reviewed, it has not been shown on American or British television. A similar fate befell *Hearts and Minds*, Peter Davis's seminal 1974 documentary on the Vietnam War. We believe that down the road our project will be more widely recognized for the light it sheds on this important war.

Another issue faced in some journalistic work is how, once the story goes public, it affects the community that is revealed. In this case, we felt confident that the individuals we interviewed knew the costs and risks of choosing to pick up arms. They also were aware of the risks of acknowledging their involvement and discussing their sentiments with us as journalists. We kept to our agreements. We did not reveal their faces on camera; nor did we pass on information we gleaned about them or point them out as resistance members to U.S. or Iraqi security services. We told the story that we found with honesty and integrity. Had we found that these were religious fanatics and a fringe element of the Iraqi society, that would have been the story that the film told. We were not seeking in any way to fill a preconceived notion of what perpetrators of this violence would be like or force what we did find into a more flattering light. Our sources had never asked for, and were never offered, any say in what parts of our interviews we used or what conclusions we would draw from our reporting. And since we left Iraq not knowing their names and with no method of contacting them, the process of putting the film together, releasing, and speaking about it has happened with no feedback or input from them. Hence, there was no impact they could have or have had on the final product.

We were often asked during Q&As while we traveled with the film whether we had shared what we learned from our reporting with U.S. military or intelligence, either in real time or after we were finished cutting the film. The reality is that what we learned is in the film and the *Vanity Fair* piece. But a more subtle answer is that journalists have a job to do, which we feel involves providing information to the public, not the government or intelligence communities. They have their own roles and jobs and we understand them. But we do not feel it is journalists' role to provide special information to any security apparatus. We publish our best knowledge, and intelligence operatives can learn from it by watching or reading it along with the public. This concept cuts both ways. We also did not and would not provide any information or insight to those we interviewed about U.S. military actions or what we had learned by being inside the Green Zone or embedded.

PART IV: CONCLUSION – MEDIA AND CONFLICT TODAY

The media role in conflict is obviously a complicated one. Media are how the world learns about events – and now almost everyone can see the same media and know how a topic is being covered. Media are also used by powerful societal elements – governments, NGOs, militaries, and corporations – to shape the discourse around those topics. These entities convey their message using data, narratives, and as the former White House spokesman Scott McClellan, in his memoirs, repeatedly chose to call the Bush White House's manipulation of the media – "propaganda" – to gain or keep public support for their policies, actions, or reactions to events (McClellan 2008).

Sadly, because of the dramatic technology and business changes in media, as well as cuts in media staffing, there are fewer people doing the same work. There is less time for journalists to think critically or chase down contradictions and leads. Because they are largely corporately held, there is less interest – at the managerial level – in challenging power structures or pursuing or publishing material that might make the public uncomfortable or cause the outlet to lose ever more crucial readership or viewers, and hence advertising revenue. These forces converge to make media today an incredibly powerful tool in building narratives and yet weak in challenging them or the structures interested in manipulating public perception. As a result, media are now regarded by the public with increasing skepticism. Journalists are no longer assumed to be impartial. They are often now viewed more as potential tools of public communication than reporters. Those you interview may not only know the media organization you are working for but have opinions on how that organization is covering their story. It also means that if you are filing (or even posting on Twitter or Facebook) regularly, they can watch or read what you have filed.

A more profound element of this same issue is that today's media – all media, as far as we can tell – are carrying a national perspective in their coverage of events. When your sources perceive this, navigating the gap in national visions of events becomes very challenging. In Iraq we found that many Iraqis saw the Western press as taking a side – and it was not theirs. For example, "The Teacher" would often ask us why the resistance was being called terrorists in the Western media, when they were simply defending their territory – something he believed was a right under international law.

There is also an increased blending among the roles of civilians and military journalists and intelligence, NGOs, and governments. The U.S. military has increasingly engaged in soft projects, intentionally co-opting, organizing, and protecting the work usually carried out independently by NGOs and civilians. Reconstruction, garbage collection, rebuilding schools, water rehabilitation projects, all drive a public perception that the foreign civilians and foreign military occupation are one and the same. Journalists, sometimes wearing parts of or only standard issue military uniform, are confusing to the public at best and at worst project a coziness and likeness of mind that dramatically impact access and perception. As well, all parties in the conflict (in Iraq, for example, the U.S. military and the resistance themselves) want to create zones where foreigners – be they military, intelligence, or journalists – will not come

poking around. All sides in any conflict may aspire to have a zone free of pry-
ing eyes. The easiest, fastest way to do this is to kidnap and/or kill an aid worker
or journalist. As a result, journalists have an increasingly difficult time accessing nonofficial information about the places and people they are covering.

More than ever, journalists are working on multiple deadlines in multiple
formats and if they do not have the time to get on the ground and report,
they will go to the press conference or cover what the local politician said.
But speaking only with those more easily accessible figures tells only part of
the story. As McClellan wrote in his book, "I still like and admire President
Bush, but he and his advisers confused the propaganda campaign with the
high level of candor and honesty so fundamentally needed to build and then
sustain public support during a time of war. ... In this regard, he was terribly
ill-served by his top advisers, especially those involved directly in national
security" (McClellan 2008, 566).

BIBLIOGRAPHY

Akbar, Arifa. 2003. Briton killed in Baghdad wanted to be a war reporter. *Independent*,
    July 7. Available at http://www.independent.co.uk/news/world/middle-east/briton-k
    illed-in-baghdad-wanted-to-be-a-war-reporter-585987.html (accessed April 15, 2011).
Associated Press. 2003. Rumsfeld blames Iraq problems on "pockets of dead-enders."
    USA Today, June 18. Available at http://www.usatoday.com/news/world/iraq/2003–
    06–18-rumsfeld_x.htm (accessed April 15, 2011).
BBC. 2003. Obituary: Sergio Vieira de Mello. *BBC News*, August 19. Available at
    http://news.bbc.co.uk/2/hi/americas/2146395.stm (accessed April 15, 2011).
    2007. Iraq poll September 2007. BBC News, September 10. Available at http://news.
    bbc.co.uk/1/shared/bsp/hi/pdfs/10_09_07_iraqpollaug2007_full.pdf(accessedApril15,
    2011).
Bingham, Molly. 2004. Ordinary warriors. *Vanity Fair*, July. Available at http://www.
    vanityfair.com/politics/features/2004/07/iraq200407 (accessed April 15, 2011).
Bloom, John. 2003. Analysis: The Baghdad museum muddle. *UPI*, June 13. Available
    at http://www.upi.com/Odd_News/2003/06/13/Analysis-The-Baghdad-museum-
    muddle/UPI-19781055529139/ (accessed April 11, 2011).
Chandrasekaran, Rajiv. 2006. *Imperial life in the emerald city: Inside Iraq's Green Zone*.
    New York: Knopf.
Connors, Steve and Molly Bingham. 2007. Meeting resistance. Available at http://
    www.meetingresistance.com (accessed April 11, 2011).
Dao, James, Richard Lezin Jones, Christine Hauser, and Eric Lichtblau. 2004.
    Visions and suspicions: The entrepreneur: Tracing a civilian's odd path to his
    gruesome fate in Iraq. *New York Times*, May 26. Available at http://www.nytimes.
    com/2004/05/26/world/visions-suspicions-entrepreneur-tracing-civilian-s-
    odd-path-his-gruesome-fate.html?ref=nicholas_E_berg&pagewanted=all
    (accessed April 11, 2011).
Davis, Peter. 1974. *Hearts and minds*. Documentary film.

Fisk, Robert. 2003. An Italian diplomat, his translator and another Iraqi tragedy. *Independent*, September 22. Available at http://www.independent.co.uk/opinion/ commentators/fisk/an-italian-diplomat-his-translator-and-another-iraqi-tragedy-580749.html (accessed April 11, 2011).

Hassan, Ahmed. 2007. Life goes on. *Islam Online*, January 28. Available at http://www.islamonline.net/servlet/Satellite?c=Article_C&cid=1169972845025&pagename= Zone-English-Family%2FFYELayout (accessed April 11, 2011).

Hersh, Seymour. 2004. Torture at Abu Ghraib. *New Yorker*, May 10. Available at http://www.newyorker.com/archive/2004/05/10/040510fa_fact (accessed April 11, 2011).

Iraq Body Count. 2004. No longer unknowable: Falluja's April civilian toll is 600. *Iraq Body Count*, October 26. Available at http://www.iraqbodycount.org/analysis/reference/press-releases/9/ (accessed April 1, 2011).

Jackson, Ashley. 2010. Quick impact, quick collapse: The dangers of militarized aid in Afghanistan. *Oxfam International*, 1 (January 26). Available at http://www.oxfam. org/en/policy/quick-impact-quick-collapse (accessed May 6, 2010).

McClellan, Scott. 2008. *What happened: Inside the Bush White House and Washington's culture of deception*. New York: Public Affairs.

Meeting Resistance. 2008. Department of Defense "Enemy initiated attacks by month" chart. Available at http://www.meetingresistance.com/DoDgraph.html (accessed April 1, 2011).

Nabulsi, Karma. 1999. *Traditions of war: Occupation, resistance and the law*. New York: Oxford University Press.

Oliver, Mark and George Wright. 2004. US faces Iraqi revolt. *Guardian*, April 5. Available at http://www.guardian.co.uk/world/2004/apr/05/usa.iraq1 (accessed April 1, 2011).

Oppel, Richard A., Jr. 2004. Early target of offensive is hospital. *New York Times*, November 8. Available at http://www.nytimes.com/2004/11/08/international/ middleeast/08hospital.html (accessed April 1, 2011).

Raghavan, Sudarsan. 2007. Marriages between sects come under siege in Iraq. *Washington Post*, March 4. Available at http://www.washingtonpost.com/wp-dyn/ content/article/2007/03/03/AR2007030300647_pf.html

Ratnesar, Romesh, Michael Weisskopf, et al. 2003. Portrait of a platoon. *Time*, December 29. Available at http://www.time.com/time/subscriber/personofthe-year/2003/poyplatoon.html (accessed April 15, 2011).

Ross, Brian, Vic Walter, and Anna Schechter. 2008. Inside account of U.S. eavesdropping on Americans. *ABC News*, October 9. Available at http://abcnews.go.com/ Blotter/story?id=5987804&page=1 (accessed April 1, 2011).

Strobel, Warren P. and Jonathan S Landay. 2006. Intelligence agencies warned about growing local insurgency in late 2003. *McClatchy Newspapers*, February 28. Available at http://www.mcclatchydc.com/2006/02/28/16299/intelligence-agencies-warned-about.html (accessed April 15, 2011).

United States Government Accountability Office. 2008. Securing, stabilizing and rebuilding Iraq: Progress report: Some gains made, updated strategy needed. *U.S. G.A.O*, June 23. Available at http://www.gao.gov/products/GAO-08–837 (accessed April 15, 2011).

Wilson, Jamie. 2003. US troops "crazy" in killing of cameraman. *Guardian*, August 19. Available at http://www.guardian.co.uk/media/2003/aug/19/iraqandthemedia. iraq (accessed April 15, 2011).

PART V

RESPONSIBILITY

Figure 9. "Mourning" May 2010, Pul-e-Charkhi, Afghanistan.
Photographer: Mònica Bernabé.

Relatives of victims honor their loved ones missing or killed during the several periods of war in Afghanistan. Dozens of men and women traveled by bus to the area of Pul-e-Charkhi outside Kabul, where it is believed hundreds of people are buried who were arrested and detained in Pul-e-Charkhi prison during the Russian regime. The relatives of the victims want to raise their voices, to be heard, and to see justice.

8

Establishing a Policy Research Organization in a Conflict Zone

The Case of the Afghanistan Research and Evaluation Unit

Paul Fishstein and Andrew Wilder

On September 11, 2001, Afghanistan was transformed from a forgotten conflict into the frontline state in the "War on Terror." The spotlight of international attention, which had long before shifted away from Afghanistan after the withdrawal of Soviet troops in 1989, returned to a country that had provided sanctuary to Al-Qaeda and its leader, Osama bin Laden. Within three months the Taliban government had been overthrown by a United States–led military operation, and the Bonn Agreement establishing an interim government in Kabul headed by Hamid Karzai was signed by a range of Afghan power brokers. Soon after, hordes of officials, consultants, and aid workers from a wide range of bilateral and multilateral donors, UN agencies, NGOs, and private sector contractors descended on Kabul to begin the task of working with the interim administration to rebuild a country devastated by more than two decades of conflict.

With the spotlight back on Afghanistan, one of the key issues that soon became readily apparent was how little was actually known about the country and its people. Two decades of war, a collapsed education system, and a decade of inattention by international actors had resulted in very little rigorous research or learning about contemporary Afghanistan. It was the recognition by some donors and United Nations and NGO officials of the need to address this gap that gave birth to the Afghanistan Research and Evaluation Unit (AREU) in February 2002. The objective of this chapter, written by the first two directors of AREU (2002–8), is to describe some of the experiences and challenges of setting up an independent policy research institution in what was originally perceived to be a "postconflict situation" but steadily deteriorated back into a full-fledged conflict zone.

BACKGROUND

In 1998, in response to growing concerns about the lack of coherence between international aid and political efforts in Afghanistan, the Strategic Framework for Afghanistan (SFA) was adopted by the United Nations, and supported by major international donors and most NGOs operating in the country. The overarching objective of the SFA was to facilitate "the transition from a state of internal conflict to a just and sustainable peace through mutually reinforcing political and assistance initiatives." In July 2000, an independent Strategic Monitoring Unit (SMU) was created to support the SFA by conducting research and analysis and to measure progress in achieving the SFA objectives. The SMU consisted of an international director, an Afghan deputy director, and two support staff and was governed by a board consisting of three representatives each from donors, United Nations agencies, and NGOs.

After the defeat of the Taliban regime, and the emergence of an internationally recognized interim government in Afghanistan in December 2001, the SFA became redundant, and with it the need for the SMU to inform and monitor its implementation. However, the need for rigorous research and analysis to inform assistance efforts in Afghanistan was recognized to be more important than ever. At a February 2002 meeting of the Afghanistan Programming Body (APB), which consisted of major donors, United Nations agencies, and NGOs, a decision was taken to change the name of the SMU to AREU, to reflect its changed purpose from analysis and monitoring of the SFA to research and analysis to inform the much more ambitious reconstruction and development efforts of the government and international community in Afghanistan.

AREU'S MISSION AND STRATEGY

The main rationale for AREU was to help address the lack of reliable data and analysis, as well as the need for an independent voice to comment on Afghanistan's reconstruction and development. A review of bibliographies on Afghanistan quickly revealed the paucity of rigorous published research on Afghanistan between 1980 and 2001. Despite large-scale cross-border aid programs into Afghanistan from Pakistan during the 1980s and early 1990s, as well as the largest refugee program in the world from 1980 to 1992 to support the estimated five million Afghans who fled to Pakistan and Iran, there is remarkably little published literature on humanitarian and aid efforts during this period.[1] During this more than two decades of aid programming, financed primarily from short-term humanitarian aid budgets, project evaluations were often the only form of analysis, if analysis was done at all. Longer-term, more in-depth and reflective analysis was rare, in part because of the unending crisis atmosphere and the lack of stability, which caused institutions (and individuals) to focus on the present and the immediate future. Only a handful of Ph.D. students conducted in-depth field research in Afghanistan during this period, generating a few well-regarded publications,[2] but most publications consisted of journalistic accounts of travels through Afghanistan with various mujahideen factions.

Post-Taliban Afghanistan therefore was in dire need of more reflective, analytical, dispassionate, and independent institutions that could provide policy makers and practitioners with relevant information (although the extent to which they were actually interested varied tremendously). This was particularly true given the vast amounts of money that were being spent within very short time frames, based on very limited understanding and untested assumptions. The urgency was compounded by the flood of new actors with no experience or knowledge of the country, and the intense political pressures and expectations for immediate results.

Partly illustrating the need for information on virtually all aspects of Afghanistan (historical, social, economic, political, and cultural), AREU was able quickly to establish its reputation and legitimacy with donors and aid practitioners engaged in reconstruction and state-building efforts. Key services provided to the community were a range of research publications, periodic seminars and workshops, briefings for senior policy makers, a library open to the public, the *A to Z Guide to Afghanistan Assistance*,[3] and a Web site containing both

[1] A search of the 187-page 5th edition of Christian Bleuer's *Afghan analysts bibliography* (2010), which focuses on social science publications on Afghanistan since the late 1970s, reveals only the following six academic publications in the 1980s and 1990s focusing on Afghan humanitarian and development assistance efforts: Inger W. Boesen (1985), Olga Baitemann (1990), S. Barakat and A. Strand (1995), Asgar Christensen (1995), David R. Howell (1982), and J. H. Lorentz (1987). While academic publications were few during this period, there were many unpublished documents related to aid and development efforts in Afghanistan, including needs assessments, program reports, and evaluations. A considerable amount of this unpublished gray material was collected by the ACBAR Resource and Information Centre (ARIC) founded by Nancy Dupree in 1989, which is now housed at the Afghanistan Centre at Kabul University (http://www.acku.edu.af/).
[2] See, for example, David B. Edwards (1996) and Alessandro Monsutti (2005).
[3] AREU's *A–Z guide to Afghanistan assistance* has been published annually since 2002 and consists of a useful handbook that deciphers the alphabet soup of acronyms, the aid architecture, and structures of government and provides key reference documents such as the Constitution, as well as maps, and a contact directory.

AREU's own publications as well as other resources. AREU covered a range of topics, including the overall aid and development framework, public health, rural and urban livelihoods, internal and regional labor migration, refugee repatriation, rural land tenure, water management, elections and political system development, public administration, gender relations, security sector reform, political economy and markets, community-level institutions, and governance.[4] Positive perceptions of AREU and its work contributed to growing donor support and the rapid growth of the organization. The SMU budget of approximately $250,000 in 2001 expanded to $750,000 during AREU's first year in operation in 2002, which doubled again to approximately $1.5 million in 2003. AREU was launched in February 2002 with two professional and two support staff supplemented by consultants, and within one year had grown to fifteen staff. By the start of 2008, AREU had an annual budget of $4.3 million and a program staff of fifty (not including administration and finance), who were from Afghanistan and eight other countries.

There were growing pains associated with this rapid growth, which required the development of stronger finance, administration, and personnel management systems. However, the presence of a relatively clear organizational mission, mandate, and strategic plan from the outset helped protect AREU from expanding in ways that could have damaged the organization by diverting it from its mission and objectives. In March 2002, the director drafted the first organizational strategic plan, which was subsequently approved by the board. During the fall of 2003, AREU held a much more comprehensive strategic planning retreat with all of its research, communications, and administration/finance staff to develop a three-year strategic plan for the period 2004–6. During the second half of 2006, AREU followed a similar process to develop its third strategic plan, for the period 2007–9. Although minor alterations were made to the wording of the statement, the essence of AREU's mission from the outset was

> To conduct and facilitate action-oriented research and learning that informs and influences policy and practice. AREU also actively promotes a culture of research and learning by strengthening analytical capacity in Afghanistan and creating opportunities for analysis, thought and debate. Fundamental to AREU's vision is that its work should improve Afghan lives.

---

[4] Some of AREU's key early studies were Taking refugees for a ride? The politics of refugee return to Afghanistan (2002); Land rights in crisis: Addressing tenure insecurity in Afghanistan (2003); Afghan elections: The great gamble (2003); A guide to government in Afghanistan (2004); and Subnational administration in Afghanistan: Assessment and recommendations for action (2004).

All three strategic plans articulated AREU's three core objectives: 1) producing high-quality policy research, 2) advocating for change based on research results, and 3) building the culture and capacity of research. Also, a number of frameworks developed in the 2004–6 plan (i.e., criteria for research activities, AREU's seven thematic areas)[5] served the institution well as a guide and reference point. Topics for research were chosen somewhat opportunistically, based on internal discussion of what was likely to be relevant in the coming period as well as the availability of qualified staff and consultants to do the research.

Each year, using the three-year strategic plan for overall guidance, AREU developed an annual plan and budget that laid out the planned research and other activities for the year ahead. The formal process, which typically started during the final quarter of the previous year, included small working groups and departmental meetings to review the current plan, followed by one to two days of all-staff meetings to conduct an environmental analysis and in turn identify important sectoral themes likely to be relevant in the coming period. On the basis of the outputs from the large group meetings, teams then drafted a work plan identifying specific research projects, planned publications, and required human and financial resources. The draft plan was then presented to the board, which usually suggested some minor modifications. Given the unpredictability of the external environment and human resource constraints, it was common for some studies to be delayed or not accomplished, and for other unplanned but particularly relevant studies to be taken up during the course of the year. The planning process also provided an opportunity to review administration and management procedures and to identify ways in which they might be improved.

AREUs board originally consisted of nine members, which was later increased to twelve, divided equally among United Nations/multilateral organizations, embassies/bilateral donors, and NGOs. Board members served in their individual rather than institutional capacities, which allowed AREU strategically to select individuals who would be motivated and effective as board members, rather than being stuck with ineffective and/or disinterested persons through a "hereditary" system. As AREU was a policy research institution, strategic considerations for selection of board members included their access to policy makers and interest in making research relevant, as well as ability to assist with funding. AREU's board

---

5 The seven thematic research areas identified in AREU's 2004–6 strategic plan were 1) political economy and markets, 2) governance, 3) livelihoods and vulnerability, 4) gender, 5) natural resource management, 6) education, and 7) health.

generally drew from people who were on the ground in Kabul and engaged in development – not scholars.

From the very beginning it was clear that AREU's intention was to be policy relevant. The first strategy document emphasized that AREU did not want just to produce reports, "but to be part of a process of change that will significantly improve the quality, impact and accountability of assistance efforts." The increased aid effectiveness and accountability AREU hoped to promote were not through the monitoring and evaluation of individual projects, but through relevant research and strategic level evaluations that increased knowledge, informed policy, and improved practice (AREU 2002, 4).

MAJOR ORGANIZATIONAL CHALLENGES FACED BY AREU

AREU faced a number of challenges as it tried to find its place in Afghanistan's reconstruction scene. The immediate challenge was to raise funding for the idea of an independent policy research organization, as the remaining funds AREU inherited from the SMU were only sufficient to cover basic operating costs for a few months. A very supportive AREU board chairman and a few brave donors that were willing to take a risk on an idea, such as the Swiss Agency for Development Cooperation (SDC) and the Swedish International Development Cooperation Agency (SIDA), soon provided AREU with a relatively stable funding base.

It is important to highlight the critically important role that undesignated core funding provided by a few key donors at the outset played in AREU's success. This core funding enabled AREU to set a large part of its own research agenda, and provided the flexibility to respond quickly to key issues as they emerged. Had it been necessary for AREU to seek donor funding for all new research on a project-by-project basis, AREU would not have been able to be nearly as independent in determining research priorities or to be sufficiently responsive in an extremely fluid policy making environment. Having flexible funding also allowed exploratory work to be done on possible topics, which could then be developed into proposals for larger research projects. Furthermore, the fact that AREU received no United States government funding enhanced its credibility as an independent body that was able to advocate for policy recommendations that were on occasion at odds with those of the most powerful international actor in Afghanistan. AREU did not refuse United States government funding as a matter of principle, but at a time when money was not a major constraint, the combination of complex administrative procedures and political strings (i.e., extensive prepublication content reviews) made such funding less attractive.

After the initial financial crisis, securing donor funding was not one of AREU's major challenges. However, that left many other challenges that AREU struggled to overcome in a very difficult and fluid operating environment. The following section describes some of the major challenges of setting up a policy research organization in a conflict zone and highlights some of the difficult decisions and trade-offs that had to be made, either as conscious choices or through the unfolding of events.

HUMAN RESOURCE CONSTRAINTS

By far, AREU's most serious challenge was how to produce high-quality policy research in a country with a collapsed education system and extremely limited human resources. Even before the conflict began in 1978, few Afghans had the opportunity to get a decent primary or secondary education, let alone higher education. In addition, during the country's development push of the 1970s, the government's emphasis was on the more "practical" areas, and the elite educational paths were engineering and medicine. With the possible exception of archaeology and anthropology, social sciences were seen as less useful to a developing country. Also, a government that was preoccupied with extending its control over a potentially unruly population was not especially interested in encouraging potentially difficult and divisive analysis of social trends and relationships. The state was responsible for all education and scholarship, and it had little interest in encouraging independent research institutions that might ask difficult questions. Consequently, with little interest or investment in the social sciences, naturally there were few trained researchers. Also, the evaluation and monitoring of projects and programs that did take place tended to be punitively focused on compliance, mainly on whether or not staff were in place and whether inventory was complete, with less interest or capacity in articulating the more complex realities on the ground.

This situation was exacerbated during the war years, when Afghanistan's educational institutions were immensely degraded and most of its educated population either were killed or migrated abroad. The insecurity also meant that only the most intrepid international doctoral students and scholars continued doing research in or on Afghanistan. While the war and the refugee crisis it generated did result in a large influx of foreign aid agencies and workers, the short-term humanitarian focus on providing basic health, education, and shelter left little time, interest, or resources to pursue more in-depth research. While some needs assessments and program evaluations were conducted, these were generally very narrowly focused and were often funded by aid agencies and donors who were not always disinterested or objective observers. Furthermore, much of the training and capacity building provided by international agencies and NGOs based mostly in neighboring Pakistan was geared to the needs of donor-funded project implementation, including project management, finance, and report writing.

As a result of the factors outlined, Afghanistan in 2001 found itself with a very limited pool of persons with the capacity to do or even understand policy research. The explosion of development projects and programs beginning in 2002 required trained Afghans, but these were primarily in the areas of project management rather than research. Given the overwhelming reliance on imported skills, systems, and ideology, the demand was for Afghans who could bridge the gap between the foreign assistance community and local realities. These tended to be those who had worked in project management with NGOs, and who had acquired the requisite skills. The key skills usually valued most by the burgeoning aid industry were English language and computers, often to the exclusion of more fundamental understanding of the country and its institutions. This meant that there was a very limited pool of skilled persons who could take leadership roles in research. It also meant that in a white-hot job market for people with management or analytical skills, staff were bid away by United Nations agencies and bilateral (i.e., USAID) contractors for often several times current NGO salaries. For instance, AREU hired a research assistant for a substantial increase over his previous position, only for him to resign without working one day, having used his new salary to extract an even higher one from a USAID-funded contractor.

In setting its salary and benefits packages, AREU tried to be reasonably competitive with international NGOs, but decided that it could not compete with the much higher salary scales of embassies, United Nations agencies, and donor-funded consulting firms. AREU tried to compensate by offering longer-term employment in a more supportive work setting, but in a resource-scarce environment with high levels of uncertainty about the future, some staff understandably opted for higher salaries with other agencies. The effects of the competitive job market were exacerbated by the uncertain external environment. As security deteriorated, there was a growing fear among Afghans that the current favorable work environment might not endure. This made it more difficult to focus staff attention on the longer term and caused staff to switch jobs to those with higher short-term salaries and perhaps a potential exit strategy. A number of staff took jobs that they knew would be less interesting and even dangerous because they paid more. A number of staff were approached by the United States military, which was in need of translators, and were offered high salaries and the eventual prospect of an immigration visa.

As a consequence, it was difficult to find qualified Afghan researchers or retain Afghan staff for long-term capacity development. This, in turn, meant that leadership of research was provided primarily by international staff and consultants. However, especially after security began to deteriorate in 2005, finding well-qualified international researchers with Afghan experience also proved to be a major challenge and constraint on what AREU could do. While AREU was able to find some excellent short- and longer-term international researchers, it was a constant struggle to find *and* retain them. Some international researchers were experienced and skilled in their technical areas, but their knowledge of Afghanistan was often limited; that meant both that they were not always incisive in their observations, and that Afghans had questions about their legitimacy. While in many cases this was overcome over time, it meant at a minimum an often lengthy learning process.

Aside from limiting the type and quantity of research that AREU could do, the shortage of qualified, senior Afghan researchers had the additional implication of limiting the extent to which AREU could establish its identity as an Afghan organization. Although AREU is technically an Afghan organization, the prominence of international staff in senior positions meant that many outsiders, both Afghan and foreign, assumed that it was an international organization. AREUs structure and staffing are partly a consequence of its origins in a United Nations system, but are also in part due to the limited availability of qualified Afghans to take on senior research positions.

AREU's identity and the consequences of that identity are somewhat complicated. In theory, a greater Afghan identity would have increased AREU's legitimacy in the eyes of Afghan citizens and institutions and resulted in a better understanding of the often opaque (to foreigners) workings of society. Also, although all major publications and the AREU Web site were translated into Dari and Pashtu, publications and communications produced originally in local languages would be more accessible to Afghans. On the other hand, a widespread Afghan distrust of most institutions, which are often seen to be representative of certain political or social factions, could have reduced AREU's legitimacy. A number of new Afghan policy research institutions that have emerged in recent years are widely seen as fronts for people and political parties or groups. Internally, while staff expressed desire for seeing more Afghans in senior positions, they also expressed concern that AREU could be "captured" by a political faction or ethnic group. Therefore, despite the downsides of AREU's international image, it may have also helped to maintain an image of independence and protected it from political pressures, although from the start it was the explicit intention to become an Afghan institution. Additionally, given the major role played by international actors in policy

making from 2002 onward and given that at least initially the government
had little demand for or capacity to utilize policy research, it made sense
for AREU to focus its policy-influencing efforts on international rather than
Afghan institutions.

Another major challenge AREU struggled with was finding a balance between
the competing priorities of producing high-quality research and building
research capacity, the first two of the three objectives in AREU's strategic
plans. Especially after initial research publications raised expectations in the
assistance community, there was a persistent tension between addressing the
demands for more good-quality research and for increased capacity of local
institutions as well as that of AREU's own staff.

Internally, AREU Afghan staff understandably had the desire to play a more
significant role in research, rather than simply functioning as research assistants and translators for international staff and consultants. Because research
was typically led by those with advanced degrees, Afghan staff could not perceive a clear career path. In addition, they sought educational opportunities,
mostly overseas, which AREU did not have the means to support. AREU was
under considerable pressure to produce research and given the immediate
human resource constraints believed that it could not afford to send staff
away for expensive long-term training, especially given the likelihood that
foreign-trained staff would join better-paying organizations on their return.
The rapid career path seen in many of the implementing NGOs and international agencies provided AREU staff with a negative comparison. The expectations of rapid career advancement created a tension between the need to be
more proactive in promoting Afghan staff, and the recognition of the risks to
research quality, especially as developing research and analytical skills is a
longer-term process.

Externally, the interest in research derived from the recognition that
the assistance community had large, gaping holes in its understanding of
Afghanistan at the same time that it was rapidly expanding the scope and
scale of state-building activities. Good research was now at a premium, and
AREU was approached by a range of actors for partnerships and for training and other forms of capacity building. For instance, the directors were frequently asked about AREU's relationship with Kabul University, often with
the suggestion either to collaborate with university professors on research or
to engage substantively with them to build their capacity. AREU was also

regularly approached about participating in capacity-building programs for Afghan and international NGOs, government ministries, emerging Afghan think tanks, and other institutions. In most cases, however, potential partners were looking for shortcuts and vastly underestimated the time and effort required to do good research.

While AREU's mission included building the capacity and culture of research, the simple realities of time and organizational capacity meant that choices often had to be made between research and capacity building. There were times when AREU attempted a number of mechanisms to do both. For instance, in a number of partnerships with Afghan and international NGOs, AREU conducted research in areas in which the NGOs operated. In exchange, the NGOs gained some insights into conditions in their areas, which they would not have gained otherwise under the pressure of day-to-day operations. Some NGOs were invited to send staff to research training conducted for AREU staff, especially during the winter months, when fieldwork was often suspended. In general, however, AREU opted to prioritize research over partnerships and capacity building. Ultimately, the opportunity cost of capacity building of other institutions would have been research not done, and it was research on which AREU's reputation was made.

CONDUCTING RESEARCH IN A DIFFICULT SECURITY ENVIRONMENT

While conducting research in a difficult security environment appeared to many outsiders as AREU's most serious challenge, in fact, relative to that of many organizations, security was less of a constraint during the first few years following AREU's establishment than one might have thought. Even in later years, AREU research teams were able to travel to areas that were off-limits to many organizations encumbered with rigid security protocols. Still, security imposed a number of constraints and limits, mainly with respect to dangerous areas of the country and in taking on difficult subjects that might put staff and the institution itself at risk.

With the Taliban-led insurgency progressively increasing in much of the south and east, security conditions increasingly eliminated areas in which research could be done. This obviously limited the extent to which social conditions could be assessed in some of the most critical areas of the country, including how populations and institutions were responding to the international aid effort. The fact that insecure areas often corresponded with areas where the Pashtun ethnic group were the majority had the extremely negative consequence that most of AREU's (and other) analyses focused more on relatively secure areas where ethnic minority groups such as Tajiks, Hazaras, and Uzbeks were dominant.

At the same time, through the use of various strategies, AREU was able to conduct more research in problem areas than would have been expected, while maintaining the well-being of staff. The security of staff was the first and foremost concern, and research was not conducted in areas in which staff did not feel comfortable. Moreover, individual staff were not required to go to places where they did not feel secure. Of course, comfort is very much a subjective thing, and some staff were clearly willing to take more risks than others. During AREU's first couple of years, when the security environment throughout much of the country was relatively good, security policies were relatively ad hoc. They relied to a considerable extent on good local partners and networks, and on the two principles of providing staff with information and staff in turn using good judgment in the field. However, as the security environment deteriorated, and as AREU grew and hired more staff that did not have much prior experience working or traveling in Afghanistan, the demand for stronger organizational security systems grew. In response, AREU's security policies and procedures were reviewed and strengthened, and more overt instructions were provided to staff. In early 2008, AREU finally engaged a security contractor (shared with another organization), although with the very explicit agreement that AREU would maintain its low-profile approach.

AREU's research teams used various approaches to enhance security, including the adoption of a low-profile "under the radar" approach to conducting field research. Staff and consultants traveled in private vehicles without radios, armed guards, and other trappings that would tend to draw unwanted attention. This was AREU's policy from the start, and it became even more sensible as the security situation deteriorated. Especially in areas that were potentially dangerous for international staff and consultants, Afghans would take the lead in conducting the field research. They were often supported by international staff in provincial centers who could on a regular basis provide feedback on interviews and help resolve methodological problems. In fact, as a result of the dynamic introduced by the presence of international staff (who were subjected to the guest treatment or seen as potential providers of assistance for the area), this had methodological benefits as well. While donors and other stakeholders were especially keen to understand conditions in difficult areas, it was necessary to maintain flexibility in the choice of research sites. In many instances, research planned for one area had to be relocated to another in response to a worsening security situation. In some cases, security issues were transient, and research could be carried out after the situation resolved itself, although in others it was necessary to relocate sites entirely to other districts or even provinces.

The choice of research subjects was also a challenge, especially given both the importance and sensitivity of a few subjects for Afghanistan, namely, corruption, narcotics, and the presence of international forces. Again, the security of staff and the institution was a primary consideration in determining what could be realistically taken on. AREU did do fairly extensive research on narcotics including work on opium production and trading (see Mansfield 2006 and Pain 2006), which highlighted the important issues without explicitly naming names, an option that was felt best left to journalists and to institutions that did not live on the ground in Afghanistan. AREU also published an issues paper on police reform efforts in Afghanistan, which highlighted the predatory nature of the police as well as problems of massive corruption in the Ministry of Interior and the police. The English version of the paper was somewhat provocatively titled *Cops or Robbers? The Struggle to Reform the National Police* (2007). However, after discussions with some of the national staff, it was decided to change the first part of the title in the Dari and Pashtu versions to the much more innocuous *Rule of Law?*

The importance for international policy makers of findings on corruption and narcotics had to be balanced with the need to maintain relationships with Afghan institutions and limit dangerous exposure of staff and consultants, and even the institution itself. The unfortunate reality of current-day Afghanistan is that security institutions are weak and incapable of protecting (or unwilling to protect) individuals or organizations from power holders threatened by public exposure. The arrest and prosecution of a few journalists for articles they have published and the sentencing of one to death on dubious charges of blasphemy (later revoked) highlight the risks of offending the powers that be. On the other hand, the fact that there have been very few cases where the authors of even explicit exposés have suffered harm suggests a level of impunity whereby power holders do not feel threatened.

(INTER)CULTURAL CHALLENGES

If culture is defined as a system of beliefs and behavior, in many ways AREU exemplified what is called a "complex, multi-cultural environment." In mid-2007, the twenty-one international staff (seven male, fourteen female) held citizenship in ten different countries, while the thirty-nine Afghan professional staff (twenty-six male, thirteen female) were from different parts of Afghanistan (urban/rural), ethnic groups, and socioeconomic backgrounds. Some had grown up and been educated in Pakistan or Iran, others had lived in Kabul throughout the years of conflict, while still others had grown up in the west – all of which provided very different social outlooks.

As is common in most postconflict settings, there were vast gaps and differences between the lives of the international staff and those of the local staff. Of course, there were the routine cross-cultural issues with the potential for misunderstanding and for communicating unintended messages, including clothing, food, language, body language, personal habits, and gestures. Many of these were the stuff of humor and were largely accommodated by staff once they understood that no ill will was intended. For instance, when a newly arrived international staff person walked straight across the middle of the tablecloth that had been set on the floor for lunch (the equivalent of walking across a dining room table with one's shoes on), the Afghan staff managed to laugh. Likewise, when one of the Afghan staff told an international female, approvingly, that she had gotten fat during her vacation, the staff person managed to recover and put it in a cross-cultural context. Most foreigners were keen to learn about Afghan culture, and most Afghans were interested to learn about what were often perceived as the more "modern and advanced" cultures of their foreign colleagues, although there were often differences with their own culture that were hard to digest or even comprehend. In addition, there were the various conversational taboos for each side. For example, direct questions about salaries, age, weight, marital status, and why they do not have children are generally fair game for Afghans but are often considered rude by Westerners, while direct questions from males about female members of the family are usually considered inappropriate and intrusive by Afghans.

Yet, there were also the more substantial issues of office culture and tone. Western and Afghan office traditions differed greatly in styles of supervision, feedback, accountability, and demeanor. There was therefore a mild tension between which set of cultural rules applied, as well as who set the agenda. The fact that the office working language was English rather than Dari or Pashtu had implications for office culture. The international staff had a whole set of administrative issues (visas, guesthouse amenities, R&R entitlements, etc.) that were irrelevant to the Afghan staff, but that in meetings could sometimes crowd out other issues. Similarly, while everyone had a common stake in security, Afghan and international staff had very different concerns and imperatives. For example, for the international staff, there was always the last resort, however unpleasant, of evacuation from Afghanistan, whereas for Afghans, there was no such concept, and in fact evacuation of their international colleagues would convey the notion of abandonment and a level of disorder that could mean disaster for them. Similarly, low key security procedures were better options against violence that might target organizations affiliated with the government or the international community. However, as security deteriorated, much of the apparatus of heightened security response for international staff (high walls, security fences, more secure vehicles) ran in exactly the opposite direction and could even make Afghans feel more vulnerable.

As noted previously, while most international staff were interested to learn about Afghan culture, living up to expectations imposed by that culture was not always easy. The lack of division between the public and the private in Afghanistan was especially difficult for international staff accustomed to being autonomous and anonymous in their after-hours lives. The notion that one's workplace and colleagues could reflect so significantly on an individual or his or her family was hard to comprehend. NGOs were new to Afghanistan and were associated with the West. Among conservative elements in Afghan society they had a reputation of being places of debauchery, where male and female staff sit together and no doubt did much worse. This was a recurrent element of Taliban propaganda, which had been absorbed by many Afghans. Therefore, it was common for the parents of prospective young female employees to enter the office to ensure that the environment was sufficiently morally upright. The need to maintain an office environment beyond reproach sometimes created conflict, as when, for instance, AREU restricted a number of the international staff from tending bar at the International Security Assistance Force (ISAF) military base.[6] What was seen by them as a way to pick up some additional income and have an innocent social outlet was potentially seen quite differently by their Afghan colleagues, for whom serving alcohol to the foreign military had all sorts of negative connotations.

Outside the workplace, the lifestyles of international and Afghan staff were vastly different, resulting in different pressures on the different staff. In general, the lives of Afghan staff revolved around their families, and they would return home at the end of the workday. Many, especially females, had extensive household and family obligations, which they often struggled to meet after (and before) a workday and a long commute. International staff, who were largely away from their families, lived together in AREU guesthouses, and their personal lives often revolved around socializing with friends and going to restaurants and parties. International staff were also largely accustomed to leading independent lives and were mostly unaccustomed to the restrictions of living in an environment restricted by security or social custom. Restrictions on mobility, especially on walking (which were sometimes half-heartedly imposed), were perceived as particularly confining.

---

[6]   The International Security Assistance Force (ISAF) is a NATO-led security mission established by the United Nations Security Council in 2001.

The expectations of the international and Afghan staff with respect to physical amenities also varied. International staff were accustomed to adequate heat, hot water, and Internet connections, while the Afghan staff who were responsible for providing these to the guesthouses often had none at home. While the Afghan administrative staff were responsive, it is likely that at times they felt that the foreigners were living a coddled, privileged life. At the same time, partly because their lives revolved largely around work, the international staff tended to work longer hours and felt that they were entitled to the amenities because of that and the fact that they were far from home and family, had given up comforts, and were potentially putting their lives at risk in working in Afghanistan. These types of intercultural challenges were certainly not unique to AREU. However, for an institution that wanted to be Afghan, but at the same time had many international staff in leadership roles, addressing some of the resulting cultural tensions proved to be a never-ending management challenge.

RESEARCH CHALLENGES IN AFGHANISTAN

Depending on the type of research being done, AREU faced a number of specific challenges related to doing field research within Afghanistan's social, cultural, and physical environment. In the complex, chaotic, and unstable environment in Afghanistan, AREU's guiding principles were practicality and flexibility. While some of the solutions (e.g., relatives accompanying female research staff, service-providing NGOs acting as intermediaries, sampling based on pragmatic calculations rather than rigid sampling frames, holding interviews in public places) were not always ideal in terms of research methodology, they were judged to be the best choices in that environment.

LOGISTICAL CHALLENGES

Afghanistan's well-documented physical characteristics and poor infrastructure created some of the more obvious practical challenges. The harsh landscape, poor roads, and weak transport networks, coupled with insecurity in much of the country, limited mobility and access to potential field sites. Much of the country, including some of the areas that were more secure and thus more amenable to research, became inaccessible during much of the harsh winter. While the winter therefore should have been the time for fieldwork in the warmer southern areas, insecurity made that impossible, so generally much of the winter was dedicated to training and preparing for the warmer months in which travel would take place. Research was possible during the fasting month of Ramadan, although productivity was reduced.

While the areas around Kabul and parts of the north were accessible by road, as time went on and parts of the countryside became less secure, teams increasingly traveled to the field by air. For instance, although the cities of Herat in the west and Taloqan and Faizabad in the northeast were themselves reasonably secure, road access was through areas that were not, and so often research teams would fly and either meet up with drivers dispatched from Kabul or use local drivers. In some cases international staff would fly, while Afghan staff would go by road, as they were judged to be at lower risk. In a few cases, international staff traveling by air would carry all of the work-related materials and identification cards of the Afghan staff traveling by road, so as to allow the Afghans to say that they were traveling on personal affairs, rather than as part of an NGO. Apart from the major cities, Afghanistan has no network of hotels or other lodging; especially in rural areas that condition required research teams to make accommodation arrangements with NGOs or local communities.

STAFF AND GENDER DIMENSIONS

The challenges for both research and implementation activities associated with gender roles and restrictions in Afghanistan are daunting. Female seclusion meant that, except in Kabul or in official settings (i.e., government or NGO offices), interviews of females usually had to be conducted only by females, and focus group discussions had to be held in separate groups of males and females. This in turn meant that, depending on the topic and where fieldwork would be done, research teams had to be composed of even numbers of male and female research assistants. However, because of cultural restrictions, it was very difficult to find female staff who were willing and able to travel outside Kabul, especially to the more conservative and conflict-ridden south, and whose families were willing to allow them to do so. In Afghanistan females generally do not travel alone or accompanied by males not related to them, and it is even more rare that they would stay in hotels or other public facilities. Therefore, the pool of potential Afghan female researchers was quite limited. Some of the females whose families did allow them to travel required that they be accompanied by a male relative (known as a *mahram*), who would be responsible for their well-being and honor. While this notion created something of a clash with Western notions of equality, practicality won out, and after some discussion AREU instituted a policy to permit and pay for the expenses of a male relative to accompany female researchers on field trips.

While this was necessary, its implementation was not without problems. First, to some extent it was seen as providing special privileges to certain staff. Also, it was not always clear whether the presence of a male relative was required by the family or was merely a preference of the staff person herself. In addition, although the *mahram*'s main function was simply to accompany the female staff person, having an additional person along could create some negative dynamics within the group. In far-flung rural areas, there is not a lot to do, and boredom could understandably push the *mahram* to interact with the female staff person or the other members of the team in ways that were not necessarily productive. Also, if the male felt that he wanted to involve himself in the decisions made in the field or even involve himself in the research, this would be problematic, especially if he was older or had higher status than the other members of the team. There were a few cases where the interaction between the *mahram* and the research teams created a serious conflict. Another option was to hire couples or close male-female relatives, but institutional restrictions on hiring family members and the low probability that both members of a couple would have equally suitable skills and experience made this a less attractive option.

ACCESSING LOCAL COMMUNITIES

Because of the characteristics of Afghan society – primarily rural, suspicious of outsiders, and insecure in many areas – it is not advisable simply to drive into a village and begin knocking on doors to conduct research. Instead, it was necessary to have some sort of intermediary, and in most cases AREU used NGOs who had some sort of ongoing relationship with the community. This was often the case even in urban areas, which were composed of communities with various levels of cohesion and were likewise wary of outsiders. In Afghanistan's current environment of suspicion, both communities and the government authorities were concerned about the presence of spies. While working in a relationship with a known and trusted NGO that was providing services or development activities to a community was necessary, it was not ideal because of a number of factors, most of which were related to potential conflicts of interest. Mostly, the arrival of any institution from outside could raise expectations of additional services or activities. This raised the risk of generating "correct" answers during interviews (which tended to overstate the deprivation of the community). But there was also the question of whether community members would be willing to criticize the NGO that had supplied them with services. At the same time, learning about the weak points of the NGO could put AREU in a difficult position in relation to the NGO, as all publications were available publicly. Moreover, if community members did not have a good perception of the NGO, this could likewise cause bias.

Generally, research teams were welcomed by communities, in part because of the strong Afghan tradition of hospitality. The downside, of course, was something that might be called "strategic hospitality." Establishing a close relationship with the research teams might have affected the objectivity of the research. At a minimum, once embedded with one group, it often became difficult to move to other areas that might have had different perspectives. Of course, communities might have put a certain slant on information in order to improve their own position and potentially attract additional assistance. They might also have exposed the NGOs, if the community had a complaint about them. It was therefore an ongoing challenge to balance the need to engage with communities with the need to maintain a certain distance.

Field sites were generally selected on the basis of areas being representative for the research at hand but also constrained by practical considerations, mainly security and entrée into the area. Where field sites were reasonably close to provincial towns with lodging or NGO guesthouses, staff commuted back and forth each day. In other places, it was sometimes necessary to rent quarters or to stay with NGO staff or even in some cases with families of local leaders. Another step that was taken to allay suspicion and fulfill legal requirements was to obtain letters of introduction from the relevant ministries and government offices in Kabul.

METHODOLOGICAL ISSUES

From its early days, AREU shied away from large-scale data collection exercises (i.e., national surveys), largely because it recognized that the management and logistical requirements would be overwhelming for a small organization and that adequate supervision and quality control in present-day Afghanistan would be extremely difficult if not impossible. As a result, most of AREU's research was qualitative, despite policy makers' general bias in favor of quantitative methodologies, which are perceived to be superior because of large sample size, numbers, and predictive powers. Unfortunately, a large sample size is often judged to indicate that research is reliable. However, there are a number of reasons why the use of quantitative methodologies, especially surveys, can be problematic in the Afghan context. First, there is a serious dearth of reliable numbers, including Afghanistan's total population or number of administrative districts. Furthermore, given the human resource constraints discussed earlier, there are very few institutions in Afghanistan with a sufficient number of well-trained survey teams to collect reliable data. Some survey practices can only be described as "drive-by" polling. It is common to hear reports of surveyors who, rather than deal with the effort and at times risk of going out to interview respondents, simply stay at home and complete survey questionnaires themselves. Another risk is that once information is quantified, to a great extent the "warts" and caveats from its collection are lost. Given an illiteracy rate of nearly 75 percent and therefore the lack of experience of most Afghans with responding to surveys, important nuances and information are lost unless one probes behind the initial question. For respondents unfamiliar with the sorts of 1–5 scales asked on surveys and with no or limited numeracy, certain types of questions that frame categories, rank choices, and ask percentages can easily be misinterpreted. Because of social desirability bias or fear of "betraying" their NGOs or giving the "wrong" answer, respondents may feel compelled to provide answers in accord with standard social norms. In fact, given the characteristics of the rural population, it is likely that many respondents are unable to grasp even the purpose and logic of research.

For the preceding reasons, AREU researchers generally assumed that for community-level research the best approach was to spend significant time with communities in order to build up trust and to be able to observe inconsistencies and triangulate responses. While there were still problems with recall, bias, and self-interest, the more time that was spent with a community, the more likely it was that some of the biases would surface and that slanted information would be detected. After some time, respondents generally felt more comfortable talking, as a result of which also rival narratives often emerged to challenge earlier ones that were presented.

In fieldwork, AREU used a variety of research techniques, mainly semistructured individual interviews, informal conversations, focus group discussions, and observation, each of which had advantages and drawbacks. While focus group discussions can elicit a broader set of views and induce respondents to draw out comments from others in the group, as a result of Afghan social hierarchy, especially in a group setting, often the voices of the elder males and the powerful will be heard, while others lower down on the social scale are expected to keep quiet and defer. In such a situation, social forces may discourage other people' willingness to talk openly or express ideas that violate social norms or may encourage a sort of groupthink. This is likely to be especially true for sensitive topics such as the influence of local power holders or the characteristics of the government.

At the same time, given the lack of privacy in many settings, it is often difficult to conduct individual interviews. It is considered rude to ask people to leave a social setting, so planned individual interviews held in government offices or in market areas often become de facto focus groups. Similarly, for most Afghans, privacy is virtually nonexistent, and so while there are exceptions, the strategy of going off into a private space to conduct a confidential interview is generally unrealistic. While this might have been convenient, for instance, when drug dealers felt no reluctance to discuss the trade in front of others, the lack of privacy was highly problematic for a study of family violence; it was unrealistic to expect family members to air their dirty laundry in front of other extended family members, who might have been a threat to impose additional violence. In fact, as a result of the communal nature of Afghan culture, there is a limited notion of an individual with his or her own personal views.

TRANSLATION ISSUES

Because of the human resource issues noted in a previous section, AREU's working language was English. Research questions, questionnaires, frameworks, publications, and so on, were all developed in English, then translated into Dari and Pashtu. Translation posed a huge challenge on a number of levels. At the simplest level, it was difficult to find Afghans who could translate the abstract and often highly technical concepts to and from English. At the dissemination stage, during workshops and seminars, a poor verbal or written translation would undermine whatever message was being conveyed – sometimes with a questionable translation providing an opening to contest controversial findings. More substantively, the translation of key abstract terms and concepts from foreign languages to Dari or Pashtu was highly problematic, as most such concepts have meanings that are highly informed by culture. For instance, that there is no Dari or Pashtu word for "gender" is indicative. Additional common terms in the postconflict environment that were problematic included the English term "democracy," which has a whole set of connotative meanings that affect the way people view it. The Dari term *komak* translates literally as "help" but can refer to charity as well as development assistance. However, the English term "sustainable," which often translates to "long-term," and "freedom," which in the West has a universally positive connotation, in post-2001 Afghanistan acquired a negative undertone of impunity and license. Even the Dari word for research, *tahqiq*, was associated with the sort of "research" done by the police and intelligence services and so had to be elaborated as *tahqiq-e elmi*, or "scientific research."

Most Afghans did not have experience with interviewing or with principles of inference, and so inexperienced research assistants would often jump to general conclusions based on a few interviews. This was especially problematic when it was augmented by Afghan social hierarchy to encourage a tendency to rely on "reliable" and "good" informants such as elders and the educated, who were presumed to know better than the poor and uneducated. There is no tradition of the "man in the street" or "everyman" interview. There could also be a tendency for educated research staff to rely on an imperious style of interaction usually adopted by government officials from Kabul or the cities.

Overcoming this lack of experience required training in advance of fieldwork and close supervision during it to ensure, for instance, that research assistants probed, rather than simply accepted a respondent's first response, and that they took careful notes. Yet because the presence of foreigners in a community can alter the atmosphere, research teams tried to find a balance: enough exposure to field sites to get an understanding of what was happening and to be able to supervise research assistants, yet not enough so that the atmosphere was unalterably polluted. (Of course, the presence of foreigners can also have benefits such as being able to meet more easily with officials.) In practice, this often meant that the international staff would participate in some initial interviews, then retreat to a nearby town and be available each evening to review transcripts and debrief on the day's fieldwork, note items for follow-up and probing, and generally troubleshoot.

ETHNIC ISSUES

Given the Afghan sensitivity on ethnic issues, it was important to try to maintain a balance on a number of different fronts, including doing research in a range of ethnic communities and regions, hiring across all ethnic groups, and making sure that publications were translated into both Dari and Pashtu. Unfortunately, the insecurity in the largely-Pashtun south put real limits on doing research there, and as time passed, ethnic sensitivities rose, mostly because the Taliban are largely a Pashtun movement, and the insurgency was therefore largely associated with Pashtuns. While in the more ethnically heterogeneous large cities this was somewhat diffused, in rural areas there was potential discomfort in having researchers from one ethnic group doing fieldwork in a community of another ethnic group, although this varied with the individual and the community. As researchers do not leave their personalities behind, especially in a tense social situation, if someone is an ethnic chauvinist this will likely be conveyed to respondents (and colleagues). In some studies, attempts were made to use researchers who were from the same area and/or ethnic group, as it was felt that this would help in reassuring respondents and building trust.

THE CHALLENGE OF INFORMING AND INFLUENCING POLICY IN AFGHANISTAN

Ultimately, the greatest challenge for AREU was that of informing and influencing policy, which were central to its mission. AREUs 2003 and 2006 strategic plans both included sections on communications and advocacy, which highlighted the need to ensure that AREU's research

- is effectively disseminated and communicated to relevant decision-makers;
- reaches Afghan and international audiences;
- informs and influences the policies and practice of its stakeholders, so that its research findings become integrated into key political and reconstruction processes and debates; and
- is effectively targeted to reach those decision makers who can ultimately improve Afghan lives. (AREU 2003)

AREU used a variety of methods to disseminate its research findings and to try to influence policy making and programming. These included producing a range of publications, including detailed issues papers on key issues, in-depth case studies, synthesis papers presenting the overall findings of longer-term research projects, a quarterly research newsletter highlighting all known research being done on Afghanistan, and shorter briefing papers targeting policy makers. There was often tension, however, between keeping publications short enough to be read by busy policy makers and not oversimplifying highly complex and nuanced issues. Briefing papers, originally intended to be four to six pages in length, often ended up being twelve to fourteen pages long, leading AREU on some occasions to produce much shorter "briefing notes."

In terms of the overall mission to improve Afghan lives, AREUs policy was that all research outputs were to be publicly available, a philosophy that differentiated it from most consulting firms, which produced reports for donors or other institutions but often did not make them publicly available. All of AREU's publications were initially published in English and Dari, and subsequently in Pashtu as well, and were available free of charge in hard copy from the AREU office as well as from its Web site. As mentioned earlier in this chapter, AREU also published annually its *A to Z Guide to Afghanistan Assistance*. These highly popular guides, which could be purchased for ten dollars in hard copy (in later years, a Dari and Pashtu hard copy version was distributed free) or downloaded free from the Web, could be seen on the desks of many of the movers and shakers in Kabul. They proved to be very popular with the steady stream of newcomers hungry for information, and an effective way to boost AREU's name recognition and brand.

Dissemination of AREU's research findings was not limited to its publications. AREU's director and researchers frequently had opportunities to communicate research findings through formal presentations and briefings for civilian and military officials, interviews with national and international media, and participation in national and international conferences. In addition to these more formal methods, more informal meetings and discussions held over lunch or dinner often proved to be the most effective way to interact with key policy makers. In an environment where many international officials lived behind prison-like walls and barricades in cramped temporary accommodations and ate breakfast, lunch, and dinner with their colleagues in cafeterias, the opportunity to escape and have dinner at the AREU director's home with outsiders was often welcomed.[7] Dinner guests could include the range of types found in Kabul, such as United Nations staff or heads of agencies, NGO workers, journalists, diplomats, visiting academics, Afghan government officials, and members of parliament. Informal dinners would provide the opportunity (or excuse) for people who would not otherwise have the chance to meet and talk in official or more formal settings of embassy compounds or military bases. Most important for many of international officials was the chance to meet and interact with Afghans.

Another important component of AREU's communications and advocacy strategy, which also contributed to AREU's third objective of building the capacity and culture of research, was its library, where students, researchers, journalists, aid officials, and others could take advantage of a wide range of primarily Afghanistan-specific publications, as well as a work area, Internet access, and library reference services. The backbone of the library's initial collection was the valuable British Institute for Afghan Studies (BIAS) holdings that were generously donated to AREU. The BIAS collection had been boxed up and stored at the British Embassy compound for more than two decades after the organization's expulsion from Afghanistan after the Soviet invasion. When AREU moved to its current office location in 2006, one of the main requirements was for a facility that would accommodate the growing collection, as well as be accessible to external students, researchers, and others interested in using the library resources. By 2010 the library contained 22,500 physical items including 11,000 unique titles. It is one of only two libraries in Afghanistan that have online catalogs, and it now serves as one of the most important information resource (physical and virtual) available to researchers in Afghanistan. This well-organized and accessible collection plays a particularly important role given the surprisingly limited value attributed to information management in Afghanistan by the Afghan government and most international organizations, not to mention the unfortunate tendency of most bureaucracies to unnecessarily classify many documents and

---

7   Several people commented (only half-jokingly) that having a good cook, especially prior to the establishment of many new restaurants in Kabul and after the deterioration in security led to restrictions on visiting those restaurants, was one of AREU's more strategic investments in terms of both communicating research findings as well as fund-raising.

reports. This tendency made it very difficult to find or access any Afghan government records in Afghanistan, or many key international assistance community documents. As a result, visitors often went to the AREU library to view documents that in theory should have been available from the Afghan ministries.

AREU's efforts to inform and influence policy making raised a number of complex issues with which the organization had to continually grapple. The first was to try to determine where on the continuum from (passively) communicating research findings to (actively) advocating specific policy changes based on research findings was appropriate for a policy research organization. AREU put a disclaimer on all of its publications that the views and opinions expressed in the reports did not necessarily reflect those of AREU. The question then arose, however, as to whether AREU should simply let research findings speak for themselves or whether it should be more outspoken in advocating the adoption of policy recommendations outlined in AREU's publications – and, if so, which ones? There was a concern that adopting more of an advocacy role could detract from AREU's reputation as a neutral policy research organization. It did not want to be perceived as an advocacy organization that did research to support preconceived advocacy positions. However, AREU's mission of using its research findings to influence policy making and to improve Afghan lives seemed to demand more than a passive dissemination of research publications. AREU ultimately adopted a somewhat pragmatic policy of "targeted advocacy," whereby some research findings were left to speak for themselves, whereas on others AREU more actively advocated policy changes.

Another challenge when it came to influencing policy was identifying the target audience for AREU's research. Initially, at least, the main decision makers with regard to Afghan policy were international rather than national actors. As a result, AREU's advocacy efforts often prioritized targeting key international military and civilian officials over Afghan government officials. Over time, however, as Afghan ministries gained capacity and the role and responsibilities of Afghan officials increased in policy making, AREU dedicated more resources and time to briefing key Afghan government officials, partnering with Afghan NGOs and civil society organizations, as well as disseminating findings through the growing Afghan media sector. However, the effectiveness of AREU's communications and advocacy efforts with Afghan policy makers and institutions was often undermined by the lack of senior Afghan researchers to communicate research findings, as well as the difficulty in finding individuals who could effectively translate AREU research publications into Dari and Pashtu.

On some key issues it was extremely difficult to influence policy making, as it was very dependent on one or two individuals. For example, when the Afghan-American Zalmay Khalilzad served as U.S. ambassador to Afghanistan from 2003 to 2005, his familiarity with the country, its languages, and the key personalities, along with his direct links back to the Pentagon and White House, made him extraordinarily influential in policy making. It also made him extraordinarily difficult to influence, as it often appeared that he did not believe he had much to learn from others about anything related to Afghanistan. This clearly had a negative impact on AREU's ability to influence policy on a few key issues, such as the selection of a voting system during the country's first parliamentary elections in 2005 (Reynolds and Wilder 2004). AREU was the first organization publicly to question the wisdom of the proposed "single nontransferable vote" (SNTV) system for the poor correlation between votes won and seats won in a parliamentary election, and the way in which it favored independent candidates with narrow appeals along ethnic, tribal, or sectarian lines over political parties with broader appeal across these social divides. While AREU's briefing papers, communications, and advocacy efforts were quite successful in raising awareness about the disadvantages of SNTV among many of the senior embassy, United Nations, and government officials in Kabul, as well as some of the major Afghan political party leaders, ultimately the inability to convince Ambassador Khalilzad and President Karzai (whose interests were best served by a weak and divided parliament, which the SNTV voting system nearly guaranteed) resulted in the adoption of the SNTV system. While the negative impact of this system is now widely recognized, it is now much more difficult to change, given the vested interests in maintaining the status quo by those who were elected through this voting system.

Managing the tension that often arose between the very different time frames within which researchers and policy makers operated was another factor to contend with when it came to trying to influence policy making. For many researchers one year was a very short time frame in which to conduct a rigorous research project. For most international policy makers in Kabul, however, many of whom were on short-term assignments ranging from a few months to usually a maximum of one year, there was a desire for immediate information to inform policy making. The eyes of many officials in Kabul would glaze over the moment a researcher began describing a project where the findings and policy recommendations might not emerge for a year or more. In terms of receptivity by policy makers, some of AREU's most effective studies were therefore not the most in-depth and rigorous ones, but the ones that were timely in terms of producing actionable information in a rapidly evolving political and security environment with a high turnover of key policy makers (Lister 2005, Paterson and Blewett 2006, and Wilder 2007).

A related challenge was the need to balance the researchers' desire for rigor and nuance in writing about the research findings with the Communications and Advocacy Department's need to communicate complex issues in a simplified and compelling manner to policy makers. AREU's staff and consultants had a range of backgrounds (e.g., academics, development practitioners, recent Ph.D.s, longtime Afghanistan hands), and some who had a more academic research background were particularly reluctant to, in their view, "dumb-down" their writing styles.

The difficulty of finding and recruiting researchers proved to be another serious constraint when it came to achieving AREU's objective of influencing policy making. The human resource constraints outlined earlier in this chapter (e.g., lack of Afghan capacity in research and unwillingness of international researchers to work in an insecure environment) prevented AREU from adequately pursuing a number of important research topics that were critical for Afghanistan's development and for which the development community was hungry for information. These included the relationship between economic policy and performance of the economy in promoting pro-poor activities, the volume and distribution of international aid flows, Afghanistan's water resources and the long-term outlook for development, and the performance of community-based education. Most notable, however, was the limited amount of research AREU was able to do on the security sector, which proved to be very inadequate relative to demand, especially as the deteriorating security situation increasingly became the priority issue for many policy makers. [8]

A final and perhaps most difficult challenge worth noting in terms of the objective of influencing policy is the one that confronts all policy research institutions – how to measure their own policy impact. While AREU generally received positive feedback on its research and publications, it continually struggled to find ways to measure its impact on policy. Efforts were made to measure success through tangible indicators such as use of AREU publications and materials by the development community, citing of research findings in meetings and documents, references made to AREU publications in media, Web site hits, and occasional readership surveys. While all of these conveyed the notion that AREU's work was well received and the organization's role was valued, they did not give any conclusive indication of its effectiveness in achieving policy impact. In fact, sometimes AREU had the suspicion that it was preaching to a somewhat

---

[8] AREU's only two research publications focusing on the security sector are Michael Bhatia, Kevin Lanigan, and Philip Wilkinson (2004) and Andrew Wilder (2007).

disempowered choir, and that while officials on the ground in Afghanistan praised AREU's work, policy was being driven by other actors – especially in Washington as well as the inner circle around Karzai – for whom there was considerably less interest in the findings of in-depth policy research.

CONCLUSIONS AND LESSONS LEARNED

This chapter has described the processes and challenges of establishing a policy research institution in a setting that initially was perceived to be "postconflict" but that over time descended back into conflict. While environments differ, a number of conclusions and generalizable lessons can be extracted from AREU's experience.

First, like all policy research institutions, AREU struggled to measure the impact that its research had on policy. The role and impact of AREU's research were particularly ambiguous when it came to Afghan actors and institutions. In an environment with very weak traditions of public discussion and involvement in policy-related matters, and where there had never before been an independent policy research organization, there was little or no prior experience engaging with or utilizing independently generated policy research. Furthermore, for many of the former warlords, commanders, and factional leaders who dominated the new Afghan government, there was no interest in research findings intended to contribute to better policy making. That AREU never encountered serious backlash or threats in response to its research on sensitive topics (e.g., opium economy, police corruption) could mean that AREU was judicious and careful in communicating its research findings, or simply that the power holders were never aware of or interested in the findings and/or did not feel threatened by them.

While the direct impact of AREU's work on Afghan policy makers seems to have been limited, it did appear to be much more successful in informing and influencing the policies of international actors and institutions. Although the impact was still difficult to measure precisely, AREU's research publications were widely cited in key bilateral and multilateral donor policy and planning documents, and more informal feedback also suggested that AREU's research had influenced donor policies. For example, World Bank officials noted that AREU's research work with the World Bank on subnational administration played an important role in shaping the bank's thinking on public administration reform and subnational governance. Given the very strong influence of the international community led by the United States on shaping many Afghan government policies, AREU's work can be seen to have had an indirect rather than direct impact on Afghan government policies.

A second lesson from the experience of establishing AREU is the importance of establishing strong institutional objectives, structures, and systems early on in a fluid environment such as Afghanistan. As noted in earlier sections of this chapter, a relatively clear mission, mandate, and strategy to guide criteria for research and other activities prevented the organization from being diverted from its fundamental mission and goals. Investing time and effort at the beginning to develop the "nuts and bolts" of sound policies and procedures can free up staff time that would otherwise be wasted in inevitable ad hoc disputes over policies and in determining how to accomplish tasks. In an environment where distrust of institutions runs high, a transparent system that conveys a sense of fairness encourages staff loyalty. Relatively sound institutional structures also encourage donor confidence and, in turn, funding.

At the same time, an organization cannot become so wedded to its policies and procedures so as not to have flexibility when required – especially critical in an environment such as Afghanistan. There is also a need to be informally linked with enough of the right external actors to be able to navigate the quasi-lawless system when confronted with resistance to findings or, more frequently, personal agendas that threaten the organization. In AREU's case, this meant, for instance, having access to those who could get the release of employees wrongly jailed or in getting special exemptions written into government regulations that would have required ministerial review of all AREU publications.

A third lesson is the need to carefully consider optimal organizational size and relationship to other institutions. Among many civil society and research organizations there tends to be a bias toward growing and becoming more visible. Perhaps because most small institutions struggle to attract sufficient resources and to be relevant, the growth instinct is almost genetically coded into young organizations. Yet, too much or the wrong kind of growth can ultimately be detrimental to the organization, either because it becomes too big or because it tries to do too much and strays from its core mission.

Some observers felt that an organization such as AREU did not neatly fit into any one category, and therefore over the long term to be sustainable it would somehow have to be institutionalized within a formal relationship to the Afghan government. This was questionable even at the time when it was conceivable that the state was on a linear path to development, and the current state of affairs has vindicated AREU's skepticism about this direction. Even under the most optimistic scenarios about the Afghan state, a close relationship with the government would likely cost AREU much of its effectiveness as it became another neglected and abused bureaucracy subject to the interests of officials. As mentioned earlier, core funding allowed AREU to be independent institutionally, but also in terms of setting research priorities.

This chapter has tried to identify the considerable challenges to establishing a policy research institution in a conflict zone, but also the significant rewards. In AREU's case, the rewards included providing a young generation of Afghans with exposure to new analytical approaches and a new perspective on their own society, and at the same time providing empirically based observations to policy makers, both Afghan and international, who were motivated to use them. The hope is that AREU's experience shows the value of such an institution and can be of benefit to others creating something similar in other contexts.

BIBLIOGRAPHY

Afghanistan Research and Evaluation Unit (AREU). 2002. Draft strategic plan. *AREU*. Available at www.areu.org.af (accessed September 10, 2010).

 2003. Afghan elections: The great gamble. *AREU*: Available at www.areu.org.af (accessed September 10, 2010).

 2003. Improving Afghan lives through research: AREU strategic plan (2004–2006). *AREU*: Available at www.areu.org.af (accessed September 10, 2010).

Afghanistan Research and Evaluation Unit (AREU) and the World Bank. 2004a. A guide to government in Afghanistan. *AREU*: Available at www.areu.org.af (accessed September 10, 2010).

 2004b. Subnational administration in Afghanistan: Assessment and recommendations for action. *AREU*: Available at www.areu.org.af (accessed September 10, 2010).

Afghanistan Research and Evaluation Unit (AREU). 2011. A-Z guide to Afghanistan assistance. *AREU*: Available at http://www.areu.org.af/ContentDetails.aspx?ContentId=19&ParentId=19 (accessed September 10, 2010).

Baitemann, Olga. 1990. NGOs and the Afghan War: The politicization of humanitarian aid. *Third World Quarterly* 12(1).

Barakat, Sultan and A. Strand. 1995. Rehabilitation and reconstruction of Afghanistan: A challenge for Afghans, NGOs and the UN. *Disaster Prevention and Management* 4(1): 21–6.

Bhatia, Michael, Kevin Lanigan, and Philip Wilkinson. 2004. Minimal investments, minimal results: The failure of security policy in Afghanistan. *AREU*: Available at www.areu.org.af (accessed September 10, 2010).

Bleuer, Christian. 2010. *Afghan analysts bibliography*. Available at http://afghanistan-analyst.org (accessed September 1, 2010).

Boesen, Inger W. 1985. From autonomy to dependency: Aspects of the "dependency syndrome" among Afghan refugees. *Migration Today* 13(5): 17–21.

Christensen, Asgar. 1995. *Aiding Afghanistan: The background and prospects for reconstruction in fragmented society*. Copenhagen: NIAS Press.

Edwards, David B. 1996. *Heroes of the age: Moral fault lines on the Afghan frontier.* Berkeley: University of California Press.

Howell, David R. 1982. Refugee resettlement and public policy: A role for anthropology. *Anthropological Quarterly* 65(3): 119–26.

Lister, Sarah. 2005. Caught in confusion: Local governance structures in Afghanistan. *AREU:* Available at www.areu.org.af (accessed September 10, 2010).

Lorentz, J. H. 1987. Afghan aid: The role of private voluntary organizations. *Journal of South Asian and Middle East Studies* 11(1–2).

Mansfield, David. 2006. Opium poppy cultivation in Nangarhar and Ghor. *AREU:* Available at www.areu.org.af (accessed September 10, 2010).

Monsutti, Alessandro. 2005. *War and migration: Social networks and economic strategies of the Hazaras of Afghanistan.* trans. Patrick Camiller. New York: Routledge.

Pain, Adam. 2006. Opium trading systems in Helmand and Ghor. *AREU:* Available at www.areu.org.af (accessed September 10, 2010).

Paterson, Anna and James Blewett (2006), Putting the cart before the horse? Privatization and economic reform in Afghanistan. *AREU:* Available at www.areu.org.af (accessed September 10, 2010).

Reynolds, Andrew and Andrew Wilder. 2004. Free, fair or flawed: Challenges for legitimate elections in Afghanistan. *AREU:* Available at www.areu.org.af (accessed September 10, 2010).

Turton, David and Peter Marsden. 2002. Taking refugees for a ride? The politics of refugee return to Afghanistan. *AREU:* Available at www.areu.org.af (accessed September 10, 2010).

Wilder, Andrew. 2007. Cops or robbers? The struggle to reform the Afghan national police. *AREU:* Available at www.areu.org.af (accessed September 10, 2010).

Wily, Liz Alden. 2003. Land rights in crisis: Addressing tenure insecurity in Afghanistan. *AREU:* Available at www.areu.org.af (accessed September 10, 2010).

9

Conducting Research in Conflict Zones

Lessons from the African Great Lakes Region

Timothy Longman

The house had a painting of a snarling guard dog on the front gate to warn potential troublemakers against entering, so the clandestine prison hidden within was known to the people of Goma as Chien Méchant – Vicious Dog – an apt warning of the horrors that took place inside. When I traveled with a Human Rights Watch (HRW) colleague on a mission in the eastern part of the Democratic Republic of Congo in March 2000, the people of the region told us about many such sites, improvised and covert places of detention where people suspected of opposing the Rwandan occupation of their territory or of organizing resistance of any sort were held indefinitely, without charge, in terrible conditions.[1] Houses, public offices, schools, or any other building could be commandeered for use as a makeshift prison. In several places, shipping containers were used as detention cells, and in a few cases, people inside reportedly suffocated to death when the sun beating down made the containers as hot as ovens. Reports of torture were common, but since these prisons were unofficial, illegal under international law, and said by the provisional government not to exist, neither the Red Cross nor the United Nations (UN) visited to investigate.

Chien Méchant was an improbable place for a prison – a good-sized home inside a large walled compound located in an old upscale neighborhood in the center of Goma. As we drove through town, we passed the compound many times, and we would never have guessed what was going on behind the gates had not numerous people told us that Chien Méchant was a detention center specializing in torture. Several people, including civil society activists and nongovernmental organization (NGO) workers, told us that they had been picked up off the streets of Goma, then taken to Chien Méchant and beaten while soldiers accused them of colluding with the Kabila government

---

[1]   The report based on this mission was published as Longman (2000).

in Kinshasa or passing incriminating information about the Congolese Rally for Democracy (RCD) administration or the Rwandan Patriotic Front (RPF) to outside groups like HRW and Amnesty International. Most prisoners were detained for only a few days before being released, but some were held in the prison for longer periods. Though we doubted we would be allowed to enter, my colleague and I determined that, at the very least, we had to show that we were aware of the illegal prison's existence and would do our best to expose it.

Late one afternoon, we knocked on the gate of the Chien Méchant compound. A uniformed RCD soldier opened a door cut into the large metal gate and stepped outside. We gave him our calling cards and told him that we were conducting a human rights investigation and had authorization to visit the detention center. This assertion was almost true, since we had paid courtesy visits when we arrived in Goma to the local military commandant and several ministers in the provisional government, who had given us grudging permission to conduct research, though not specifically in clandestine prisons. The soldier was not flustered and did not deny that this was in fact a prison. He simply took our cards and told us that his commanding officer was not there and that we should return in the morning.

When we returned the next day, the same soldier greeted us at the gate, and without further question, he led us inside. The compound of the colonial era home, which had probably once boasted attractive gardens, had been converted into a military camp. Whatever grass there had once been was replaced by a wide expanse of well-trod dirt dotted with piles of wood, the remains of campfires, and a few olive green military pup tents. A few soldiers were loitering about an open cooking fire to the side of the house. The soldier led us to a side door, where a young RCD officer met us and told us that he was in charge. We told him that we were human rights researchers and that we had heard reports that civilians were being detained and tortured in this facility. Specifically, we reported the accusation we had heard that a number of intellectuals and NGO leaders were briefly detained here and tortured after a citywide protest in Goma three weeks earlier. Remarkably, the commander objected only to the charges of torture, not the illegal detentions. He told us openly that the arrests were only meant to frighten people. "We arrested all of these people, and everyone was afraid because they did not know what would happen to them, whether we would kill them or beat them. But they were fine, and we released them the next day. Really this was only intended to intimidate the population."[2]

---

[2] Interview in Goma, March 9, 2000.

We asked to see the facility, and he willingly took us into the house where prisoners were kept. There were only three prisoners there at the time, and he pointed to them and said, "See, you can see for yourself that they are being well treated, that there is no torture. These are men accused of stealing." My colleague walked on with him into another room, engaging him in loud conversation, while I quickly stepped over to the prisoners and asked them about their experience. One told me that he was not accused of theft but was a worker at a local business that they had accused of making contact with people in Kinshasa. He hastily lifted the back of his shirt to show me the fresh wounds from where he had been whipped. He said that he had been there for more than a week and that although there were only three in detention today, a few days before there had been more than a dozen. People were brought in for a couple of days, beaten repeatedly, and then either transferred to another facility or released. The other two corroborated his story. I heard my colleague moving on with the commander, so I thanked them and rushed into the next room. The commander led us out through an open door onto the patio, where we asked him a few more questions, before he accompanied us back to the entrance gate and sent us on our way.

I begin my chapter with this story, because it highlights several of the points that I hope to make about doing human rights research in conflict zones – the surprising availability of evidence, the importance of local knowledge, the value of popular sources, and the impossibility of scholarly neutrality. As my work as both an academic researcher and a human rights advocate in the strife-torn Great Lakes region of Central Africa has shown me, conducting research in conflict zones clearly poses major problems. As a researcher, you put your personal safety at risk when you explore politically sensitive issues in areas under authoritarian rule or military occupation. The potential risks to those who work with you and provide information are even greater, and you have to take special precautions to protect your sources. Because of the risks, many potential sources may be afraid to speak openly, and those who do speak may avoid divulging information that incriminates those in power.

Yet even in places where violence is endemic and governments regularly persecute people who criticize them, good, systematic research is still possible. Sometimes information that one would expect to be secret is readily available. People are often much more willing to speak openly than one would expect. In fact, many people who are critical of military occupation, authoritarian political tactics, and other offenses will speak out of principle, as a means of disseminating information about the abuses their country is experiencing. And it is not simply civil society activists and other elites who will be willing to provide information. Average people – farmers, day laborers, market women – not only are much better informed than most elites (whether domestic or international) assume, but are also often very willing to reveal what they know. Even when people are afraid of the consequences of speaking out and evade questions or tell untruths, a well-developed knowledge of the local culture can help a researcher break through this barrier and persuade people to open up.

While conducting research on human rights abuses and the effects of war and authoritarian rule can be systematic and scientifically valid according to the best standards of the social sciences, such research places a heavy burden on the researcher. The challenge of protecting sources can be quite difficult and may force one to limit the research conducted and what is done with information collected. People participate in sensitive research, providing information that could potentially put them at risk, for a purpose; they want the researcher to use the information they provide to make a difference in their communities. As a result, researchers in conflict zones have a moral responsibility to ensure that their research has a maximum impact. Focusing purely on academic publication – and the resultant rewards of teaching positions and promotions – without trying to improve conditions by disseminating information to a general audience (through public lectures, popular publications, and other means) is irresponsible. A researcher can conduct scientifically valid inquiries without remaining neutral on how the results are applied.

BACKGROUND ON THE CONFLICTS IN THE GREAT LAKES REGION OF CENTRAL AFRICA

In this chapter, I draw on my experience conducting research in Rwanda, Burundi, and DRC, three countries whose conflicts in recent decades have been deeply interconnected. Tension between the minority Tutsi and majority Hutu ethnic groups has troubled Rwanda and Burundi since the colonial era. Ethnic violence in one country has usually encouraged reactions in the other. For example, the Hutu uprising in Rwanda in 1959 and subsequent attacks on Tutsi moved the Tutsi leaders of Burundi to harden their control. Likewise, attacks on Tutsi in Burundi in 1972 helped inspire pogroms against Tutsi in Rwanda in 1973. In the early 1990s, democracy movements in both countries challenged the established ethnically based political order, but resistance by powerful elites led to civil wars. In Burundi, the assassination of the first Hutu president only three months after he took office in 1993 launched a ten-year civil war. Elections in 2006 installed the former Hutu rebel leader as president but also inaugurated a system in which public positions were formally reserved for all ethnic groups. In Rwanda, the RPF invasion helped fuel the fear that motivated participation in the 1994 genocide, a radical program of ethnic scapegoating implemented by Hutu elites seeking to protect their power. But the genocide was so disruptive that it allowed the RPF to seize control of the country. Their control was consolidated in elections in 2003 that ended a formal period of transition.

Despite the DRC's very different demography and geography, with more than three hundred different ethnic groups scattered across a vast territory, the violence in Rwanda and Burundi in the 1990s spilled over into the DRC. In 1996, Rwanda, Burundi, and Uganda created and fought alongside a Congolese rebel group that ultimately deposed the longtime dictator Mobutu Sese Sekou. When the new Congolese president sought to assert his independence from his former allies, the three countries created a new rebel movement that attacked Congo in 1998. This time, however, other African states backed the government of the DRC, stopping the advance of the rebels, who fractured into several groups, each controlling a portion of Congo's territory. The conflict ultimately descended into a brutal contest among warlords. Despite several peace deals, a massive UN peacekeeping operation, and successful 2006 elections, the DRC remains deeply fractured and violence remains pervasive.

The examples in this chapter are from research that I conducted in these three countries throughout this period of upheaval. I lived in Rwanda conducting dissertation research in 1992–3, in the midst of the 1990–4 civil war. I returned to Rwanda a year after the 1994 genocide as the head of the field office for HRW and the International Federation for Human Rights (FIDH et al.). From 2001 through 2006, I directed a major research project based at the Human Rights Center of the University of California, Berkeley, on postgenocide reconstruction in Rwanda. I have also traveled repeatedly to Burundi and the DRC both for human rights missions and for research. I conducted human rights research in Burundi in 1997, at the height of that country's civil war, and I returned a decade later in 2007, a year after the return to civilian rule. Similarly, I was in the DRC during a particularly bloody and chaotic period of its war and returned to the country a year after its transition to civilian rule.

EVIDENCE MAY BE READILY AVAILABLE

Human rights organizations operate largely under an approach commonly referred to as "naming and shaming" (Rubenstein 2004, 845–65). Working under the assumption that most human rights violations happen under cloak of darkness and that most perpetrators of unjust detention, torture, and political murders do not want their actions publicly exposed, Amnesty International in the 1960s pioneered the method of investigating disappearances, detentions without trial, and other human rights abuses; naming the specific individuals responsible; and then seeking to disseminate the information as widely as possible in the hopes of pressuring the perpetrators into releasing the detained, stopping torture, or ending other human rights abuses. HRW, Physicians for Human Rights, Amnesty International, the International Crisis Group, and many other human rights groups, both international and domestic, now regularly conduct field research and issue reports that seek to expose abuses and shame perpetrators into changing their behavior.

Yet as the story of Chien Méchant suggests, human rights abuses are not necessarily carefully hidden. In fact, since the purpose of many abuses is to intimidate the population and scare them away from opposing the regime, abuses often need to be relatively open to serve their purpose. The fact that Chien Méchant was situated in such a central location and that its ostensibly secret existence was so poorly concealed seemed to indicate that the prison, with its arrests and torture, served as a warning to the people of Goma against resisting RCD control. The commander's openness about their attempt to intimidate activists after the February 2000 protest clearly reinforces this conclusion.

While uncovering the facts about human rights abuses is not always as easy as knocking on a gate and being ushered inside, the truth is often more easily accessed than people who have not conducted this type of research are aware. Perpetrators may feel no particular shame about their actions, because they feel they are justified, they are merely following orders, or they are acting with impunity, with no fear of negative consequences. As a result, like the commander of Chien Méchant who willingly told us that they had arrested civil society activists just to intimidate them, police and military personnel and others may be much more forthcoming than one might expect. This is particularly true when the setting of an interview is more casual – over a meal in a restaurant or over drinks at a bar. Outside a formal interview context, when the notebook is put away, many informants will speak quite freely – though to cite this information a researcher needs to be clear that everything said is on the record or to use it as a basis for pursuing information through other means.

The lack of immediate shame among perpetrators of human rights abuses does not mean that the name and shame approach does not work. The purpose of human rights research is not merely to expose hidden abuses but to point out that certain practices – such as regularly beating all prisoners – are in fact unacceptable under international law and widely held moral principles. Pressure is ultimately directed against civilian leaders and against the military chain of command to ensure that their subordinates are aware of international human rights law and that they engage in practices that are consistent with international standards.

Often when a regime is engaged in systematic human rights abuses, there are those inside the regime who, even if they agree with the goals of the regime's policies, object to illegal and violent tactics. Military officers, government ministers, and others working for a regime should not be assumed to be hostile to the cause of human rights; they may serve as excellent sources of information, able to confirm the complicity of the government or the military in abuses, though usually off the record. During an international human rights mission that visited Rwanda in early 1993, several individuals who had participated in official government meetings, including one high-level official within the regime still in office, were willing to provide the researchers with information. They verified that a series of massacres of Tutsi that took place from October 1990 (when an RPF invasion launched the civil war) through February 1993 were not only organized by local officials but also approved by those at the very top of the regime. One journalist who had previously worked directly for the president was even willing to go on record with details about meetings where plans for massacres were discussed (FIDH 1993). Similarly, in the months prior to the 1994 genocide, senior military officers contacted the head of the United Nations Mission, General Romeo Dallaire, to inform him, "More massacres of the same kind are being prepared and are supposed to spread throughout the country" (quoted in Des Forges 1999, 145).

Conducting forms of research more reliable than key informant interviews is often more possible in a conflict zone than many on the outside realize. In 2002, as part of a larger research project on postgenocide social reconstruction in Rwanda, I worked with several colleagues to organize a survey in four representative communities. While the genocide had ended nearly a decade ago and there was little active violence in Rwanda at the time, the political situation was still quite restrictive, with the government tightly controlling the press, limiting civil society, and intimidating the general public into silent acquiescence. Despite this less than propitious research environment, in conducting a number of semistructured interviews with both elites and the general population, we found that it was still possible to induce people to talk with a degree of candor. Drawing on our qualitative research and directly involving several Rwandan colleagues, we crafted a survey that probed sensitive subjects such as attitudes toward justice and reconciliation, interpretations of the past, and even ethnic relations in a delicate and culturally sensitive manner. The survey was revised and improved in response to numerous trials. We chose a group of twenty-six student interviewers evenly divided ethnically, and we spent a week conducting intensive training, emphasizing tactics for approaching survey participants that diminished class barriers and put them at ease. In the end, our survey went off with surprising success, and most people were willing to speak forthrightly (Longman, Pham, and Weinstein 2004, Pham, Weinstein, and Longman 2004). Some reviewers of our publications resulting from the survey challenged the very possibility of conducting research in a country like Rwanda (Nemery 2004). We were confident in our results, not simply because of cross-checking questions built into the survey but more importantly because of the willingness that people showed to say things at variance with the official government line. We were fortunate to have conducted our research at a moment in time before the government implemented its major crackdown against discussing ethnicity. Key to our success, however, were the team's depth of understanding of the Rwandan context and the qualitative work that provided the basis for our survey.

LOCAL KNOWLEDGE IS IMPORTANT

Despite the sometimes surprising accessibility of information, the most easily obtained answers to research questions are not always the most accurate. Conducting good research requires finding ways to check and cross-check results. In a context of ongoing violence or authoritarian oppression, people are, not surprisingly, quite savvy at protecting themselves by avoiding saying things that could get them into trouble. Unless people trust you and have confidence that you will protect their interests, they are likely either to remain largely silent or merely to feed you the official line. A surprising number of researchers are willing to accept whatever they are told at face value, which generally reinforces the claims of those in power. To get beyond superficial, false answers – and to be able to assess when you are being misled – an understanding of the local culture is quite helpful. Speaking local languages puts potential informants at ease, and understanding the constraints they are under allows you to address them in a fashion that can make them comfortable speaking openly with you.

For example, when Molly Bingham and I conducted a mission for HRW in Burundi in 1997, most of the news coverage at the time focused on attacks by Hutu rebel groups and the civilian deaths that were supposedly resulting. The idea that the rebels were attacking communities and massacring unarmed civilians in various parts of Burundi was not only widely reported by journalists but also widely believed within diplomatic circles. Asking around, however, raised doubts. Burundians with whom we spoke in Bujumbura told us that they questioned the veracity of the reports. Nearly all of the international

journalists and foreign diplomats admitted that they had visited areas of
reported attacks either with a government minder or with an armed escort.

In contrast, when we went into the countryside to conduct investigations
in communities where attacks had taken place and civilians had been killed,
we traveled without escort of any kind, only an interpreter. We made a point
of addressing people with a few greetings in Kirundi. We often stopped along
the road before we arrived at a community – and before we had introduced
ourselves to local government officials and thereby drawn attention to our
visit – and questioned people about the situation. Despite these attempts at
putting people at rest, nearly all people responded to our initial questions
with the official government line, telling us that Hutu rebels had attacked
their community and killed people. But we knew to push further. We asked
people whether they were eyewitnesses of massacres, and if so whether they
could describe exactly what happened. For those who had seen events themselves, we asked them to describe those who opened fire, where they came
from, and how they were dressed, for example, questions that often revealed
that those who had shot civilians were actually dressed in Burundi army uni-
forms. Sometimes after people had repeated to us the official interpretation of
events, we told them of an alternative explanation that we had heard in which
it was actually government troops who had opened fire on the population.
After only a little prodding, most people would laugh and then change their
story. In almost all cases, it turned out, what had actually happened was that
rebels had raided the community to steal, sometimes from an arms depot, but
often just seeking provisions. The army would arrive after they had fled and,
either frustrated at missing their target or believing that the local population
was working in collusion with the rebels, opened fire on whoever had the misfortune of being present. After confirming this version of events, people would
sometimes laugh and say, "We didn't think we could tell you that at first." As a
result of understanding Burundian culture enough to know to push beyond
initial responses, we were able to present a report that was at sharp variance
with most other contemporary reports on human rights in Burundi, pointing
a finger squarely at government forces for many of the abuses. Though the
rebels unfortunately became increasingly abusive themselves in subsequent
years, the version of events that we presented was generally shown to be more
accurate (Longman 1998).

The case of Rwanda puts the need for local knowledge into sharpest relief.
As someone who was in Rwanda prior to 1994, I was struck deeply and personally by the genocide. I lost a number of friends and colleagues and was
confronted as well with the reality that I knew some of those who carried out
the massacres. Prior to my going to Rwanda in 1992, the country was little

known in the rest of the world. Yet in the years after 1994, the genocide began to attract increasing international attention, with treatments in the popular press, like Philip Gourevitch's articles and book, and even attention in Hollywood. Many journalists and researchers approached Rwanda exclusively through the lens of the genocide, and many people inaccurately equated the 1994 genocide of Tutsi with the Jewish Holocaust during the Second World War. As Johan Pottier has effectively analyzed, the Rwandan Patriotic Front (RPF) that took power in 1994 very effectively promulgated an international image of itself as reluctant warriors who had put a halt to the genocide that the international community failed to stop. The RPF promoted a Manichean worldview that depicted them as good guys who opposed the bad guy *genocidaires*, ignoring the reality that their invasion of Rwanda had facilitated the genocide by sowing insecurity in the population and that the RPF itself had engaged in extensive human rights abuses as they marched across Rwanda after seizing power, and in particular during their two invasions of the DRC (Pottier 2002).

As a result of the way that Rwanda attracted international attention and because of the RPF's very effective propaganda campaign, a major divergence has emerged in interpretations of the social and political situation in postgenocide Rwanda. Many of those whose interest in Rwanda began with the 1994 genocide – in particular, many scholars of the Holocaust, journalists looking for a positive story, and people involved in development work – present Rwanda as a model of good governance and successful recovery from violence. They point to the rhetoric of the RPF-led regime, which has regularly articulated a commitment to reconciliation, and they emphasize the high level of energy, low level of corruption, and general competence demonstrated by regime operatives. Stephen Kinzer's hagiography of President Paul Kagame, *A Thousand Hills* (2008), is perhaps the paradigm of the approach that focuses only on the positive aspects of the RPF while ignoring or justifying any evidence of RPF massacres, regional imperialist aims, suppression of dissent, and other authoritarian tendencies.

In contrast, nearly all of the scholars who worked on Rwanda before the genocide (like Catherine and David Newbury, the late Alison Des Forges, René Lemarchand, and Filip Reyntjens) as well as a handful of newer Rwanda scholars who have done intensive, long-term research in Rwanda (like Scott Straus, Lee Ann Fujii, Susan Thomson, Lars Waldorf, and Jennie Burnett) take a more nuanced approach, acknowledging the horrors of the genocide while also recognizing the failings of the new regime. The source of the divergence seems to be the much greater depth of knowledge about Rwanda among the latter group. Most serious scholars have spent substantial time in the Rwandan countryside, and they have developed intimate understandings of local communities and their dynamics.

Language is one of the major barriers to many recent converts to Rwandan studies. Many of those who have approached Rwanda more recently and more superficially do not speak French, which was the language of intellectual discourse in Rwanda prior to 1994, much less Kinyarwanda, the national language. They are therefore limited to working with anglophone interpreters and informants, most of whom arrived in Rwanda after the RPF occupation of the country. While the anglophone RPF perspective is certainly valid and should be included in any serious analysis of the country, it is a particular and limited perspective. Most anglophone Rwandans were not in the country at the time of the genocide, and they therefore have only secondhand knowledge of what happened. In fact, most of these returned anglophone refugees had no experience of Rwanda at all prior to 1994, growing up in Uganda, where they may have had interactions with members of various Ugandan ethnic groups but where most had no experience with Rwanda's majority ethnic group, the Hutu. In contrast to most Tutsi who lived in Rwanda prior to 1994, the repatriated Tutsi generally are not members of families with ethnically mixed marriages. As my research in the past decade has found, many of the repatriated former refugees (including many of the francophone repatriated from Congo and Burundi) have no close Hutu friends, and they tend to view Hutu with substantial suspicion, often regarding them as inherently genocidal. Finally, the fact that French is absolutely essential for conducting research in Burundi and the DRC may explain the lesser degree of academic attention their conflicts have received in the United States.

My point here is not to invalidate all research that does not adhere to my own perspective – Gourevitch and Kinzer, for example, provide excellent insights into how the RPF leadership perceives its mission and justifies its behavior. Rather, I want to balance my assertion about the relative accessibility of some supposedly hard to find information with a warning that one needs appropriate training and background to be able to perceive distortions and winnow the false from the true. Seeing evidence of torture – both on the body of the prisoner I spoke with at Chien Méchant and on the bodies of others who told me they had been tortured there – as well as speaking with a number of eyewitnesses who could corroborate one another's stories were key to making a confident assertion about the behavior of RCD and RPF troops in eastern Congo. My knowledge of Kinyarwanda, Swahili, and Lingala and my decade of academic research on Congo have proved invaluable in my efforts to get at the truth about events like the torture that took place at Chien Méchant. In contrast, there is a troubling trend in my own discipline, political science, as well as in economics, sociology, and certain other fields, to encourage only general and comparative studies and to disparage an area studies approach that involves in-depth knowledge of particular places. The approach of conducting quick, superficial surveys and other forms of drop-in research that are not complemented with more intensive, long-term qualitative studies and do not benefit from the knowledge of people with a deep understanding of the local culture can lead to incomplete and inaccurate scholarship.

DON'T OVERLOOK POPULAR SOURCES

Undoubtedly, the most common form of research, particularly in conflict zones and other sensitive contexts, is interviewing elites – government officials, civil society activists, journalists, and other community leaders. These influential individuals are the people who are easiest to find (they usually have offices, secretaries, and cell phones), are generally well informed (their government ministry or NGO may be directly involved in issues a researcher is investigating), and are simplest to interview (in Africa, they are usually conversant in French or English or Portuguese, thus obviating the need for a translator from other languages). Many assessments and other quick research junkets – like the Democracy and Governance Assessments that I have conducted for USAID – consist primarily of a series of elite interviews of this sort, in which well-informed individuals are pumped for information and analysis. As a methodology, this approach is now often called "key informant interviewing," a term that lends an air of formality and authenticity to an approach that is unfortunately often not very systematic.

Interviewing elites is often an important first step in beginning a research project, but it cannot substitute for more extensive and rigorous research methodologies. In most African countries, elites – whether inside or outside the government, whether regime supporters or regime critics – often share a common perspective that separates them from the general population. Through their Western education and their integration into the formal job market, most have become heavily influenced by a Western worldview that shapes how they understand phenomena such as group identity, politics, and morality. One reason that many foreign researchers focus much of their interviewing on these elites is that this shared worldview facilitates communication – but it also means that research results are likely to be distorted and incomplete.

Unfortunately, the exclusion of average people from research is driven not simply by a desire to facilitate investigations but also by an arrogant assumption that common people have little useful to say – in part because they do not understand the very concepts with which we are working. International actors and national governments often make important decisions about how to resolve conflicts, which political reforms to implement, which focus economic development should take, and other life-and-death issues for the public without ever taking popular will into account in any formal fashion. While representatives of civil society are commonly consulted, in Africa civil society tends to be based in urban areas and dominated by intellectuals with little connection to the majority of the population. The assumption that systematic research is not possible in conflict situations reinforces the tendency to ignore popular sources of information.

The tendency to ignore popular perspectives is particularly pronounced in the area of transitional justice. The use of judicial or quasi-judicial mechanisms after violent conflict has become a major tool that both governments and the international community have adopted as a means of helping to rebuild societies. Yet the decision to establish courts or truth commissions is generally made without any attempt to understand public attitudes, let alone the survivors' views, toward justice or public opinion about what is most needed for a society to rebuild. Much of the initial academic work on transitional justice (particularly in legal studies and political science) was based on principles of international law or theories of peace building rather than on empirical evidence about the impact that trials and truth commissions actually have on postconflict societies (cf. Kritz 1995, Mendez 1997, Neier 1998, Teitel 2002). Although empirical assessments of transitional justice mechanisms now indicate a frequent disconnection between the intentions of policy makers and the public reaction to trials, truth commissions, and other accountability mechanisms (cf. Stover and Weinstein 2004, Theidon 2006, Clarke and Goodale 2010, Olsen, Payne, and Reiter 2010, Shaw and Waldorf 2010), diplomats and government officials continue to promote transitional justice giving little consideration to local culture and carrying out no meaningful consultation with the very people who are expected both to participate in and to benefit from the processes.

In my own work on transitional justice over the past decade, I have found that while many elites have adopted Western understandings of accountability and justice, local conceptualizations of these ideas remain dominant within the general population. For example, when I was in Burundi in 2007, I asked a couple of women who were involved in a local community group in Bujumbura – women, I should point out, who did not have a formal education and did not speak French – what they thought about an amnesty for perpetrators of atrocities that could be part of a proposed truth commission. They told me that they absolutely opposed the idea of amnesty. "Someone who has committed atrocities should have to come before the public, admit what they did wrong, and ask forgiveness, and only then will we welcome them back into our communities." To Westerners and those who share Western understandings of justice, what the women described was, of course, amnesty. Yet within Burundian concepts of justice, having to go before the public and open oneself up for humiliation by admitting to error was in fact a form of accountability.

Even uneducated people have strong opinions about justice and accountability, and their opinions are often at variance with the ideas of elites. For example, many scholars and journalists have claimed that the Rwandan public is hostile to the International Criminal Tribunal for Rwanda (ICTR), basing their conclusion on the unrelentingly negative propaganda from the regime and the disparaging comments about the ICTR common among elites. Yet in our 2002 survey in Rwanda, we found that the general public had a mildly positive opinion of the ICTR, despite some criticisms. The main complaint that people expressed was that they were not better informed about the activities of the court, but this was at least as much the fault of the government as of the ICTR itself. Nevertheless, decisions about trials and truth commissions continue to be made without research into public opinion. In the DRC and Burundi, for example, plans for transitional justice were integrated into the country's postconflict political transitions without any attempt to consult the population in any meaningful fashion. Yet the success or failure of transitional justice depends on how it is received by the population. The practice of imposing judicial structures on the population from above has proven deeply flawed, yet it continues.

Everyday people are important sources of information not simply because public opinion affects the success or failure of policies but also because ordinary people – the kind who may not have finished school, who work with their hands, who are often struggling for daily survival – offer a perspective that originates in the grass roots. Living in communities where they are overlooked or discounted by the more powerful members of society, common people often have access to information that the elite do not. Sadly, they frequently bear the brunt of war-related violence and other human rights abuses, so they have important eyewitness accounts to report. They are also much more willing than one might expect to share their stories, even when doing so is dangerous. When we were in Congo in 2000, people were literally lining up at our door to tell us about the killings and torture and rape they had experienced.

Average citizens have a clear understanding of how conflicts take place in their communities and why people choose to participate or not. Much of the national-level literature on conflicts tends to treat the general population as an undifferentiated mass, completely prone to manipulation. A number of works

on the Rwandan genocide, for instance, Mahmood Mamdani's *When Victims
Become Killers* (2002), depict the Hutu masses as having been aroused to murder by an ideology that promoted hatred of the Tutsi. Yet my own research
on the genocide, which involved several long periods of fieldwork in local
communities in various parts of the country, including extensive interviewing
and focus groups with the general public, as well as ethnographic observation of local communities, found that people's reasons for participating were
much more complex. While some of the elites who organized the killings
were motivated by real hatred of Tutsi, most participants in the slaughter were
not driven primarily by hatred; they had lived at peace with their Tutsi neighbors for many years, and most had ethnically mixed families. Instead, people
participated out of obedience and fear. People were ordered to participate by
the government, and they feared the consequences of failing to do so. The
RPF advance across the country created additional fear and uncertainty,
which inspired some people to act. People also were motivated by greed, by
the chance to settle scores with rivals, and by opportunities to empower themselves and advance their social standing. My results are similar to those of
others who conducted local-level studies involving extensive interviewing of
average people, such as Lee Ann Fuji (2009) and Scott Straus (2006).

Sadly, most of the policies that the postgenocide government has implemented to promote reconciliation in Rwanda have been based on the idea
that the Hutu population was blinded by ideology and filled with hatred of
Tutsi. The new RPF regime, having a conception of Rwandan society shaped
by the experience of exile, failed to conduct their own research on the actual
causes of the genocide. Reconciliation programs – including reeducation
camps, school curricular reform, and various workshops and programs – have
focused on changing people's attitudes to diminish hatred rather than on promoting responsible citizenship. This didactic approach has been backed up
by coercive force as well. Genocide trials, including the local, nonprofessional
gacaca trials, have tried more than a million Hutu for even the smallest of
genocide-related crimes, holding culpable even those who acted under duress
and condemning people for merely being present when crimes were committed. An approach to justice informed by the voices of common people would
have focused more on establishing command responsibility and punishing
the leaders and organizers of the genocide while helping to empower common people to avoid manipulation in the future.

RESEARCHERS CANNOT BE NEUTRAL

As the discussion here should make clear, throughout my career, I have
attempted to bridge the worlds of academics and practice. When I first traveled

to Rwanda and began to conduct research on religion and politics, I could never have predicted the terrible calamity that would soon befall the country. Yet by the time I concluded my year of fieldwork and left Rwanda, I had seen enough ominous signs to be deeply concerned about the future. At a conference at the University of Leeds in November 1993, I remember speaking about the very dark times that Rwanda was going through and warning that something needed to be done. I was merely a graduate student when the genocide began, and I was deeply frustrated at my impotence, at my inability to raise public awareness of what was happening in Rwanda and to correct the misperception that the violence was merely another African instance of "ancient tribal hatreds." Alison Des Forges of HRW was one of the few individuals who spoke with moral authority and passionately called people to action to stop the Rwandan tragedy. When a year later, having just finished my dissertation, Alison offered me a position at the HRW office in Rwanda, I jumped at the opportunity. I spent a year as a human rights researcher for HRW, primarily participating in the massive exploration of the genocide that became *Leave None to Tell the Story*.

Since my first position with HRW in 1995–6, I have traveled to Africa many additional times, sometimes for formal academic research, sometimes for HRW and other organizations working in the field. Far from finding these two types of research to be contradictory, I find them to be complementary. I find that my social science research skills are highly useful for investigating human rights abuses or for helping the U.S. government analyze the principal challenges for democratic consolidation in a country. My social scientific training pushes me to conduct more systematic research, to go beyond key informant interviews and talk to the sorts of people – the poor and uneducated – who are often overlooked in brief assessments, and to push outside the capital cities into the countryside as much as possible. My knowledge of local languages and cultures helps me ask better questions and allows me to assess the veracity of answers.

On the other hand, working for governmental and nongovernmental groups has forced me to revise both my research and my writing. I have been forced to consider the potential impact that my research might have. I have been challenged to think about priorities for research projects based (at least in part) upon perceived needs for the societies that I am studying rather than simply choosing a topic that I might find personally most intriguing. In writing, I have been pushed to avoid jargon and to write in a fashion that will be accessible to people outside a narrow academic field.

Scholars who study sensitive issues like conflict, human rights conditions, democratization, and social and political activism have unique responsibilities. One responsibility about which nearly all researchers on sensitive subjects would agree is the need to protect sources. Our research depends on the willingness of individuals to risk punishment, including arrest and even potential death, to speak out against the government, expose abuses, and otherwise provide information that those in power would rather keep hidden. As researchers, we need to protect our sources not only in order to make them feel free to speak openly, but also because we have a moral obligation to see that our research does not cause harm. The widespread establishment of institutional research boards (IRBs) has occurred in response to unethical researchers whose inquiries failed to take the interests of research subjects into account.

Yet ensuring that research in human rights and conflict studies does not cause harm to subjects remains a great challenge. IRBs developed in the hard sciences, and their approaches to protecting human subjects are not always well adapted to the social sciences. They emphasize informed consent as a means of diminishing risk, but in countries experiencing war and authoritarian rule, many people will make a principled decision to provide information about human rights abuses even if doing so puts them at clear risk. Researchers have a responsibility to be more cautious than their subjects about decreasing the potential for negative consequences of the research. The responsibility to protect sources may occasionally force us as researchers to compromise our research methods, for example, preventing us from going to locations to see evidence firsthand. Yet reliable research can still be conducted even in many dangerous settings if sufficient care is taken. And the need for research in these settings is great. Where conditions make safe research impossible, other alternatives must be pursued, such as interviewing recent refugees or displaced persons.

One important factor in protecting sources is to be careful about the location of interviews. During my 2000 human rights mission in the eastern Congo, because of the extensive ongoing violence in the region and high level of paranoia of the rebel regime, we chose not to interview people in their homes or offices. Instead, we had people go to us where we were staying. Just before going to Congo, we had several Congolese human rights organizers travel to Uganda to meet with us in a safer atmosphere where we could speak freely and at length about the situation and strategize on how to conduct research safely in the occupied region. When they returned to Congo, they spread the word through local civil society networks that we were in town gathering data, and we were greeted by lines of people willing to speak to us at the Baptist Guest House in Goma and at the Catholic Episcopal Center in Bukavu. We also went to a few other locations where people's arrival would not raise suspicions, such as churches. To our Congolese colleagues, we emphasized the need for eyewitnesses. As a result, we had numerous people talk to us about the attacks on their villages, their imprisonment and torture, and their experience of being forced to mine coltan.[3] While security concerns prevented us from undertaking the preferred form of research, going out into the field to see evidence of abuses with our own eyes, a number of people showed us photographs of burned villages, dead bodies, and people showing scars from torture to back up their accounts. Precautions such as these could help to decrease risk while still allowing reliable research to be conducted.

I would further assert that researchers need to commit themselves to improving conditions in the societies they study rather than preserving scholarly detachment. Researchers who study conflict and human rights cannot remain neutral. In the tradition of critical theory (Horkheimer 1972, Guess 1981), we are called not simply to explain what has gone wrong in places like DRC, Rwanda, and Burundi, but to participate in the transformation of the countries. As outsiders, we cannot ourselves produce lasting positive transformation, but we can play a role in helping to promote it. During our Congo research, one of the reasons so many people talked to us, they explained, was that they could not themselves safely publicize what was happening in their communities – and they charged us with taking the information and disseminating it.

Taking a proactive approach to research need not compromise scientific rigor. In fact, if one is committed to using research to help transform society, then conducting reliable research is essential. A commitment to diminishing human rights violations or helping to resolve conflict peacefully should push one to explore particular topics and ask certain questions, but it should not cause one to distort results. Having worked in Rwanda prior to 1994, I knew both the victims and many of the killers in communities where I conducted research. The killers were not fundamentally different from their victims. They were not thoroughly and irrevocably evil individuals predestined to commit these crimes. Instead, the political and social situation, their social position, and their own irresponsible choices combined to bring about their participation in atrocities. In a different context, the tables might have been turned, a fact that Mamdani (2002) notes about Rwanda in *When Victims Become Killers*. Today's human rights activist can become tomorrow's brutal government official, a circumstance I confronted in Congo in 2000 when I encountered Congolese I had previously worked with on human rights causes then holding posts in the RCD regime.

---

3   Coltan is a metallic ore that, once refined, yields a substance called tantalum (Ta), a heat-resistant powder capable of holding high electrical charge. Tantalum is used in the manufacture of cell phones, pagers, and computers.

In postgenocide Rwanda, a number of scholars regard the RPF favorably because of its role in stopping the genocide and competently managing post-genocide reconstruction. Because of their belief in the RPF, a regrettable number of scholars have been willing to overlook evidence of human rights abuses, persecution of civil society, censorship of the press, and suppression of dissent. As someone who lived in Rwanda prior to the genocide and who was critical of the abuses of the Habyarimana regime, I understand well the danger of allowing political considerations to overshadow honest consideration of evidence. Much like under the RPF today, many people willingly overlooked the authoritarian practices of the Habyarimana regime, because of its competent management of economic development. The results of this selective vision were ultimately disastrous. A commitment to improving society does not mean choosing sides and blindly allying with the apparent "good guys." Instead, it means conducting honest research and respecting the facts, even if they are uncomfortable.

CONCLUSIONS

Conducting research on politically sensitive topics in conflict zones and in countries under authoritarian rule clearly poses serious challenges to researchers. Yet research in these societies is more desperately needed than in relatively peaceful and democratic places. Tragically, the countries that are in the worst shape and in the most need of development – places like Somalia, North Korea, and Burma – are the most challenging in which to conduct research and thus are the most neglected and least studied. Yet in most other countries in conflict and or under dictatorial rule, research remains possible, even if constrained. Research conditions in DRC, for example, are highly challenging, yet the Congolese people speak with a surprising frankness, and I have heard of few consequences for people who have served as sources for research. Despite the difficult conditions and the need to protect sources, rigorous and reliable research remains possible in most cases and is essential to help rebuild societies that have suffered from violence. In particular, researchers play a role in helping to ensure that the voices of average people, those usually overlooked and ignored by policy makers, be included in discussions about the future of their own countries. Researchers should have a commitment to studying societies in conflict not simply to advance scholarly knowledge but also to help contribute to their transformation. As outside researchers, we have the capacity to tell the world about places like Chien Méchant and to help see that such places are eradicated, and I would argue that we have a moral responsibility to do so as well.

BIBLIOGRAPHY

Clarke, Kamari Maxine and Mark Goodale, eds. 2010. *Mirrors of justice: Law and power in the post–Cold War era.* New York: Cambridge University Press.

Des Forges, Alison. 1999. *Leave none to tell the story: Genocide in Rwanda.* New York: Human Rights Watch.

Federation International des Ligues de Droits de l'Homme, Africa Watch et al. 1993. Rapport de la Commission Internationale d'Enquere sure les Violations des Droits de l'Homme au Rwanda depuis le 1er Octobre 1990 (7–21 janvier 1993). Paris: FIDH, March.

Fujii, Lee Ann. 2009. *Killing neighbors: Webs of violence in Rwanda.* Ithaca, NY: Cornell University Press.

Gourevitch, Philip. 1998. *We wish to inform you that tomorrow we will be killed with our families: Stories from Rwanda.* New York: Farrar, Straus & Giroux.

Guess, Raymond. 1981. *The idea of a critical theory: Habermas and the Frankfurt School.* Cambridge: Cambridge University Press.

Horkheimer, Max. 1972. *Critical theory: Selected essays.* New York: Continuum.

Kinzer, Stephen. 2008. *A thousand hills: Rwanda's rebirth and the man who dreamed it.* Hoboken, NJ: John Wiley & Sons.

Kritz, Neil J., ed. 1995. *Transitional justice.* Washington, DC: United States Institute of Peace Press.

Longman, Timothy. 1998 (March). Proxy targets: Civilians in the war in Burundi. New York: Human Rights Watch.

    2000. Eastern Congo ravaged: Killing civilians and silencing protest. *Human Rights Watch* 12(3) (May).

Longman, Timothy, Phuong Pham and Harvey Weinstein. 2004. Connecting justice to human experience: Attitudes toward accountability and reconciliation in Rwanda, in *My neighbor, my enemy: Justice and community in the aftermath of mass atrocity*, eds. Eric Stover and Harvey Weinstein. Cambridge: Cambridge University Press.

Mamdani, Mahmood. 2002. *When victims become killers: Colonialism, nativism, and the genocide in Rwanda.* Princeton, NJ: Princeton University Press.

Mendez, Juan. 1997. Accountability for past abuses. *Human Rights Quarterly*, 19(2): 255–82.

Neier, Aryeh. 1998. *War crimes: Brutality, genocide, terror, and the struggle for justice.* New York: Random House.

Nemery, Benoit. 2004. Letter to the editor. *Journal of the American Medical Association.* 292(17) (November 3): 2082.

Olsen, Tricia D., Leigh A. Payne and Andrew G. Reiter. 2010. *Transitional justice in balance: Comparing processes, weighing efficacy.* Washington, DC: United States Institute of Peace Press.

Pham, Phuong, Harvey Weinstein, and Timothy Longman. 2004. Trauma and PTSD symptoms in Rwanda: Implications for attitudes toward justice and reconciliation. *Journal of the American Medical Association.* 292(5) (August 4): 602–12.

Pottier, Johan. 2002. *Re-imagining Rwanda: Conflict, survival and disinformation in the late twentieth century.* Cambridge: Cambridge University Press.

Rubenstein, Leonard S. 2004. How international human rights organizations can advance economic, social, and cultural rights: A response to Ken Roth. *Human Rights Quarterly* 26(4) (November): 845–65.

Shaw, Rosalind and Lars Waldorf, eds. 2010. *Localizing transitional justice: Interventions and priorities after mass violence.* Stanford, CA: Stanford University Press.

Stover, Eric, and Harvey Weinstein, eds. 2004. *My neighbor, my enemy: Justice and community in the aftermath of mass atrocity.* Cambridge: Cambridge University Press.

Straus, Scott. 2006. *The order of genocide: Race, power, and war in Rwanda.* Ithaca, NY: Cornell University Press.

Teitel, Ruti. 2002. *Transitional justice.* Oxford: Oxford University Press.

Theidon, Kimberly. 2006. Justice in transition: The micro-politics of reconciliation in post-war Peru. *Journal of Conflict Resolution* 50(3) (June): 433–57.

PART VI

PRACTICALITIES

Figure 10. "Sweet Potatoes and Laundry" December 2003, Kono, Sierra Leone.
Photographer: Kate Lapides

Mr. Bah had recently repatriated to Sierra Leone from a refugee camp in
Guinea and we were visiting him and his family to see how they were faring.
After lunch, our research assistant took the video camera and began to film in
the ruins of the house across the street. We realized that people were actually
living in the roofless house, hanging their laundry, raising chickens, and cultivating sweet potatoes in the shadow of the wrecked car.

10

Preparing for Research in Active Conflict Zones

Practical Considerations for Personal Safety

Dyan Mazurana and Lacey Andrews Gale

There is something ironic about going to a war and becoming overly concerned with security. It may seem obvious to say so, but a war is a very dangerous place to be. Risk can be mitigated but it cannot be eliminated. That is not to say it should be taken lightly, but these are concerns that should be thought through as fully as possible before the decision is made to go to an area where there is active conflict. It is easy to adopt the self-delusion that the war is happening to others and that it will not impact me. But going to the war removes all choice in the matter.

> – Molly Bingham and Steve Connors on interviewing
> and filming insurgents in Iraq

Conducting research in situations of armed conflict where hostilities (i.e., acts of overt warfare) are taking place necessitates careful, practical preparation and planning. Part of this preparation and planning must include clearly assessing how to keep yourself and your team physically safe and emotionally healthy. Researchers who lack the knowledge, ability, and/or discipline to make good decisions to stay physically and emotionally healthy and safe are a risk to themselves, the other people on their team, and the people they are interviewing. Writing on this subject, Julie Mertus contends that

> care of the self is related to care for others ... a researcher who overlooks the potential risks of their work and who disregards their own vulnerability may endanger not only their own security but also the security of their interview subjects. (2009, 166)

The editors of this book received training for their own work in conflict zones from a variety of sources, including growing up in a country experiencing civil unrest and armed conflict, advanced training courses through the United Nations and human rights organizations, wilderness survival and orienteering courses, volunteering through the U.S. Peace Corps, emergency medical response courses, leadership courses, and working as a journalist or with humanitarian and human rights organizations. The contributors to this book, in the course of their work, have relied on their training and years of experience to survive armed attacks, arrests and detention, numerous armed roadblocks and checkpoints, minefields and unexploded ordnance, violent threats and intimidation, being taken hostage, a variety of injuries, diseases, and illnesses, and other challenging and unpleasant situations. In this chapter, we draw from our own experiences and training, as well as key lessons from other recognized experts in the field, to discuss practical steps to help ensure the researcher's physical safety and mental well-being while carrying out research in conflict zones where open hostilities are taking place.

TRAINING TO WORK IN CONFLICT ZONES

The United Nations and the major humanitarian and human rights NGOs require that staff going into areas experiencing armed conflict are up-to-date on all immunizations, are physically healthy (certified by a physician), and have completed security training to help ensure their personal safety and the safety of their teams. Such increased security awareness is necessary as violent attacks against humanitarian and human rights actors have significantly increased over the past decade, concentrated in a small number of exceptionally insecure countries (Egeland and Stoddard 2011). The most widely recognized and respected publications on staff security include the United Nations' *Security in the Field: Information for Staff Members of the United Nations System* (United Nations, Office of the United Nations Security Coordinator 2003); the recently updated *Operational Security Management in Violent Environments: A Field Manual for Aid Agencies* (Overseas Development Institute 2010); the NGO designed *The People in Aid Code of Best Practice in the Management and Support of Aid Personnel* (People in Aid 2003); and the International Federation of the Red Cross' (IFRC) excellent guide *Stay Safe – International Federation's Guide to a Safer Mission* (Tangen, Dryer and Julisson 2007). For researchers who are not working for the United Nations, the IFRC, or an NGO, these training guides are nevertheless worth studying as they offer practical and important information on a range of safety issues such as conducting situational, threat, and vulnerability analyses and the resulting risk assessment; staying safe while walking or driving; avoiding and surviving hijacking and kidnapping; and exit strategies. While the internal institutional security measures in these guides will not apply to all researchers, understanding the threat level as perceived by the United Nations or INGOs in the area the researcher is working should be an important component of her/his own security assessment and response.

Staff training for humanitarian and human rights workers is backed up with institutional protocol and health and security measures to keep staff safe. The United Nations Department for Safety and Security is the lead agency providing leadership, operational support, and oversight of the United Nations' security management system. The IFRC and the major humanitarian and human rights NGOs all have their own security divisions or experts to help prepare and ensure the security of field staff. While the focus of these measures remains on physical security, over the last decade there have been important measures established to enable staff to receive the necessary mental health care – something that previously existed only on an ad hoc basis, where it existed at all.

Compared with their humanitarian aid counterparts, most researchers carrying out work in zones of armed conflict have had little training or preparation regarding their own health and security in the field; most have gained their knowledge through their own hard-won experience. Additionally, unlike United Nations staff or the staff of large NGOs, most researchers conduct fieldwork with little institutional backing or security measures in place if help is needed. Yet, given the increase in contracting of researchers by governments, the United Nations, and NGOs, and the increased interest of academics in studying and working in situations of active armed conflict, it is imperative that researchers working in such situations be as well prepared as possible. A foundational element of this preparation concerns the researcher's personal security and well-being.

One of the best ways for researchers to become familiar with the key security threats and risks they may encounter in working in active conflict zones and how to mitigate such threats and risks, is to review the manuals noted here and complete both basic and advanced security training courses. A number of organizations offer these courses, and we recommend those focused on training for humanitarian and human rights workers. When selecting courses, researchers should ensure they receive training on the topics of how to keep safe in selecting a place to live, daily movements, and traveling around the country. Such training includes basic but vital information such as the following: in larger hotels do not stay on the ground floor (easy for assailants and thieves to break in), and do not stay above the sixth floor, as most fire rescue ladders do not reach higher than the seventh floor. Link up with NGOs where possible for transport and if hiring a driver ensure he or she is a licensed professional driver as most injuries in the field occur in car accidents caused by drivers driving recklessly. If working in an area where fighting is likely or is occurring, the radio should remain off as the driver needs to be alert to all sounds. Do not give lifts or offer to transport any armed person, including army or police.

Researchers should also receive training in avoiding and or remaining safe when encountering armed roadblocks, which they may frequently encounter in active conflict zones, as well as armed ambushes or being caught in an armed attack (both on the ground and from aircraft). Such training will include protocol both for the driver and for passengers. Here are some examples of what these training courses cover: Make sure to review with your driver the expected protocol for approaching armed roadblocks – switch off the high beams so as not to blind those at the checkpoints, approach them slowly so they can see your vehicle is coming, and do not attempt to turn around and avoid them as this may draw attention and perhaps fire or pursuit. The researcher should take off sunglasses, make sure the radio is completely turned off, and have all necessary identification and travel documents (in the national and local language) available. Do not make direct eye contact with those manning the checkpoint as this can be misinterpreted. Be respectful and professional, keep the hands where those manning the checkpoint can always see them, and move slowly. Roll down the window to answer questions and turn off the engine if requested to (otherwise leave it on). Do not get out of the vehicle unless ordered, and if so ordered try first to show them the necessary documents and remain in the vehicle. Never attempt (or appear to be attempting) to take photographs of any roadblock or armed forces or groups. If the roadblock is manned by child soldiers, remember to treat child soldiers as one would treat adult soldiers as they can be extremely dangerous.

Researchers should be trained on how to find and travel to (relatively) safe spaces during an attack or prior to a suspected attack. For example, when staying in guesthouses or hotels in areas where there is a possibility of fighting or an attack, the researcher should identify a safe place in the room or guesthouse where someone can take cover and stay away from windows. The researcher should identify safe routes in and out of the town. He or she should also know when it is best to stay in the vehicle and when to get out and take cover during an attack. The researcher should know that in almost all circumstances it is best to drive through an armed attack (once the firing begins), and not to stop (i.e., hesitate) or try to back up.

Kidnappings are the fastest growing form of attack affecting humanitarian aid workers (Egeland and Stoddard 2011). Researchers should know how to avoid or survive hijacking and kidnapping. The first few hours of a hijacking or kidnapping are the most deadly, as the abductors are tense and full of energy, so researchers should know the appropriate survival skills and be ready to put them to use. These include such basics as remaining quiet and calm and paying attention to where you are taken, doing what the hijackers or kidnappers tell you to do, not arguing or trying to talk your way out or showing feigned sympathy for their cause, and continually looking for possible escape routes.

Researchers working in areas of active conflict should be familiar with basic navigation and survival skills in case of being stranded or abandoned in remote or unknown areas. They should know how to build a variety of emergency shelters appropriate to the particular geography and circumstances. They should be able to navigate using the sun and the stars as guides. The researcher should wear appropriate clothes and shoes to enable trekking over distances and carry on their bodies a pack with water and a medical kit, which they should try to ensure they keep with them at all times.

Researchers should also be aware of how to avoid and detect antipersonnel, land mine, and unexploded ordnance; this is essential in working in conflict areas that are mined. Researchers need to know what local and international signs for land mines look like, so they are aware that certain symbols and painted rocks along fields and roads indicate the area is mined. They need to know what to do if they inadvertently walk or drive into a minefield. If working in an area that is mined, only walk on well-worn paths and do not go into areas that have overgrown bush or that look uninhabited.

Good security training courses also provide necessary information regarding how to use a variety of radios and other communication devices. A researcher who is working in areas where she/he will travel using armed convoys should receive training on communication and security protocols for such convoys.

While the preceding information may seem intimidating, we want to reassure researchers that it is possible to develop these skills and that having them will help ensure the safety and well-being of the researcher and the team members.

LEARNING IN THE FIELD

While training manuals and security courses can give the researcher a foundational overview of key issues, linking up with an experienced researcher or a very solid local partner such as a key NGO staff or civil society member is crucial for those entering active conflict affected areas, especially if those areas are new to them. This is true even for senior researchers working in their primary field site – the work is strongly enhanced by linking up with a strong, well-informed local partner. Our contributors strongly supported this point in their chapters. Bingham and Connors relied heavily on their female translator in Iraq to establish their credibility, to provide introductions, and to gauge their security on a continual basis. Wessells worked closely with national and international field staff over the course of his research projects, relying on their feedback to fine-tune research methods and to design relevant and appropriate interviews and focus groups with aid recipients and community members. Hébert relied on academics with deep knowledge of the conflict in Uganda along with key Ugandan nationals to help her create a narrative that was true to the experiences of her subjects.

The ability to read and respond correctly to the more subtle signs of an insecure landscape is developed over time as the researcher becomes more and more tuned in to life in the area in which he/she works and develops a network of local contacts that can provide daily updates. Hébert writes of her reliance on local contacts to assess when and how to move into rebel-affected areas. In the rural regions of east Africa where Mazurana works, signs of increased insecurity may include fields that are left unharvested, even those close to roads; fields that have been planted but are full of weeds and look unattended; fewer and fewer livestock (large and small) and fowl around homesteads or in fields; few if any cattle grazing in fields away from homes; compounds that are falling into disrepair and have not had the grounds swept of leaves; people who are gathered tightly together in trading centers (in which there is little trading going on) and make no attempt to greet new arrivals; and, perhaps most tellingly, little to no foot traffic on the sides of the roads.

If a researcher should be caught up in a violent attack, although it may sound obvious, it is essential to remain calm and not to panic. The authors' experience is that given the biochemical responses to fear – such as high adrenaline levels and increased heart rate – time appears to slow and there are a few fleeting moments to make good decisions to attempt to keep oneself uninjured and alive. Because the researcher has already considered what to do in such a situation (i.e., has planned a response to a variety of security threats and risks), she/he can nearly instantaneously scan the options and, keeping in line with earlier training, pick the one most appropriate to the situation. If a researcher has not had training and has not prepared and practiced for the eventuality of a serious security threat, fear can trigger panic or freezing, both extremely bad reactions for survival.

INTUITION

It is important for the researcher to pay attention to and trust his/her intuition – when something feels wrong, it is important to pull back, get oneself and/or the team to a safe place, and carefully assess the situation. Self-care is crucial and should include, as possible, exercise and space to reflect (e.g., meditation) and other forms of downtime. If your intuition tells you something does not feel right, you should not hesitate to delay the work, appear rude, or break social rules.

To keep one's intuition honed, the researcher should make sure to take breaks and leave the conflict zone, as the longer one stays in a violent and insecure location without taking a break, the less likely one is to assess threats and risks realistically (Mertus 2009). For Bingham and Connors, once they had defined their project and knew they were going to undertake risky work with the armed insurgency fighting against the United States–led occupation of Iraq, they took several weeks off in a relaxing location to lay their plans and prepare for the intense upcoming work. Hébert carried out three lengthy trips, giving herself several weeks in between to review her film footage carefully, assess what was needed, and determine how best to go back in and get it. Brun continually assessed the security situation and shifted her research goals and methods accordingly, while giving herself time out of the country to make those decisions.

SECURITY PLANS

Researchers should also develop their own security plans, which they follow, assess, and update daily. Researchers' security plans should be based on their best assessment of the security conditions and should include a situation analysis, threat analysis, vulnerability analysis, and risk assessment (Tangen, Dyer, and Julisson 2007, Mertus 2009). As is detailed in the manuals cited, a situation analysis lays out the key factors influencing the general security situation in the country and the region where the researcher is working; it includes

- history and current dynamics of the country, including any regional influences
- politics within the country or region
- economy/resource base and infrastructure
- crime profile (overall and in particular in the area the researcher is working)
- likelihood and/or frequency that the country or region will be affected by a natural disaster
- nature and structure of conflict or violence
- up-to-date information on the level of hostilities (including ground movements, aerial bombings, indiscriminate attacks, land mines) and military developments (including troops moving into particular areas and raising of militias)
- reminder always to seek up-to-date information and informed advice, as situations in active conflict zones can change quickly

From this assessment the researcher can identify the threats that exist and need to be monitored and his/her vulnerability to such threats. Those threats should be assessed and prioritized according to their frequency, severity, and likelihood of occurrence.

Researchers can cultivate a range of primary information sources to inform these assessments before entering the field, including well-placed individuals such as academics operating on the ground, government sources, local communities, and contacts at humanitarian or human rights agencies. Other valuable resources include press, media, or Internet security incident reports (available via the United Nations Office for the Coordination of Humanitarian Affairs [UN OCHA] if they are present in country) and current academic reports.

Once the researcher is in country, local contacts are increasingly relied upon for the most current security assessments. The researcher would also want to identify the important actors (e.g., state armed forces, nonstate armed forces, criminal elements, government offices, NGOs, local power brokers) also operating in the area and what impact, if any, they would have on the researcher's proposed project and security. Once the threats have been identified, the researcher would evaluate his/her vulnerability to them and assess where and why he/she would be at greatest risk. The researcher should assess how serious the affect of an incident resulting from a threat would be, determine his/her capacity to confront these threats, and determine the acceptability of risk and lay out measures to mitigate against risks he/she is willing to incur or may incur.

For example, in this book, Brun decides to pull out of Sri Lanka and later changes the location and focus of her work after her colleague is abducted and killed. Bingham and Connors close their project when the political and military climate shifts to the extent that they determine that the risk of kidnapping or harm to them is likely. Jok constantly monitors his relationships with the rebel commanders, who cannot understand why he is not joining the rebellion. In Afghanistan, Wessells determines that his identity as an American and the possible repercussions by Western aid agencies or the United States government if he is harmed outweigh his ability to contribute in insecure regions of the country.

Finally, researchers should also establish contact with the United Nations, NGOs, or some other reputable civilian organization in the area that they trust, and have someone within those bodies who has agreed to provide help if they are injured or do not make their call to their check-in (discussed later). However, unlike staff in the United Nations or the large NGOs, at the end of the day, independent researchers on the ground are ultimately responsible for their own safety.

CHECK-INS AND COMMUNICATION

Researchers' security plan should also include a regular check-in with some-one in their organization/university whom they could count on to help make clear, careful decisions and who would know how to get the researchers help if they needed it. This person is likely a professional colleague in the researchers' institution or a long trusted colleague who carries out similar work. The per-son selected as the check-in should have experience in working in situations of armed conflict and should have all the necessary contact information for United Nations and/or humanitarian or human rights groups working in the area where the researchers are based that have agreed to provide emergency assistance. When working in insecure areas, researchers should keep their secu-rity contact regularly updated on developments, sometimes several times a day if the situation is quite insecure and/or there is ongoing fighting or attacks.

While seemingly obvious, it is a good idea to keep the cell phone or satellite phone charged and with plenty of credit, as it can literally become a lifeline. In areas of high insecurity and spotty electricity (the two often seem to go hand in hand), carry two cell phones and keep both charged in case one runs out of power.

MEDICAL CARE

The greatest threats to researchers' physical health are unhygienic conditions and resultant diseases. A researcher working in situations of armed conflict should ensure that she/he has sound physical and mental health, that all necessary immunizations are current, and that all medications that she/he might need are taken to the field. Researchers should be in good physical shape to engage in the kinds of activities needed to undertake the research. A well-stocked medical kit is essential and should include a supply of neces-sary antibiotics to treat a range of infections and illnesses. Researchers are advised to carry a concise yet comprehensive medical guide for common and possible illnesses and injuries while working in remote locations (ranging from malaria to gunshot wounds). It is important that the researcher be famil-iar with all the contents of the medical kit, know how to use them, and be thoroughly familiar with the accompanying medical book. Both the medical kit and the guide should remain in their bags and travel with them wherever they go in the field.[1]

---

[1] Adventure Medical Kits and Lonely Planet offer a variety of excellent kits and very useful medical guides.

During fieldwork the researcher should be sure to carry a day's supply of water and drink it. If working in remote areas, a high-quality, lightweight water filter to ensure access to clean water is a good investment. If traveling by vehicle, ensure that there is at least a two-day supply of water in the vehicle in case one becomes stranded by vehicle breakdown or military shutdowns. If there is a likelihood of being called before military or government personnel in the area one is working, it is a good idea that the vehicle contains a clean set of clothes to look presentable and professional.

Working in active conflict zones means that the researcher will likely be working among populations and in areas where rates of disease and illness are high and health care provision is scarce to nonexistent. Therefore, part of the researcher's initial security assessment includes identifying and making contact with medical NGOs and local doctors in the area who are both willing and able to treat the researcher for a variety of ailments or injuries. If the conflict is quite intense in the area, anticipate that local clinics and hospitals will not have medicines, oxygen, or supplies on hand to treat injuries or major illnesses. Also anticipate that most of the medical personnel have left and that a researcher might need to have money to pay immediately for a physician for treatment, even under life-threatening conditions. A researcher who becomes injured or ill should contact the medical NGO or local doctor with whom he/she has already established contact to seek immediate assistance.

LANGUAGE, INTERPRETERS, AND RESEARCH ASSISTANTS

Fluency in the language of the populations one is studying is ideal. As a native Arabic speaker, Nusair in her chapter eloquently illustrates the importance and power of using Iraqi women's words to convey the subtle ways in which war and displacement limit their freedom and sense of self. For Jok, his ability to detect nuanced shifts in language underpinned his work on key changes in gender relationships that have occurred over years of violent conflict in Sudan. Longman's linguistic skills enable him quickly and quietly to interview prisoners and persons being subjected to torture while his colleague distracts the prison commander. Even without fluency, knowing basic vocabulary and local greetings is key, as Longman notes in his chapter, to gaining entrée into a particular scene, to setting a tone of respect, and to placing the researcher within a social frame.

Unless the researcher is a native or fluent speaker, most fieldwork requires a local interpreter, who often functions as a research assistant, helping to orient the researcher in nuances of culture and language. In active conflict settings, the government or party controlling the area has a stake in ensuring information is shaped in particular ways. It is not uncommon for them to assign interpreters to journalists or others who will spend brief periods in the conflict zone. At times, these interpreters are intelligence agents or informants for the state or controlling party, and interviewees know or suspect as much and so are guarded and careful about what they say (Macklin 2004).[2] It makes more sense for the researcher to seek out his/her own interpreter through trusted channels.

A trusted research assistant is invaluable for the cultural interpretations he or she offers – the finer nuances of what is meant by a particular turn of phrase, the importance of a certain event, and the effects of crisis on individuals and communities. Local research assistants not only help turn a social blunder into a comic gaffe, but open the researcher's eyes to meaningful interactions or scenes as they unfold, helping to see as those around see.[3]

In active conflict settings, a local research assistant may also be instrumental in providing security information and advising the researcher how to avoid dangerous situations or how to behave if caught in an unavoidable situation. Bingham and Connors discuss at length their relationship with their research assistant, in particular how she vouched for their character in interactions with Iraqis and helped steer the project through their frequent debriefs.

As researchers, journalists, filmmakers, and human rights workers, we have the ultimate freedom in the form of a plane ticket out of the active conflict zone. But what about the research assistants who cannot leave countries embroiled in conflict? Brun gives examples of how her research assistants were pressured into assisting armed forces and groups or asked for assistance by research participants after their work with her. As Brun states, "*Their* closeness to the field meant that I and others who had employed them to work in the conflict zone, and their own work in the north, had placed them in danger. The safe spaces that we had jointly developed for the research participants in Sri Lanka were challenged and turned into spaces of insecurity for the research assistants." Often, research assistants become more than hired support and are considered friends and confidantes. This is both rewarding and complicated, particularly in conflict settings, where there is much at stake. There are no easy

---

[2]   The use of undercover intelligence officers assigned as interpreters to foreign journalists entering the area to report on the war (who had to get government permission and papers to enter the war zone) was common practice in one of the countries where Mazurana has worked for many years.

[3]   The opening photo to this section, "Sweet Potatoes and Laundry," is a perfect illustration. Lacey Andrews Gale and the photographer Kate Lapides were led by their research assistant on several occasions to explore apparently empty houses that in reality housed multiple families of returning refugees.

answers to the dilemma of how to create and maintain an ethical relationship with research assistants in an unsafe environment. Perhaps the answer lies in continuing to ask the hard questions: Could I defend the current level of risk to a colleague? Am I willing to recalibrate my decisions and wrap up this project at any moment? What questions or circumstances related to my research and my presence could place my research assistant at risk and how do I mitigate against those?

TRAUMA AND VICARIOUS TRAUMA

Another concern that is important, though difficult, to address for both researchers and the research assistants they employ is that of mental and emotional health. It is ethical and standard practice that researchers who conduct interviews with victims of serious human rights violations and crimes, including torture and sexual violence, be skilled and trained to work with such populations and work in tandem with local (or locally based) mental health professionals who can offer support to interview participants who may be reliving traumatic events in the telling of their story. But what of the effects on the researchers, journalists, or filmmakers witnessing these stories, translating these stories, and being in situations of violence? How does one keep oneself and the research team mentally healthy?

Researchers in extreme cases may suffer from secondary trauma due to "the sustained effects on witnesses of observing gross human rights violations" (Cramer et al. 2011, 6). McCann and Pearlman (1990) coined the term "vicarious traumatization" in 1990 specifically in reference to the experience of psychotherapists working with trauma survivors. "Vicarious traumatization" has since become a term that is relevant to a range of persons who work with trauma survivors. Symptoms of vicarious trauma include somatic illness and pain as well as emotional and spiritual distress, all of which have the potential to negatively affect one's abilities to make decisions and function well (McCann and Pearlman 1990). The Headington Institute offers a training module on their Web site created by experienced psychotherapists designed to help humanitarian workers understand and address vicarious trauma, a resource that is equally applicable to researchers, students, and journalists and their research assistants.

CLOTHES, SHOES, AND RINGS

It is important to choose clothes that are considered modest and respectful in the culture where you are working; what is acceptable in New York or London or other capital cities may be offensive in different locales, particularly rural ones. Tight clothes or garments that reveal the body are not appropriate and may solicit unwanted attention and actions. As Connors and Bingham detail in their chapter, it is key to look like who you are, particularly avoiding clothes and sunglasses that resemble military issue. Heavy-soled flat shoes that cover the feet or boots are the best choices for footwear. They may not be the most attractive choice, and they may be warmer than open shoes or flip-flops, but sturdy shoes ensure that you can run far and fast if a situation deteriorates. For researchers working in rural areas and moving around in the brush, consider boots to help protect against snakebite. Females – married or not – should consider wearing a plain metal wedding ring. It can help prevent unwanted attention or advances. Similarly, it can help to carry photos of one's children or family. Everyone can relate to the idea of family, and it is also a way of beginning conversations and making links with people, whether they are interviewees or those met on the journey.[4]

MONEY

It makes good sense to ensure one has enough money to carry out the work and address emergency concerns. At the everyday level, always carry small denomination local currency and have a few small denomination dollar bills. Do not carry around large sums of money on one's body; do not carry all the money in one pocket, wallet, or purse; and be careful not to show large amounts of money to anyone. Lock up the rest of the money in the hotel or another safe location.

OFFICIAL PAPERS AND LETTERS OF INTRODUCTION

It is a good idea always to carry a copy of one's passport to prove one's identity along with an official letter of identification and introduction (written in both the official language of the country as well as the local language) from the researcher's university or the government, United Nations office, NGO, or agency that contracted the work. This letter of identification and introduction should include the names of the local partner organization, local contact, and/ or translator working with the researcher and have necessary contact information and official seals or stamps. Carry multiple copies of this document that

---

[4]   BBC News Magazine has published an article entitled "Women reporters on the frontline: 15 survival tips" that may be of interest to female researchers.

have original, official seals or stamps as the researcher may be expected to leave copies with key government and or military officials.

INSURANCE

Researchers working in conflict settings should ensure they have insurance to cover injury and disability due to civil unrest and war. Most standard insurance policies exclude injury, disability, or death due to civil unrest or war, so it is imperative that the researcher have coverage that reflects the reality of where he/she is going. Those with families should ensure they have life insurance policies that will still be valid if they are killed as a result of civil unrest or war. If the researcher is a graduate student or consultant and does not receive insurance as part of her/his position, it is possible and highly advisable to purchase short-term insurance (injury, disability, and life) for going into zones of civil unrest or war.[5] If the researcher carries out research in sites of civil unrest or war as part of his/her permanent job, it is essential that the company or university provide insurance that covers work in those locations. Persons working in regions where kidnapping is a real risk should consider kidnapping insurance, which might enable one's family, company, or university to pay a ransom to secure one's release. Different countries have different policies regarding paying ransom for their nationals, so it is important for researchers to have resources available to pay their own ransom if necessary.

DIGITAL PROFILES

One of the important components of safely carrying out research is that researchers must look and act like who they say they are (see also Introduction and Bingham and Connors in this book). Researchers should anticipate that persons interested in checking up on who they are will go to the Internet and search for information about them. This is especially the case for persons carrying out research on or interacting with nonstate armed groups or researchers whose work has drawn or is likely to draw the attention of political elites. Researchers working in active conflict zones should ensure that their digital profiles are in line with who they claim they are, and that those digital profiles present their work and them in a professional light. Groups

---

5   Companies providing this short-term insurance can be found on the Internet by searching companies that provide coverage for religious or humanitarian missions or extreme sports/adventure travel. Be sure to indicate you are going into an area experiencing armed conflict.

will draw conclusions about the researcher based on past work assignments, research or publications, affiliations, even Facebook pages. In cases where those doing the checking up are nonstate armed groups, the results of their Internet search can have serious consequences for the researcher. Bingham and Connors discuss how Bingham's earlier assignment for the newsmagazine *Newsweek* documenting a day in the life of Bernard Kerik, the Interim Coalition Provisional Authority interior minister responsible for Iraq's security, could have been disastrous and possibly life-threatening for them had it been discovered. David Rohde, a reporter for the *New York Times* held hostage by the Taliban for seven months, said that his captors frequently searched the Internet for information about him to determine whether he was a spy and to assess how much they could demand and possibly receive for his ransom (Rohde and Mulvihill 2010).[6] The bottom line is that researchers should ensure their digital profile is exactly in line with who they claim to be.

CONCLUSION

Carrying out rigorous research in active conflict zones is an essential component of revealing what is actually happening to people experiencing war. Only when people think differently will they act differently. Consequently, accurate and grounded analysis of people's lives and livelihoods in active armed conflict zones is indispensable in helping to shape knowledge and action in response to violence. Yet entering areas of active armed conflict requires that researchers be as prepared as possible for the many challenging situations they may encounter. We are hopeful this chapter is a step in that direction.

BIBLIOGRAPHY

BBC News Magazine. 2012. "Women reporters on the frontline: 15 survival tips," Available at http://www.bbc.co.uk/news/magazine-17288577 (accessed January 5, 2012).
Cramer, Christopher, Laura Hammond, and Johan Pottier. 2011. *Researching violence in Africa: Insights and experiences.* Leiden and Boston: Brill Publishing House.
Egeland, Jan and Abby Stoddard. 2011. *To stay and deliver: Good practice for humanitarians in complex security environments.* New York: United Nations Office for the Coordination of Humanitarian Affairs. Available at http://ochanet.unocha.org/p/Documents/Stay_and_Deliver.pdf (accessed January 5, 2012).
Headington Institute. Available at http://www.headington-institute.org/Default.aspx?tabid=2647 (accessed January 3, 2012).

[6] David Rohde, personal communication with Dyan Mazurana, March 15, 2011, Medford, Massachusetts.

Macklin, Audrey. 2004. "Like oil and water with a match: Militarized commerce, armed conflict and human security in Sudan." In *Sites of violence*, eds. J. Hyndman and W. Giles, 75–107. Berkeley: University of California Berkeley Press.

McCann, I. L. and L. A. Pearlman. 1990. Vicarious traumatization: A framework for the psychological effects of working with victims. *Journal of Traumatic Stress* 3(1): 131–49.

Mertus, Julie. 2009. "Maintenance of personal security: Ethical and operational issues." In *Surviving field research: Working in violent and difficult situations*, eds. Chandra Lekha Sriram, John King, Julie Mertus, Olga Martin-Ortega and Johanna Herman, 165–76. New York: Routledge.

Overseas Development Institute. "Operational security management in violent environments: A field manual for aid agencies," Good Practice Review, *Humanitarian Practice Network* no. 8 (December 2010). Available at http://www.odihpn.org/report.asp?id=3159 (accessed January 5, 2012).

People in Aid. 2003. *The People in Aid code of best practice in the management and support of aid personnel*. London: People in Aid. Available at http://www.peopleinaid.org/pool/files/code/code-en.pdf (accessed January 5, 2012).

Rohde, David and Kristen Mulvihill. 2010. *A rope and a prayer: A kidnapping from two sides*. New York: Viking Press.

Tangen, Lars, John Dyer and Karl Julisson. 2007. *Stay safe – International Federation's guide to a safer mission*. Geneva: International Federation of the Red Cross Security Unit (2007). Available at http://reliefweb.int/sites/reliefweb.int/files/resources/853 28A9953AD7D3CC125741F004E9E0D-113700-stay_safe_management-EN.pdf (accessed January 5, 2012).

United Nations, Office of the United Nations Security Coordinator. 1998 (updated 2003). *Security in the field: Information for staff members of the United Nations system*. New York: United Nations. Available at http://www.eisf.eu/resources/item.asp?d=1606 (accessed January 5, 2012).

AFTERWORD

If peace returns, I will give up this work and go home
~ Caroline

Figure 11. "Caroline in the Quarry" April 2006, Larro quarry near Gulu, northern Uganda.
Photographer: Sébastien Gros

Caroline, twelve years old, told us she was working in a quarry in order to provide food for herself and the family she lived with, as she had lost both her parents to the war. We walked with her to the quarry the day this photograph was taken to see what kind of work she was doing. It was a ten-kilometer walk each way. She hammered rocks for eight hours in a row – difficult, monotonous work. The sound in the quarry was like a hundred hammers responding to one another, creating a sad and regular rhythm that haunted us.

Reflections on the Challenges, Dilemmas, and Rewards of Research in Conflict Zones

Elisabeth Jean Wood

This excellent volume documents and analyzes the practical, methodological, and ethical challenges of research in conflict and postconflict zones, particularly those occurring in research focused on voices "from below." Across a diverse range of disciplines, including the social sciences, policy development, advocacy and implementation, and journalism, the authors encountered dilemmas that went well beyond those emphasized by ethical review boards that oversee human subject research by researchers in many contexts. Across a wide range of settings, from Africa to the Middle East to South Asia, the authors convey their failures as well as successes. The volume compiles a rich variety of lessons learned by these experienced field researchers, many of whom faced demanding situations characterized by violence, profound and well-grounded distrust, and social fragmentation. The hard-earned wisdom of these authors offers insights not only to the novice. Field researchers with many years of experience should be spurred (as I was) to rethink our own practices along lines laid out in these chapters.

In this Afterword, I summarize the authors' insights into field research in conflict and postconflict settings that I judge most important, challenging, provocative, or promising. I first discuss the challenges as well as the promise of gathering data in such settings – including the importance of participant observation alongside more structured encounters with subjects, the complexity of the construction of trust with subjects, and the role of respect for the agency of our subjects. I assess the process of "learning from the field," including subjects' capacity for resilience as well as suffering, the dilemmas of working with research assistants or partners, and the importance for most projects of deep local knowledge on the part of the researcher, which often implies returning time and again to the same setting. I then discuss the ethical challenges and dilemmas that researchers confront in conflict settings and argue that the ethical principles held central by academic researchers and institutions of "do no harm," data security, and informed consent are particularly challenging to implement in such settings. I then turn to the ongoing responsibilities of the field researcher, including the dilemma about how best to reciprocate the support extended by host communities and networks. I argue that some standard reciprocity practices are not appropriate but that a more generalized exchange is possible, including through policy engagement. Throughout, my discussion makes frequent reference to the volume's overarching themes of representation, do no harm, safe spaces, trust, and responsibility, as well as to practicalities. I draw from my own experience as well as that of some students. After noting the value of the chapter on practicalities for both novice and experienced field researchers – particularly those working in conflict zones – I conclude with reflections on some additional questions raised by this important work.

RESEARCH DURING AND JUST AFTER CONFLICT

Despite the many security challenges of working in conflict and postconflict areas, the authors gathered data – transcripts or footage of formal interviews and focus groups, physical evidence of serious crimes and violations, notes from participant observation, or coded survey protocols – in a range of demanding settings through face-to-face encounters with ordinary people, as well as with "elites" of different kinds. The authors share a conviction that the narratives and judgments of ordinary people in the midst of violence are a source of important insights for understanding conflict, violence, and its aftermath; for documenting the history and legacy of society-shattering events; and for denouncing suffering and injustice. Timothy Longman argues that ordinary people living in the midst of violence share what they know – and they often know more than elites – because they want the researcher to use it. Isis Nusair approached the often-recited aim of "giving voice to the voiceless" with skepticism, noting the limits of research in effecting meaningful change. Yet she nonetheless found that her subjects – women displaced from Iraq by violence – constructed life narratives profound in the articulation of their struggle to cope with the complexity of their refugee identities and the erosion of their agency as months in exile turned into years. Perhaps Catherine Hébert stated the promise and the challenges of the representation of lives lived among such conditions most eloquently: she sought to show suffering without self-indulgence or affectation, and to convey the dignity, courage, and anger of her subjects.

   That people living in the midst of conflict and its aftermath choose to share those insights with a researcher is of course not to be presumed. Indeed, why in the midst of what is often a very difficult struggle to sustain self and family with some degree of dignity from one day to the next should they want to do so? As the authors convey very clearly, surprisingly people often do decide to engage with the researcher, for a range of reasons. Some authors note that their subjects made an active choice to speak out in order to denounce injustice because they believed it might make a difference, or because they wanted to bear witness to past suffering and injustice, or because they simply needed to share their suffering with someone. Hébert found that one abducted girl deeply needed to tell someone her story. In southern Sudan, local women eventually agreed to work with Jok Madut Jok in order to draw attention to how wartime social transformations exacerbate women's suffering. Iraqi insurgents spoke with the investigative journalists Molly Bingham and Steve Connors to correct the profound misunderstanding of the Iraqi insurgency among Western observers. As Longman points out, some subjects talk with researchers in part because they feel no shame about their past actions.

Of course, such engagement depends on the subject's "trust" in the researcher, as the literature often notes. Yet "trust" is too often treated as a binary: either the researcher is trusted or she is not. Several authors demonstrate (sometimes implicitly) that trust has degrees. Trust – that is, some degree of trust, a degree that often evolves – is *earned* by the researcher, often through returning to speak with the same subject again and again. Hébert noted when those she approached about her work learned that she would be returning, she saw "the first glimmers of trust." Yet even for an insider, return to a conflict area may be fraught with distrust, as Jok's chapter on his research among fellow Dinka makes clear. The local commander distrusted him, so the European aid director had to vouch for him, and it took him a year to develop rapport with local women.

Bingham and Connors are adamant that "trust is much too strong a word to describe the human interaction that allowed us to all be in the same space and talk for periods of time." They and their Iraqi research partner carefully constructed a degree of trust sufficient to repeatedly engage with their insurgent subjects by carefully conveying the nature of the project and making very clear the kinds of information they would ask their subjects to discuss and the topics about which they would never ask (including some topics about which they would refuse to listen). Key to the limited, contingent, and fragile trust of their subjects was the fact that they never collected contact information – each time they wanted to speak with a subject, they returned to the neighborhood and let the subject find them – and mentioned the insurgency only after extensive discussion.

Consistency in self-presentation is also essential to the construction of (some degree of) trust. Because trust is likely fragile in the at-best-tenuous security circumstances of research in these settings, inconsistent presentation of the researcher or the project – articulating distinct researcher identities or advancing different project purposes to different audiences – may lead to the erosion of participation unless the researcher has been at pains to explain beforehand why apparent inconsistencies do not in fact threaten subjects. Bingham and Connors emphasize the point most explicitly – dress in the clothes, drive the vehicles, and ask the questions expected given subjects' understanding of the project. And avoid looking like or acting like soldiers.

Yet such consistency is often in tension with the need to avoid drawing unwanted attention of authorities whose hostility would threaten participants or the researcher. While a few authors engaged in essentially covert research (Hébert when she filmed in northern Uganda in order to evade government minders and Bingham and Connors when they concealed the topic of their documentary from all but an extremely small circle of trusted colleagues), other researchers gave distinct but not inconsistent descriptions of the research project. When I carried out research on a unique reconstruction project in the midst of El Salvador's civil war – the town of Tenancingo was repopulated as a *zona inerme* (essentially, an unarmed zone) as the result of an agreement negotiated by the Archdiocese of San Salvador between the state and the insurgents – I presented the project to state authorities as one on repopulation more generally (which was true as I also researched other repopulated villages), and in interviews with officials I asked questions about those other projects as well as Tenancingo. As I stayed with Catholic nuns (in Tenancingo as well as in the sites of a later project) and dressed modestly, I was often mistaken by soldiers and insurgents alike at checkpoints (both armies had them) for a nun, a misconception I did not always correct though I never explicitly confirmed it.

In conflict zones, subjects' engagement with researchers – even those they trust highly – depends on the existence of "safe spaces." The chapters make clear that engaging successfully depends on a well-developed understanding of the local setting. In some contexts, safe spaces were open sites in public view; in others, they were private homes or work spaces. For some authors, working in safe spaces also meant not asking some questions or pursuing those topics only if raised by their subjects. Although the chapters show that the construction of safe spaces is often possible despite challenging and even threatening circumstances, in some settings, it is impossible. In her analysis of research in highly militarized societies, Cathrine Brun concludes that sometimes the best – and perhaps only – safe space is simply staying away and doing what is possible from a distance. More specifically, Brun relied on her subjects – for example, university students in Jaffna during the Sri Lankan civil war – to decide what constituted the multiple, contingent "safe spaces" in which she worked. Wessells concluded that after the U.S. invasion of Afghanistan, he could no longer work in rural Afghanistan as the presence of American aid workers led to excessive harm to the local community. In the course of developing a policy research organization in Afghanistan, Paul Fishstein and Andrew Wilder found that there were some topics that they and their researchers could research at best infrequently and superficially, given the logistical, cultural, and security constraints of the setting.

Participant observation –informal participation with local groups and individuals to observe their everyday (or sometimes extraordinary) activities – is often a crucial method for gathering the type of deep knowledge of particular field settings that enables the researcher to construct such safe spaces. Though most authors did not explicitly make a case for the centrality of this research method (they may have presumed it obvious), their deep familiarity with their research sites and frequent anecdotes show that they engaged in it often. Longman argues that the "drop-in" style of field research in which many social scientists engage may lead not only to incomplete but to inaccurate research. Judging by my own experience, political scientists are particularly slow to recognize the importance of this kind of data gathering both for the building of trust with subjects and for the evaluation of alternative interpretations of data of all kinds. For example, it was only after writing my second (and most ethnographic) book that I realized the extent to which my argument – and my confidence in it – drew on the hours and hours and hours spent "hanging out" with a wide variety of residents of El Salvador's conflict zones. Yet, to my lasting regret, I included few of those data in the published work although they were in fact crucial evidence for its claims.

Also essential to the construction of some degree of trust and to the willingness of subjects to engage with the researcher is her ability to convey her respect for her subjects, their life experience, perceptions, opinions, and analyses. While open-minded curiosity is essential, it may not be sufficient in the challenging settings of conflict and post conflict. Respect implies treating subjects as *persons*, and not merely as sources of needed data. For some authors, the way to convey respect was explicitly to hand over to their subjects a significant degree of control of the research encounter. Nusair invited her subjects to construct life narratives with minimal intervention on her part. Bingham and Connors began their interactions with Iraqi insurgents with long conversations about their personal history before ever discussing the insurgency itself. Similarly, my interviews with (mostly former) military and insurgent officers

and combatants are essentially oral histories – narratives entirely controlled
by the subject with minimal interruption – followed by a discussion of their
analysis of particular issues. For Hébert, persuading her potential subjects that
her film would be made with them, and not merely about them, was a core
part of her approach. For Brun, respect for her subjects meant respecting the
many silences in her interviews while being sensitive to other ways of communicating what they preferred not to discuss: that is, how they "communicate
the unspeakable." Such silences occurred not only in her interviews but also
within her research group: some topics could not be discussed.

Learning from the Field

Researchers in conflict settings often gain respect for their subjects through
their own experiences. As many researchers discover or confirm, living in
conflict and immediately postconflict settings impels the development of
analytical skills on the part of ordinary people in order to cope with pervasive uncertainty and insecurity. In her research among Sudanese refugees in
Uganda, Tania Kaiser explicitly relied on her subjects for her safety as their
judgment about security conditions was better informed than hers. Wessells
is eloquent in his description of the agency and resilience of young people in
conflict settings: many were capable of exercising agency in pursuit of their
goals (rather than being passive victims) despite witnessing and sometimes
wielding horrific violence. Longman's respect for the courage of ordinary people (as well as internal dissidents in institutions) to help document human
rights abuses despite threatening settings emerges very clearly throughout his
chapter, as does his confidence that people choose to do so only when they
deem it safe enough.

   Several researchers not only left the management of the interview to their
subjects, but developed the project itself (or subsequent projects) in light of
their preferences and insights, or even with them. Jok, for example, decided
that his next project would focus on humanitarian assistance. Wessells transformed his research practices over time as his understanding of local knowledge and practices as a source of resilience and healing deepened. (Also
contributing to this shift was his growing awareness of the ethical dilemmas
of research in conflict zones, to which I return later.)

   Several authors learned to read the field from their research partners and
assistants. Bingham and Connors convey clearly the centrality of their interpreter, Amina, to their research: she vouched for them and their project,
gave it credibility through her knowledge of Iraqi culture and the Quran,

addressed misgivings, and was often able to persuade the initially reluctant to participate. Only the three of them knew the real contours of the project, an essential precaution during a time of widespread violence and well-grounded suspicion of foreigners in Iraq. In addressing the challenges of policy research in postinvasion Afghanistan, Fishstein and Wilder found they often needed to match the gender and ethnicity of the researcher with the community being studied – a necessity that entailed innovations such as allowing family members to accompany female researchers. Some topics simply could not be pursued given the paucity of researchers (for whose services their organization was often outbid by other international and bilateral agencies).

Engagement with local experts, including assistants and partners, may also serve to continuously re-orient the researcher toward local priorities, avoiding the tendency of research (especially but not exclusively policy research) to be driven by short-term trends of the international donors and sponsors. One such trend is the overtargeting of some populations as the subjects of research and the beneficiaries of services and the resulting neglect of others. For example, Wessells points out that despite the recent international emphasis on child soldiers, researchers and policy makers often neglect to document and analyze the experience of girl soldiers. Similarly, despite the sharp increase in funding for victims of wartime sexual violence, male victims (who in some cases constitute a third or more of victims) are neglected by nearly all agencies and ignored by many researchers.

However, local assistants and partners may also have objectives that differ from those of the researcher, introducing unrecognized bias and incomplete or inaccurate data. Such divergence in objectives (which may have damaging results) is not necessarily malicious in intent. Local partners may deem ethical constraints overly scrupulous and so pursue topics and subjects in ways the researcher has prohibited – in the best interest of the project, in their view. They may have a different assessment of risk, on which they may act without necessarily divulging it (in order to protect their reputation as a go-to local researcher, for example), and so report "work" that was not in fact done as assigned. Other bias may result from some social, political, or economic agenda of which the researcher is unaware. As a result of any of these forms of divergence, data gathered may be biased and the research manipulated – and the researcher may not be aware of it.

So "learning from the field" may therefore be quite problematic. Once again, deep local knowledge on the part of the researcher herself will sharpen her ability to assess potential assistants and partners and their work.

Ethical Challenges and Dilemmas

That field research in conflict and postconflict zones poses sharp ethical challenges and dilemmas is one of the strongest themes across the chapters of this volume. Three broad findings are evident across the authors' research sites. First, while many challenges are shared across the authors' research settings, others are specific to particular sites; as a result, researchers confronted a variety of ethical challenges and dilemmas. Whether or not a particular challenge occurs frequently, the authors' response was invariably shaped by local conditions.

Second, the twin imperatives most often emphasized by human subject research review boards in their evaluation of proposed research projects – data security and informed consent – may be challenging to implement (and are rarely the only challenges researchers confront). To maintain security of their data, for example, Bingham and Connors only discussed their project during walks through the city, never in their hotel room. Security officials (as well as border officials) may confiscate laptops or demand to see material on hard drives. Universities may not be both willing and able to protect oral history archives from demands for them from prosecutors (for example, this is evident in the recent controversy concerning oral histories of the Irish Republican Army held by Boston College, which led to a federal appeals court ruling that the researchers must turn over their confidential research recordings (Mole 2012). Securing informed consent may also be challenging. Desperate living conditions may impel poor families to participate in research against their better judgment and despite informed consent protocols that are very explicit in their denial of any assistance conditioned on participation, as discussed by Wessells. The presence of researchers (particularly foreign researchers) may raise expectations that aid projects will nonetheless arrive, or at least that the researcher will follow cultural norms of reciprocity and assist the subject in some way.

Third, the ethical imperative "do no harm" poses particular dilemmas to the researcher working in conflict and postconflict settings. As Wessells notes in his chapter, such research may have unintended consequences even when led by a well-intentioned, experienced researcher (for example, his focus groups with children were rumored to be recruitment meetings). Moreover, the suggestion that research should lead to no harm to anyone surely violates other ethical principles. For example, if those who carry out human rights abuses suffer no harm from research that documents those abuses, the principles of justice and accountability are violated. So "do no harm" needs more elaboration for research in conflict and post than its breezy assertion suggests. One way that researchers often circumscribe the principle is to follow a narrower principle, "carry out research such that no foreseeable harm comes to participants as a result of their participation in my project." Yet "participation" is vague: does it refer to those who participate as "human subjects" in the technical sense of the term only, or does it include various elites who may be interviewed but are not subjects in that technical sense? And the principle allows research that brings foreseeable harm to nonparticipants.

Moreover, who is the best judge of "harm" balanced against potential benefits? The principle of informed consent emphasizes the judgment of the potential human subject, but the chapters contain several examples of researchers' deciding against using some material although they had their subject's permission to use it. Hébert decided against using what surely would have been very dramatic footage of a child seeking his family in a displaced persons' camp only to find his father gone and his grandmother dying. This is an instance of a recurring dilemma: the ethical imperative of doing no harm to the subject may be in tension with the responsibility to represent that subject as he presents himself. Kaiser notes that she did not include in her publications particular ways in which her subjects coped with life in exile: she did not report how some refugees took advantage of certain loopholes in regulations, falsified legal documents or personal narratives, or engaged in illicit activities. Yet she also felt an ethical obligation to the government (whose permission she had for her project) and refused to enter the camp when it was closed despite ample opportunity (and concrete invitations) to do so.

A particular concern often at the center of the "do no harm" imperative in the conflict and postconflict context is the danger that participation in the research project (through recounting devastating experiences or confronting painful truths) may "retraumatize" the subject. The authors' approaches to this challenge vary across the chapters. Some authors identified questions that they would never ask (and some asked their subjects not to raise the relevant topic). Others emphasized the choice by subjects to pursue such topics and then edited the material using their own judgment.

Review boards that govern research with human subjects often address this challenge by requiring that researchers halt the interview if *any* indication of traumatization emerges and that they offer to possibly traumatized subjects a list of organizations from which they can seek counseling. Both are problematic. In my experience, many subjects who cried, lamented, or showed other signs of significant and even profound emotional distress as they recounted their story, when asked whether they would like to end the encounter or change the subject, insist on continuing – and often express relief in having done so. And some explicitly stated that they had never told anyone else. While this may be more frequent in research with present and former members of armed groups focused on violence, other researchers who work with victims have similarly come to question the presumption that revisiting the painful past is likely to be traumatizing. I should clarify, however, in my present research on wartime sexual violence, I have not sought to interview victims as I did not think it ethically justifiable for an essentially academic project. Instead, I draw on the many narratives from victims gathered by colleagues in human rights and women's groups for the victims' perspectives.

Second, in many contexts, this requirement is impractical for various reasons: there may be no such organizations, if they do exist they may impose fees for services, or they may be associated with some political agenda with which the subject fears association, and so on. Mazurana and Gale urge that researchers themselves obtain the skills and training to work with human rights victims as well as work with mental health professionals. Yet even this degree of preparation may not adequately address this challenge if the counseling offered is culturally inappropriate and/or displaces local alternatives that might have been more beneficial.

Of course, researchers themselves may suffer from their ongoing exposure to human suffering and violence. Humanitarian organizations understand "vicarious traumatization" (Mazurana and Gale) as a significant threat to their staff, but researchers may fail to recognize its potential to affect them or their assistants.

Identifying ethical challenges and addressing the dilemmas that arise in confronting them are likely to be very dependent on the particular research context (yet another reason that researchers themselves should develop such contextual knowledge). As Wessells argues in his chapter, there is little consensus among researchers about the appropriate standards for evaluating different approaches to these challenges and dilemmas, and little evidence available to assist researchers in their evaluation of the consequences of their choices. Yet this uncertainty should not mean that research cannot be conducted, he argues, but that the researcher should engage continuously in critical analysis, self-reflection, and dialogue in order to remain alert to unintended consequences of the project. As Brun emphasizes, the practice of such thoughtful engagement should not suggest that ethical research is always possible: there are settings in which there is no persuasive argument that the potential benefits outweigh the harm to the subjects, the research team, or local people.

Ongoing Responsibilities

The challenges and dilemmas that researchers in conflict and postconflict zones face do not end when they leave the field. Unintended consequences may occur in the wake of departure (or later if local conditions change). Indeed, departure may leave research assistants and subjects exposed to increased risk if the researcher's presence ensured their protection (and this possibility should be considered from the beginning of project design, argue Bingham and Connors). So returning "home" does not mean leaving the field: responsibilities to subjects continue, as does the researcher's responsibility for foreseeable consequences of her work. As Brun writes, "We are part of the field when we are away." Yet, as argued previously, to carry out research only in conflict zones that guarantees no unintended consequences is too strong a standard. This would essentially prohibit all research – including clearly justified projects. Leaving the field for home – however connected they remain – is often a painful process for ethnographic researchers as well as those they leave behind. Hébert writes: "In reality, I do not handle it; I endure it.... My feelings of unhappiness are inconsolable." Nonetheless, she recognizes that leaving is part of her work.

All researchers face the challenge of how to reciprocate the gift of their subjects' time, their willingness to recall the painful past, and their sharing of valued materials including their own perceptions and analyses. There is a well-developed literature in anthropology about the responsibility to reciprocate, which often takes the form of returning data to communities or local museums (artifacts or recordings of oral histories, for example), inviting participants to comment on and respond to key research findings, or contributing in some substantial way to community resources, perhaps through support for local schools or ongoing collaboration with local researchers. Jok recounts how he held meetings with his subjects on later trips: "However joyous and rather comical it was, reading sections of my dissertation did not really afford them ample opportunity to comment." As a result, Jok not only founded a primary school for girls but shifted his research agenda toward themes important to his subjects. Hébert supported children in boarding schools; Nusair returned to make a film with her subjects; others "gave back" through contributing to the building of institutions of various kinds in the host society. Such engagement is not without risk, as Brun notes. In doing the latter, she found herself entangled in power relations she never fully understood. Such measures definitively exceed an older standard, that the ethnographer should deposit copies of publications in relevant scholarly and national libraries.

Yet many such ethnographic practices are inappropriate for research in conflict and postconflict zones. In communities wracked by conflict, the return of data such as oral histories may result in violence or at least discord and polarization. Moreover, such data are often gathered under assurance of confidentiality (if not anonymity), which is likely to be difficult to maintain if detailed data are returned to research sites. One way out of this dilemma is to understand reciprocity as a more generalized exchange, whereby the researcher's return "gift" is political or policy engagement in ways the subjects would value. For example, in my work on wartime sexual violence, I give workshops and talks to policy audiences not only because I hope to affect policy but also because I know the many staff members of women's and human rights organizations who have spent many hours answering my questions would value my doing so.

Several of the authors engage with policy work, though not all solely as a way to reciprocate. Indeed, Longman argues it is irresponsible not to do so. He contends that neutrality and objectivity in this field are not options; researchers must participate in the transformation of the society in which they work. Yet in some settings, the best way to contribute to such transformation is precisely to engage in neutral and objective research – and to disseminate it appropriately.

Moreover, the balance (for academic researchers) between advocacy and policy, on the one hand, and academic publication and teaching, on the other, is one challenging to maintain: time frames are distinct, not all topics are relevant, important qualifications are often lost in the course of dissemination, and advocacy on some topics may undermine perceptions of the neutrality of research on others, as discussed by Fishstein and Wilder. Some authors, particularly Longman and Wessells, argue that, though difficult, moving between the two worlds offers positive synergies: research questions are sharpened through policy engagement, alternative (perhaps comparative) perspectives are encountered, and research agendas are clarified. Yet policy work has its own challenges and dilemmas, as Wessells also recognizes, including the possibility of displeased gatekeepers' closing down access to key research sites or populations, the risk of being drawn into debates and rivalries that offer little promise either to academic work or to policy advocacy, and the perhaps ill-informed reaction of assistants and subjects "on the ground" in the field. Moreover, more junior (though not necessarily less experienced) researchers may find such dilemmas particularly vexing given that they often face the demands of both building a strong record in their particular discipline and at the same time finding ways to combine field research with family life. Getting the work "right" may feel more than sufficiently challenging without the added expectation of reciprocating in whatever form.

Practical Advice

I cannot adequately summarize the superlative chapter on researcher security and other practicalities by Dyan Mazurana and Lacey Andrews Gale.

Particularly powerful is the detailed enumeration of how best to ensure the safety of the researcher and his/her team: the need for detailed situational analysis and risk assessment, the development of protocols for approaching armed roadblocks and responding to an armed attack or kidnapping, navigational and first-aid skills, and the importance of regular "check-ins" with colleagues who can provide backup should it become necessary. The authors emphasize the importance of the researcher's adequate care of herself as crucial not only to her safety but to that of her team:

> Researchers who lack the knowledge, ability, and/or discipline to make good decisions to stay physically and emotionally healthy and safe are a risk to themselves, the other people on their team, and the people they are interviewing. (Mazurana and Gale)

Researchers need specialized skills and training to work with victims of serious human rights violations and perpetrators of those crimes and should work with local (or locally based) specialists who can offer support. The authors also underscore the potential for vicarious traumatization to undermine the researcher's ability to make sound decisions. The practical advice covers a wide range, including the need to edit one's digital profile (you *will* be Googled). The chapter also includes an extremely useful compendium of sources on the identification and management of the logistical and security challenges of research in conflict zones, including international training manuals and courses.

CONCLUSION

These chapters comprise an invaluable collection of reflections on field research in the challenging but also rewarding setting of conflict and postconflict context. While the approach that best addresses the ethical, methodological, and practical challenges and dilemmas of field research in conflict zones depends on the specific conditions of the particular setting, the ability of any researcher to identify that approach will be significantly increased after studying this volume.

The volume raises many questions and concerns for further reflection and research. Under what conditions is a resilient response by individuals, families, and communities possible? On what cultural resources do people draw? On what new resources? For example, what role does religious conversion play? When are violence and suffering best understood as a continuation from the past, and when as a rupture? What difference does it make for the lived experience of violence? How (and to what extent) do postconflict communities cope with the presence of victims and victimizers, and with those who are both?

How should field researchers respond to the blurring of boundaries of humanitarian aid, counterinsurgency projects, and academic research? How should we respond to the lack of consensus on ethical standards for research in conflict zones, and our lack of knowledge about its unintended consequences (both noted by Wessells)? Given the differences in local contexts, is a consensus on standards possible? On principles?

Even as we struggle with these questions, we should draw inspiration from the authors' commitment to the documentation and analysis of persons whose voices and life experience are often lost, misrepresented by uninformed interlocutors, or displaced by the well-meaning, whose assumed authority to speak for others is too little questioned. The chapters vividly demonstrate not only the challenges and dilemmas of field research in conflict zones, but also the courage and moral clarity of these researchers.

The relationship between the researcher and her subjects not only makes possible this type of research but provides its ethical and moral grounding. Sound research on the life experience of ordinary people during and after conflict is necessary to an understanding of the suffering that violence imposes, often on the innocent who are caught up in its path through no fault of their own. All of us who attempt to convey what we have learned in the course of our work in conflict zones are indebted to the authors of this volume for speaking frankly of failures as well as triumphs, of tragic mistakes as well as judgment well exercised, and for sharing their reasons for engaging in such work.

BIBLIOGRAPHY

Mole, Beth. 2012. Boston College must release records in IRA oral-history case, Appeals Court says, *Chronicle of Higher Education*, July 7. Available at https://chronicle.com/article/Appeals-Court-Affirms-Ruling/132779/ (accessed September 27, 2012).

Index

A to Z Guide to Afghanistan Assistance, 225
Abaya, 193
ABC News, 206
abduction, 30
    children, 17, 29, 31–2, 43, 143, 284
    colleagues, 143
    digital profiles, 199
    kidnapping, 40, 121, 208, 278, 280, 284, 290, 292
    precursor to, 204
    women, 32
Abdul Sattar abu Risha, 170
Aboke girls, 31, 40, 50–1
abortion, 153, 159
Abu Ghraib, 10, 189, 202, 204, 220
abu Risha clan, 170
access, 6–7, 13–6, 19, 20, 22, 39, 85, 93, 101, 111, 115–22, 135, 137–8, 142, 149, 158, 163, 181–3, 204, 208, 213, 216, 218, 227, 238–9, 246, 251, 267, 286
    government permission, 115
accountability, 81, 147, 228, 236, 266, 267, 273
Acholi (people), 29, 30, 42, 109, 113, 117
Acholiland, 30
action research, 95
activism, 30, 39, 40, 145, 271
Adhamiya, 177–8, 181–3, 188, 190, 191, 197, 198, 206, 209–10
Afghanistan, 3–5, 15–16, 20, 91, 93, 103–4, 178, 179, 190, 199, 207, 220–53, 284, 299, 301
    Elections, 248
Afghanistan Programming Body (APB), 224
Afghanistan Research and Evaluation Unit (AREU),
    access to communities, 240
    advocacy, 247
    Afghan staff, 20, 231–2, 236, 237, 238, 239
    briefing notes, 245
    challenges of research informing policy, 244
    communications and advocacy strategy, 246
    community relationships, 240
    competition for skilled staff, 230
    confidential interviews, 243
    corruption, 235
    dissemination strategy, 247
    ethnicity, 244
    library, 246
    logistical challenges, 238
    measuring policy impact, 249
    multi-cultural environment, 235
    narcotics, 235
    publications, 245
    security constraints, 233
    translation issues, 243
African Union, 3
agency, 6, 84, 87–8, 91, 95, 100–2, 119, 141, 156, 279, 289
aid agencies, 19, 156, 159, 229, 284, 292
aid delivery, 159
aid workers
    as targets, 141
Akbar, Arifa, 219
Al Qaeda, 173, 176, 179, 194, 206, 223
alcohol, 42, 154, 237
Allen, Tim, 108, 124
Altorki, Soraya, 164
Amin, Idi, 107
"Amina", 180, 182–4, 189, 192, 194–6, 204, 212–3, 300
Amman, 57–8, 64–5, 68, 72, 74
Amnesty International, 255, 259
Anbar Awakening, 170
Angelina, 39–41, 49–50
Angola, 82, 84, 88, 90–1, 103–4
Anguleta, 9, 37–8, 41–2, 48, 52

Anthropology, 149
    areas of specialization, 111
    cultural models, 154
    discipline, 19, 22, 85–6, 107, 124, 147–8, 151,
        154, 160–3, 229
    methods, 12, 151, 161
apprenticeship, 7, 281
Arabic language, 170, 177, 195, 286
    translation, 181
area studies approach, 265
Armbruster, Heidi, 164
armed forces
    definition, 3
armed groups
    blurring between criminal and political
        motivations, 143
    cell structures, 190
armed road blocks
    safety protocol, 280
assessment fatigue, 94
assistance
    as connected to research participation, 302
    requests from informants, 93, 118, 213, 287
Associated Press, 177, 219
atmospheric film, 23, 31, 81, 115
Ayatollah Khomeini, 172

Ba'athist, 171, 172
Badr Corps, 172–3
Baghdad, 169–70, 177, 180, 182, 193, 196, 202,
        208, 210, 219
Baitemann, Olga, 252
Bar On, Bat-Ami, 26, 41
Barakat, Sultan, 252
Barnett, Clive, 134, 147
Barnett, Michael, 21–2
BBC, 173, 175, 216, 219, 291
Bell, Sharon, 147
belligerent forces, 3–4, 11
Bernard Kerik, 198, 208, 291
Bhatia, Michael, 252
bin Laden, Osama, 223
Bingham, Molly, 8, 10, 13, 16, 19, 167, 169, 176,
        188, 205, 219, 261, 277, 281, 283–4, 287,
        289, 290, 291, 297, 298, 299, 300, 302, 305
Blackwater Security, 202
Bleuer, Christian, 252
blind spots, 189, 190, 196
Bloom, John, 219
Boesen, Inger, 252
Bonn Agreement, 223
Breytenbach, Breyten, 145
British Institute for Afghan Studies (BIAS),
        246
b-roll
    defintion of, 190
Bronwyn, Bruton, 22

Brun, Cathrine, 8, 15–6, 19, 127, 129, 132–4, 142,
        145, 147, 283–4, 287, 298–9, 300, 304–5
Bujumbura, 261
Bukavu, 270
Burma, 272
Burundi, 20, 178, 257–8, 261–2, 264, 266–7,
        271, 273
    concepts of justice, 267
    human rights, 262

Caliphate, 176
capacity building, 89, 232, 233
Cardone, Pietro, 209
Caroline, 9, 44–5, 48–9, 52–3, 165, 293
Carter, Kevin, 215
Carter, Sean, 147
ceasefire, 127, 132, 138–40
censorship, 53, 133
Central African Republic, 30
Chandrasekaran, Rajiv, 219
Charlotte, 39–40, 50
Chechnya, 190
checkpoints, 9, 127, 129, 133, 139–40, 144, 209,
        278, 280, 298
child soldiers, 97, 280, 301
childbirth, 158–9, 164
children
    armed conflict, 81
    casualty of war, 45, 84, 152
    dangerous labor, 97
    definition of, 82
    invisible, 81
    legal category, 11
    night commuters, 18, 47
    pregnancy, 94
    protection, 94
    recruitment into armed forces, 96
    sexual abuse, 10
    sexually exploitation, 97
    vulnerability, 82
    war affected, 11
Christensen, Asgar, 253
Christian Children's Fund (CCF), 88
Christine, 43, 219
Civil Defense Units, 96
civil society, 20, 110, 247, 251, 259–60, 266,
        272, 281
civil society activists, 254, 256, 265
Clarke, Kamari, 273
"Clear, Hold and Build", 194
clothing 115, 236, 288–9,
    avoid military issue, 207 289
cluster system, 100
coalition forces
    Iraq, 188, 194
Coalition Prvisional Authority of Iraq, 171
Coetzee, John Maxwell, 147

cold war, 151
Colin Powell, 173
collaboration
    institutional vs. individual, 142
    politics of universities, 138
    with local universities, 101–2, 130, 142–4,
        147, 305
    with NGOs, 145
Colombia, 3, 4, 101
Colombo, 129, 139, 143, 147
colonialism, 90, 97, 150–1, 257
Colson, Elizabeth, 124
coltan, 271
communal riots, 131
community health, 164
complex citizenship, 19, 132, 139
confidentiality, 14–15, 92
    research ethics, 14
conflict analysis, 21
conflict zone
    defintion, 3
Congolese Rally for Democracy (RCD), 255,
    259, 264, 271
Connors, Steve, 8, 10, 13, 16, 19, 169, 219, 277,
    281, 283–4, 287, 289, 290, 297–300, 302,
    305
consent
    voluntary vs. coerced, 47
consequences of displacement, 112
Constitution of Medina, 176
continuum of violence, 10
Convention against Torture and Other
    Cruel, Inhuman or Degrading
    Treatment or Punishment, 11
Convention on the Elimination of All Forms
    of Discrimination Against Women, 11
Convention on the Elimination of All Forms
    of Racial Discrimination, 11
Convention on the Rights of the Child, 81, 97
Convention relating to the Status of
    Refugees, 11
coordination
    emergencies, 95, 99, 100, 101, 102
courtesy, 94, 115, 193
covert, 115, 181, 254, 298
Cramer, Christopher, 22
critical theory, 271
critical thinking, 99
culture, 20, 23, 38, 42, 85, 90–1, 98–9, 124,
        134, 147–8, 151–2, 157, 160–1, 165, 189,
        192–3, 205, 213, 220, 226–7, 233, 235–6,
        243, 246, 261–2, 266, 286, 288
    beliefs, 89–91, 178, 189, 235
    farming, 42, 110–1
    positive practices, 98
    static, 98
    traditional healers, 89–90

Dallaire, Romeo (General), 260
Dancygier, Rafaela, 22
Dao, James, 219
Dari, 231, 235–6, 243–5, 247
data
    public domain, 188
    connection with aid delivery, 95
data security, 196, 198
Davis, John, 124
Davis, Peter, 219
de Alwis, Malathi, 147
de Laine, Marlene, 164
de Mel, Neloufer, 147
demeanour
    with government officials, 115
Democracy and Governance Assessments,
    265
Democratic Republic of Congo, 3, 20, 30,
        254, 257–8, 263, 264, 267, 271–2
    human rights organizers, 270
Dennis, 9, 43, 48–9, 52–3
depression, 87–8, 99–100
Des Forges, Alison, 273
detainees, 104
detention, 254–9, 278
digital profile
    monitoring, 198
dignity, 29, 34, 44, 52, 155,
        163, 192
Dinka (people), 150, 164–5, *See* Jieng 297
disappearances, 132, 147
discrimination, 10, 16, 96–7
disease, 35, 286
dissemination of research findings, 124, 130,
        146–7, 247, 256–7, 271
    informal methods, 246
    timeliness, 248
do no harm, 7, 17–9, 82, 130
documentary, 13, 17, 28–9, 31, 33, 37, 38–41,
        55, 170, 188, 216
domestic violence, 115, 123, 158
Donald Rumsfeld, 171
Donini, Antonio, 22
double role
    researcher/aid worker, 156
"drive- by" polling, 241
Dudley, Sandra, 124
Duffield, Mark, 5, 10, 22

East Africa, 282
East Timor, 94
Eastern Equatoria, 109
Eastern University of Sri Lanka, 143
educated population
    migration abroad, 229
education, 82, 85, 98, 101, 117, 131, 150, 158, 164,
        170, 186, 223, 229, 249, 265–6, 268

Edwards, David, 253
Egeland, Jan, 291
Egypt, 150
elderly
    older people, 9–10
    older women, 29, 37, 42, 48
elections, 226, 252–3, 258
elites, 20, 162, 256–7, 260, 265–8
embedded journalism, 182
    limitations of, 197
England, Jan, 27, 122
English, 13, 34, 110, 195, 220, 230, 235–6, 243,
    245, 265
epistemic privilege, 6, 117
ethics, 82, 92, 117
Ethiopia, 16
ethnicity, 30, 109, 122, 144, 153, 164, 171, 175,
    231, 233–5, 244, 248, 257–8, 260, 264
    government control, 261
ethnography, 149
    contrast with needs assessment, 157
    methods, 12, 84, 98, 114, 152, 161, 162
evaluation, 20, 88–9, 91, 228–9, 252
Evans-Pritchard, E. E., 164
everyday lives, 10, 48, 149
    farmers, 20, 42, 114, 118, 153, 256
    market women, 20, 257
evil spirits, 37
exclusion, 134, 141
exit strategies, 278
expectations
    community, 42, 93–5, 115, 118, 137, 157, 225,
        232, 240
    of researcher, 137

Faizabad, 239
Fallujah, 170, 202
family violence, 243
famine, 150, 152, 157, 215
Federation International des Ligues de
    Droits de l'Homme, 273
female genital mutilation/cutting, 98
female researchers, 42, 123, 138, 289
femininity, 154
feminist scholarship, 18
the field
    bringing the field home, 144
    constructed category, 118, 147, 148
    definition of, 130, 134
film, 8, 9, 18, 32–33
    crew, 33, 36–37, 40, 45, 47, 48, 196
    post-production, 49
    preparation, 4–9, 14–18, 21, 25, 28–55, 180,
        187, 190–193, 201, 210, 211, 219, 283, 288
    process, 14, 33, 46, 48
    production, 36, 136, 216, 217
    sound recorder, 33, 36, 48
    technical issues, 36

techniques, 192
Finnstrom, Sverker, 125
Fishstein, Paul, 8, 15, 20, 223, 299, 301, 306
Fisk, Robert, 220
fixer, 180, 214
    protection of, 212
    short-cuts, 184
flexibility
    research method, 19, 228, 234, 238, 251
focus groups, 12, 114, 120, 135, 160, 268, 282,
    296, 302
    de-facto focus groups, 242
    social hierarchy, 242
food aid, 34, 35
food insecurity, 88, 149
forced marriage, 94
forced migrants. *See* refugees
forced migration studies, 12, 109,
    114, 123
forced wives, 32
formal data- gathering, 115
formerly recruited children, 96, 97
    reintegration, 96
freedom of movement
    lack of, 139, 208
freedom of speech, 133
French, 34, 47, 189, 264, 265, 266
Fujii, Lee Ann, 273
funding
    documentry film, 46
    humanitarian aid, 95
    program assesments, 95

Gacaca , 268
Gale, Lacey, 8, 21, 277, 304, 306, 307
Garner, Jay, 171
gate keepers, 13, 133
Gauthier, Mélanie, 25, 38
Gaza, 3, 178, 190
gender
    division of roles, 154
    dynamics on a research team, 192
    inequality, 149
    language, 154
    modified, 152
    norms, 15
    relationships, 19, 152, 154, 159, 161, 226
    socialization, 152, 159
    static roles in changing environment, 158
gender blindness, 117
gender- based violence, 82, 154
Romeo (General), 260
generational affects of conflict, 6, 17, 29, 39,
    86, 131, 170
Geneva Conventions, 3
genocide
    command responsibility, 268
    Rwanda, 268

Geography, 147, 258, 281
  academic field, 19
George W. Bush, 170
global north, 151, 163, 164
global south, 151, 163
globalization, 151
Goma, 254–5, 259, 270
Goodhand, Jonathan, 147
gossip, 113, 121
Gourevitch, Philip, 273
"Governing Council" (Iraq), 171, 174
Grabska, Katarzyna, 125
grave violence, 16
Great Lakes region, 254, 256–7
Gros, Sébastien, 294
group identity, 265
Guantanamo Bay, 104
the *Guardian*, 177, 220
Guess, Raymond, 273
Guiding Principles on Internal
  Displacement, 11
Gulu, 25, 44, 110, 293
Gupta, Akhil, 8, 134, 147, 148

Habyarimana regime, 272
Hamas, 190
Hammond, Laura, 16, 22, 112, 123, 125
hanging out
  research method, 13, 15, 136, 148
Harvey, Paul, 22
Hassan, Ahmed, 220
Hazaras (people), 234, 253
Headington Institute, 288, 291
healing practices, 89–90
health, 21, 93, 96, 99–100, 110, 125, 149, 153–4,
  158, 163, 229, 279, 285–6, 307
health care workers, 153
health cluster, 100
"hearts and minds", 216
Hébert, Catherine, 9, 12, 14, 16, 18, 282, 283,
  296, 297, 298, 300, 303, 305
Herat, 239
Hersh, Seymour, 220
HIV/AIDS, 164
Hoffman, Daniel, 22
Holocaust, 263
honorary male status
  female researchers, 117
hooks, bell, 6, 22
Horkheimer, Max, 273
hors de combat, 11
Horst, Cindy, 125
hospitality, 93, 105, 121, 177, 241
"Hostile Environment" courses, 207
hostilities
  definition of, 277
hosts, 16, 113, 121, 131, 137
  relations with refugees, 115

Howell, David, 253
human rights, 6, 8, 17, 35, 41, 48, 82, 97–8, 100,
  105, 125, 149, 156, 255, 259, 269–1, 274, 284
human rights abuses, 257, 259–60, 267,
  269–70, 272, 300, 302
human rights activists, 48
Human Rights Center of the University of
  California, Berkeley, 258
human rights mission, 255, 258, 270
human rights organizations, 258, 277
  security training, 278
human rights research, 256, 258–9, 269
human rights violations, 17, 98, 258, 271, 288,
  307
Human Rights Watch, 20, 132, 147, 254, 255,
  258–9, 261, 269, 273
humanitarian aid, 97
  distribution, 156
  institutional protocol, 279
  militarization of, 199
  security training, 278
  targeting, 156
  violent attacks, 278
humanitarian cinema, 46
hunger, 9, 46, 149, 154
Hussein, Saddam, 170–2, 177, 179, 186, 197–8,
  215
Hutchinson, Sharon, 164
Hutu (people), 257, 261–2, 264, 268
Hyndman, Jennifer, 125

Inter-Agency Standing Committee (IASC)
  Guidelines on Mental Health and
  Psychosocial Support , 101
identity, 13, 19, 85, 102–5, 113, 121, 144, 150, 159,
  175, 178, 182, 187–8, 231, 284, 289
  affiliation, 199
  citizenship, 189
  class, 139, 157, 186
  ethnicity, 8, 114
  "passing", 16, 122
  spy, 104, 179, 204, 291
  visa, 103
  militarism, 131
idioms, 154
improvised explosive device (IED), 200
Ikafe Refugee Settlement, 107–11, 125
illegal prison, 255
illiteracy , 242
illness , 88, 285, 286, 288
"The Imam", 193
inclusion, 134
indentity cards, 49, 139
independent research, 5, 20, 229
India, 132, 142, 173
indigenous researcher. *See* Native researcher
infant health, 158
infant mortality rates, 158

information
  as power, 114
  as economy, 116, 119
initiation, 82
insider
  researcher identity, 19, 98, 149–50, 153–4, 157
Institute of Development Studies, 22
Institutional Review Board (IRB), 270
insurgency
  definition of, 174
insurgent groups
  military and civilian lives, 159
insurgents, 3, 11
intelligence agencies
  payment of subjects, 213
intelligence collection
  wiretaps, 196
internally displaced person (IDP), 11, 19, 25, 30–35, 38, 41–42, 51–52, 108, 131, 161
International Covenant on Civil and Political Rights, 11
International Covenant on Economic, Social and Cultural Rights, 11
International Criminal Tribunal for Rwanda, 267
International Crisis Group, 259
International Federation for Human Rights, 258
International Federation of the Red Cross, 278
international human rights law, 260
international law, 4, 174, 218, 254, 259, 266
interpreters, 40, 139, 195, 262, 286–7, 300
  inelligence agents, 287
interview, 12–15, 19, 21, 48, 49, 52, 114, 133, 135–137, 144, 162, 180–181, 185, 186–193, 195, 196, 198, 199, 201, 204, 206, 214, 242–244, 265, 268, 286, 288, 307
  as conversation, 185
  barriers to expressing personal views, 243
  exclusion of average people, 265
  grassroot perspective, 267
  informal interview, 259
  key informants, 260, 265, 269
  lack of privacy, 242
  principles of inference, 243
  questions to avoid, 185
  techniques, 185
Intifada, 87
Irish Republican Army (IRA), 190, 308
Iran, 172, 176, 224, 235
Iran – Iraq war, 172
Iran's Revolutionary Guard, 172
Iraq, 3–5, 16, 19, 103, 167–218, 281, 283, 291
  definition of, 170
Iraq Body Count, 220
Iraqi exiles, 172

Iraqi resistance, 203–4, 206, 216–8
  indigenous, 215
The Islamic Supreme Council of Iraq (ISCI), 172
Israel, 86, 190

Jackson, Ashley, 220
Jaffna, 138, 139, 140, 141, 146, 299
Jieng, 150n2, 152n5, 153–4, 156, 159, 161–3 *See* Dinka
Jihad, 193–4
Jok, Madut Jok, 8, 12, 16, 19, 149, 157, 162, 164, 284, 286, 297, 300, 305
Jordan, 9, 18, 86, 87
journalism,
  advocacy film, 216
  blurring of roles, 218
  embedded, 208
  emotionally embedded, 208
  ethics of humanitarian work for subjects, 214
  payment of subjects, 213
  responsibility, 209
  vested interests, 215
justice system, 155

Kabila, Laurent-Désiré, 254
Kabul, 20, 223, 228, 236, 239, 241, 244, 245–6, 248
Kabul bubble, 20
Kabul University, 232
Kagame, Paul, 263
Kaiser, Tania, 12, 13, 16, 18, 106, 108, 120, 125, 300, 303
Kampala, 16, 30, 35, 109, 110, 122, 124
Kapuściński, Ryszard, 27, 55
Karuna, 132
Karzai, Hamid, 223, 248, 250
Katz, Cindi, 147
Keen, David, 22
Khalilzad, Zalmay, 248
khawaja edge, 151
kidnapping. *See* abduction
Kinshasa, 255, 256
Kinyarwanda, 264
Kinzer, Stephen, 273
Kirundi, 262
Kiryandongo refugee settlement, 108–123
Kobayashi, Audrey, 148
Kono, 79, 275
Kony, Joseph, 30, 52
Koran, 192, 300
Kritz, Neil, 273
Kurds (people), 172

labor migration, 226
land, 18, 38, 42, 106, 107, 113–114
  tenure, 226

land mines, 281
landscape, 13, 238, 282
Lango (people) , 29, 42
language
    barrier, 14
    changing speech patterns, 152
    generational affects, 152
    native researcher, 286
    safe spaces, 145
    subversion, 145
    translation issues, 243
Lapides, Kate, 79, 275
Latin America, 86
Lawrence, P., 148
legitimacy, 13, 102, 108, 172, 225, 231
Leopold, Mark, 125
libraries, 225, 246–247
    affects of conflict, 145
Lienhardt, Godfrey, 164
"The Lieutenant", 191, 200, 209
Lingala, 264
Lira, 38, 43
listening, 14, 34, 51, 54, 88, 113, 174, 177, 183, 189
Lister, Sarah, 253
literacy, 163
livelihoods, 85, 87, 112, 116, 123, 142, 226, 291
local knowledge, 91, 256, 257, 262, 300, 301
local stakeholders, 145
location
    affective relationship with, 113
    long term research, 8, 13, 28, 106, 108, 110, 111, 114, 116, 118, 120, 134, 137, 148, 181, 201, 270
    safety, 200
    significance of, 139
Loescher, Gil, 125
Loizos, Peter, 125
London Sunday Telegraph, 177
London Times, 177
Longman, Tim, 6, 8, 20, 254, 261, 262, 273, 286
Lords Resistance Army (LRA), 29–32, 35, 39, 43–44, 49, 50, 51, 107–109, 121
Lorentz, J. H., 253
loyalists
    Iraq, 179, 215
Liberation Tigers of Tamil Eelam (LTTE), 15, 81, 129–133, 137–141, 147

Macklin, Audrey, 292
Madi (people), 109
Mafeje, Archie, 165
Mahdi Army, 202
mainstream media, 28
Malkki, Liisa, 148
Mamdani, Mahmood, 273
Mangos for Charlotte, 27, 39

Mano River region, 11
Mansfield, David, 253
marginalized populations, 5–7, 10, 84, 89
marriage, 113, 125, 153, 186, 264
    early marriage, 158
Marriage, Zoe, 125
Marx, Karl, 6, 22
masculinity, 131, 154
massacres, 108, 260–3
Massey, Douglas, 148
maternal health, 158
Maxwell, Daniel, 23
Mazurana, Dyan, 5, 8, 21–2, 27, 277, 282, 304, 306–7
McCann, I. L., 292
McClatchy Newspapers, 216, 220
McClellan, Scott, 218
Meeting Resistance, 170, 174, 177, 188, 199, 201, 211, 213, 216, 220
memory, 147, 155, 157, 198
Mendez, Juan, 273
mental health, 99–101, 279, 285, 288
Mertus, Julie, 148, 292
Middle East, 86, 190, 253
militarism, 129–131, 135, 136, 149, 153, 162
military, 129, 144, 153
    gender socialization, 159
    intimidation, 255, 259
Milner, James, 125
Mobutu Sese Sekou, 258
Mònica Bernabé, 221
Monsutti, Alessandro, 253
Montreal, 36, 52, 53
Moqtada al Sadr, 171, 202
motherhood
    as political, 158
Mozambique, 90
Mujahideen, 225
Mukhabarat intelligence services, 179
Muonjang. *See* Dinka
Muqawama
    definition of, 177
Museveni, Yoweri, 29–31, 35, 51–3, 107
Mvepi settlements, 111
Mwenda, Andrew, 51, 52

Nabulsi, Karma, 174, 220
"name and shame", 259
narrative, 28, 119, 147, 178, 186, 188, 191, 215, 282
Nast, Heidi, 148
National Intelligence Council Director, 215
National Intelligence Estimate on Iraq, 215
National Security Agency, 206
nationalism, 105, 132, 139, 147, 173, 175, 188
native researcher, 151, 153, 157, 164
    challenges, 157
NATO, 3

needs assessment, 116, 157, 229
    poverty mapping, 157
Neefjes, Koos, 125
Neier, Aryeh, 273
Nemery, Benoit, 273
neutrality, 4, 14, 256
New York Times, 177, 219, 220, 291
The New Yorker, 202, 220
Newsweek, 177, 198, 291
NGOs, 82, 93, 96, 100, 109, 123, 171, 199, 208,
    217–8, 223–4, 227, 230, 232–3, 237–42,
    247, 252, 278–9, 284, 286
night commuters, 31, 44, 47
1972 Addis Ababa Agreement, 106
"no go" lists, 208
Noah's Ark, 44, 47, 49
non-state armed groups, 3
Nordstrom, Caroline, 5, 10, 22, 148, 154, 165
Norman, Julie, 22
North Korea, 272
Northern Ireland, 178
Norwegian Centre for International
    Cooperation in Higher Education, 142
the Norwegian University of Science and
    Technology, 142
Nuer (people), 161, 162, 164, 165
Nusair, Isis, 9–11, 13, 16, 18, 296, 299, 305
nutrition, 163, 164

Obeysekere, Ranjini, 148
Obote, Milton, 107
the *Observer* of London, 177
occupation
    US in Iraq, 19, 103, 169, 174–178, 183, 186,
        188, 197, 202–203, 215, 216, 218, 254, 283
Oliver, Mark, 220
Olsen, Tricia, 273
Operation Lifeline Sudan, 163
*Operational Security Management in Violent
    Environments: A Field Manual for Aid
    Agencies*, 278
Oppel, Richard, 220
Optional Protocol on the Rights of the Child
    on the Involvement of Children in
    Armed Conflict, 11
oral history, 114, 300, 302, 305
Ottoman era, 170
Overseas Development Institute (ODI), 125,
    278, 292
Oxfam, 107–11, 125, 220

Pain, Adam, 253
Palestinian, 13, 18, 86–8
Pan Muonyjang, 150
Parkin, David, 125
participant observation, 12, 114, 154
participatory action research, 87
partitionists

Iraq, 175
partnership
    Afghan NGOs, 247
    Afghanistan Northern Alliance, 103
    competing interests, 233
    local expertise, 146
    local universities, 232
    with communities, 94
    with informants, 33
    with organizations, 7, 233
Pashtu (language and people), 231, 235–6,
    243, 244–7
Paterson, Anna, 253
Paul Bremer, 171
Payne, Linda, 125
peace activism, 86, 104
Pearlman, L. A., 292
*The People in Aid: Code of Best Practice in
    the Management and Support of Aid
    Personnel*, 278, 292
perpetrators, 10, 155, 217, 258–9, 307
    amnesty, 266
    impunity, 259
personal safety
    aid workers, 130
    armed road blocks, 280
    changing conditions, 188
    check-ins, 307
    clothing, 281, 288
    digital profile, 290
    emotional health, 277
    freedom of movement, 141
    health protocol, 21
    hotels, 279
    identifying safe spaces, 280
    intuition, 282
    kidnapping, 280
    landmines, 281
    linking with local partner, 281
    medical kit, 285
    money, 289
    network of local contacts, 282
    phones, 285
    physical health, 285
    reading the landscape, 282
    security plans, 21, 121, 283
    security teams, 208
    self care, 282
    signs of increased insecurity, 282
    sources and resources, 284
    survival skills, 281
    working with drivers, 40, 196, 279
Peshmerga militia, 172
Davis, Peter , 216
Pham, Phuong, 273
photo elicitation techniques, 114
photojournalism, 169, 177, 179
    affects of security detail, 207

blurring of roles, 208
concealing identity of informants, 201
distribution, 216
look like who you are, 207
political implications, 216
preserving anonymity through nicknames, 201
security measures, 201
policy, 17–20, 23, 34, 111, 118–119, 122–124, 146, 148, 170, 176, 220, 225–230, 234, 239, 244–250, 252, 253, 306
impact of research, 122, 124, 224
policy research institution, 20, 223, 227, 250, 252
political activism, 269
political elites, 290
political violence, 131
polygyny, 161
Portuguese, 90, 265
post-genocide, 258, 260, 263, 268, 272
post-traumatic stress disorder (PTSD), 87, 96, 99, 273
Pratt, Geraldine, 148
prayer, 167
preparation for fieldwork
communication devices, 281
insurance policies, 290
letter of introduction, 289
press
control by government, 260
impression of Iraqi resistence, 188
press relations with armed groups, 183
taking sides, 203
prison, 145, 179, 202, 246, 254–5, 259, 286
prisoners, 10, 202, 255–6, 259, 286
private security forces, 51
program evaluation, 81, 95, 229
propaganda, 43, 139, 218–9, 237, 267
Protection Cluster, 100
protracted conflicts, 152
protracted displacement, 132, 147
Psychologists for Social Responsibility, 104
psychosocial, 82, 84, 88–9, 91, 94, 99, 100, 102, 104
clinical, 99
community-based, 99
holistic needs, 100
psychological operations (PSYOPS) 164
publishing, 164
alternate venues, 145
funder demands for, 145
jargon, 269
Puttalam, 131

quantitative methodology, 241

Raghavan, Sudarsan, 220
rape, 9–10, 47, 155, 267

children, 50, 96
children born of, 31–2, 40
Ratnesar, Romesh, 220
Ravindranath, S., 143
rebels, 9, 11, 30, 32, 36–37, 41, 44, 47–48, 258, 261–262
reciprocity, 93, 121
reconciliation programs, 268
recruitment into armed groups, 82
Red Cross, 254, 292
reflexivity, 118
refugee camps, 13, 18, 88, 114, 120, 275
rations, 111, 122
refugee resettlement, 119, 124, 253
Refugee Welfare Council, 111, 115
refugees, 10–12, 16, 18, 87, 106–125, 252–253, 264, 270
education, 122
local integration, 131
repatriation, 125, 226
reintegration, 49, 88, 96
relationships
importance of, 12
religion, 8, 30, 87, 186, 269
religious extremists
description by press, 179
representation, 7–9, 13, 17, 39, 125, 133–6, 159, 165, 180, 208
dangers of, 118
refugees, 124
reproduction of violence
family life, 159
reproductive front, 154
reproductive health, 149, 152, 158
reputation, 103, 121, 160, 193, 225, 233, 237, 247, 301
research agenda
shifts in, 116, 130, 153, 156, 228, 305
research assistants
aiding research participants, 141
anonymity as protection, 213
class, 261
contact with militant groups, 141
driver, 40–41, 46, 48, 141, 182, 196–197, 206, 212, 214, 280
"vouching" for researchers, 180, 184
research ethics
benefit, 4–5, 33, 40, 83, 92–3, 95, 110, 116, 118, 121, 143, 179, 213, 252, 265–6
children, 83
compassion, 84, 214
consequences, 14, 18, 20, 22, 48, 81–83, 113, 124–125, 141, 144, 195, 198, 206, 213–214, 231, 257, 259, 270, 272, 291
emotional support, 138
extractive approach, 94, 95
impact on subjects, 34, 49

research ethics (*cont.*)
  informants at risk, 206
  informed consent, 15, 92, 93, 270
  no feedback from subjects, 217
  precautions to protect identity, 49
  protection of sources, 257, 270
  responsibility, 130, 270
research fatigue, 136, 157
resilience, 21, 84, 87–88, 105, 295, 300
resistance, 6, 19, 32, 52, 87, 169, 170, 174–179,
    181–188, 191, 194, 198, 200, 210, 219–220,
    251, 254, 257
respect, 299
responsibility, 7, 17, 19–20, 48, 52, 87, 92, 135,
    139, 146–8, 158, 159, 171, 173, 184, 200–1,
    257, 269, 272
responsibility to subjects, 38, 40, 53,
    140, 173
restrictions on mobility, 237
return
  ethics of leavetaking, 48
  home, 115
  research method, 28, 31, 34, 40, 43, 94, 129,
    137, 139, 150, 179, 232, 237, 253, 258
Revolutionary United Front, 96
Reynolds, Andrew, 253
Rhino Camp, 111
Richards, Paul, 22
risk, 13, 21, 37, 46, 48–9, 51, 81, 109–10, 121–2,
    133, 139, 150, 158, 160, 195, 212, 228, 233,
    239, 241, 256–7, 270, 283–4, 288, 290
  mitigation not elimination, 197
  monitoring, 144
  political expression, 48
  real vs. perceived, 144
risk assessment, 278, 307
rite of passage, 82
  rituals, 88, 90, 111, 113–4, 123
  burial rituals, 88
  cleansing ritual, 89
road blocks, 278, 280, 307
Rodgers, Graeme, 148
Rohde, David, 291, 292
Ross, Brian, 220
rocket-propelled grenade (RP), 210
Rubenstein, Leonard, 274
rumour, 113, 116, 121
Russia, 5, 13, 14, 86, 161, 190
Rwanda, 20, 178, 257–8, 260, 262–4, 267, 268,
    269, 271–4,
  ethnically mixed marriages, 264
  genocide trials, 268
Rwandan Patriotic Front (RPF), 255, 257, 260,
    263, 268, 272
  anglophone pespective, 264
  human rights abuses, 263
  propaganda campaign, 263

Saad Mohamed Sultan, 209
Sadr City, 202
safe spaces, 7, 14–17, 130, 131, 133, 138–140, 145,
    146, 280, 287, 298
  becoming insecure spaces, 141
  public places, 200
  researcher residence, 270
  scouting locations, 188
  staying away, 146
  variation in, 138
  vehicles, 140
safety
  accents, 16
  as an illusion, 199
  personal safety, 21, 91, 256, 278
  research assistants, 279
  responsibility for assistants, 48
sample size, 241
scapegoating, 258
secondary trauma, 288
security
  assessment, 144, 278, 286
  abduction, 204
  differences between researcher and
    humanitarian agencies, 141
  email/phone communication, 206
  plans, 283
  protocols, 142, 307
  regular check-in, 285
  responsibility for informants, 201
  training courses, 279
security sector reform, 226
security services, 21, 179
self-censorship
  security vs. disseminating findings, 145
  writing, 145
self-reflexivity, 135, 146
sex workers, 153, 161
sexual autonomy, 158, 164
sexual blackmail, 149
sexual health, 164
sexual relations, 10, 154, 159
sexual reproduction, 154
sexual violence 149, 152–5, 288, 304
  male victims, 301
sexuality, 8, 152–3, 159
sexually transmitted diseases, 153, 159
Shandy, Dianna, 165
Shaw, Rosalind, 12, 16, 22, 266, 274
Sheikh Harith al Dhari, 170
Shi'a, 172, 175
Shi'ite, 171–2
Sierra Leone, 12, 16, 22, 79, 82, 94, 96, 98–9,
    104, 275
silence, 16, 18, 28, 31, 39, 132, 136, 138, 155
  as a form of protection, 132, 139
  as protest, 136

becoming invisible, 132
empowering, 136
multiple meanings, 300
muteness of trauma, 132, 136
respect for, 146
self-censorship, 144
self-silencing, 90
survival strategy, 132, 144
understanding, 16, 130, 135–8, 140, 145, 146
Simmel, Georg, 148
"single non-transferable vote" (SNTV)
  system, 248
Sinhalese, 132
slavery, 31, 149, 153
Slim, Hugo, 8, 9, 22
Sluka, Jeffrey, 148
Smith, Linda, 165
social events
  baptisms, 13
  funerals, 13, 137–8
  weddings, 13, 137
social networks, 120, 152, 182
  informant networks, 213
social status, 13, 120, 158, 161
social violence, 131
soft law, 11
"The Soldier", 185, 191
Somalia, 3, 4, 22, 272
songs
  recording-research technique, 114
South Africa, 82
South Sudan, 19, 106, 149, 150–1, 156, 158
space,
  family space, 15
  as gendered, 137
  meeting space, 15
  private vs. public, 15
  private space lack of, 242
spaces of thoughtfulness, 136, 138
special forces soldiers, 207
Sphere Project, 4, 22
spirits of the dead, 88
spiritual beliefs, 84, 89, 90, 161, 288
Spivak, Gayatri Chakravorty, 23
Sri Lanka, 15–6, 19, 81, 104, 127–148, 284, 287,
  299
staff security, 20, 278
standards gap, 82
state intelligence, 133
state-sponsored violence, 131
*Stay Safe – International Federation's Guide
  to a Safer Mission*, 278
Stover, Eric, 274
Strategic Framework for Afghanistan (SFA),
  224
Strategic Monitoring Unit (SMU), 224, 226,
  228

Straus, Scott, 274
street children, 6, 9, 38, 42–3, 48, 49
strela, 191
Strobel, Warren P., 220
Sudan, 3, 5, 8, 19, 30, 106–9, 111, 113, 115, 118,
  149, 150, 152, 158, 161, 164, 215, 286, 292
Sudanese People's Liberation Army, 30, 107,
  118, 150
suffering, 9, 21, 29, 32, 84, 106, 111–2, 115, 124,
  148, 151, 158, 169, 295–7, 304, 307–8
Sunni, 175, 192
Supreme Council for Islamic Revolution, 172
surveillance, 133
surveys, 241, 260
  "betraying" NGOs, 242
  1–5 scales, 242
  social desirability bias, 242
Swahili, 264
Swedish International Development
  Cooperation Agency (SIDA), 228
Swiss Agency for Development Cooperation
  (SDC), 228

"The Syrian", 186
Tajiks (people), 234
Taliban, 92, 103, 223–225, 233, 237, 244, 291
Taloqan, 239
Tamil (people), 81, 127, 129, 140, 144
Tangen, Lars, 292
targeted advocacy, 247
targeting, 96–7, 124, 159, 174, 245, 247
tea
  research methods, 13, 137, 177, 178, 181, 183,
    184, 188, 200, 212
"The Teacher", 181, 190–1, 198, 204, 218
teaching, 42, 85, 86, 257
  dissemination of information, 145
  research method, 13
  filming, 36
Teitel, Ruti, 274
Tenancingo, 298
terrorists, 206, 218
  testimony, 34, 46, 50–1, 114–5, 135, 192
Theidon, Kimberly, 274
therapeutic feeding centers, 152
Thrift, Nigel, 148
Time magazine, 197
torture, 9–10, 87, 104, 189, 202–3, 254, 255,
  256, 258–9, 264, 267, 271, 286, 288
  Abu Ghraib, 189
  forced killing, 50
  survivors, 87
toubab, 33, 42
traditional birth attendants, 153
traditional healer, 89
trafficking, 82
training guides, 278

transcripts, 192, 194–95, 296
transitional justice, 266–7, 274
    local conceptualizations, 266
translation
    abstract concepts, 243
    challenges, 195
    challenges with translating "research", 243
    insider perspective, 151
    issues with gender, 243
    risks associated with poor translations, 243
translator, 14, 35, 212, 230, 232
transparency, 20
    in gaining permission, 115
trauma, 7, 18, 21, 40, 46–47, 84, 87–89, 96,
    100–101, 119, 132, 136
    children, 96
    impact of exposure, 88
    trauma program, 89
    trauma scales, 90
"The Traveler", 186, 196
triangulation, 242
    research method, 13, 116, 139, 191
trust, 14, 17, 20, 22, 33–34, 39, 50, 93, 95, 102,
    116, 121, 140, 156, 159, 180–181, 199, 213,
    242, 244, 261, 282, 284
    gradations of, 297
truth commissions, 266–7
Tsunami, 132, 134, 142
Turton, David, 125, 253
Tutsi (people), 257, 260, 263, 264, 268

United Nations (U.N.), 3–4, 7, 23, 27, 34, 79,
    101, 215, 223, 230, 231, 246, 248, 252, 254,
    258, 260, 277, 278, 279, 284, 285, 289,
    291, 292
U.N. Department for Safety and Security, 279
U.N. Security Council, 173
U.N. Special Representative in Iraq Sergio
    Vieira de Mello, 173
U.N. weapons inspectors, 196
United States of America (U.S.) Defense
    Department, 209
U.S. Department of Defense, 174
U.S. Government, 269
U.S. military
    soft projects, 218
U.S. Peace Corps, 277
U.N. peacekeeping forces, 79
Uganda, 5, 12, 14, 17–18, 25–47, 51, 53, 54, 100,
    106–109, 111, 112, 115, 117, 119, 120–125,
    258, 264, 270, 282, 293, 300
UNHCR, 110–1, 117–8, 120, 124
UNITA, 103
United Kingdom, 16, 111, 122
United States, 16, 22, 82–6, 103–4, 150, 172–4,
    220, 230, 250, 264, 273, 283–4, 284

USAID, 89, 104, 230, 265
Uzbeks (people), 234

Vanni, 139
vetting process
    by research subjects, 115
vicarious trauma, 21, 288, 304, 307
victims, 9–11, 16, 39, 46, 84–87, 122, 155, 271,
    273, 288, 292
    retraumatization, 47
Vietnam War, 85
volunteer
    research method, 16, 110, 122

Walker, Margaret Urban, 4, 9, 10, 23
Walker, Peter, 23
war, 9, 22, 39, 46, 81, 85, 86, 125, 153, 252, 253,
    263, 273
"War on Terror", 223
war-affected children, 82–84, 88, 91, 97
warlords, 250, 258
Warrap State, 164
"The Warrior", 191, 193, 204
Webster, Mackinnon, 23
well-being, 18, 90, 92, 98, 104, 155, 234, 239,
    279, 281
Wessells, Mike, 10–11, 16, 18, 81, 281, 284,
    299–2, 304, 306, 308
West Nile Bank Front, 107–9
"The Wife", 186, 193
Wild, Richard, 207
Wilder, Andrew, 8, 15, 20, 223, 248–9, 253,
    299, 301, 306
Wilson, Jamie, 220
Wily, Liz Alden, 253
wire taps, 196
women
    abandoned, 27, 35, 160, 281
    abuse, 10
    commentary on daily lives, 160
    deferral to men in interview situations, 162
    deviance, 161
    elderly, 48
    grandmother, 37, 41–3
    health, 158
    household duties, 139, 162
    influence on men's participation in the
        resistance, 193
    labelling, 161
    marital status, 154
    protection of secrets, 160
    relations with men, 15
    reproductive issues, 160
    as research assistant, 192
    as researcher, 18, 33, 42, 50–1, 98, 110, 115,
        116, 137, 155, 158, 186, 192–3

revolutionary roles, 158
single, 12, 14, 28, 32, 35, 40, 49, 100, 118,
    175, 209
status, 161
suffering, 158
testimony, 51
traditional expertise, 153
unmarrried, significance of, 161
voices, 160
widowed, 155
Wood, Elisabeth, 23
World Bank, 250, 252
World Food Program, 34–5, 110
World War I, 170
World War II, 263

Young, Iris Marion, 7, 22–3, 134–5,
    146–8

youth, 300
    agency, 87
    capacity building, 252
    defintion of, 82
    disappearances, 132
    "Lost Generation", 87
    narratives, 87
    political activism, 87
    recruitment by armed forces, 81
    reintegration of formerly
        recruited, 88
    resilience, 87
    safe spaces, 138
    sampling, 160
Yugoslavia, 190

Zaire, 107, 178
zona inerme, 298

Lightning Source UK Ltd.
Milton Keynes UK
UKHW021315111218
333800UK00026B/1118/P